The Blackwell Encyclopedic Dictionary of Strategic Management

About the Editors

Cary L. Cooper is Professor of Organizational Psychology at the Manchester School of Management (UMIST), UK. He has also been appointed Pro-Vice-Chancellor at the University of Manchester Institute of Science and Technology (UMIST). He is the author of over 80 books, has written over 250 scholarly articles and is editor of the *Journal of Organizational Behavior*. He is also the Founding President of the British Academy of Management.

Chris Argyris is James B. Conant Professor of Education and Organizational Behavior at the Graduate School of Business, Harvard University. He has written many books and received numerous awards, including the Irwin Award by the Academy of Management for lifetime contributions to the disciplines of management. Recently, the Chris Argyris Chair in Social Psychology of Organizations has been established at Yale University.

About the Volume Editor

Derek F. Channon is Professor of Management at Imperial College, London. Prior to this he was Professor of Strategic Management and Marketing at the Manchester Business School and a founder and Director of the International Financial Services Centre there.

Before becoming an academic he worked in a variety of marketing roles for the Royal Dutch Shell Group in the UK and overseas. He attended the Harvard Business School where his thesis won the Irwin Prize. He was a founder of the Strategic Management Society in the UK and its President from 1985 to 1988. He has consulted widely around the world for many major corporations and is the author of numerous books, articles and cases in the field of strategic management.

The Blackwell Encyclopedic Dictionary of Strategic Management

Edited by Derek F. Channon

Imperial College

Copyright© Blackwell Publishers Ltd, 1997

Editorial organization© Derek Channon, 1997

First published 1997

First published in USA 1997

2 4 6 8 10 9 7 5 3 1

Blackwell Publishers Ltd
108 Cowley Road
Oxford OX4 1JF
UK

Blackwell Publishers Inc.
238 Main Street
Cambridge, Massachusetts 02142, USA

Library of Congress Cataloging-in-Publication Data

The Blackwell encyclopedic dictionary of strategic management /edited by Derek Channon.
    p.   cm. — (The Blackwell encyclopedia of management)
    Includes bibliographical references and index.
    ISBN 1-55786-966-9 (alk. paper)
    1. Strategic planning – Dictionaries.   I. Channon, Derek F.
    II. Series.
    HD30.28.B59   1996   96–30369
    658.4′012′03—dc20   CIP

British Library Cataloguing in Publication Data
A CIP catalogue record for this book is available from the British Library.

ISBN 1557869669

Typeset in 9½ on 11pt Ehrhardt by Page Brothers, Norwich
Printed in Great Britain by T. J. Press (Padstow) Ltd

This book is printed on acid-free paper

To Charlotte and Toffee – the Golden Wonders

Contents

—— Preface ——

This book is the volume in the Blackwell Encyclopedia of Management devoted to the subject of strategic management. This relatively recent area of study in management stems from the 1970s, but its origins go much deeper. The literature of the subject builds upon the early pioneers of management thought, such as Urwick, Fayol, Taylor, Simon, Barnard, Chandler, and the like. Notice that nearly all of these names are from the USA. The list could be broadened to include others from Europe, such as Crozier, Woodward, Edwards, and Townsend. The field has also drawn somewhat on writers on military strategy, such as Clauzwitz, Liddell Hart, Sun Tzu, Machiavelli, and Mao Tse Tung. Not all of these conceptual thinkers are represented in this book; nor are the writers in decision theory, game theory, and such like. Regrettably, there is a finite length to any volume.

The concept of strategic management in its present form developed in the 1960s with the emergence of two very different approaches – which ultimately became complementary – at the Harvard Business School and at Carnegie Mellon. At Harvard, by recognizing that something "different" occurred at the top management level of the large corporation, and based on many of the behavioral studies by practitioners and academics such as Barnard, Drucker, Selznick, Fayol, and Urwick, case-based material was developed which attempted to explain this behavior. Eventually, in 1965, Ken Andrews articulated the concept of corporate strategy as developed at Harvard. He combined the views of Drucker and the seminal work of Alfred Chandler to define strategy as:

> The pattern of objectives, purposes or goals and major policies and plans for achieving these goals; stated in such a way as to define what business the company is in or is to be in and the kind of company it is or is to be.

In contrast, Igor Ansoff, coming from the Carnegie school and influenced by rational decision-making concepts, developed the view of strategy as the "common thread" among an organization's activities and product/markets that defined the essential nature of the business that the organization was in and planned to be in in the future.

At the same time as these two schools were developing within the academic world, in consultancy a number of important concepts were developing. Bruce Henderson and the Boston Consulting Group had developed the experience curve concept which, coupled with the observable diversification trend in large US corporations, led to the introduction of the growth share matrix, a recipe for balancing the cash flow profiles of different businesses based on expected cost advantages secured from the experience effect, the surrogate for which was subsumed to be relative market share. Similarly, Chandler's structure findings were being widely disseminated by McKinsey and Company, both amongst diversified US corporations and around the world, to introduce the profit centered (and later strategic business unit centered) form of organizational structure.

During the next decade the field developed with some dichotomy between behavioral models of strategy and analytic methods. At Harvard, interestingly, the behavioral school tended to dominate in the area now known as Business Policy, while analytic techniques, such as those of the Boston Consulting Group, found root in the marketing faculty. Ansoff visited Europe where he was instrumental in establishing a European network of scholars and helping to establish the discipline of corporate strategy there, in an environment exhibiting substantial skepticism that the area existed as a business discipline at all.

In the late 1970s, the strategic management movement in its present form was born. At perhaps the first international conference on the theme of corporate strategy, hosted by the University of Pittsburgh, it was decided by an international group of scholars that the term "Strategic Management" might be used to help coalesce the diversity between the concepts developed at Carnegie and at Harvard. Further, it was proposed that the new movement should endeavor to be truly international and embrace not only academics, but also business consultants and practitioners. This was cemented at a conference in Aix en Provence, hosted by Henry Mintzberg and attended by Dan Schendel and Derek Channon, who together with Igor Ansoff set out to create the Strategic Management Society and *Journal* in the next few years. The first international meeting of the Strategic Management Society was held in London in 1979, hosted by Hugh Parker of McKinsey and Company and Derek Channon, and attended by Dan Schendel and visitors from Harvard and around the world from business, academia, and consultancy.

The second meeting, hosted in Montreal by Henry Mintzberg, led to the creation of the Strategic Management Society. Meanwhile, Igor Ansoff, Derek Channon, and especially Dan Schendel had launched the *Strategic Management Journal*, which became and remains the leading professional journal in the area.

Since the beginning of the 1980s the area has expanded dramatically. Today it has become a leading area of management consultancy. It is a required area in the curriculum of virtually all graduate business administration and executive programs. In business, the concept of strategy is taken as an accepted norm and the search for strategic advantage has become a key element in corporate success. Notably, the work of Michael Porter in the early 1980s has built heavily upon the concepts of industrial economics, and the work of Mintzberg has challenged the analytic themes of rational economic strategy. The work of C. K. Prahalad and Gary Hamel has introduced new or modified concepts of core competence and globalization; and the consultancy industry has built upon finance theory to develop value based planning, re-engineering, benchmarking, and the like.

Seriously neglected in the literature of strategic management have been concepts from the East, and especially from Japan. This volume has, however, attempted to redress the almost total omission of the strategies, structures, and management techniques developed by Asian corporations. On average, the present major texts in the area devote less than one per cent of their content to this region, and yet in economic terms over the past several decades these countries have been the winners. Moreover, many of their management practices tend to be in almost direct contradiction of the best practices espoused in the West. We have therefore devoted a number of entries to attempting to describe and understand their management methods. While much of this discussion has been devoted to descriptions of actual practices, some attempt has also been made to show how, structurally, many of the strategies actually work. We hope this feature will add to the strategic management literature and help redress the imbalance.

The volume has also been designed to try to reflect the ideals established with the formation of the Strategic Management Society, namely to add value to the three constituencies of Academic, Business executives and Consultants, the ABCs that were the foundation of the Society. Thus, while the entries develop the theoretic concepts of the field, there is also an emphasis on the practical use of these.

Derek F. Channon

—— Acknowledgments ——

In producing this volume I have been supported by many others, without whom the task would have been impossible. In particular, I would like to single out Stephanos Avgeropoulos, who has worked with me both in producing many of the entries and in constructively criticizing what is in and what is out. I would also like to thank Peter Dempsey, formerly of Anderson Consulting, for his contribution in arranging and writing many of the entries on manufacturing. I am also heavily indebted to the leading consultancy companies which have provided contributions to this volume and to my strategic management specialization offered at Imperial College. These include McKinsey and Company, Cap Gemina, Marakon Associates, Barclays de Zoete Wedd, Charterhouse Bank, Price Waterhouse Consultants, Coopers and Lybrand, Arthur D. Little, Braxton Associates, and PIMS Europe. Thanks go to Kevin Jagiello and Gordon Mandry for the section on PIMS, which they were instrumental in establishing in Europe, and to my former colleagues at Manchester Business School. Other colleagues at The Management School, Imperial College have also contributed to and encouraged this effort; especially the director, David Norburn, and Richard Schoenberg, Dot Griffiths, Joe Tidd, Mike Brocklehurst, Benita Cox, and Kaye Loveridge. I would also like to thank Mrs Yvonne Doyle who has tolerated and worked assiduously on the numerous drafts of the book, and Paul and Christine Halliday of Quay Office Services who prepared much of the artwork. I would also thank all those academicians, business executives, and consultants, the ABCs of what Igor Ansoff, Dan Schendel, Henry Mintzberg, and I saw as the foundation for the subject in the very early years when it was very much just a dream in our eyes, and which have very much influenced my thoughts over the years.

While I thank all of the above, any mistakes, omissions, and errors are entirely mine.

Derek F. Channon

—— Figure and Table Acknowledgments ——

I would like to thank the many individuals and organizations who have granted permission for the reproduction of their copyright material. While every effort has been made to contact copyright holders, I apologize in advance to any who have inadvertently been omitted from the following list:

acquisition strategy Figure 1 reprinted with the permission of The Free Press, a division of Simon & Schuster, from *Managing acquisitions: creating value through corporate renewal* by Phillipe C. Haspeslagh & David B. Jemison. Copyright © 1991 by Simon and Schuster.

activity-based costing Table 1 and figure 1 reprinted by permission of Prentice-Hall Inc. from *The complete guide to activity based costing* by M. C. O'Guin. Copyright © 1991 by Prentice-Hall Inc./Career and Personal Development.

advantage matrix Figure 1 reprinted by permission of the Boston Consulting Group Inc.

benchmarking Table 1 reprinted by permission of The McGraw-Hill Companies from *Benchmarking for best practice* by C. Bogan & M. English. Copyright © 1994 by The McGraw-Hill Companies.

break even analysis Figure 1 reprinted by permission of the Asian Productivity Organisation from *100 management charts* by S. Nagashima. Copyright © 1992 by the Asian Productivity Organisation.

cause–effect analysis Figure 1 reprinted by permission of the Asian Productivity Organisation from *100 management charts* by S. Nagashima. Copyright © 1992 by the Asian Productivity Organisation.

chaebol structure Figure 1 reprinted by permission of Greenwood Publishing Group, Inc. from M. Hattori, in *Korean managerial dynamics*, Kae H. Chung & Hak Chong Lee (eds). Copyright © 1989 Frederick A. Praeger Inc.

competitive position – market attractiveness matrix Figure 1 reprinted by permission of D. F. Channon and Stratpack Ltd.

core process Figure 1 reprinted by permission of McKinsey and Company from R. B. Kaplan and L. Murdock, Core process redesign, *The McKinsey Quarterly*, 1991.

cross-functional management structure - Table 1 and figures 1–3 reprinted by permission of the Asian Productivity Organisation from Kozo Koura, in *Cross functional management*, Kenji Kurogane (ed.) Copyright © 1993 by the Asian Productivity Organisation.

customer profitability matrix Figure 1 reprinted by permission of *Harvard Business Review*. An exhibit from "Manage customers for profits (not just sales)" by Shapiro et al. Copyright © 1987 by the President and Fellows of Harvard College; all rights reserved.

directional policy matrix Figures 1 and 2 reprinted by permission of the Royal Dutch Shell Group. Tables 1 and 2 reprinted from *Long Range Planning*, vol. 11, S. J. Q. Robinson, R. E. Hitchens, and D. P. Wade, "The directional policy matrix – tool for strategic planning", pp. 8–15. Copyright © 1978 by Elsevier Science Ltd.

diversification Figure 1 reprinted by permission of B. R. Scott. Figure 2 reprinted by permission of D. F. Channon.

divisional structure Figure 2 reprinted by permission of John M. Stopford.

experience and learning effects Figure 3 & 5 reprinted by permission of Arthur D. Little Inc. and Prentice-Hall Inc. from *Strategic management: an integrative perspective* by A. C. Hax & N. S. Magiluf. Copyright © 1984 by Prentice-Hall Inc. Figure 4 reprinted from G. B. Allan & J. S. Hammond, "Note on the use of experience curves in competitive decision making" (Case No. 175-174). Boston: Harvard Business School. Copyright © 1975 by the President and Fellows of Harvard College. Reprinted by permission.

five forces model Figure 1 reprinted with the permission of The Free Press, a division of Simon & Schuster, from *Competitive strategy: techniques for analyzing industries and competitors* by Michael E. Porter. Copyright © 1980 by Simon and Schuster.

gap analysis Figure 1 reprinted by permission of Alan J. Rowe from *Strategic management*, 4th edn, by A. J. Rowe et al. Copyright © 1994 by Alan J. Rowe.

generic strategies Figures 1 and 4 reprinted by permission of Prentice Hall from *Exploring corporate strategy* by G. Johnson & K. Scholes. Copyright © 1993 by Prenice Hall UK – International Book Distributors Ltd. Figure 2 reprinted by permission of Alan J. Rowe from *Strategic management*, 4th edn, by A. J. Rowe et al. Copyright © 1994 by Alan J. Rowe. Figure 3 and table 1 reprinted with the permission of The Free Press, a division of Simon & Schuster, from *Competitive strategy: techniques for analyzing*

industries and competitors by Michael E. Porter. Copyright Copyright © 1980 by Simon and Schuster.

growth share matrix Figure 7 reprinted by permission of Simon & Schuster from *Corporate strategic analysis*, by M. C. Bogue & E. S. Buffa. Copyright © 1986 by Simon & Schuster.

holding company structure Figure 3 reprinted by permission of D. F. Channon.

horizontal structure Figure 1 reprinted by permission of McKinsey and Company from f. Ostroff and D. Smith, The horizontal organization, *The McKinsey Quarterly*, 1992.

just in time Figure 1 reprinted with the permission of The Free Press, a division of Simon & Schuster, from *Japanese manufacturing techniques: nine hidden lessons in simplicity* by Richard J. Schonberger. Copyright © 1982 by Simon and Schuster.

keiretsu structure Figures 2 & 3 reprinted by permission of Dodwell Marketing Consultants.

Lanchester strategy Figure 1 reprinted by permission of the Asian Productivity Organisation from *100 management charts* by S. Nagashima. Copyright © 1992 by the Asian Productivity Organisation.

life cycle strategy Figures 1–4 and tables 1 & 2 reprinted by permission of Arthur D. Little Inc.

manufacturing strategy Table 1 adapted and reprinted by permission of John Wiley & Sons Inc. from *Restoring our competitive edge – competing through manufacturing* by R. W. Hayes & S. C. Wheelwright. Copyright © 1984 by John Wiley & Sons Inc.

McKinsey 7S model Figure 1 reprinted by permission of McKinsey and Company from R. Waterman, Jr, et al., Structure is not organization, *The McKinsey Quarterly*, 1980.

organizational life cycle Figure 1 reprinted by permission of Alan J. Rowe from *Strategic management*, 4th edn, by A. J. Rowe et al.

Copyright © 1994 by Alan J. Rowe. Figure 2 reprinted with the permission of H. Mintzberg from *Mintzberg on management* by H. Mintzberg. Copyright © 1979 by H. Mintzberg.

Pareto analysis Figure 1 reprinted by permission of the Asian Productivity Organisation from *100 management charts* by S. Nagashima. Copyright © 1992 by the Asian Productivity Organization. Figure 2 reprinted with the permission of John Wiley & Sons Ltd from *Bank strategic management and marketing* by D. F. Channon. Copyright © 1986 John Wiley & Sons Ltd.

PDCA cycle Figure 1 reprinted by permission of The McGraw-Hill Companies from *Kaizen* by Masaaki Imai Copyright © 1986 by The McGraw-Hill Companies.

PIMS structural determinants of performance Figures 1–6 reprinted by permission of PIMS.

product market diversification matrix Figure 1 & 2 reprinted by permission of Igor Ansoff.

radar mapping Figure 1 reprinted by permission of the Asian Productivity Organisation from *100 management charts* by S. Nagashima. Copyright © 1992 by the Asian Productivity Organisation. Figure 2 reprinted by permission of The McGraw-Hill Companies from *Benchmarking for best practice* by C. Bogan & M. English. Copyright © 1994 by The McGraw-Hill Companies.

SBU structure Figure 1 reprinted by permission of Richard D. Irwin Publications from W. Hale (1978), General Electric. Reprinted in A. Thompson & A. Strickland *Strategic Management*. Copyright © 1993 by Richard D. Irwin Publications.

segmentation Table 1 reprinted by permission of Prentice-Hall Inc. from *Principles of marketing*, 4th edn, by P. Kotler & G. Armstrong. Copyright © 1989 by Prentice-Hall Inc.

served market Figure 1 reprinted by permission of John Wiley & Sons Ltd from *Bank strategic management and marketing* by D. F. Channon. Copyright © 1986 John Wiley & Sons Ltd.

Stakeholder analysis Figure 1 reprinted by permission of A. Rowe from Rowe et al., *Strategic Management*. Figures 2 and 3 reprinted by permission of John Wiley & Sons from W. C. King, Formulating strategic and contingency plans, in Gardner et al. Copyright © 1986 John Wiley & Sons Ltd.

strategic groups Figure 1 reprinted by permission of Richard D. Irwin Inc. from *Strategic management*, 7th edn, by A. Thompson & A. J. Strickland. Copyright © 1993 by Richard D. Irwin Inc.

strategic management Figure 2 reprinted by permission of McKinsey and Company from Gluck et al., Strategic management for competitive advantage, *The McKinsey Quarterly*, 1980.

strategic planning Figure 1 reprinted by permission of D. F. Channon. Figure 2 reprinted by permission of John Wiley & Sons Inc. from W. C. King, Formulating strategic and contingency plans, in *Handbook of strategic planning*, J. R. Gardner, R. Rachlin, & H. W. A. Sweeny (eds). Copyright © John Wiley & Sons Inc.

structuring organizations Figure 1 reprinted with the permission of The Free Press, division of Simon & Schuster, and H. Mintzberg from *Mintzberg on management* by H. Mintzberg. Copyright © 1989 by The Free Press.

strategic planning Figure 1 reprinted by permission of D. F. Channon. Figure 2 reprinted by permission of John Wiley & Sons Inc. from W. C. King, Formulating strategic and contingency plans, in *Handbook of strategic planning*, J. R. Gardner, R. Rachlin, & H. W. A. Sweeny (eds). Copyright © John Wiley & Sons Inc.

structuring organizations Figure 1 reprinted with the permission of The Free Press, a division of Simon & Schuster, and H. Mintzberg from

Mintzberg on management by H. Mintzberg. Copyright © 1989 by H. Mintzberg.

sustainable growth rate Table 1 reprinted by permission of the Boston Consulting Group.

technology assessment Figure 1 reprinted by permission of Alan J. Rowe from *Strategic management*, 4th edn, by A. J. Rowe et al. Copyright © 1994 by Alan J. Rowe.

time-based competition Figure 1–3 and table 1 reprinted by permission of Rossmore Dempsey & Co. Ltd.

total quality control Table 1 reprinted with the permission of The Free Press, a division of Simon & Schuster, from *Japanese manufacturing techniques: nine hidden lessons in simplicity* by Richard J. Schonberger. Copyright © 1982 by Simon and Schuster.

value-based planning Figures 1, 5 & 6 reprinted by permission of Marakon Associates. Copyright © 1995 Marakon Associates. Figure 2 reprinted by permission of Lily K. Lai from Corporate strategic planning for a

diversified company (1983 thesis). Figure 3 reprinted by permission of Mercer Management Consultants.

value chain analysis Figure 2 reprinted with the permission of The Free Press, a division of Simon & Schuster, from *Competitive advantage: creating and sustaining superior performance* by Michael E. Porter. Copyright © 1985 by Simon and Schuster.

value-driven re-engineering Figure 1 reprinted by permission of Rossmore Dempsey & Co Ltd.

vulnerability analysis Figure 1 reprinted by permission of Alan J. Rowe from *Strategic management*, 4th edn, by A. J. Rowe et al. Copyright © 1994 by Alan J. Rowe.

workout Figure 1 reprinted from *Control your destiny or someone else will* by Noel M. Tichy and Stratford Sherman. Copyright © 1993 by Noel M. Tichy and Stratford Sherman. Used by permission of Doubleday, a division of Bantam Doubleday Dell Publishing Groups Inc.

—— Contributors ——

Chris Adams
Andersen Consulting

Stephanos Avgeropoulos
The Management School, Imperial College

Michael Brocklehurst
The Management School, Imperial College

Derek F. Channon
The Management School, Imperial College

Julia Channon
Price Waterhouse

Benita Cox
The Management School, Imperial College

Peter Dempsey
Rossmore Dempsey & Co.

Mike Freedman
Partner and Executive Vice President, Kepner-Tregoe Inc.

Dorothy Griffiths
The Management School, Imperial College

Alan Harrison
Cranfield School of Management

Ed Heard
Rossmore Dempsey & Co.

Kevin Jagiello
Manchester Business School

David Johnston
Andersen Consulting

Bill Lattimer
Andersen Consulting

Kaye Loveridge
The Management School, Imperial College

Gordon Mandry
Manchester Business School

David Norburn
The Management School, Imperial College

Richard J. Schoenberg
The Management School, Imperial College

Joe Tidd
The Management School, Imperial College

A

acquisition strategy Acquisition provides a rapid means of gaining an established product market position. Compared to the alternate routes for achieving growth or diversification, acquisitions overcome the relatively long time-scales and potential resource constraints of internal development and do not involve the dilution of control inherent within STRATEGIC ALLIANCES.

Acquisitions may be a particularly attractive means of corporate development under certain strategic and financial conditions. In mature industries containing a number of established players, entry via acquisition can avoid the competitive reaction that can accompany attempts to enter the industry by internal development: rather than intensifying the rivalry by adding a further player, the potential competition is purchased. In other industries in which competitive advantage is held in assets built up over considerable periods of time, for example the back-catalogs in the record or film industries, acquisitions can immediately achieve a market position that would be virtually impossible to develop internally. The Japanese electronics company Sony, for example, has achieved this with its acquisition of CBS Records and Columbia Pictures.

Financially, acquisitive growth may be particularly attractive to a quoted company if its price: earnings ratio is relatively high compared to that of potential target companies. Under such circumstances an acquisition funded by shares may provide an immediate earnings per share enhancement to the acquiring firm. A further stimulus to the acquisition boom of the late 1980s in Britain was the existence of accounting standards that permitted acquirers to offset the goodwill element of an acquisition's cost against reserves rather than treating it as an asset that had to be depreciated over time, reducing future stated profits.

The importance of acquisitions is evidenced by the volume of activity. In 1994, US companies spent in excess of $222 billion on domestic acquisitions and a further $24 billion on cross-border transactions. Comparative figures for companies within the European Union are $67 billion and $60 billion respectively (data source: *Acquisitions Monthly*). However, acquisitions are not without their risks: empirical studies have consistently shown failure rates approaching 50 per cent, regardless of the criteria used.

A recent study by McKinsey and Company revealed that 43 per cent of a sample of international acquisitions failed to produce a financial return that met or exceeded the acquirer's cost of capital (Bleeke & Ernst, 1993). Nonfinancial studies show little improvement over John Kitching's (1974) early finding that between 45 per cent and 50 per cent of acquisitions are considered failures or not worth repeating by the managements involved. Further support comes from Michael Porter's (1987) examination of the diversification record of large US firms over the period 1950–86. He found that 53 per cent of all acquisitions were subsequently divested, rising to 74 per cent for unrelated acquisitions.

As one would expect given this performance record, a significant amount of research has been conducted to examine the factors determining acquisition success or failure (see Haspeslagh & Jemison (1991, pp. 292–309) for a concise review of the research literature). Two key success criteria emerge. First, there must be clear opportunities to create value through the acquisition and, second, the acquired company must be effectively integrated into the new parent in a way that takes account of both strategic and human considerations. Each is discussed in turn below.

The purchase price of an acquisition typically includes a bid-premium of 30–40 per cent over the previous market value of the target company. Premiums of that order in general make it difficult for acquisitions to be a financial success for the acquiring company. Many acquisitions fail because the perceived benefits of increased market share and technological, manufacturing, or market synergies fail to increase profit margins or raise turnover by the amount necessary to justify the price paid to conclude the deal. Acquisitions can only be justified in cases in which the post-merger benefits have been solidly defined. In order to successfully create value through acquisition, the future cashflow stream of the acquired company has to be improved by an amount equal to the bid-premium, plus the often overlooked costs incurred in integrating the acquisition, and the costs incurred in making the bid itself. Four basic value-creation mechanisms are available to achieve this:

1. *Resource sharing*, in which certain operating assets of the two merging companies are combined and rationalized, leading to cost reductions through economies of scale or scope. (The British pharmaceutical company Glaxo planned to save $600 million annually following its acquisition of Wellcome by combining headquarters operations, rationalizing duplicated R&D facilities onto selected sites, and adopting a single sales force in overlapping product areas.)
2. *Skills transfer*, in which value-adding skills such as production technology, distribution knowledge, or financial control skills are transferred from the acquiring firm to the acquired, or vice versa. Additional value is created through the resulting reduction in costs or improvement in market position. The effective transfer of functional skills involves both a process of teaching and learning across the two organizations, and therefore tends to be a longer-term process than resource sharing. Nevertheless, it is often the primary value-creating mechanism available in *cross-border* acquisitions, in which the opportunities to share opera-

tional resources may be limited by geographic distance. For example, in its acquisition of the Spanish brewer Cruz del Campo, the drinks company Guinness planned to recoup the acquisition premium by using its marketing expertise to establish Cruz as a major national brand in the fragmented Spanish market.

3. *Combination benefits*. These are size-related benefits such as increased market power, purchasing power, or the transfer of financial resources. A company making a large acquisition within its existing industry, or a series of smaller ones, may succeed in raising profit margins by effecting a transformation of the industry structure. The emergence of a dominant player within the industry should reduce the extent of competitive rivalry, as well as providing increased bargaining power over both suppliers and customers for the acquiring company. The European food processing industry, for example, has consolidated rapidly through acquisitions, driven both by a desire to reduce competitive rivalry and a belief that larger brand portfolios will help to maintain margins in the face of increasing retailer concentration. Financially based combination benefits may be available. The superior credit rating of an acquirer may be used to add value by refinancing the debt within an acquired company at a lower interest rate. In other instances in which the acquired company has been a loss-maker prior to acquisition, the associated tax credits can be consolidated to the new parent, thereby reducing the latter's tax charge.
4. *Restructuring* is applicable when the acquired company contains undervalued or underutilized assets. Here, acquisition costs are recouped by divesting certain assets at their true market value, and by raising the productivity of remaining assets. The latter may be accomplished by closing down surplus capacity, reducing head office staff, or rationalizing unprofitable product lines. Very often the two elements are combined: for example, the closure of surplus capacity may lead to a vacant factory site which can then be sold off at a premium for redevelopment. A further

Need For Strategic Interdependence

		Low	High
Need for Organisational Autonomy	High	Preservation	Symbiosis
	Low	Holding	Absorption

Figure 1 Types of acquisition integration approach.
Source: Haspeslagh & Jemison (1991).

form of restructuring is the concept of "unbundling." This involves acquiring an existing conglomerate (or other portfolio of businesses) the market value of which is less than the sum of the individual constituent businesses. The businesses are then sold off piecemeal, creating a surplus over the acquisition cost. Restructuring is essentially financially based, in that it does not require any strategic capability transfer between the two firms. Rather, the skill of the acquirer is in recognizing and being able to realize the true value of the targets' assets. A classic illustration of value-creation through restructuring is Hanson plc's acquisition of the diversified tobacco company, Imperial. Hanson paid $5 billion for Imperial and within a year had sold off its food and brewing interests, along with its London head office, for $3 billion, leaving it with the core tobacco business that generated 60 per cent of Imperial's previous profits for only 40 per cent of the acquisition cost.

The presence of value-creating opportunities does not in itself guarantee a successful acquisition. Plans have to be effectively implemented before the benefits can be realized in practice. This is the second area in which acquisitions frequently fail. In many instances organizational issues block the ability of the acquirer to create the planned value. Key personnel may depart following the acquisition, clashes of organizational culture may lead to mistrust and lack of communication, or inappropriate control systems may hinder the efficiency of the newly acquired firm.

Haspeslagh & Jemison's (1991) comprehensive study of the acquisition process has highlighted the fact that the appropriate form of post-acquisition integration will depend on two principal characteristics of the acquisition. First, the value-creation mechanism(s) will determine the degree of *strategic interdependence* that needs to be established between the two companies. Resource sharing and skills transfer imply high to moderate strategic interdependence respectively, while combination benefits and restructuring imply little or no interdependence. Second, the extent to which it is necessary to maintain the autonomy of the acquired company in order to preserve its distinctive skills will determine the need for *organizational autonomy*. Where critical employees are loyal to a distinctive corporate culture, as in many service businesses, it may be important to preserve that culture post-acquisition. Consideration of these characteristics suggests the appropriate form of post-acquisition strategy, as illustrated in figure 1.

Effective implementation also depends on creating an atmosphere of mutual cooperation following the acquisition. Resource sharing, skills transfer and, to a lesser extent, combination benefits all create value through the transfer of strategic capabilities between the acquiring and acquired firms. Because of the high degree of change often involved, and the uncertainty likely to be felt by employees on both sides following the acquisition, it is critical that the acquirer works to create an overall atmosphere that is conducive to the required capability transfer. Haspeslagh & Jemison (1991) argue

Table 1   Types of acquisition integration approach.

Absorption integration	The aim is to achieve full consolidation of the operations, organization, and culture of both companies, ultimately dissolving all boundaries between the acquired and acquiring firms.
Symbiosis integration	The acquiring company attempts to achieve a balance between preserving the organizational autonomy of the acquired company while transferring strategic capability between the two organizations.
Preservation integration	The acquired organization is granted a high degree of autonomy, typically positioned within the acquiring organization as a stand-alone subsidiary.

that there are five key ingredients to such an atmosphere:

1. *Reciprocal organizational understanding.* In order to work together effectively, both companies need to understand each other's history, culture, and management style. This two-way learning process is particularly important in the context of skills transfer, as the acquirer must ensure that the source and origins of the sought-after skills are not inadvertently destroyed during the integration process.
2. *Willingness to work together.* Employees of both companies may have a natural reluctance to cooperate together post-acquisition. Fears over job security, changes in management style, or simple distrust of the new organization may all hinder the willingness to work together. Research suggests that the negotiation stage of an acquisition can play an important role in creating an atmosphere of cooperation. Successful implementation is more likely where there is a clear vision of the future, assurances are maintained, and concern is shown for the people involved. Post-acquisition, reward and evaluation systems also can be used to encourage cooperation.
3. *Capacity to transfer and receive the capability.* In order for skills transfer to occur, it has to be possible to accurately identify and define the skills and to actually effect their transfer. In some smaller acquisitions, for instance, it may prove difficult to transfer the acquirer's control and reporting systems, as the receiving management does not have the time both to collect substantial amounts of additional data and continue to run its business as before.

4. *Discretionary resources.* Managements need to keep in mind that acquisitions frequently take up more managerial resource than was planned initially. Once a fuller understanding of the newly acquired company is developed post-acquisition, new opportunities and problems will often emerge that require managerial time and attention.

5. *Cause–effect understanding of benefits.* Finally, the correct atmosphere for implementation can only be generated when there is a clear understanding of how value will be created through the acquisition. Those involved in the value-creation process must understand the benefits sought and the costs involved in achieving them. The detailed knowledge about these two elements may be held at different organizational levels. Executive management will have conceptualized the benefits of acquisition, but operating management who will conduct the day-to-day implementation frequently hold the knowledge about the associated costs. Open communication between those charged with planning and implementing the acquisition becomes critical. Value can only be created when the acquisition benefits outweigh the implementation costs.

Bibliography

Bleeke, J. & Ernst, D. (eds), (1993). *Collaborating to compete: using strategic alliances and acquisitions in the global marketplace.* New York: John Wiley.

Cartwright, S. & Cooper, C. (1992). *Mergers and acquisitions: the human factor Oxford4 Butterworth–Heinemann.*

Haspeslagh, P. & Jemison, D. (1991). *Managing acquisitions: creating value through corporate renewal.* New York: Free Press.

Kitching, J. (1967). Why do mergers miscarry? *Harvard Business Review*, 45, 84–101.

Kitching, J. (1964). Winning and losing with European acquisitions. *Harvard Business Review*, 52 124–36.

Norburn, D. & Schoenberg, R. (1994). European cross-border acquisition: how was it for you? *Long Range Planning*, 27 (4) 25–34.

Porter, M. (1987). From competitive advantage to corporate strategy. *Harvard Business Review*, (May–June), 43–59.

RICHARD SCHOENBERG

activity-based costing Activity-based costing (ABC) was developed to understand and control indirect costs. It also provides management with a tool which enables them to understand how costs are generated and how to manage them. By contrast, historic cost analysis tends to allocate costs according to some arbitrary formula which often fails to truly reflect actual costs.

ABC assigns costs to products and/or customers upon the basis of the resources that they actually consume. Thus an ABC system identifies costs such as machine set-up, job scheduling, and materials handling. These costs are then allocated according to the actual level of activities. All overhead costs are thus traced to individual products and/or customers, as the cost to serve all customers is far from equal.

As a result, ABC forms an integral component in the strategic planning process and, unlike conventional accountancy, provides a vehicle for assuming future costs rather than purely measuring past history. It allows management to identify systems, policies, or processes that operate activities and thus create cost. ABC permits management to identify actual cost drivers and address these, and so reduce fixed cost.

While ABC assigns material costs to products in the same manner as conventional accounting, it does not assume that direct labor and direct material automatically generate overhead. Rather, it assumes that products incur indirect costs by requiring resource consuming activities, and these costs are specifically assigned rather than being estimated as a function of the direct costs.

In a traditional cost system it is usually assumed that these costs are related to volume. However, in reality some activities are not necessarily triggered by individual units but, rather, may be generated by a batch of units. For example, doubling a product's volume does not double the number of machine set-ups. Rather, set-ups are determined by the number of batches produced, and an ABC system assigns cost accordingly. Purchasing is another cost driven by batches. Traditional cost accounting allocates purchasing costs according

Table 1 Allocation bases for traditional and ABC.

Indirect cost	Traditional	ABC
Production control	Labor hours	Parts planned
Inspection	Labor hours	Inspections
Warehousing	Labor hours	Stores receipts and issues
Purchasing	Labor hours	Purchase orders
Receiving	Labor hours	Dock receipts
Order entry	Labor hours	Customer orders
Production setups	Labor hours	Production changeovers

Source: O'Guin (1991).

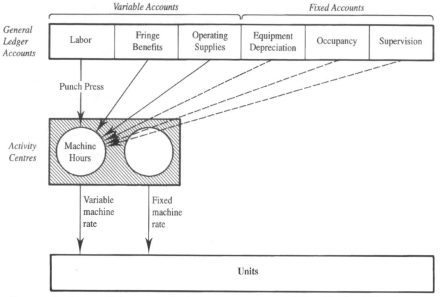

By segregating the general ledger accounts flowing to parts one can create variable and fixed cost drive rates

Figure 1 Using ABC to calculate variable and fixed costs.
Source: O'Guin (1991).

to material cost. However, this method fails to account for the true cost of purchasing, which is directly proportional to the number of purchase orders made. ABC allocates cost according to purchase order numbers. ABC also reflects economies of scale in the factory, allocating actual costs based on set-ups, materials handling, warehousing costs, and the like. Such differences are illustrated in table 1.

In addition to allocating costs specifically to products, ABC assigns below-the-line costs, such as those attributable to sales, marketing, R&D, and administration. When such a subdivision is meaningful, this can be done by class or segment of customers. Usually, customer costs can vary substantially as a result of differences in the following factors:

- customer segment
- order size
- pre- and after-sales service levels
- service levels
- product size
- distribution channel

- geography
- selling and marketing service

From such an understanding of the costs to serve, management can devise policies to improve profits and reduce costs. These might operate on:

- average number of units per customer order
- number of locations supplied
- type and volume of sales promotions used
- alternate pricing strategies
- number of returns sent back
- channels of distribution used
- number of sales calls required
- speed of bill payment

An ABC system separates product- and customer-driven costs. PARETO ANALYSIS can then be used to focus on key costs on each and both dimensions concurrently, with a view to eliminating serious loss-making customer and product combinations.

Assigning Costs in an ABC System

ABC allocates all resources to either products or customers to reflect actual operations. Just as traditional accounting does this in a two-stage process, so too does ABC. However, ABC uses more cost pools and assigns costs to a wider variety of more appropriate bases. In particular, a wider choice is made of second-stage cost drivers, allowing ABC to model more complex situations in a superior way.

Activity Centers

ABC first assigns all key manufacturing and business process costs to activity centers. Being based more on actual activity measures, this analysis tends to be more rigorous than traditional methods. These first-stage cost drivers are then allocated to products, as shown in figure 1. The truly differentiating feature of ABC, however, is the much greater sophistication in the treatment of second-stage drivers. Here the ABC system recognizes that many costs are not directly proportional to volume but, rather, that many are proportionate to the number of batches produced. As such, costs are assigned to batches while some, such as design engineering, are related to entire products.

Activity centers come in two groups: product-driven activity centers and customer-driven centers. Activity centers themselves are either homogeneous processes such as the punch press, machining, or assembly, or a business process such as marketing, procurement, or distribution.

Second-stage Drivers

These are activity measures used to assign activity center costs to products or customers. In traditional cost accounting, such second-stage drivers usually consist of direct labor costs, material costs, machine hours, or other indicators of value. In ABC systems, in addition to these costs, second-stage drivers might include set-up times, inspection costs, warehouse moves, sales calls, and customer orders. These drivers thus reflect how an activity center consumes cost by product and/or customers. As a result, by not assigning such costs on the basis of volume can reflect the different costs of complex products or customer groups.

Hierarchical Costs

A further significant difference between ABC and traditional costing is the formal systems recognition; these costs can be stimulated at different hierarchical levels. While individual units trigger some costs, others occur at the level of the batch and even at the market segment. As a result of this recognition, ABC separates costs for management decision making. Such hierarchical costs can also be separated by product and customer as follows.

Product-driven Activities
- *Unit level*: production costs assigned once for each unit (e.g., drilling a hole)
- *Batch level*: manufacturing costs assigned once for each batch (e.g., machine set-up)
- *Product level*: costs to support the design or maintenance of a product line (e.g., product engineering and process design)

Customer-driven Activities
- *Order level*: costs attributable directly to selling and delivering orders to individual customers (e.g., order entry, shipping, billing, and freight)
- *Customer level*: non order related costs attributable to individual customers (e.g., sales force costs, credit and collections, pre- and post-sale service costs)
- *Market level*: costs required to enter or remain in a particular market (e.g., R&D, advertising and promotion, and marketing)
- *Enterprise level*: costs required to remain in business that are unassignable to any lower level (e.g., pensions, board of management, central staff).

These might apply for higher or lower levels for a business dependent upon the cost structure of the firm; the ABC system distributes all such costs in a way which reflects actual operations.

ABC by Business Type

ABC principles have mainly been applied in manufacturing industry, but are becoming increasingly important in the service sector as cost analysis becomes an important strategic factor in a deregulated, more competitive environment.

In capital-intensive process industries, ABC costing is very important. Many process industries utilize time-based costing as a representative of capacity utilization as a cost driver, with factors such as direct labor being assigned to a process, not a product. Process time is charged to products on the basis of machine hours. Capital costs and thus change-over costs tend to be high in process industries and should not be assigned on a volume measure such as time.

As fixed costs are so high in capital-intensive industries, high-capacity utilization is a critical determinant of business profitability. Variable pricing may well therefore be necessary and the cost of excess capacity needs to be calculated so that fixed costs do not incorrectly influence pricing decisions. An ABC system needs to reflect this and, in addition, the large fixed costs required to maintain the process, such as maintenance and process engineering, are annually allocated to production lines rather than being arbitrarily spread.

In some process industries, such as food and brewing, logistics costs can form an extremely large element in overall costs. Furthermore, the costs to some specific customer segments may also vary widely. Customer sales volume, location, and product mix will all affect logistics costs. This, coupled with the need for high-capacity utilization rates, can allow traditional costing systems to suggest unprofitable policies, such as the pursuit of small customers with specialist product needs. Limited production flexibility may well compound this problem. By allocating indirect costs more accurately, ABC pinpoints profitable opportunities and encourages exit from loss-making segments.

Many process industry firms actually have very primitive cost systems, offering little more than aggregate values for labor, supplies, utilities, raw materials, and the like. In addition, in many process industries the joint cost problem exists, in which a variety of products are produced as a result of a drive to produce one. ABC does not address all of these issues, and managerial decisions will need to be taken about costing system assumptions.

Service industries similarly have notoriously weak costing systems. Again, many costs (such as branch premises for a bank) are joint costs, and it may be impossible to exit part of the business without fatally damaging that part the firm wishes to retain. The use of ABC, while not providing clear answers to these problems, nevertheless identifies profitable customer and profit segments in a superior manner to traditional costing.

Designing an ABC System

The key element in designing a successful ABC system is in the choice of cost drivers. To choose these variables it is essential to identify correctly what generates activity; these activity triggers are cost drivers.

The first key principle in designing an ABC system is to keep it simple. Efforts should be concentrated on the significant costs, with the focus being on relevance rather than precision, reflecting on how the firm actually incurs cost. Moreover, many costs have no precise measures and common sense needs to be used to assign such costs in the most equitable way. Care must also be taken to avoid attempting to track every small cost, to avoid the creation of an overly expensive, complex system. All unnecessary detail increases the need for more cost drivers, which adds to the expense of designing and operating the system. Finally, keeping matters simple makes understanding easier and actually stimulates acceptance and use of the system.

Second, it needs to be recognized that each firm is somewhat individual and that the nature of costs may vary widely from company to company. As a result, different cost drivers may be employed in different corporations; thus the same type of costs may be allocated using cost drivers that are not applicable to another concern.

Third, it is imperative to understand what objectives top management wishes the cost system to support. A substantial number of decisions must therefore necessarily be made before the final design is set. Such decisions affect the choice of cost drivers, the level of system complexity, and whether or not the system is to be on line.

Designing the system therefore involves the following steps:

1. Develop fully "burdened" departmental costs from the general ledger.
2. Segregate costs into product-driven or customer-driven.
3. Split support departments into major functions, each of which:

- has a significant cost

- is driven by different activities

4. Split departmental costs into function cost pools.
5. Identify activity centers.
6. Identify first-stage cost drivers.
7. Identify second-stage cost drivers on the basis of:

- available data

- correlation with resource consumption

- effect on behavior

8. Identify activity levels.
9. Choose the number of cost drivers on the basis of:

- system use

- company complexity

- available resources

ABC provides a new insight into the true profitability of products and customers by allocating indirect costs in a much more realistic way than traditional costing systems. As a result, product and customer profitability is often shown up in stark relief and in a new way, causing significant rethinking of policies and overall corporate strategy. This is especially true in industry sectors which historically have not really been required to compete vigorously. New technologies and deregulation are transforming competitive conditions in many industries, and this is leading to widespread efforts to incorporate this alternate means of costing.

Bibliography
Cooper, R. (1988). The rise of activity-based costing, part one: What is an activity-based costing system? *Journal of Cost Management* (summer).
Cooper, R. (1990). Implementing an activity-based costing system. *Journal of Cost Management* (spring).
Cooper, R. & Kaplan, R. S. (1991). Profit priorities from activity-based costing. *Harvard Business Review*, **69**, 130–5.
O'Guin, M. C. (1991). *The complete guide to activity based cost.* Englewood Cliffs, NJ: Prentice-Hall. See chapters 2, 3, and 4.
Rotch, W. (1990). Activity-based cost in service industries. *Journal of Cost Management* (summer).
Turney, P. B. B. (1989). Activity based costing: a tool for manufacturing excellence. *Target* (summer.)

DEREK F. CHANNON

advantage matrix   During the 1970s, the Boston Consulting Group recognized that the GROWTH SHARE MATRIX had a number of

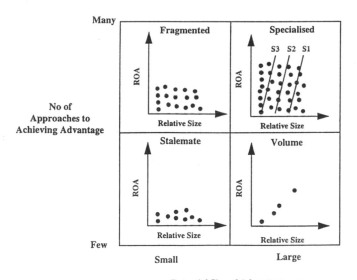

Figure 1 The BCG Advantage Matrix.
Source: Boston Consulting Group.

limitations, in that an underlying experience effect (*see* EXPERIENCE AND LEARNING EFFECTS) was not always present and that differentiated products need not be as price-sensitive as undifferentiated or commodity products. As a result, the Advantage Matrix, was developed, as shown in figure 1. In this system four generic environments were identified on the basis of the potential size of competitive advantage that could be generated, and the number of ways in which a competitor could establish a leadership position within an industry.

VOLUME BUSINESSES, STALEMATE BUSINESSES, FRAGMENTED BUSINESSES, and SPECIALIZED BUSINESSES are identified within this system. As shown in figure 1, only in volume businesses does the historic experience effect (*see* EXPERIENCE AND LEARNING EFFECTS) analysis tend to hold. In specialized businesses a relationship also exists between size and profitability within specific but different segments. In stalemate and fragmented businesses, size *per se* does not necessarily determine relative cost. Despite the BCG's modification of the Growth Share Matrix for portfolio planning, the revised matrix is much less well known and, regrettably, the deficiencies of the original concept remain insufficiently discussed.

Bibliography

Boston Consulting Group (1974). *Segmentation and strategy*. Boston, MA: Boston Consulting Group.
Boston Consulting Group (1974). *Specialization*. Boston, MA: Boston Consulting Group.
Rowe, A.J., Mason, R. O., Dickel, K. E., Mann, R. B. & Mockler, R. J. (1994). *Strategic management*, 4th edn, Reading, MA: Addison-Wesley. See pp. 119–22.

DEREK F. CHANNON

agency theory   Agency theory deals with situations in which one party (the "principal") delegates responsibility to another party (the "agent") to take decisions on its behalf. Typical agency relationships exist between shareholders and managers; employers and employees; professionals such as lawyers, doctors, or investment advisers and their clients; and elected politicians or civil servants and citizens. Delegation does not need to be explicit, and this brings into the scope of agency a wider range of transactions, such as insurance contracts, where the insurer delegates responsibility to the insured to reduce the likelihood and/or cost of the insured event occurring. Variations include multiple principals and/or multiple agents.

The establishment of an agency relationship typically increases total utility. Nevertheless, several costs are involved, including the costs of drawing up, monitoring, and enforcing the contract. Jensen & Meckling (1976) classified agency costs as follows: (i) monitoring costs, incurred by the principal to regulate the agent's behavior (including the use of incentive schemes designed to induce the agent to act in the way in which the principal would act if he had the information available to the agent, and also the costs of organizing multiple agents to act in unison); (ii) bonding costs, incurred by the agent to assure the principal that he will not take inappropriate actions; and (iii) the residual loss, which is the loss to the principal due to actions by the agent which the principal would not have undertaken (or would have undertaken differently, or actions which the principal would have undertaken but the agent did not) if he had the agent's information. Overall, agency costs are affected by the respective utility functions of the principal and the agent, including their risk attitudes, and the degree to which information asymmetries prevail, and a trade-off exists between monitoring costs and the residual loss.

Information asymmetries obstruct effective delegation in two principal ways. In the first case, the agent may hold information before the contract is drawn up which, if known by the principal, would influence the latter's choice. Such private information (often the rationale behind the delegation in the first place) can be withheld by the agent to increase his own utility from the contract. In the second case, the principal cannot accurately observe the agent's actions, either because these are difficult to distinguish from environmental factors, or because the agent again withholds information. These two cases of pre- and post-contractual difficulties are known as the hidden information (adverse selection) and hidden action (moral hazard) problems, respectively.

An important agency relationship of interest is the contract of shareholders (residual risk bearers/beneficial owners) with management (risk takers/those exercising control). In this case, shareholders may have goals such as profit maximization or value maximization, subject to a minimum level of security against variability, while management may, in addition to the above, value high levels of discretionary expenditure, sales maximization, "empire building," cost minimization, accumulation of power and prestige, promotion, and stress and effort minimization. There may be situations in which shareholders may be sufficiently dispersed so as to make the formulation and implementation of a coherent shareholder utility function difficult, in which case the agents are likely to find it easy to pursue their own objectives.

A poorly structured relationship of this sort may lead to high rates of corporate growth if managers pursue practices such as "empire building" and budget maximization; diversification, as a means of achieving growth or to reduce corporate and personal risk; allocative inefficiency, as a result of sub-optimal firm size (*see* EFFICIENCY); or productive inefficiency, if, for example, an executive uses a more expensive airline at company expense to take advantage of a frequent flier scheme, the benefits of which accrue to himself personally. Shareholders can reduce the likelihood and extent of such behavior by modifying managers' interests to converge to their own, by such methods as share option and profit sharing schemes.

Most interesting in this context is the historical development and role of pension funds, mutual funds and other like vehicles. As advances in transportation made distant markets more accessible and new technologies encouraged firms to pursue ECONOMIES OF SCALE and diversify (*see* DIVERSIFICATION), so firms' size and capital requirements increased. Close family or joint stock arrangements became increasingly unsatisfactory, and stock had to be offered to a broader range of investors of increasingly lower affluence. While investors in general welcomed traded stock as a savings method which offered particularly good liquidity, smaller ones could only buy into few companies and found the risk of doing so too great.

As a result, intermediary vehicles such as the above started to manage portfolios of stocks on behalf of those investors who entrusted them with their funds. Beneficial stock ownership became separated from the exercise of the

associated voting power (Berle & Means, 1932), and it was up to the fund managers to ensure that corporate management were adequately supervised. This, although capable, they did not always do, often preferring portfolio-based risk reduction to active involvement in the affairs of the companies, and it was only recently that competition between funds started to squeeze managements to perform better, contributing to the "short-termism" they are sometimes accused of.

Bibliography

Berle, A. A. Jr & Means, G. C. (1932). *The modern corporation and private property.* New York: Macmillan/Commerce Clearing House.
Grossman, S. & Hart, O. (1983). An analysis of the principal and agent problem. *Econometrica*, **51**, 7–46.
Jensen, M. C. & Meckling, W. H. (1976). Theory of the firm: managerial behaviour, agency costs and ownership structure. *Journal of Financial Economics*, **3**, 305–60.
Williamson, O. E. (1964). *The economics of discretionary behavior, managerial objectives in a theory of the firm.* Englewood Cliffs, NJ: Prentice-Hall.

STEPHANOS AVGEROPOULOS

area-based divisional structure Several variants of this form of organizational structure occur. They are especially to be found in multinational corporations; but they may exist in relatively undiversified national concerns, and particularly in service industries such as retailers, banks, railroads, utilities, insurance, and restaurants. The advantages of such a structure include the ability to tailor strategy to the needs of each geographic market; that it takes advantage of local market, fiscal, and tax opportunities on a local basis; and that it produces a cadre of multifunctional general managers. Disadvantages include problems of coordination with product divisions and functions; problems of maintaining a common corporate image/reputation from area to area; problems of standardizing marketing, and especially pricing policies; and potentially additional costs due to an extra tier of management.

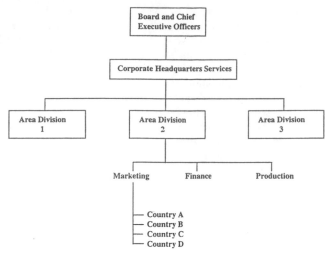

Figure 1 Area-functional organizational structure.

Area-functional Structure

This variant of area structure is commonly found under conditions where there are:

- low levels of product diversification

- high levels of regional market differentiation

- economies of scale in production, transportation, and/or distribution that occur on a regional basis

- low levels of interregional trading

This structure is illustrated in figure 1. Such firms tend to organize their global interests on a highly integrated basis in any region of the world, and to link individual national manufacturing and marketing activities within a region into integrated, interdependent operations. In some cases regional product design may be undertaken, while pricing, distribution, promotion, and production within a region tend to be centralized and determined at the regional divisional headquarters. This structure is often found where regional influences are more important than global influences, while production ECONOMIES OF SCALE are limited. Such industries include specialist foods, products subject to climatic variation (e.g., tropical versus arctic); and products meeting specific ethnic and cultural requirements. However, an increasing number of traditionally regional markets are globalizing, and as this tendency increases the regional structure becomes potentially unstable. For example, the Ford Motor Corporation, which for many years operated an area-based divisional structure, was undergoing a fundamental change toward a global product-based structure in the mid-1990s.

Area Product Divisional Structure

This structure is illustrated in figure 2. It tends to be found where:

- there are large MNCs involving a network of product and geographic interests, and where there is no home market dominance

- there is a need to provide significant coordination on an area basis between local activities

- product flow is high between national subsidiaries within a region, but is relatively low between regions

This type of organization is an extension of the local umbrella HOLDING COMPANY STRUCTURE and is widely used in diversified companies as a means of coordinating and controlling operations for a variety of product areas within a specific geographic region. This type of organization is also close to a MATRIX STRUCTURE requiring multilevel product and geographic coordination and integration, and also usually involving multiple executive reporting relationships. The area division becomes in many

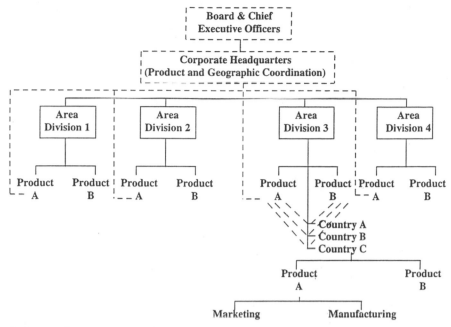

Figure 2 Area product organizational structure.

respects a regional headquarters and is often seen as a localized extension of the corporate headquarters. As MNC overseas operations become an increasingly important component of corporate strategy, there is a need to closely supervise these activities to prevent serious potential losses of control. Such organizations may also act as localized cash centers which, because of their time zone differences, may require localized inputs in addition to central cash, leads and lags, foreign exchange, transfer pricing, and tax management.

A regional headquarters, therefore, performs this type of role, as well as reducing local frictions and local legal and fiscal conformity. Moreover, it is still possible to use expatriate managers to fill key positions in regional offices, to ensure that close linkages with the headquarters culture are maintained and that the corporation can generate general managers with a global perspective.

Such structures have tended to be introduced first in particular areas. Thus many US corporations have initially established European and/or Latin American headquarters, before extending the principle on a global scale, the ultimate move being the treatment of North America as similar to other regions. Regional headquarters tend to be located in favorable tax environments such as Switzerland, but many companies may use such operations as booking centers, while main personnel locations have favored cities or countries with central location, transportation, and communication facilities, together with proximity to business information, governments, and supranational authorities. As a result, major centers in Europe would include Brussels, London, and (to a lesser extent) Paris.

Bibliography

Channon, D. F. & Jalland, M. (1979). *Multinational strategic planning.* New York: Amacom.

Prahalad, C. K. & Doz, Y. L. (1987). *The multinational mission.* New York: Free Press.

DEREK F. CHANNON

B

balanced score card A critical element in successful strategy implementation is an appropriate management control system. Many systems do not provide the critical information required by management to assess the corporations progress to achieving its strategic vision and objectives. The balanced score card is a performance measurement system developed by Kaplan and Norton which, although including financial measures of performance, also contains operational measures of customer satisfaction, internal processes, and the corporation's innovation and improvement activities, which are seen as the key drivers of future financial performance. The approach provides a mechanism for management to examine a business from the four important perspectives of:

- How do customers see the firm? (*customer perspective*)

- What does the firm excel at? (*internal perspective*)

- Can the firm continue to improve and create value? (*innovation and learning perspective*)

- How does the firm look to shareholders (*financial perspective*)

The system also avoids information overload by restricting the number of measures used so as to focus only on those seen to be essential. The balanced score card presents this information in a single management report and brings together often disparately reported elements of the firm's strategic position such as short-term customer response times, product quality, teamwork capability, new product launch times and the like. Second, the approach guards against suboptimization by forcing management to examine operation measures comprehensively.

The system requires management to translate their general mission statements for each perspective into a series of specific measures which reflect the factors of critical strategic concern. A typical scoreboard is illustrated in table 1.

The precise score card design should reflect the vision and strategic objectives of the individual corporation. The key point is that the scorecard approach puts strategy and corporate vision rather than control as the key element of design and is consistent with the development of CORPORATE TRANSFORMATION techniques, CROSS-FUNCTIONAL organizations, and customer–supplier interrelationships.

Building the Balanced Score Card

While each organization is unique, to improve acceptance and commitment to the revised measurement system, a number of companies have sought to involve teams of managers in the design of their scorecards. This also insures that line management create a system which reflects their needs, rather than with traditional systems which tend to be control driven by finance and accounting specialists. A typical score card design project might involve the following stages:

(1) *Preparation.* SBU's should be selected for which a score card measurement system is appropriate. These should have clearly identifiable customers, production facilities, and financial performance measures.

(2) *Interviews: first round.* Each senior SBU manager is briefed on the approach and provided with documents on the corporate vision, mission, and strategy. A facilitator interviews the senior managers to obtain their views and suggestions, as well as a number of

Table 1

Goals	Measures	Goals	Measures
Financial perspective		*Customer perspective*	
Survival	Operating cashflow	New product	Percentage of sales from new products
Success	Quarterly sales growth and operating income by SBU	Speed of response	Customer measure of on-time delivery
Future prosperity	Increase market share; increase productivity; reduce capital intensity	Preferred supplier	Customer ranking survey; customer satisfaction index
			Market share
Internal business perspective		*Innovation and learning perspective*	
Higher productivity	Value added per employee	Technology leadership	New product design time; patent rate versus completion
	Waste as % output		No employee suggestions
	Capital intensity; machine utilization rate	Product focus efficiency	Percentage of products equal to 80% of sales; revenue per employee
Design productivity; new product introduction	Engineering efficiency – actual versus scheduled; time to market	Employee motivation	Staff attitude survey

key customers to learn about their performance expectations.

(3) *Executive workshop.* The top management team is brought together to begin the development of an appropriate score card which links measurements to strategy.

(4) *Interviews: Second Round.* The output of the workshop is reviewed and consolidated and views are sought about the process of implementation.

(5) *Executive workshop: second round.* A second workshop is then held with senior managers together with their direct subordinates and a larger group of middle managers to design the appropriate measures, link them to any change

programs under way, and to develop an implementation plan. Stretch targets should also be developed for each measure, together with preliminary action programs for their achievement. The team must also agree on an implementation program, including communication to employees, integrating the score card in management philosophy, and developing an appropriate information system.

(6) *Implementation.* A newly formed team develops an implementation plan for the score card, including linking the measures to databases and information systems, communicating the system through the organization, and facilitating its introduction.

(7) *Periodic review*. The score card should be constantly reviewed to insure that it meets the needs of management.

Bibliography

Gouillard, F. J. & Kelly, J. N. (1995). Transforming the Corporation. New York: McGraw-Hill.
Kaplan, R. S. & Norton, D. P. (1990). The balanced scorecard – measures that drive performance. *Harvard Business Review*, January–February, 71–9.
Kaplan, R. S. & Norton, D. P. (1993). Putting the balanced scorecard to work. *Harvard Business Review*, Sept.–Oct., 134–47.
Kaplan, R. S. & Norton, D. P. (1996). *The Balanced Scorecard*. Boston, MA: Harvard School Press.

DEREK F. CHANNON

barriers to entry and exit   One of Porter's Five Forces (*see* FIVE FORCES MODEL), barriers to entry are strategies or circumstances that protect a firm from competition by making new entry difficult, or by putting potential entrants at a disadvantage. Viewed another way, barriers to entry can be considered to be the additional costs which a potential entrant must incur before gaining entry to a market. Bain (1956, pp. 3–5) argues that entry barriers should be defined in terms of any advantage that existing firms hold over potential competitors, while Stigler (1968, pp. 67–70) contends that, for any given rate of output, only those costs that must be borne by the new entrants but that are not borne by firms already in the industry should be considered in assessing entry barriers. The main effect of barriers to entry is that they may keep the number of companies competing in an industry small, and allow incumbents to earn super-normal profits in the long term. For them to be effective, they must, in principle, increase costs for the challenger more than they do for the incumbent.

Viewed from their function as entry deterrent conditions, there are three broad categories of activities that lower the threat of entry; namely, structural obstacles to entry, risks of entry, and reduction of the incentive for entry. Seen from another dimension, barriers to entry can exist naturally (e.g., natural monopolies), or they can be the result of specific action by the company concerned (although this latter distinction is sometimes misleading, as competing in a naturally monopolistic industry may well be the result of strategic decision). Finally, barriers can generally be classified as either dependent on or independent of size.

Size-independent Structural Barriers

Size-independent cost conditions include: government subsidies, tariffs, and international trade restrictions (anti-dumping rules, local content requirements, and quotas); regulatory policies; licensing; special tax treatment; restrictions on price competition; favorable locations; proprietary information; proprietary access to financial resources, raw materials, and other inputs; proprietary technologies, know-how, or proprietary low-cost product design; EXPERIENCE AND LEARNING EFFECTS and proprietary access to distribution channels and markets.

To constitute credible barriers, the above need to be defensible and to continue holding in the long term. They can be obtained by encouraging government policies that raise barriers by means of trade protection, economic regulation, safety regulation (product standards and testing, plant safety, or professional body membership or accreditation requirements), or pollution control. Barriers can also be set up: by limiting access to raw materials; by exclusive ownership of the relevant assets or sources; by, for example, purchasing assets at pre-inflation prices; by tying up suppliers (by means of contracts, for example, and also by convincing them that it is risky to take on products which lack consumer recognition); by raising competitors' input costs (for example, by avoiding passing on scale economies through suppliers and bidding up the cost of labor if they are more labor-intensive); by foreclosing alternate technologies (and obliging challengers to take defenders head-on); by investing in the protection of proprietary know-how (by means of patents, secrecy, etc.); by blocking channel access; by raising buyer SWITCHING COSTS and the costs of gaining trial (e.g., by targeting the groups most likely to try other products with discounts); or, finally, by molding of customer preferences and loyalty (through, for example, advertising and promotional activities that increase the costs that the new entrant will have to incur to attract customers), by filling product or positioning gaps, and by brand proliferation (which reduces the market share that will become available to the new entrant).

Size-dependent Structural Barriers

In addition, depending on the size of the firm, other barriers may become available. ECONO-MIES OF SCALE and minimum efficient scale effects, for example, force the aspiring entrant to come in on a large scale (with all the risks and costs this entails, particularly if incumbents are unable to accommodate the new entrant, and are thus expected to retaliate), or accept a cost disadvantage. In addition, the absolute size of the required investment in certain industries and the fact that such investment may have to be made up front, and can be unrecoverable, limits the pool of potential entrants and may act as a deterrent for smaller potential entrants.

To make use of these barriers, scale econo-mies can be pursued in production, if feasible. They can also be pursued in marketing and R&D, and it is in those areas where they are likely to be a more readily available tool as, there, scale thresholds are largely determined competitively. Similarly, although the amount of capital necessary to compete in an industry is not controled by the firm, it is possible to increase it by methods such as raising the amount of financing available to dealers or buyers, or employing more investment-intensive technologies (*see* INVESTMENT INTEN-SITY).

Risks of Entry

Once a company has decided that it can find ways in which to circumvent such barriers, it has to consider how risky its prospective industry is, and how easy it will be to survive there.

In principle, there are three industry char-acteristics which are said to affect this. High industry concentration makes incumbents more powerful, high investment intensity can raise the cost of failure (it may bear the risk of further financial demands, or it can simply make the firm more prone to technological obsolescence) and, finally, high advertising intensity can also act as a deterrent because of the brand loyalties and switching costs involved.

Nevertheless, high concentration is also an indication of a profitable or new industry, high investment intensity can allow the technological innovator to leap-frog incumbents, and high

advertising intensity may similarly be a tool to be exploited to enter concentrated markets. As a result, there are few industry characteristics which can be depended upon as effective barriers to entry.

Instead, it may be more effective to indicate to prospective entrants that their efforts will be contested (*see* SIGNALING). For such indication to be effective, the incumbent must show that there are good causes for not accommodating the entrant and that the incumbent is able to fight. Upon entry, the strategies to be deployed against the new entrant must also be deter-mined.

Starting from a consideration of the credible signals that the incumbent can use to indicate his intention to defend, the most effective deterrent is to make combat unavoidable upon entry (this is the most committing, and also the riskiest way, as the potential entrant may be stronger). This can be done by foreclosing or raising the cost of one's own exit routes, by means of matching competitor guarantees or anything else that increases the economic need to maintain share, such as the setting up of high fixed cost operations, or the building up of excess capacity. Slow industry growth makes such signals even more credible, as it implies that the entrant cannot be accommodated without serious loss of share.

On a less committing level, any known particular threat can be delayed by signaling incipient barriers, such as by early announce-ment of product launches or capacity expansion.

As far as the ability to fight is concerned, the maintenance of a healthy financial state may act as a good deterrent, as well as an indication that the firm is able to expand output, cut prices, and the like.

Some methods that can be employed before entry to prepare for combat involve the estab-lishment of blocking positions. These are for use mainly against prospective entrants that are established in other industries, but which are likely to move into the defender's markets. Protection may be achieved by setting up small business units in the main markets of such competitors, so that conflict can be threatened in those markets too, with only limited losses for the defending firm but more extensive ones for the prospective challenger. In addition, ϵ preemption can be used: this involves obtaining and maintaining a head start in critical projects that any prospective entrant would have to undertake, the size of the head start being marginally greater than the incumbent's response delay.

The response of the firm immediately upon entry is also significant. At this time, the challenger is likely to be very sensitive to new information, and its confidence dependent on early results. Causing uncertainty can help in such situations, and this can be done by disrupting test or introductory markets with high but erratic levels of marketing and sales promotion activity. Being able to introduce a new product just after a competitor has entered with an imitation of earlier products can also set him back, and the threat of legal action can also raise the risks, costs, and uncertainty involved, and delay entry. In any case, putting on a good defense even against entrants that are not considered particularly harmful can be useful in establishing a good track record which may help to prevent further attacks.

Finally, the role of pricing is deemed to require special attention. In principle, the threat of a price war would normally be expected to act as a deterrent, particularly in an industry with excess capacity or slow growth. Upon closer consideration, however, there may appear to be no reason for prices to be used as an entry barrier, as they can be changed easily, allowing the incumbent to enjoy high profits before entry and still be able to fight entrants with lower prices once they have entered the market. Nevertheless, limit pricing can be used to signal a cost function that is difficult to imitate, and it allows prices to act as a deterrent for higher-cost producers, at the cost of sacrificing short-run profits in order to maximize long-run profits (Salop, 1979, in Milgrom & Roberts, 1982). Having said that, however, lowering prices after entry does not necessarily indicate anti-competitive strategies, as it may be done simply to accommodate a new entrant (Stiglitz, 1981, 1986).

Lowering the Inducement for Attack

Another method of preventing entry is to make the industry itself appear uninviting. It is difficult to deceive potential rivals completely, but some shaping of their expectations and information regarding future and current profit-ability may well be possible. To this effect, it is well worth publicizing realistic industry growth forecasts if it is suspected that potential challengers may be overestimating the industry's prospects, and also to make some effort to disguise large profits, as they are highly visible.

As a solution of last resort, poison pill strategies or licensing of a proprietary technology when a competing technology appears may also be effective.

Barriers to Exit

Barriers to exit are the activities and circumstances that commit a firm to its industry and its position within it.

Typical exit barriers may take the form of specialized assets, vertical integration, long-term contracts with suppliers or buyers, or inter-relationships and synergies with other businesses, which would be adversely affected should the business unit in question be shut down.

The higher the exit barriers are, the more costly it is to abandon a market, so the stronger the incentive will be for firms to remain and compete as best they can. As a result, the barriers to exit of established firms imply that any potential entry will be contested and, as such, also act as barriers to entry for prospective entrants.

Bibliography

Bain, J. S. (1956). *Barriers to new competition.* Cambridge, MA: Harvard University Press.

Harrigan, K. R. (1981). Barriers to entry and competitive strategies. *Strategic Management Journal*, **2**, 395–412.

Porter, M. E. (1979). How competitive forces shape strategy. *Harvard Business Review*, **57** (2), (March–April). Reprinted, with deletions, in H. Mintzberg & J. B. Quinn, *The strategy process: concepts, contexts, cases* 2nd edn, Englewood Cliffs, NJ: Prentice-Hall. See pp. 61–70.

Porter, M. E. (1980). *Competitive strategy: techniques for analyzing industries and competitors.* New York: The Free Press.

Porter, M. E. (1985). *Competitive advantage: creating and sustaining superior performance.* New York: The Free Press.

STEPHANOS AVGEROPOULOS

benchmarking   In the late 1970s, the Xerox Corporation woke up to the fact their Japanese competitors were selling copiers at prices at which Xerox could sometimes not manufacture. After realizing this, Xerox set out to understand why and to learn, from their competitors, concepts such as VALUE ENGINEERING and TEAR DOWN. Xerox also began to learn from competitors about other best practice techniques. This has developed into the now widely practised methodology of benchmarking, and has been extended to all elements of a business.

There are usually around ten generic categories for designing benchmarking architecture:

- customer service performance
- product/service performance
- core business process performance
- support processes and services performance
- employee performance
- supplier performance
- technology performance
- new product/service development and innovation performance
- cost performance
- financial performance

In designing a benchmark architecture, the first step is to design a system that enables management to achieve the organization's strategic objectives.

Second, it is necessary to create a common language for measuring performance. This should be consistent with the corporate culture.

Third, it is necessary to develop plans to collect, process, and analyze the performance measures. It is likely that while the organization possesses much of the data needed, it is not in a useful form to encourage management action. The information is collected to reflect the organization's position on a radar chart (sometimes called a "spider chart"; *see* RADAR MAPPING).

In addition to careful design of the benchmarking system architecture, other critical success factors include:

- top management support
- benchmarking training for the project team
- suitable management information systems
- appropriate information technology

Table 1   The Xerox 12-Step Benchmarking Process.

Step	Description
Phase 1 – planning	
1	Identify what to benchmark
2	Identify comparative companies
3	Determine data collection method and collect data
Phase 2 - analysis	
4	Determine current performance gap
5	Project future performance levels
Phase 3	
6	Communicate findings and gain acceptance
7	Establish functional goals
Phase 4 - action	
8	Develop action plans
9	Implement specific actions and monitor progress
10	Recalibrate benchmarks
Phase 5 - maturity	
11	Attain leadership position
12	Fully integrate practices into processes

Source: Bogan & English (1994, p. 82).

- internal corporate culture

- adequate resources

The precise process used for benchmarking varies from company to company according to internal culture and needs. The process used by one of the pioneering US corporations, Xerox, used one of the more comprehensive systems which involves 12 steps divided into five phases, and is illustrated in table 1.

Successful implementation of benchmarking systems favors simplicity. The system recommended by the Strategic Planning Institute Council on Benchmarking advocates a five-step process. This is illustrated in figure 1. These phases are explained in the following subsections.

Launch

The launch phase requires management to decide which improvement areas have the greatest impact or potential for the corporation. These usually flow from the STRATEGIC PLANNING process, from an analysis of the corpor-

ation's internal and external best practices. Continuous monitoring should also be undertaken to identify opportunities for improvement in CORE PROCESS functions and businesses.

The Organize Phase

In this phase, benchmarking projects to a clear focus, a benchmarking project team is organized, and a project plan is developed.

The Reach Out Phase

During the third phase the benchmarking team reaches out to understand its own and other organizations' processes. This involves:

- documentation of the process to be studied, based on customer needs

- collection of secondary data

- determination of variables by which to evaluate performance

- design of a questionnaire through which to solicit performance information, both from within the corporation's own operations and from external corporations

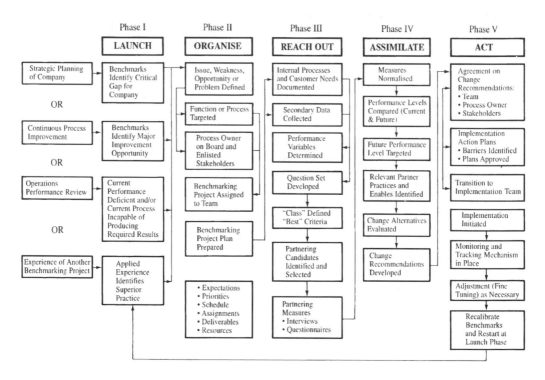

Figure 1 The benchmarking process.

Table 2 Integrating benchmarking and re-engineering

Seven-step re-engineering process	*Tools applied*
Step 1. Identify the value-added, strategic processes from a customer's perspective.	Performance benchmark analysis (cost, quality, cycle time, and the like). Customer satisfaction benchmark analysis. Value analysis.
Step 2. Map and measure the existing process to develop improvement opportunities.	Flowcharting and process management tools. Performance measurement tools.
Step 3. Act on improvement opportunities that are easy to implement and are of immediate benefit.	Informal benchmarking for short-term solutions. Implementation planning tools.
Step 4. Benchmark for best practices to develop solutions, new approaches, new process designs, and innovative alternatives to the existing system.	Best practice benchmarking among processes and performance systems.
Step 5. Adapt breakthrough approaches to fit your organization, culture, and capabilities.	Process redesign tools. Implementation planning tools.
Step 6. Pilot and test the recommended process redesign.	Training, and pilot test techniques. Apply lessons learned from past successful pilots.
Step 7. Implement the re-engineered process(es) and continuously improve.	Train employees. Implementation techniques. Use benchmarking to maintain continuous improvement process.

- collection of data

- selection of benchmarking partners

- on-site visits to the best performing partners

Assimilation Phase

Best practice information is assimilated and prepared for a report for top management. Data gathered is normalized, performance gaps identified, future performance goals targeted, and implementation for changes recommended.

Act Phase

In this final phase the benchmarking team works with senior management and core process owners to develop an agreed implementation program. This leads to the development of formalized action plans, implementation schedules measurement and monitoring systems, and benchmark recalibration plans. Once this has been done, responsibility passes to an implementation benchmarking team.

Benchmarking is not only a tool in its own right but also forms an essential component in re-engineering projects (*see* RE-ENGINEERING DISADVANTAGES; VALUE-DRIVEN RE-ENGINEERING). The integration between these two activities is illustrated in table 2.

Bibliography

Anonymous (1987). *Leadership through quality: implementing competitive benchmarking.* Xerox Corporation Booklet, Part 1.

Anonymous (1992). *Benchmarking: focus on world class practices.* AT&T.

Anonymous (1993). *Benchmarking. PIMS Letter on Business Strategy No. 54.* PIMS Europe Ltd.

Bogan, C. E. & English, M. J. (1994). *Benchmarking for best practices, winning through innovative adaptation.* New York: McGraw-Hill. (This is one of the best books to date on the benchmarking process and this entry has drawn heavily on this work.)

Garvin, D. (1993). Building a learning organization. *Harvard Business Review,* 71, 78–91.

McNair, C. J. & Leibfried, K. H. J. (1992). *Benchmarking.* New York: HarperCollins.

Walleck, S. A., O'Halloran, D. & Leader, C. A. (1991). Benchmarking and world class performance. *McKinsey Quarterly,* no. 1, 3–24.

DEREK F. CHANNON

best practices   This was a related activity which formed part of the WORK OUT process in the US General Electric company. Historic success had led to a degree of complacency in the company and, as part of his radical campaign to modify the culture of GE, Jack Welch instituted a program of effectively BENCHMARK-ING GE against a carefully selected group of companies that were also seen as excellent in terms of management practices. Nine companies, including seven major US corporations and two leading Japanese multinationals, participated in a year-long study to identify these concerns' best practices. The main findings of the study were that these highly productive concerns exhibited the following characteristics:

● They managed processes rather than people.

● They used process mapping and benchmarking to identify opportunities for improvement. This involved writing down every single step, no matter how small, in a particular task.

● They emphasized continuous improvement and praised incremental gains.

● They relied on customer satisfaction as the main measure of performance, so overcoming the tendency to focus on internal goals at the customer's expense.

● They stimulated productivity by introducing a constant stream of high-quality new products for efficient manufacturing.

● They treated suppliers as partners.

Bibliography

Tichy, N. M. & Sherman, S. (1993). *Control your own destiny or someone else will.* London: HarperCollins. See p. 205.

DEREK F. CHANNON

bid defenses   In the face of a major growth in contested acquisitions (*see* ACQUISITION STRATEGY) in the late 1980s, managements of companies subject to such actual and potential hostile attacks, in conjunction with investment banking advisers, developed a number of defense tactics. A number of the better known of these include the following, although some defenses may not be possible in some markets due to local stock exchange regulations and corporate law.

The "Pac Man" Defense

Based on the popular video game of the 1980s, the "Pac Man" defense occurs when a company subject to a bid turns around and tries to swallow the aggressor. There are two main variations of the defense. In the first of these a counter tender offer is made by the target company for some portion of the shares of the corporation attempting to purchase it. The second variation of the "Pac Man" defense, whereby the target purchases the acquirer's shares in the open market, is called "counter accumulation." The major difference between the two variants is that the latter can be carried out with less commitment than the tender offer. No offering circular with legally binding statements needs to be issued, although the firm's intentions need to be filed with the Securities Exchange Commission (SEC). In addition, counter accumulation defense avoids the cost of paying a price premium that is usually associated with a tender offer.

Problems with the "Pac Man" defense are that it stimulates both parties to behave irrationally, and also makes the fight especially reckless. Moreover, it creates considerable uncertainty in the marketplace as, first, it is difficult to discern who will be the winner and, second, one counter offer seems to stimulate another. "Pac Man" also tends to shorten the time frame of an acquisition, as each party races to acquire the other.

As with most defensive strategies, "Pac Man" is usually adopted with a "golden parachute" scheme whereby, for the losing executives, substantial payments need to be made to those who are removed following victory by one party or the other, since with "Pac Man" the initial aggressor also needs to develop a defense as it too becomes a target. Raising the funds needed to finance a "Pac Man" defense may also result in the depletion of assets or a substantial increase in leverage in the original target, possibly leading it to also adopt a "scorched earth" defense. In this, a company liquidates a substantial portion of its assets to make itself less attractive.

Lock-up Strategies

There are basically three forms of lock-up strategy. The first of these, called target company stock lock-up, involves a "white knight" being given the right to purchase authorized but unissued shares or treasury shares of the target company. This sharply increases the cost of the acquisition to any hostile bidder, as it forces the raider to purchase the newly issued shares in addition to those already outstanding.

The second variant that is often used is referred to as an asset lock-up, under which the white knight has the right to purchase a specific asset of the target, in the event of a hostile bid. The asset in question is usually that component of the target of specific interest to the acquirer, making the target much less attractive.

The third variant, much less used, is the shareholder stock lock-up. This invites the option to purchase a block of the target's shares from one or more of its major shareholders. This purchase is often large enough to block a potential acquirer from gaining a controlling percentage of stock, so locking the bidder out.

The lock-up strategy is frequently used in conjunction with other defenses. While a lock-up strategy does not give the board uncontestable control, an appropriately contracted lock-up defense enables it to substantially influence the outcome of any bid.

The Self Tender Defense

This defense, which is an important weapon, occurs when a firm undertakes a tender offer for its own shares as a method of defending against a hostile bid. After purchase such shares are retired, and are commonly referred to as treasury stock. The defense is usually employed to defend against a "two-tier" or "front end loaded" hostile bid. A two-tier bid occurs when a raider achieves majority control and then endeavors to force any remaining shareholders to sell out for an undisclosed amount of cash and/or securities. It is this second step, in which shareholders are unsure of the potential value of the acquirer's offer, that triggers a defense by the incumbent management. Similarly, the defense can be deployed against a one-tier offer when the target feels that the raider's offer is too low relative to the underlying value of its shares.

The self tender is usually for fewer shares than the offer it is defending against. The reason for the smaller offer is that most managements are looking to defend against the hostile bid, rather than selling assets to raise cash necessary for a large-scale self tender. The offer size also tends to be limited by corporate and contractual covenants and other legal constraints. The price offered in a self tender offer may, on occasion, be higher than the hostile bid, but in most cases is the same, on the premise that, all other factors being equal, shareholders will back existing management. The use of a self tender also places the hostile bid in a time frame. As tender offers have an expiration date, a self tender offer usually ensures that the battle will conclude within a relatively short period. Moreover, when the target firm specifies the date on which it will commence purchasing shares, this forces the raider to decide what action to take before that date or otherwise be left without a strategy.

Most self tender defenses are initiated by a contingent trigger, which is set off when a raider starts to carry out his tender offer in part or in full. The delay is caused to avoid serious cash outlays unless absolutely necessary. To support the cash need, this requires asset sales or burdening the target with heavy extra debt.

As with most defense strategies, self tenders tend to be used in conjunction with other defenses, notably "golden parachutes." Anti-attack measures such as staggered board elections also help to discourage raiders, because they may increase the time from the initial investment by a raider to achieving control. Legal proceedings are taken by all parties, suing for everything from arbitration to market manipulation. A self tender defense may also be used as a means of restructuring the corporate balance sheet to make the target less attractive.

Self tender therefore raises the cost to an aggressor in several ways. First, if the aggressor initiates a two-tier bid the defense increases the cost by establishing a floor share value, so raising the aggressor's cost. Second, the defense may undermine the aggressor's own financing; for example, by pledging assets being used by the bidder to secure bid finance. Third, balance sheet restructuring to finance the self tender may render the target unattractive to the bidder by substantially increasing the level of debt. Fourth, if a significant block of target company stock is placed in friendly hands prior to a bid, retiring the self tendered and bought shares increases the voting power of the bloc. Finally, the self tender defense creates a timing advantage for the target.

The Kamikaze Defense

There are a number of variants of the Kamikaze defense, all of which involve the loss of important corporate assets, such that if successful the corporate remainder is a poor shadow of its former self. At one extreme is the "scorched earth" strategy, in which the target liquidates a significant portion of its assets to frustrate an attack by an aggressor. A less drastic version of this, the "sale of the crown jewels," occurs when the target liquidates assets that are particularly desired by a raider. At the other extreme is the "fatman" defense, whereby the target purchases an "ugly duckling" business to make itself less attractive.

"Scorched earth" strategy. A "scorched earth" strategy is characterized by the sale of all, or substantially all, of a target firm's assets. The strategy is usually employed only as a threat or last resort. It works only when the price offered by a raider is substantially below that to be obtained by a quick sale of assets. The major problem for its successful implementation is when the firm fails to obtain a satisfactory price for the assets to be sold.

"Sale of the crown jewels". The motivation for this strategy is similar to that of the "scorched earth" strategy, but the effects are not necessarily as severe. In this defense the target usually sells the assets of most interest to the bidder. It is therefore used widely by conglomerate firms, which may be raided because their break-up value may well be greater than market capitalization. If the sale is substantial it may well lower the value of the target to a level at which the raider withdraws its offer. This is especially true when the proceeds of the sale are distributed to existing shareholders.

This strategy can be an effective defense, especially when a raider is targeting a specific business or division. The sale of a key asset

where the proceeds are distributed deprives the raider of the sold business's benefits and also provides shareholders with cash. Proceeds from a sale can also be used by the target to purchase new assets, which might be in business areas that cause problems for the raider with regulatory or stockmarket authorities. However, a sale under pressure carries the downside risk of a firesale price. Furthermore, any sale may make the target rich in cash, so adding to the attractiveness of the target to other raiders.

"Fatman" strategy. The "fatman" defense involves the purchase of assets by the target company which reduce the attractiveness of the target; such as, for example, the acquisition of a business that reduces the short-term earnings prospects of the combined group or adds significantly to balance sheet debt. As a result, the "fatman" defense may be an attractive long-term deterrent, while decreasing short-term vulnerability without selling off attractive assets. When used as an integral component in corporate strategy, it may add to the long-term earnings prospects of the total corporation by offering potential operating synergies. Moreover, the short-term decrease in the target's cash or increase in debt may increase the deterrent. To achieve these advantages, however, "fatman" acquisition targets must be carefully selected, and suitable candidates should be identified in advance of a raid.

The "Poison Pill" Defense

The "poison pill" defense is designed to prove a lethal dose for a raider to swallow if it successfully purchases the target. The primary mechanism for achieving this is the issue of a stock dividend to the target's shareholders. The keys to the effectiveness of the pill are the special conversion and redemption features of the issue, which significantly reduce any raider's control of the target. In particular, the conversion of the stock dividend into shares of the acquirer poses a major problem for the raider.

For the strategy to be most effective, stockholders need to have previously authorized a large block of blank check preferred stock. This is not issued until the time at which a defense is required. In addition, management should authorize an issue of common stock; otherwise, the board cannot institute a "poison pill" without going through the lengthy process of obtaining shareholder approval, thus making the defense less effective. The importance of the blank check is not only its prior authorization but the fact that it does not contain specific provisions – these are tailored later to maximize the discomfort of any raider. Once these authorizations have been obtained the "poison pill" can be administered by a simple vote of the board.

The special issue preferred stock can be converted in a number of ways and customized to maximize the effectiveness of the defense. This should hit the raider in an area of greatest vulnerability by tailoring the conversion features accordingly. Typical alternatives include the following:

- The preferred can be "flipped over" into convertible preferred stock of the raider. This feature poisons the raider in two steps. First, the target's convertible preferred is converted into that of a raider. Second, the raider's convertible preferred is converted into the raider's common stock – a move that potentially seriously dilutes the raider's position.

- The preferred can give the target's shareholders the right to directly convert the stock into the raider's common shares at a large discount to market price.

- The preferred can be swapped for notes which must be honored by the raider – a tactic that is very effective against hostile bids from highly leveraged aggressors.

To determine which option to use, target company management needs to evaluate which has the most devastating effect on a raider and select accordingly.

While the "poison pill" defense can prove to be very effective it needs to be used with caution. For example, once implemented, it may be a serious deterrent for any white knight or friendly merger partner. The customization therefore needs to take such a future position into consideration. Second, a successful "poison pill" defense could leave the target in financial difficulties; for example, by paying dividends on the newly issued preferred stock. Third, the issuance of large blocks of new stock may change the target's capital structure, making future stock issues difficult.

The Employee Benefit Plan Defense

A number of companies have made use of the employee benefit plan as an element in a defense strategy. Four methods of such a defense have been identified. First, the company may use stock held in benefit plans to assist in achieving a leveraged buyout. Second, the employee plan trustees can refuse to tender its shares, or can tender its shares to a friendly bidder. Third, the plan trustees can purchase the target company's stock; while the fourth option entails using the plan's surplus assets.

These tactics are often subject to significant legal restrictions and constraints, partially as a result of management abuses and of policies introduced by raiders that are deemed to have been against employee interests. As a result, there have been strong moves in many countries to ensure that benefit plans are in the hands of independent trustees and fall outside the control of management.

The "Shark Repellent" Defense

Most major corporations contain amendments within their articles and bylaws to deter undesired bids. These amendments, termed "shark repellents," are somewhat simpler provisions than the more complex defenses developed in recent times. Amongst the more widely used repellents are the following:

- *Staggered board.* Under this system the board is divided into three groups, each of which comes up for election once every three years. As a result, a majority shareholder can elect at most one-third of the board each year.

- *Controled board changes.* To support the staggered board concept, some companies have adopted special amendments to their Articles that permit shareholders to remove directors only with a specific cause, not simply by majority vote. The corporate charter usually also fixes the size of the board. This helps to prevent an acquirer from packing the board with its nominees at a single annual meeting.

- *Specific directors' qualifications.* Some companies require board members to fulfil certain conditions to be eligible as directors.

- *Supermajority as a defense.* Under this provision shareholders must approve any business combination by a vote substantially higher than that normally required by law. The provision, which is widely used, usually requires the approval of 75–95 per cent of the target's shareholders for a two–step merger. The required percentage is also sometimes based on a sliding scale, depending on the percentage of the company already owned by the acquirer.

Fair price amendments. These are used to protect shareholders who have not tendered their stock in the first step of a merger so that they obtain a "fair price" in the second step. Such amendments are designed specifically to prevent "front loaded" transactions that pressurize stockholders to tender at the first offer stage.

"Golden parachute" agreements. These are aimed at protecting top management in the target company. They provide significant compensation for loss of office and are custom tailored to the individual executive.

Bonding up the acquirer. Instead of authorizing more stock, some corporations have amended their charters so that they are in a position to issue bonds which are convertible with shares of common stock. Conversion of these bonds can significantly dilute the position of an acquirer.

Changing location. In the USA, the permitted "shark repellents" vary widely under the different corporate statutes in different states. The State of Delaware for example, is a popular choice for reincorporation because its statutes permit corporations to adopt a wide choice of defensive tactics. Reincorporation in a more favorable state is often easier than changing the corporation's charter.

While the best defense against raiders is to maintain a share price that is sufficiently high to prevent attack, and while "shark repellents" lead to the adoption of anti–repellent tactics by raiders, failure to have any repellents in place in today's atmosphere of potential hostile attack, which can now operate on a global basis, seems to be an invitation to unwelcome aggressors.

Bibliography

Michel, A. & Shaked, I. (1986). *Takeover madness.* New York: John Wiley.

DEREK F. CHANNON

blind spots In a remarkable number of cases, firms fail to recognize changes in competitive conditions which may severely impact their strategic position. Frequently, such blind spots fail to identify the nature of substitute products, or the entry of new competitors which may bypass the existing industry cost structure by adopting new ways of competing. These may enjoy dramatic advantages, thus negating possible historic cost positions in a stable industry structure achieved by high MARKET SHARE. Indeed, high market share positions may actually become a positive disadvantage, because to respond to such an attack, firms may be forced to transform the elements which had gained them their traditional competitive advantage.

Areas in which blind spots have been particularly common have been in newly deregulated industries, those in which channel shifts are possible and in which information technology provides the possibility of gaining substantial cost advantages. Classic examples of such blind spots would include the Merrill Lynch Cash Management Account, a product carefully designed to avoid being classified as a banking product, but in practice offering a comprehensive series of banking services, including checking, credit card, and brokerage management, and paying a superior rate of interest on all account balances. As a result, consumers withdrew their deposits from savings and loans banks, and from commercial banks, in the USA to open such accounts, while still using these institutions for most of their personal transactions. Initially not recognizing the new form of competition, the savings and loan banks found that the cost of their deposits had risen so much that they were forced to take on increasingly risky property projects to cover their increased cost of deposits, such that by the end of the 1980s many had been forced to close, leaving the US taxpayer to pick up the bill of several hundred billion dollars.

Channel shifts have also occurred in a number of industries. IBM has been forced to make dramatic price cuts in the early 1990s and to introduce a fighting brand in personal computers. As prices have tumbled and new channels have opened, it has become impossible for IBM to retain its high-cost personal selling approach. Instead, first, companies such as Amstrad began to sell IBM-compatible machines at a deep discount to IBM through consumer electronics retail outlets. Second, new entrants such as Dell Computer opened direct marketing at an even lower cost than using retailers. As a result, IBM was forced to close its own retail outlets, cut back on its sales force overhead, and add a direct sale fighting brand.

Similarly, in Europe oil companies have dramatically lost their share of retail gasoline sales to superstores and hypermarkets. Faced with serious overcapacity, low-share oil companies were happy to supply the superstores with product, sold increasingly under the store brand name rather than that of the oil companies. The large-share oil companies, with their heavy investment in retail gasoline outlets, have thus seen their market shares eroded by competitors able to lock in cost advantages on what for them was a marginal product.

The impact of information technology can be seen in the insurance industry where, for motor and household insurance, direct writing has transformed the industry. Traditional insurers, especially those with high market shares achieved by sales through brokers, have again been placed on the horns of a dilemma. Unable to compete because of the margins demanded by the brokers, the insurers have only reluctantly opened direct writing subsidiaries themselves for fear of alienating their traditional channels.

The careful assessment of industry boundaries, both at present and as they may be in the future, is therefore a critical element in achieving sustainable competitive advantage. The careful avoidance of blind spots is an essential ingredient in this analysis.

DEREK F. CHANNON

branding Branding is often viewed by consumers, both personal and institutional, as an important determinant in the purchase decision. As such, brand can add value to a product and also to its parent company. For example, products such as perfumes and cosmetics are priced heavily on the basis of brand – similar products in unbranded bottles would not command a fraction of the price. Indeed, undifferentiated products, such as vodka, can command brand-based price differentials of up to 40 per cent, despite the fact that the leading brand may be chemically indistinguishable from a store private-label brand.

Today, branding has been successfully applied to almost everything, although not always with success. Furthermore, channel brands have grown significantly in importance, to the detriment of manufacturer brands. Successful brand names can also be valuable franchise properties. Name and character licensing has thus become a business valued at many billions of dollars. Clothing and accessories producers are the largest users of licensing, with fashion leaders such as Cardin, Gucci, and the like using their names to brand a wide variety of merchandise from luggage to cosmetics, in addition to clothing. Virgin is perhaps one of the widest ranging examples of brand stretch. Having started in recorded music, Richard Branson's company initially moved into air transportation, music and computer games, stores, and cinemas, and most recently into soft drinks and liquor and mutual funds – many of these activities having apparently little or no relationship with one another.

Products such as toys, games, and food are also often linked back to names and characters such as Walt Disney, Power Rangers, and Jurassic Park. These tie-in linkages can often be an important ingredient in the overall economics of specific projects and enterprises. Such franchise and brand extension strategies can become key components of brand-based strategies. Harley Davidson, for example, originally the largest producer of US "heavy" motor cycles, now sees the motor cycle as essentially the ultimate fashion accessory! Today, the company franchises its name to a wide range of casual clothing, toys, motor cycle accessories, and the like.

Brand names and positioning are important strategic decisions. Successful brand development may take many years and, once developed, requires constant and steady investment. Ironically, the accountancy treatment of brands is ambiguous. Many accountants would argue that, as an intangible, a brand has no balance sheet value. Nevertheless, the value of many mergers and acquisitions has been decided on the purchaser's idea of the underlying value of brands to be acquired; as for example, in the purchase of Rowntree by Nestlé.

Among the required qualities of brand names are: (1) the need to suggest some of a product's benefits or attributes; (2) easy pronunciation (one-syllable words tend to be best, e.g., Mars, Daz, Lux, and Crest); (3) a distinctive quality, such as in Firebird, Fiesta, and Canon; and (4) ease of translation into other languages, as in the case of Sony, Coca Cola, and Shell.

Branding has also become important in institutional markets. For example, in financial services, maintenance products, and manufactured goods, products increasingly are named rather than being given a specification number.

The cost of brand support tends to be high in most markets. Unless a strong brand position can be achieved in a company's SERVED MARKET, therefore, a proprietary brand strategy must be questioned. Normally, unless a number one or two market position is achievable, lower-share competitors might consider exiting or becoming private-label suppliers.

Bibliography

Davidson, H. (1987). *Offensive marketing*. Harmondsworth, UK: Penguin. See pp. 293–304.
Kotler, P. & Armstrong, G. (1989). *Principles of marketing*, 4th edn, Englewood Cliffs, NJ: Prentice-Hall. See Chapter 10.

DEREK F. CHANNON

break even analysis   The break even point chart (figure 1) shows the total cost and total revenue expected at different levels of sales volume.

For each product there is a variable cost which, when deducted from the sales value, generates a contribution. The variable cost itself can be disaggregated to identify its individual constituents. In addition, to support the product there are a number of costs which are not volume-dependent but, rather, are fixed as shown. The volume level of sales at which the sum of unit product contributions equals the

fixed cost plus the variable costs is the break even point, as illustrated. For most businesses, there is also a desired level of profitability. This is illustrated as volume B, at which the difference between total revenue and total costs represents the profit impact target. Analysis of the chart enables management to also readily identify which cost items make up most of total expenditure, how much reduction could be made to these, and which expenses are controllable and which are not. Care should be taken in the allocation of fixed costs. Some costs which were previously considered to be fixed can be made variable by adopting techniques such as re-engineering (*see* RE-ENGINEERING DISADVANTAGES; VALUE-DRIVEN RE-ENGINEERING) and ACTIVITY-BASED COSTING methods.

In calculating the break even and target profits it is also important to check what these volumes represent in terms of MARKET SHARE. Such a share position should be both obtainable and sustainable at an acceptable level of cost. Frequently, firms do not undertake this check. Where substantial share gains are required to be made to achieve break even, careful assessment

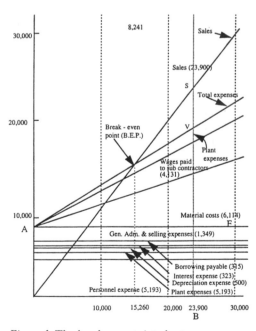

Figure 1 The break even point chart.
Source: Nagashima (1992).

should be made that this is in fact achievable. Similarly, sensitivity analysis should be undertaken on price to assess the impact on contribution margins and the consequent effect on break even volume and market share.

Bibliography

Nagashima, S. (1992). *100 management charts*. Tokyo: Asian Productivity Organisation. See pp. 30–31.

DEREK F. CHANNON

C

cartel Producers in almost every industry face risks and uncertainties that have an adverse impact on profitability. Some of these risks are associated with the activities of competitors, so it may be possible to reduce them by overt or tacit cooperation between producers on such matters as the determination of prices and output, the marketing of new products or services, and the like. Such cooperation, if extensive, is called collusion, and the organizations which take part in it are said to be members of a cartel.

Cartels are quite distinct from oligopolies, as an oligopoly simply refers to the population of an industry by only a few competitors, for whatever reason; while a cartel is the result of conscious collusive activity in order to take advantage of opportunities for cooperation. Nevertheless, the two are interrelated, as cartels are difficult to institute and operate in non-oligopolistic environments.

Methods

There are a number of methods of coordination, and collusion may be overt, as in the Organisation of the Petroleum Exporting Countries (OPEC), or tacit, as in independently devised modes of behavior or price leadership models; whereby, for example, promises to match prices or advance price notifications ensure uniformity without any communication taking place between the colluding organizations.

Turning to methods of sharing the market and the profits that it generates, a cartel can be, in principle, either profit maximizing or market sharing. A profit maximizing cartel attempts to maximize the aggregate profits of all firms, and makes the same price and output decisions as the multiplant firm, equating the cartel's overall marginal cost with the industry's marginal revenue. The distribution of the market between the firms is determined by marginal cost considerations, and agreement is reached between firms as to the redistribution of profits, with the firms producing most of the output (the lowest-cost ones) making payments to higher-cost firms in order to reduce the incentive of the latter to expand their output. Market sharing cartels, on the other hand, allow each firm to maintain a set segment of the market, defined in terms of either market share or geographic area. The segment of the market that each firm is allowed is specified by reference to a host of factors, including historic shares and the power of each firm inside the cartel.

Requirements for Success

In order for a cartel to remain successful, it must ensure that it is able to defend its market from all possible threats, including the power of buyers and suppliers (*see* FIVE FORCES MODEL), the threat from SUBSTITUTE PRODUCTS and the threat of entry (*see* BARRIERS TO ENTRY AND EXIT).

In addition, a cartel faces the requirement to keep its members under the terms of their agreement, so it must ensure that each considers itself better off as part of the cartel than outside it. The reason why this may be difficult is that cartel-operated markets face inelastic demand (*see* ELASTICITY), so firms have an incentive to expand output beyond their allowed quotas, as this would be expected to increase their individual profitability. Precisely because demand is inelastic, limited cheating has little impact on prices, but extensive cheating can destroy the cartel. As a result, each firm will only have an incentive to cheat as long as it expects others not to cheat much; and it would prefer to keep overall cheating to low levels, as dismantling of the cartel and return to competitive conditions would be expected to make each firm worse off.

With these broad requirements in view, there are a number of factors that can enhance the stability of a cartel. These include: (i) conditions of economic and industrial growth, as a booming market can allow firms to expand output without breaching any agreement; (ii) a small number of firms in the industry/cartel, as the more firms there are, the more difficult it is for cheating to be identified and exposed; (iii) a slow pace of product and process innovation, as the faster this is, the more negotiations will have to be carried out; (iv) similarity in producers' cost functions, as the more similar (or symmetrically differentiated) these are, the simpler coordination and the establishment of a single price will be; (v) the marketing of necessity types of products, as products facing inelastic demand do not significantly reduce profitability when prices are raised; (vi) the marketing of homogeneous products, as this simplifies coordination by reducing it to the price dimension only; (vii) the marketing of a small number of products, this also aiding monitoring and enforcement of the agreement; and (viii) the availability of price information, to provide early warning signs of cheating.

Implications, Dangers, and Benefits

Cartels have significant implications in three main respects; namely, the relative power of their members and, more importantly, allocative and productive EFFICIENCY.

An immediate impact of cartel organization is that weaker firms become more important than they would be under competitive conditions. This is because every single member, whether large and profitable or small and otherwise insignificant, is able to expand output and threaten the integrity of the entire cartel. As a result, the importance of any single firm for the cartel no longer depends on its market share or profitability, as it would under competitive conditions, but on its ability to upset the delicate balance of the cartel. Therefore, larger members find it worthwhile to gain the cooperation of the smaller ones by allowing them a greater share of the market and profits than they would be able to obtain in competitive conditions.

Turning to efficiency considerations, it can be said, in principle, that collusion and cartels are undesirable, and they are often illegal too, although some survive, especially those that operate across national boundaries. The undesirability of cartels is largely based on the fact that collusion reduces the forces of competition. Cartels constrain production below the socially optimal levels, and raise prices. This transfers wealth from consumers and society to the members of the cartel, which are able to earn supernormal profits in the long run. The result is that allocative efficiency is reduced, and less of the product than is socially optimal is produced and consumed.

Restrictive practices also reduce productive efficiency. As cartel members face little competition and they are able to earn excess profits irrespective of their efforts to optimize their processes, their incentive to produce cheaply and effectively is reduced.

In addition, because of the unstable nature of such organizations, their members have to be prepared for the dissolution of the cartel and a return to more competitive production. As a result, they can often only agree to restrict output if they are each allowed to maintain their best facilities in operation. This means that, unless they all have plants of comparable technology and size, firms with inefficient plants may have to be allowed to produce while a more efficient plant which belongs to other firms remains idle. This would imply that the marginal cost of the cartel is higher than is otherwise necessary, so that productive efficiency is also compromised at the aggregate level.

Cartels and Monopolies

The above arguments imply that the more a cartel restricts competition, the more undesirable it is. At the extreme, a monopoly would thus be the most undesirable industry organization. To keep the discussion in perspective, however, it is worth mentioning two characteristics of cartels which may on occasion compromise the validity of this last argument.

First, a cartel involves direct maintenance and administrative costs, such as the costs of negotiations and SIGNALING, and also indirect maintenance costs, such as the deviations from the lowest-cost production for the purposes of fairness to all members, as just described. Because monopolists have no such costs, it is possible to envisage a situation in which high coordination costs make a monopoly preferable to a cartel.

Second, the effect of cooperation on R&D and innovation must be considered. Technology sharing cartels distribute the costs and risks of research, so it is possible that they may spend more on R&D than even a competitive industry would. Moreover, even if spending on research is not increased, the net consequence for growth and welfare may still remain beneficial because of the lower cost and enhanced rapidity of dissemination. In the long term, therefore, it is possible that collusion may speed productivity and output growth, and even reduce the cost of the growth process.

Bibliography

Baumol, W. J. (1992). Horizontal collusion and innovation. *Economic Journal*, **102**, 129–37.
Katz, M. L. & Ordover, J. A. (1990). R&D cooperation and competition. *Brookings Papers on Microeconomics*. 137–203.
Salop, S. C. (1986). Practices that (credibly) facilitate oligopoly co-ordination. In J. E. Stiglitz & G. F. Mathewson (eds), *New developments in the analysis of market structure*. London: Macmillan. See pp. 265–94.

STEPHANOS AVGEROPOULOS

cash cow   A cash cow business is usually defined as one which enjoys a high relative market share in an industry in which the growth rate has slowed. Because of its high market share, in a traditional Boston Consulting Group GROWTH SHARE MATRIX analysis such a business should enjoy a value added cost advantage, relative to its competitors, assuming that an average 80 per cent experience effect (*see* EXPERIENCE AND LEARNING EFFECTS) underpins the basic industry cost economics. Such businesses should supply the cash required to finance new businesses or STAR BUSINESSES should they need it, to develop market share while the industry growth rate is high.

Such businesses are extremely valuable, but are hard to manage. Psychologically, managers of such businesses often wish to invest the surplus cash flows that they are generating, as it

is depressing for both management and workforce to run a business into decline. As a result, sophisticated control systems are usually required to ensure that any surplus cash is extracted for redistribution within an industrial group.

Moreover, despite their growth share matrix positions, many cash cow businesses may not actually generate cash. There can be a number of reasons for this, including the following:

1. *Incorrect market definition.* In the early 1980s, the US General Electric company appeared to enjoy high market share positions in the US electricals and electronics markets. However, these markets were globalizing, and in world market terms US companies were rapidly losing ground to Japanese and other Far Eastern competitors.

2. *Inappropriate experience curve assumptions.* The positioning of a business on the growth share matrix assumes that a cost advantage is generated as a result of a high relative market share, with this term being used as a surrogate for superior cumulative production volume. This phenomenon may apply, but can also be circumvented when customers redefine the value chain (*see* VALUE CHAIN ANALYSIS) of their industry to gain lower cost structures. Japanese competitors with techniques such as JUST IN TIME production methods have been especially successful in achieving this; but competitors such as Dell Computer, Amstrad, and Schneider have successfully entered markets such as personal computers with substantially lower costs than the industry leader. Variations in channel strategy have been especially effective in achieving such cost gains.

3. *Exchange rate variations.* The advantage of high market share can be severely eroded by exchange rate variations. The rate of such movements has accelerated in recent years, causing dramatic changes in international prices which are impossible to match through normal improvements in relative productivity.

4. *Capital intensity variations.* Despite cost advantages which may exist as a result of high market shares, high capital intensity

businesses, especially those which high net working capital needs, are rarely attractive cash cows. This problem is exacerbated under conditions of moderate to high inflation. Moreover, competitors such as the Japanese have been highly successful at reducing capital intensity by just in time and work-in-progress stock turn improvements.

5. *Use as a market attack business.* A dangerous tactic, but one that is occasionally used, is to destroy the cash generating ability of a competitor's market position by predatory pricing supported by cash flows from a successful business in a protected market. Japanese competitors have often been accused of such practices. For example, many Japanese products are often more expensive in the home market than in overseas markets, or competitors are excluded by the blocking of access to the distribution system. Kodak has therefore felt blocked in Japan by Fuji Film. This practice is also common in undifferentiated product markets, where the desire for capacity utilization will often lead to high capital intensity competition to erode margins by cutting price to fill the factories.

See also **Growth share matrix**

Bibliography

Bogue, M. C. & Buffa, E. S. (1986). *Corporate strategic analysis.* New York: The Free Press. See chapters 2 and 5.
Hax, A. L. & Majiluf, N. S. (1984). *Strategic management.* Englewood Cliffs, NJ: Prentice-Hall. See chapter 7.
Henderson, B. D. (1973). *The experience curve reviewed, IV. The growth share matrix of the product portfolio.* Perspectives no. 135. Boston, MA: Boston Consulting Group.
Lewis, W. W. (1977). *Planning by exception.* Washington, DC: Strategic Planning Associates.

DEREK F. CHANNON

cash trap   This refers to a business the strategic position of which is such that it needs all the cash generated from operations to maintain this position. Such a business is not creating shareholder value and may actually be destroying it.

Cash trap businesses tend to have a high level of capital intensity and limited or uncertain cash flows. The typical manufacturing company with typical growth rates and asset turnover must have a pre-tax profit of around 7 per cent or the entire company becomes a cash trap. High growth and high capital intensity businesses require even higher margins. At maturity, such businesses will tend to convert themselves into cash traps. Such businesses have a tendency to accept that change cannot happen due to difficulty in modifying corporate culture. Ironically, this attitude may create a window of opportunity for a new competitor that is not afraid to challenge the existing rules. This will almost invariably mean changing one or more aspects of product market positioning. For example, capital intensity can be reduced by OUTSOURCING, a technology bypass may negate experience curve expectations; a reconfiguration of the value chain (*see* VALUE CHAIN ANALYSIS) may be possible; and re-engineering may be possible (*see* VALUE-DRIVEN RE-ENGINEERING).

In general, cash trap businesses exhibit a low share and high capital intensity in markets with little or low product differentiation. In building defenses against cash trap situations it is important to recognize and evaluate the existing position realistically and to design counter measures before the situation becomes irretrievable. Real cash traps destroy shareholder value and should either be changed, closed, or divested. Only a few high-share competitors in any product market can expect to avoid becoming a cash trap.

Bibliography

Henderson, B. (1972). *Cash traps.* Boston, MA: Boston Consulting Group.

DEREK F. CHANNON

cause–effect analysis   The cause–effect diagram (also known as a fishbone diagram) sets out to identify the various factors making up the causes and effects in the cost structure of a business. It indicates the mutual relationships between the trunk, the branches, and the twigs

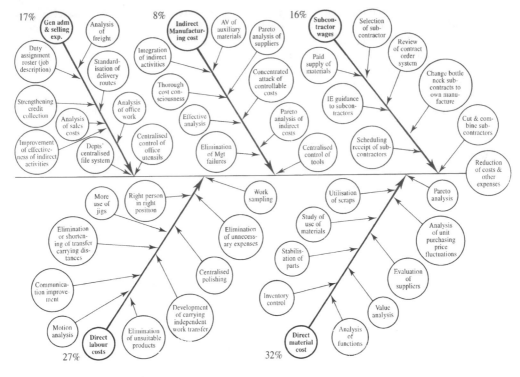

Figure 1 The cause and effect diagram for cost reduction.
Source: Nagashima (1992).

of a tree. In the example shown in figure 1, attempts are made to reduce costs in a particular business.

To produce such a diagram, the relevant group can brainstorm both causes and effects, usually writing down all the factors that can be thought of. These factors can then be grouped into a lesser number of major factors and a multitude of smaller ones. Having undertaken this analysis, a diagram such as that shown is drawn up. Careful analysis then enables the firm to plan a feasible cost reduction program to re-establish competitive advantage, which can be integrated into the overall cost structure.

Having identified cause and effect, priorities and responsibilities need to be established for cost reduction programs. These can be allocated to specific individuals, product groups, geographic areas, and the like. The identification of interrelationships between the factors provides a mechanism for establishing contingency plans and reducing political pressures within organizations.

Bibliography

Nagashima, S. (1992). *100 management charts.* Tokyo: Asian Productivity Organisation. See pp. 38–9.

DEREK F. CHANNON

chaebol structure The Korean chaebol is that country's near equivalent of the Japanese KEIRETSU STRUCTURE. Unlike the keiretsu, however, it is usually still managed at the top level by members of the founding family, and strategy is still set centrally, as in the prewar Japanese ZAIBATSU STRUCTURE. Furthermore, these concerns do not contain banking institutions within their structures; and although trading companies exist, these act mainly as exporting agencies rather than as in the SOGA SHOSHA.

The main reason for these differences is the late development of the Korean economy, in which industrialization took place mainly after the Korean War of the early 1950s. The industrial base left after the World War II period of Japanese colonialization was largely destroyed in the war, which also led to the division of the peninsular into North and South Korea.

After the War the South Korean economy was almost solely dependent upon the USA for military and economic aid. Some import substitution projects were undertaken, but the then President, Mr Sygman Rhee, was not especially interested in heavy governmental intervention.

Nevertheless, the late 1950s saw the rapid development of the early chaebol, fueled by favorable import license concessions, access to scarce foreign exchange, and governmental properties seized from the Japanese. However, in 1960 the Rhee government was overthrown and the emerging chaebol were coerced to accept government guidance from the Ministry of Trade and Industry, in a similar manner to MITI in Japan. The position of the Korean government was also strengthened by their control over the banking industry. As a result, a partnership was developed between the chaebol and government, yielding a dramatic growth in the Korean economy from the 1960s to the present day.

In the 1970s, government concern at the rising economic dominance of the chaebol led to the introduction of laws to curb their growth. Some firms were pushed to reduce the level of family ownership by issuing their stocks on the capital market; tax payments and access to bank credits were also closely controled. Some real estate disposals and divestments of subsidiaries by the leading 20 chaebol were also introduced by government. Nevertheless, industrial concentration by the top ten chaebol increased, and by the early 1980s these concerns held around a 25 per cent share of Korea's manufacturing industry.

By the mid-1980s the Korean economy was heavily dependent upon the chaebol, and to restrict their activity would have been to enforce a slowdown in the nation's economic growth. There was, however, an increase in competition between the leading chaebol, as they came to compete for market share both at home and overseas. Moreover, after initially copying the evolution of Japanese industry in the postwar period, the companies began to develop their own competence in R&D, technology, market-ing, and management skills. Development in industries similar to those behind the Japanese economic miracle, such as shipbuilding, heavy engineering, consumer electronics and, more recently, automobiles, formed the backbone of the emerging Korean economy. The changing nature of the chaebol also led to a reduction in government intervention and greater corporate independence. Nevertheless, the chaebol were not given control of the banking industry, as was the case with the keiretsu. By the late 1980s the top 30 chaebol groups held around 40 per cent of the Korean market.

The Korean chaebol were much younger than their Japanese counterparts which, prior to World War II, had developed as family-dominated zaibatsu groups following the Meiji Restoration and the subsequent industrialization of Japan. The oldest of the "big four" groups, Samsung, was created in 1938, while the remainder were mainly established in the 1950s. As a result, many were still owned by the families of their founders, with on average some 30 per cent of listed company stock in their hands. This figure was relatively higher for the larger chaebol groups.

The family ownership patterns of the Korean chaebol have been classified into three types, as shown in figure 1. In the first of these types, ownership is direct and complete, with the founder and his family owning all the chaebol affiliated companies. In the second form, the family own a holding company which, in turn, owns affiliated subsidiaries: the Daewoo group is an example of this form. The third type enjoys interlocking mutual ownership, with the founding family owning the group holding company and/or some form of foundation which, in turn, owns the affiliated companies: this form is typified by the Samsung group. As the chaebol evolve, the trend has been to move progressively from the first structure to the third.

While family ownership of keiretsu groups is generally very low, or presently nonexistent, it has been shown that more than 30 per cent of the executives of the top 20 chaebol groups are members of the founding family. Family members thus play significant roles in the direction of the chaebol and, in particular, the eldest of the founder's sons is usually groomed to succeed the father when he retires. Fathers-

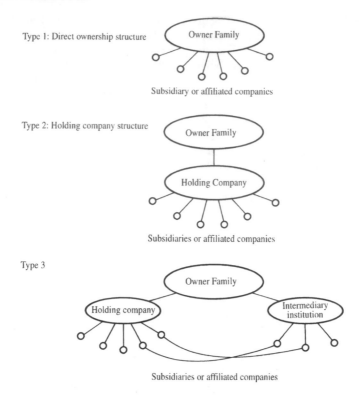

Figure 1 The organizational structure of Korean chaebols.
Source: Hattori (1989, p. 88).

in-law, sons-in-law, brothers, uncles, and nephews are also recruited into management.

The four leading chaebol are all dominated by family executives. The Samsung group has one of the highest rates of non family member executive management, but family members still dominate the most important positions. In Hyundai the founder had seven sons, five of whom manage ten major group operations: a sixth is being groomed to succeed his father, while the founder's brother heads Hyundai Motors. In the LG group, the founder has six sons and five brothers, many of whom occupy senior positions. Daewoo, created only in 1967, is still led by its founder and, apart from his wife, no other members of the family are actively involved in management, although the future position of the founder's children is still unclear.

While family ownership is a critical factor in the management of chaebol, it is also important to understand that Korean tradition allows the unequal distribution of family wealth clearly in favor of the eldest son. Moreover, the Korean concept of the family is defined strictly on the basis of blood ties, whereas in Japan zaibatsu families could absorb non blood tie related managers by adoption, marriage, or appointment. Thus, in Korea, chaebol successors are generally confined to family members related by blood.

In chaebol structures, the central office still maintains strict control over strategy and monitoring the performance of operating units. By contrast, after the elimination of the zaibatsu holding companies, Japanese keiretsu groups have a much looser system of influence over the strategies of member corporations via their presidents' councils and other integrating mechanisms.

Unlike the keiretsu groups, the Korean chaebol contain neither powerful trading companies nor significant internal financial service institutions. General trading companies within the chaebol only began to develop from the mid-1970s, as a result of discussions with government on how to stimulate exports. By the mid-1980s each of the major groups had created general trading companies, but the focus of these concerns was exports rather than the much wider role undertaken by the SOGA SHOSHA. Nevertheless, by the early 1990s, the nine largest general trading companies were responsible for over 50 per cent of Korean exports.

The lack of financial service institutions within the chaebol structure has meant that they have been forced to rely heavily on external finance to fuel their growth. In particular, they have been dependent upon government funds, which has provided the state with a major mechanism for influencing chaebol strategies, especially with regard to focus and diversification. Major groups have, however, been actively attempting to build their positions in the financial services sector, but these efforts are still weak by comparison with the position of the keiretsu.

In terms of management style, the Korean chaebol are more influenced by Japanese systems than by those of the West, despite the heavy US influence in the period after the Korean War and until relations with Japan were restored in the mid-1960s.

From the influences of the USA and Japan, coupled with Korea's own history and traditions, Korean companies have evolved their own system of management, sometimes referred to as K-Style management. This includes top down decision making, paternalistic leadership, clan management, *intival* (or harmony-oriented cultural values), flexible lifetime employment, personal loyalty, seniority and merit-based compensation, and conglomerate diversification strategies.

Bibliography

Chen, M. (1995). *Asian management systems.* London: Routledge. See chapters 12 and 15.

Chang, C. S. (1988). Chaebol: the South Korean conglomerates. *Business Horizons*, 51–7.

Hattori, T. (1989). Japanese zaibatsu and Korean chaebol. In Kae H. Chung, Hak Chong Lee (eds), *Korean managerial dynamics.* New York: Praeger. See pp. 79–98.

Korean Development Institute (1982). *Ownership structure of Korean Chaebols.* Seoul, Korea: KDI.

Lee, S. M. & Yoo, S. J. (1987). Management style and practice of Korean Chaebols. *California Management Review*, **95**, 95–110.

Lee, S. M. & Yoo, S. J. (1987). The K-type management: a driving force of Korean prosperity. *Management International Review*, **27** (4), 68–77.

DEREK F. CHANNON

cherry picking As markets mature, the opportunities to carefully segment them increase. Usually, cherry picking tends to mean that a competitor selects an upmarket segment to attack with a product/service package which is differentiable and which is perceived by customers to be superior to alternate offerings. For example, Harley Davidson motor cycles has been reborn by appealing to a particular group of dedicated enthusiasts in the USA and overseas, who are looking for values such as distinctiveness, individualism, power, and the like, rather than a simple means of transport. Some purchasers of expensive hi-fi systems can actually detect superior sound qualities; others buy such systems to feel good in front of their friends. Most golfers have high handicaps, but many buy expensive clubs because it makes them feel better.

Such upmarket segmentation is common and readily observed. However, it is possible to segment other market areas in which cost leadership can be combined with differentiation to achieve significant competitive advantage. Direct Line Insurance thus transformed the motor insurance market by offering a direct telephone service, so eliminating the need for brokers; and with a built-in cost advantage of at least 30 per cent and by carefully selecting the motor risks that the company was interested in insuring, achieved a higher level of profitability and lower risk while providing customers with lower prices and superior service quality. As a result they have grown at over 70 per cent per annum in a mature, slow growth market.

In most markets opportunities for cherry picking exist provided that careful analysis is undertaken to identify definable segments which can be serviced in a way that creates both differentiation and sustainable competitive advantage.

DEREK F. CHANNON

Chinese family business   Overseas or expatriate Chinese dominate the economies of Hong Kong, Taiwan, and Singapore, and form a significant minority in economic terms in Thailand, Indonesia, Malaysia, and the Phillipines. Apart from Singapore, where subsidiaries of Western multinationals are very significant, the major form of business organization amongst the Chinese in these countries is the Chinese family business (hereafter CFB). Interest in the phonemenon of the CFB can be attributed to a number of factors.

First, these countries have been highly successful in terms of economic performance. This success has been achieved in a variety of different contexts *vis-à-vis* the state. In some cases the state has been highly supportive and interventionist, in others largely indifferent and, in some cases, even overtly hostile, to the Chinese community.

Second, on the surface at least, the CFB has achieved this success by flouting some of the nostrums of good Western business practice. Firms are often small and little attention is paid to formalized management development. As Tam says: "Egalitarian employment measures, consensus decision making, high wage homogeneity, employee empowerment and delegation are thought to be positively associated with performance. However the reverse of all these normally cherished principles is enshrined within a typical Hong Kong enterprise" (Tam, 1990, p. 169).

Leading on from the first and second points, there is now a growing belief that the form of business organization matters. It cannot be treated as unproblematic (as implied by early neoclassical economics). Rather, the black box, the decision making agent, needs to be opened up and examined. Furthermore, the *context* in which the agent makes these decisions must also be considered, since such decisions are always grounded in an institutional context rather than being purely determined by market forces (Granovetter, 1985). Indeed, Whitley and Redding both argue that understanding any form of business organization (including the CFB) requires seeing it as forming part of a Business System (Redding & Whitley, 1990; Whitley, 1992).

Key Features

The CFB is not coterminous with a firm. The CFB may well control a number of legally distinct firms, but it is the family which is the key decision making unit (Tam, 1990). Nevertheless, CFBs are generally small. The structure tends to be simple and centralized on one dominant decision maker who operates in a highly paternalist and particularist style, often by-passing middle management. Relationships and coordination are mainly hierarchic and there is little horizontal coordination. Ownership and control are usually confined to a family and business tend to be focused on a restricted range of products or markets.

Close attention is paid to cost and financial controls. Competitive advantage is often sought by cost-cutting, by being prepared to accept low margins on a high turnover.

There are also close links with other businesses through a personalized network system (often underpinned by kinship connections). Other businesses will often contribute other elements of the value chain (components, marketing, and distribution) or be partners in a joint venture in order to reduce risk. However, each family business will retain a large degree of independence of decision making and control. Furthermore, such arrangements are often temporary and unstable (Tam, 1990). The small scale of operation permits a high degree of strategic adaptability. However, where diversification occurs, it is generally opportunistic and undertaken to capitalize on family or network connections.

Few of the procedures covering conditions of employment are formalized or institutionalized. Recruitment and selection of non-family members are often on the basis of personal recommendation or prior acquaintance. Indeed, the use of existing employees to make recommendations ensures that these employees will have a stake in the performance of the new hire. Job flexibility is the norm. Young female workers earning low wages tend to predominate in light manufacturing, textiles, and garments, particularly in Hong Kong and Taiwan (Deyo, 1989). Labor unions have little influence; partly because unions are at odds with the paternalistic ethos and partly, in the case of Taiwan, because of state opposition.

The Institutional Background

The institutional underpinning for the CFB, which helps to explain its unique characteristics, is complex. Whitley (1992) carries a full treatment. The following aspects are of particular significance.

The state can play a number of different roles, as has already been discussed. In general, banks do not play a very significant role in the CFB; this is largely because the family wish to retain financial control, although in Taiwan the banks have also been wary of lending to what is seen as a risky business sector.

It is also of interest to try to account for the specific values and attitudes that underpin the CFB. The key issue here is the enormous stress placed on family and kinship. The family, rather than the individual, assumes much greater importance in non-Western societies as a general rule (Ferrano, 1990), but amongst the Chinese it goes even deeper; Whitley (1992) observes how this can be traced back to pre-industrial China, when the village had relatively little autonomy from the state and where very little property was held as a unit by the village; hence it was the family rather than the village that became the focus of allegiance (cf., pre-industrial Japan).

Conclusions

The high value placed on family membership is a source of both strength and weakness. On the one hand, it permits a high degree of consistency in terms of values and expected behavior of those within the business, and breeds acceptance of the paternalistic style. On the other hand, the low level of trust of non-family members inhibits the degree of delegation and restricts the size of the organization and the pool of senior managerial talent available. It also limits the loyalty that CFBs can expect from non-family employees.

The form of kinship structure, whereby family assets are equally divided amongst inheritors, and the preference for vertical over horizontal relationships, encourages fragmentation. Indeed, Wong (1985) has noted how many CFBs last for only three generations, as each brother or cousin strives to set up independently. However, this process has advantages; it

ensures constant revitalization and the rapid diffusion of new innovations (Tam, 1990).

In terms of long-run developments of the CFB, Deyo (1989) has noted that as CFBs move into more sophisticated sectors, then training and development, and other employment practices designed to hold on to those with scarce skills, become more prevalent. Whitley (1992) observes how at present the CFB is a relatively homogeneous phenomenon compared to business systems in the UK and USA, where industrialization is much more established and the system much more highly differentiated. As the CFB matures, it could be that it will become less homogeneous. Indeed, there is evidence of this in Singapore, where there is a highly qualified managerial cadre and a large multinational presence which, together, are leading to a decline in the employment of family members in the CFB (Wu, 1983).

Nevertheless, the CFB remains a powerful demonstration of how forms of business organization are embedded within a set of social institutions which make up a coherent system. Such systems sound a note of caution to those who might try to seek universal principles of managerial good practice divorced from the institutionalized context in which such practices occur.

Bibliography

Clegg, S. & Redding, G. (eds), (1990). *Capitalism in contrasting cultures.* Berlin: de Gruyter.

Deyo, F. C. (1989). *Beneath the miracle: labour subordination in the New Asian industrialisation.* Berkeley, CA: University of California Press.

Ferrano, A. (1990). *The cultural dimension of international business.* Englewood Cliffs, NJ: Prentice-Hall.

Granovetter, P. (1985). Economic action, social structure and embeddedness. *American Journal of Sociology*, 91, 481–510.

Redding, G. & Whitley, R. (1990). Beyond bureaucracy: towards a comparative analysis of forms of economic resource coordination and control. In S. Clegg & G. Redding (eds), *Capitalism in contrasting cultures.* Berlin: de Gruyter.

Tam, S. (1990). *Centrifugal versus centripetal growth processes: contrasting ideal types for conceptualising the developmental patterns of Chinese and Japanese firms.* Berlin:

Whitley, R. (1992). *Business systems in east Asia: firms, markets and societies.* London: Sage.

Wong, S. L. (1985). The Chinese family: a model. *British Journal of Sociology*, **36**, 58–72.
Wu, Y.-Li (1983). Chinese entrepreneurs in South-East Asia. *American Economic Review*, 73, 112–17.

MICHAEL BROCKLEHURST

Cinderella business Such a business is one with opportunity, but which fails to receive the resources or attention it deserves. Examples are found when such businesses are located within divisions which the corporate center has designated as mature or declining, and has therefore deprived of resources overall. In these circumstances growth Cinderella businesses act as a threat to the existing divisional operations, as to reach their potential they require a disproportionate percentage of resources allocated to the division as a whole. In large corporations in which scale is such that small business units tend to get lost in the overall corporate structure, the position can become acute. Similarly, small growth businesses were given little or no attention in industries such as oil when their size did not justify attention at board level and, as a result, many such DIVERSIFICATION moves by acquisition have failed.

Cinderella businesses often occur as a result of acquisition strategies in which firms attempt to diversify into growth markets with relatively small scale, tentative moves, especially when moving into unrelated areas of industry. While sanctioned by the main board in large, diversified and especially dominant business concerns (*see* DOMINANT BUSINESS STRATEGY), such moves receive little or no attention in terms of main board reporting relationships. In oil, banking, tobacco, brewing, and the like, diversifications by acquisition have led to the introduction of many Cinderella businesses which have received little attention from boards composed largely of executives from the original CORE BUSINESSES. The problem may well be compounded by the introduction of executives from the acquiring company who have little or no understanding of the industry or needs of the small business; the imposition of parent company bureaucratic procedures, management information, planning, and control systems inappropriate to the Cinderella organization; and the addition of overheads similar to those of the parent. As a result, many such moves have resulted in significant losses, and in some cases predator attacks on the parent concerns with a view to breaking them up and reselling the constituent businesses.

DEREK F. CHANNON

competitive position – market attractiveness matrix During the 1970s, the US General Electric company (GE) developed a portfolio model measuring the relative attractiveness of its multiple businesses for investment purposes. In conjunction with McKinsey and Company, GE developed a portfolio model which differed from that of the Boston Consulting Group's GROWTH SHARE MATRIX in that it

Market attractiveness	Strong	Medium	Weak
High	Grow – penetrate	Invest for growth	Selective investment or divestment
Medium	Selective harvest or investment	Segment and selective investment	Controlled exit or divestment
Low	Harvest for cash generation	Controlled harvest	Rapid exit or attack business
	Competitive position		

Figure 1 The market attractiveness – competitive position matrix.
Sources: Channon, D. F. (1993), *Australia Pacific Bank Case*; and Stratpack Limited.

examined those variables assessed by management to be the critical success factors affecting a business. These factors were then used to identify the position of a business in a three by three matrix, each cell of which indicated a recommended investment strategy. A number of factors, the identification of which is found useful, and the matrix itself, are illustrated in figure 1.

The process of positioning a business is similar to that of the Shell DIRECTIONAL POLICY MATRIX. The position of each business on the two composite dimensions is determined by a qualitative scoring system described in the measurement of "market attractiveness" and "competitive position." Businesses are plotted on the matrix, with their relative size indicated by the area of the circle representing each one. An alternate method of weighting each variable has been used in some companies, the values of the main PIMS (*see* PIMS STRUCTURAL DETERMINANTS OF PERFORMANCE) variables being subdivided to determine the two composite variables and then used to calculate the relative matrix position of a business.

Each cell in the matrix suggests an alternate investment strategy for the businesses contained in it, as shown. Businesses in the top left-hand corner are high in market attractiveness and enjoy a strong competitive position: such businesses enjoy high growth and should receive priority for any investment support needed. Businesses in the grow/penetrate cell are also primary candidates for investment, in an effort to improve competitive position while growth prospects remain high. Defend/invest position businesses are in less attractive markets, but investment should be maintained as needed to defend the strong competitive position established. Businesses in the bottom left-hand corner are candidates for harvesting: the market attractiveness is low, probably indicating that growth is low but the relative competitive position remains high. Such businesses are therefore usually producing good profits which cannot justifiably be reinvested. Surplus cash is therefore extracted for use in investing in businesses that are short of funds, or to be used to provide other types of resource.

Businesses in the center are candidates for selective investment, usually on the basis of

Table 1 An example of the business strength assessment with the weighted score approach

Critical success factors	Weight*	Rating†	Weighted score
Market share	0.10	5	0.5
SBU growth rate	x	3	—
Breadth of product line	0.05	4	0.2
Sales distribution effectiveness	0.2	4	0.8
Proprietary and key account advantages	x	3	—
Price competitiveness	x	4	—
Advertising and promotion effectiveness	0.05	4	0.2
Facilities location and newness	0.05	5	0.25
Capacity and productivity	x	3	—
Experience curve effects	0.15	4	0.6
Raw materials costs	0.05	4	0.2
Value added	x	4	—
Relative product quality	0.15	4	0.6
R&D advantages/position	0.05	4	0.2
Cash throw-off	0.1	5	0.5
Calibre of personnel	x	4	—
General image	0.05	5	0.25
TOTAL	1.00		4.3

Key: * x means that the factor does not affect the relative competitive position of the firms in that industry;
   † 1 = very weak competitive position, 5 = very strong competitive position.
Source: Hofer & Schendel (1978)

careful market segmentation. Businesses at the bottom center and right center are candidates for withdrawal/divestment or for the pursuit of niche strategies. Businesses in the bottom right cell are both in unattractive markets and have a weak competitive position. Such businesses may well be making losses and are not likely to produce a strong positive cashflow. As a result they are clear candidates for divestment or closure. A more sophisticated but difficult alternative is to deploy them as attack businesses against a competitor's harvest businesses, to depress their cash-generating capability. Note that each strategy also implies different objectives, and the company's management information systems and reward systems need to be tuned to reflect this.

The Competitive Position – Market Attractiveness Matrix and the DIRECTIONAL POLICY MATRIX provide more sophisticated methodologies for assessing the strategic position of a business, and can allow management to incorporate due consideration of critical variables that influence individual businesses.

Competitive Position

In assessing the competitive position of an individual business, a number of variables are usually taken into consideration. The calculation of relative competitive position can be operationalized by scoring a company's position along a series of appropriate dimensions. The precise dimensions can be selected by management on the basis of their detailed knowledge of the business, and weighted according to their assessment of the relative importance of each dimension. This is illustrated in table 1. A number of such factors based on the critical variables identified in the PIMS program are used in one such system as follows.

Competitive position measures:

- Absolute market share: measured as a company's market share of its defined SERVED MARKET.
- Relative share: using the PIMS definition, this is defined as a percentage of the company's share divided by the sum of that of its three largest competitors.
- Trend in market share: the trend in the company's share over the past three years.
- Relative profitability: the relative profitability of the company's product as the percentage of

the average of that of the three largest competitors.
- Relative product quality: an assessment of the relative level of the quality of a company's product compared with those of its three largest competitors, from the customer's perspective.
- Relative price: the relative price of a company's product as a percentage of the average of those of its three largest competitors.
- Customer concentration: the number of customers making up 80 per cent of the company's business; the fewer the number of buyers, the greater the buyer power.
- Rate of product innovation: the percentage of sales from products introduced in the past three years, which indicates the degree of maturity of a business.
- Relative capital intensity: the capital intensity of a company's business, as a percentage of that of its three largest competitors: high relative capital intensity is usually a weakness.

Each of these factors, which may or may not be weighted, can be scored from 1 to 5, with the high score representing a very strong position and the low score a weak one. Summarizing the score for each dimension and dividing this by the total possible score provides a coordinate for competitive position on the matrix.

Market Attractiveness

This is assessed from data on the market/industry characteristics of a business. While the factors that determine attractiveness may vary, managerial input can be used to assess these and the relative importance of each variable by weighting them. An example is shown in table 2.

The following variables have also been found to be useful:
- Size: the size of a market is obviously important. However, in assessing size careful market definition is imperative and eventually needs to be conducted on a segment-by-segment basis. The size should also be sufficiently large for the firm to make it worthwhile to provide products or services.
- Historic growth rate: this is useful as a guide for predicting future trends.
- Projected growth rate: this needs to be carefully assessed and overoptimism avoided.

Table 2 An example of the industry attractiveness assessment with the weighted score approach

Attractiveness criterion	Weight*	Rating†	Weighted score
Size	0.15	4	0.6
Growth	0.12	3	0.36
Pricing	0.05	3	0.15
Market diversity	0.05	2	0.1
Competitive structure	0.05	3	0.15
Industry profitability	0.2	3	0.6
Technical role	0.05	4	0.2
Inflation vulnerability	0.05	2	0.1
Cyclicality	0.05	2	0.10
Customer financials	0.1	5	0.5
Energy impact	0.08	4	0.32
Social	GO	4	—
Environmental	GO	4	—
Legal	GO	4	—
Human	0.05	4	0.2
TOTAL	1.00		3.38

Key: * Some criteria may be of the GO/NO GO type; † 1= very unattractive. 5 = highly attractive
Source: Hofer & Schendel (1978)

Sensitivity analysis can be used to assess the impact of different growth rates.

- Number of competitors: the larger the number of competitors, the greater is the level of rivalry that may be expected.
- Competitor concentration: more concentrated markets are generally more attractive, whereas fragmented markets are usually more price competitive.
- Market profitability: more profitable markets are obviously more attractive.
- Barriers to entry: markets with high barriers to entry are more attractive than those in which the entry of new competitors is easy.
- Barriers to exit: high barriers to exit tend to increase competition, especially in high capital intensity industries, as competitors erode away margins in order to maintain capacity utilization.
- Supplier power: a small number of suppliers of critical raw materials and the like reduces market attractiveness.
- Buyer power: a small number of large customers enhances buyer power, especially in fragmented industries, and reduces market attractiveness.

- Degree of product differentiation: the higher the level of differentiation, the more attractive the market is, as high differentiation tends to reduce price competition.
- Market fit: markets that are truly synergistic with other corporate activities enhance attractiveness.

Having measured the position of a business along these and any other relevant dimensions, market attractiveness is assessed by assigning a value between 1 and 5 to a business according to its relative position. If the variables are weighted, this weight should also be applied and the scores summed to arrive at an overall total. This is divided by the maximum possible score to generate the value of the market attractiveness coordinate in order to plot a business's position on the matrix.

Criticisms of the system are that it requires accurate identification of the multiplicity of variables required to position a business correctly. The weighting and numerical scoring system can deceive with its pseudo-scientific approach. There is also a desire on the part of managers to attempt to avoid the disinvest cells. Data is often not available to provide an accurate assessment of the position of a business and therefore, as a consequence, there is a tendency to drift toward the moderate score. Furthermore, it is difficult to ensure consistency between the businesses. Finally, when markets change, very misleading positionings can occur in terms of market attractiveness. Thus, in GE when the electronics industry was globalizing in the 1980s, the company was often measuring its position on the basis of the US market. During the 1980s, therefore, under the leadership of Jack Welch, positioning shifted to the concept of being either number one or number two in the world or that businesses should be sold, closed, or fixed. As a result the portfolio of GE was dramatically changed. Nevertheless, when used well, the multivariate approach offers management a more realistic tool than the simplistic approach of the original BCG bivariate model. Moreover, in the 1990s, such a tool can be coupled with VALUE-BASED PLANNING to provide a very sophisticated portfolio planning tool.

Bibliography

Hax, H. & Majluf, N. T. (1984). *Strategic management: an integrative perspective*. Englewood Cliffs, NJ: Prentice-Hall.

Channon, D. F. (1993). *Australia Pacific Bank Case*. Management School, Imperial College, University of London.

Hofer, C. W. & Schendel, D. (1978). *Strategy formulation: analytical concepts*. St. Paul, MN: West.

DEREK F. CHANNON

competitor analysis   In conducting competitor analysis, it is necessary to examine those key competitors that presently and/or in the future may have a significant impact on the strategy of the firm. Usually this means the inclusion of a wider group of organizations than the existing immediately direct competitors. In many cases, it is the failure of firms to identify the competitors that may emerge in the future that leads to BLIND SPOTS. Competitors for evaluation therefore include the following.

Existing Direct Competitors

The firm should concentrate upon major direct competitors, especially those growing as rapidly as or faster than itself. Care should be taken to

uncover the sources of any apparent competitive advantage. Some competitors will not appear in every segment but rather in specific niches. Different competitors will therefore need to be evaluated at different levels of depth. Those which already do, or could have an ability to, substantially impact on CORE BUSINESSES need the closest attention.

New and Potential Entrants

Major competitive threats do not necessarily come from direct competitors, who may have much to lose by breaking up established market structures. New competitors include the following:

- firms with low barriers to entry (*see* BARRIERS TO ENTRY AND EXIT)

- firms with a clear experience effect (*see* EXPERIENCE AND LEARNING EFFECTS) or SYNERGY gain

- forward or backward integrators

- unrelated product acquirers, for whom entry offers financial synergy

- firms offering a potential technology bypass to gain competitive advantage

Competitor Intelligence Sources

Collecting legal detailed information on actual and potential competitors is surprisingly easy if the task is approached systematically and continuously. Moreover, the level of resource needed for the task is not extensive. It is therefore, perhaps, surprising how few firms actually undertake the task, and set out their strategies while being almost oblivious to the behavior of competitors. Key sources of competitive information include the following:

- Annual reports and 10 k's and, where available, the annual reports or returns of subsidiaries/business units.

- Competitive product literature.

- Competitor product analysis and evaluation by techniques such as TEAR DOWN.

- Internal newspapers and magazines. These are useful in that they usually give details of all major appointments, staff background profiles, business unit descriptions, statements of philosophy and mission, new products and services, and major strategic moves.

- Competitor company histories. These are useful to gain an understanding of competitor corporate culture, the rationale for the existing strategic position, and details of the internal systems and policies.

- Advertising. This illustrates and identifies themes, choice of media, spend level, and the timing of specific strategies.

- Competitor directories. These are an excellent source for identifying the organization's structure and strength, mode of customer service, depth of specialist segment coverage, attitudes to specific activities, and relative power positions.

- Financial and industry press. These sources are useful for financial and strategic announcements, product data, and the like.

- Papers and speeches of corporate executives. These are useful for details of internal procedures, the organization's senior management philosophy and strategic intentions.

- Sales force reports. Although they are often biased, intelligence reports from field officers provide front line intelligence on competitors, customers, prices, products, service, quality, delivery, and the like.

- Customers. Reports from customers can be actively solicited internally or via external market research specialists.

- Suppliers. Reports from suppliers are especially useful in assessing competitor investment plans, activity levels, efficiency, and the like.

- Professional advisers. Many companies use external consultants to evaluate and change their strategies and/or structures. The knowledge of such advisers is usually useful, in that most adopt a specific pattern in their approach.

- Stockbroker reports. These often provide useful operational details obtained from competitor briefings. Similarly, industry studies may provide useful information about specific competitors within a particular country or region.

- Recruited competitor personnel. The systematic debriefing of recruited personnel provides intimate internal details of competitive activity.

- Recruited executive consultants. Retired executives from competitors can often be hired as consultants, and information about their former employers can be effectively determined by requesting their assistance in specific job areas.

Competitor Analysis Database

In order to evaluate competitor strengths and weaknesses, systematic data collection on each actual and potential competitor is necessary. The most important competitors need to be comprehensively and continuously monitored. Competitors that pose a less immediate threat can be monitored on a periodic basis. The data to be collected should include the following:

- name of competitor or potential competitor
- numbers and locations of operating sites
- numbers and nature of the personnel attached to each unit
- details of competitor organization and business unit structure
- financial analysis of parent and subsidiaries, stock market assessment, and details of share register; potential acquirers/acquisitions
- corporate and business unit growth rate/profitability
- details of product and service range, including relative quality and price
- details of served market share by customer segment and by geographic area
- details of communication strategy, spending levels, timing, media choice, promotions, and advertising support
- details of sales and service organization, including numbers, organization, responsibilities, special procedures for key accounts, any team selling capabilities, and the method of the sales force segmentation approach
- details of served markets (including identification and servicing of key accounts), estimates of customer loyalty, and market image

- details of niche markets served, key accounts, estimates of customer loyalty, and relative market image

- details of specialist markets served

- details of R&D spending, facilities, development themes, special skills and attributes, and geographic coverage

- details of operations and system facilities, capacity, size, scale, age, utilization, assessment of output efficiency, capital intensity, and replacement policies

- details of key customers and suppliers

- details of personnel numbers, personnel relations record, relative efficiency and productivity, salary rates, rewards and sanctions policies, degree of trade unionization

- details of key individuals within the competitor organization

- details of control, information, and planning systems

From such a database, the strategy of a competitor can be analyzed and assessed as to future strategic actions and suggestions can be made as to how the firm can gain and sustain competitive advantage.

Analyzing Competitor Strategy

The strategy of key competitors should be analyzed and evaluated with a view to assessing their relative strengths and weaknesses, in order to identify strategic alternatives for the firm. Most large firms are multibusiness and competitor strategy needs to be evaluated at several levels:

- by function – marketing, production, and R&D

- by business unit

- by corporation as a whole

From this analysis likely competitor moves and responses to external moves can be assessed.

Function Analysis

For each competitor business, the main functional strategies should be identified and evaluated. While all of the desirable details may not be immediately available, continuous competitor monitoring will usually permit a comprehensive picture to be built up over time. The objective is not merely to gain competitive details but to evaluate the relative position of the evaluating firms to assess competitive position, BENCHMARKING opportunities, and the like.

Marketing Strategy

- What product/service strategy is adopted by each competitor relative to yours? What is the market size by product market/customer segment? What is the market share for each competitor by served market segment?

- What is the growth rate for each product/service market segment? What is the growth rate of each competitor by segment? What are the degree and trend in market segment concentration?

- What is the product/service line strategy of each competitor? Is it full line or specialist niche?

- What is the policy toward new services adopted by each competitor? What has been the rate of new product introduction?

- What is the relative service/product quality of each competitor?

- What pricing strategy does each competitor adopt by product/service line/consumer segment?

- What are the relative advertising and promotion strategies of each competitor?

- How do competitors service each product market segment?

- What are the apparent marketing objectives of each competitor?

- How quickly do competitors respond to market changes?

- How does marketing fit in competitor cultures? Has the function been the source of key executives in the past?

Production/Operations Strategy

- What are the number, size, and location of each competitor's production/operations complexes? How do these compare with each other? What product range does each produce? What is their estimated capacity? What is capacity utilization?

- What is the level of each competitor's capital employed in depreciable assets? Is it owned property?

- What working capital intensity is employed in debtors, stocks, and creditors?

- How many people are employed at each unit? What salaries are paid? What is the relative productivity?

- What is the degree of trade unionization? What is the labor relations record?

- What sales are made to other internal business units? What supplies are received from other internal business units?

- What incentive/reward systems are used?

- What services are subject to OUTSOURCING? Is this increasing or decreasing?

- How does production fit into each competitor's organization? Has production/operations been a source of key executives?

- How flexible is each competitor to changes in market conditions? How fast has each competitor been able to respond to changes?

Research and Development Strategy

- Where are new services developed?

- What is the estimated expenditure level on R&D? How does this compare? How has this changed?

- How many people are employed in research, and how many in development?

- What is the recent record for each competitor in new product introductions and patents?

- Are there identifiable technological thrusts for individual competitors?

- How rapidly can each competitor respond to innovations? What sort of reaction has typically been evoked?

Financial Strategy

- What is the financial performance of each competitor by business in terms of return on assets, return on equity, cashflow, and return on sales?

- What dividend payout policy appears to be in place? How are cashflows in and out controled?

- What is the calculated SUSTAINABLE GROWTH RATE on the existing equity base?

- How does the competitor's growth rate compare with the industry average? Is adequate cash available to sustain the business and allow for expansion? Do other businesses have priority for corporate funds?

- How well are cash and working capital managed?

Business Unit Strategy

Each competitor also needs to be evaluated at the business unit level to see where the business fits within the overall competitor strategy. Such questions should address the role of the business unit, its objectives, organizational structure, control and incentive systems, strategic position, environmental constraints and opportunities, position of SBU head, and performance.

Group Business Objectives

The position of each business within a competitor's total portfolio also needs to be evaluated. Questions that may influence behavior at the business unit level include: an evaluation of overall group financial objectives, growth capability and shareholder expectations, key strengths and weaknesses, ability to change, and the nature of the overall portfolio; GENERIC STRATEGIES adopted, values and aspirations of key decision makers, and especially the CEO; historic reactions to earlier competitive moves; and beliefs and expectations about competitors.

From this analysis, the objective is to assess likely competitor future strategies and responses to competitive moves. In most industries success is dependent on gaining an edge on competitors, and this type of evaluation is therefore as important as basic market or customer analysis.

Bibliography

Ansoff, I. (1987). *Corporate strategy*. Harmondsworth, UK: Penguin. See chapter 8.

Channon, D. F. (1986). *Bank strategic management and marketing*. Chichester: John Wiley. See chapter 4.

Garner, J. R., Rachlin, R. & Sweeny, H. W. A. (1986). *Handbook of strategic planning*. New York: John Wiley.

Sammon, W. L. (1986). Assessing the competition: business intelligence for strategic management. In J. R. Gardner, R. Rachlin, & H. W. A. Sweeny (eds), *Handbook of strategic planning*. New York: John Wiley.

DEREK F. CHANNON

complementary products In contrast with
SUBSTITUTE PRODUCTS, complementary products are those which have a negative cross-price
elasticity of demand. As with substitutes, there
can be "strong" or "weak" complements.

The strategic importance of complementarity
is somewhat inferior to that of substitutability.
Nevertheless, complements raise the question of
a firm's scope of activities. A number of
decisions have to be made by a firm engaged
in the production of complementary goods,
namely with respect to control over complementary products (and industries), pricing, and
the combined sale of complementary goods
(bundling). The most important complements
are those which have a significant impact on
each other's position (e.g., in terms of cost or
differentiation), and those which are associated
with each other by the buyer.

*Implications for Involvement in the Industry of the
Complement*

There are a number of advantages that can be
gained by being active in and controling
complementary products/markets, including
economies of scale in marketing (as demand
for one good also boosts demand for the other),
and other shared activities such as logistics (*see*
ECONOMIES OF SCALE; ECONOMIES OF SCOPE).

Controling complements, however, may have
its own problems. The two most important ones
are that the industry of the complement may not
be as attractive as that of the base good, and that
the organization concerned may not have the
skills, abilities, or any relevant competitive
advantage to compete effectively in that industry.

In any case, it should be kept in mind that
some complements may change over time, so

the firm's involvement in the industry of the
complement may not have to be as committed.
Morover, full scale operations in the complement's industry are not always necessary. Just
being active in that industry may allow the firm
to sufficiently influence it, so that other firms
may feel obliged to follow its examples when it
sets lower prices or provides a higher level of
service. As a result, controling only a relatively
small share of the complement's industry may
well be sufficient to considerably improve the
sales and profitability of the industry with which
the main interest of a company lies.

Implications for Pricing

The profitability of complementary goods may
well require pricing to be pitched at levels
different from those that would have been
appropriate if the two products were not
complements, or were not produced by the
same firm.

Implications for Capacity Planning

Finally, the relationship between complementary goods may be exploited to forecast demand
for one of them, given changes in the demand
for the other (*see* ELASTICITY). Similarly, if the
price of one good rises or falls, demand for the
other would also be expected to be affected
because they are required together by the buyer
and the price of the bundle is affected. These
relationships can be used for capacity planning
purposes, particularly where the firm only
controls one of the complements.

See also **Cross-subsidization**

Bibliography

Porter, M. E. (1985). *Competitive advantage: creating
and sustaining superior performance*. New York: The
Free Press.

STEPHANOS AVGEROPOULOS

conglomerate strategy Conglomerates are
corporations that have no apparent STRATEGIC
FIT between the activities of their constituent
businesses. They were defined by Wrigley in the
early 1970s as businesses in which no one
business accounted for 70 per cent of sales and
in which there was no readily apparent relation-

ship between the activities. Conglomerates are also characterized by a small central office which is heavily oriented to finance and control plus, in addition, acquisition analysis and implementation. Such businesses were popular in the USA in the late 1960s, when it was argued that it was desirable to build a portfolio of strategic businesses at different stages of the life cycle which could financially compensate one another. In the early period of the use of the GROWTH SHARE MATRIX, this strategy was strongly advocated by the Boston Consulting Group, and the success of companies such as Textron, Litton Industries, and Ling Temco Vought (LTV) seemed to support the theory.

There was no particular effort by firms adopting a conglomerate strategy to seek SYNERGY or STRATEGIC FIT between businesses, with the exception of seeking out financial synergy which could be released by the purchase of companies with underutilized assets, debt capacity, complementary cashflows, and the like. Typically, acquisition screens used by conglomerates emphasized criteria such as the following:

- the ability of target companies to meet corporate targets for profitability and return on equity

- whether an acquired business would be cash using to finance capital investment, growth, and working capital

- the growth rate of the industry in which the acquisition operated

- whether the acquisition was large enough to make a significant contribution to the parent

- potential problems due to customer relations and government or regulatory constraints

- industry vulnerability to inflation, interest rates, and local government policy

The financial emphasis of conglomerate strategy leads such active acquisitive firms to seek out targets with the following like characteristics:

- *Asset strips*: situations in which the market capitalization is substantially less than the underlying asset value. Substantial capital gains are possible by selling off surplus assets in order to recover acquisition costs.

- *Financially distressed businesses*: businesses which can be purchased at deep discounts but which can be turned around provided that the acquirer has the necessary management skills to implement a TURNAROUND STRATEGY. Such businesses can then be held or sold on to realize a significant gain for the acquirer.

- *Capital short growth companies*: such companies possess attractive growth prospects but lack the financial resources to exploit their advantage.

Advantages of Conglomerate Diversification

There are a number of financial advantages which can be attributed to a conglomerate strategy:

- Business risk can be dispersed across a portfolio of businesses, reducing the risk from over-concentration in any one industry. While related diversification also spreads risk, it is confined to industry areas with strategic fit, whereas no such constraint applies to conglomerates.

- Capital can be invested into businesses that justify it in terms of creating shareholder value and withdrawn from cash generating businesses. At one time, the Boston Consulting Group thus advocated a conglomerate strategy as a logical outcome of the active pursuit of a growth share portfolio strategy.

- Corporate profitability can be stabilized by investments in businesses which are traditionally counter-cyclical to each other.

- Companies with skills in identifying asset-rich situations, and with the skills to turn around ailing businesses which can create shareholder value.

- Mergers between businesses with complementary asset investment and cashflow characteristics and/or complementary capital structures which can release financial synergy, so increasing shareholder value.

Disadvantages of Conglomerate Diversification

At the same time many conglomerates actually under-perform in the market, and rather than adding to shareholder value may be worth more in break-up situations than as conglomerate corporations. Reasons for this include the following:

• The management needs of conglomerates are primarily financial and general management skills in turnaround situations. They do not possess operational business skills, nor can they be expected to. It is, therefore, noticeable that major conglomerate failures have occurred in high-technology businesses, where the central management fails to recognize projects going out of control despite sophisticated financial reporting systems.

• Without strategic fit providing operating synergy and competitive advantage, there is a tendency for the component businesses of a conglomerate to do no better (and sometimes worse) than the market average. In addition, tight financial controls might reduce entrepreneurial spirit in the business units while the centre provides no real support other than financial.

• Counter-cyclical businesses often do not actually behave with perfect timing, so failing to smooth the corporate earnings stream.

Nevertheless, overall, there is some evidence that high acquisition rate conglomerates do successfully perform in terms of return on equity and growth rate by comparison with related diversified concerns. Furthermore, despite an apparent trend toward reduced diversification in the late 1980s and encouragement to retreat to the CORE BUSINESSES of the corporation, the number of conglomerates has not diminished significantly. Indeed, there has been a tendency in North America and the UK for diversification to continue, especially with the development of mixed manufacturing and service industry corporations. Meanwhile, in the Korean CHAEBOL STRUCTURE, the Japanese KEIRETSU STRUCTURE, and within the typical CHINESE FAMILY BUSINESS, the major industrial groups have virtually all continued their strategies of conglomerate diversification.

During the 1970s the number of conglomerate businesses grew sharply in the USA and the trend spread to other countries, including the UK. The failure of Litton Industries and LTV, however, made the conglomerate form unattractive to the US stock market. In the boom years of the stock market in the 1980s, conglomerates again became attractive in the USA, but in the late 1980s some such corporations came under predatory attack, on the basis that breaking them up might create greater shareholder value than allowing them to remain intact. This led to the belief that retreating to a core business was a more desirable strategy.

The answer, however, as to whether a conglomerate strategy is less viable than a RELATED DIVERSIFIED STRATEGY strategy is far from clear. There are many corporations in the developed economies which have little or no relationships between their businesses but which are highly successful financially, and are well received by the stock market. Such concerns would include US General Electric, BTR, and Hanson Trust. These companies are very highly diversified and manage the businesses within that framework. They also operate with very tight financial control. Similarly, in Japan the KEIRETSU STRUCTURE and in Korea the CHAEBOL STRUCTURE have become ever more diversified.

Bibliography

Channon, D. F. (1973). *The strategy and structure of British enterprise.* Cambridge, MA: Harvard Division of Research.

Rumelt, R. P. (1974). *Strategy structure and economic performance.* Cambridge, MA: Harvard Division of Research.

Thompson, A. A. & Strickland, A. J. (1993). *Strategic management.* Homewood, IL: Irwin. See pp. 173–7.

Wrigley, L. J. (1970). Diversification and divisional autonomy. Unpublished doctoral dissertation, Harvard Business School.

DEREK F. CHANNON

core businesses Made popular as a theme in the late 1980s, many Western companies, especially in the USA, found that their strategies of DIVERSIFICATION had not achieved the improvement in profit performance that was expected. Successful corporations were identified as usually having developed a "core" business around which related activities had been developed. In companies that had adopted a RELATED DIVERSIFIED STRATEGY new activities had been added, usually as a result of common technology or skill, mode of marketing and distribution, and the like. Financial SYNERGY was not significantly recognized, although in practice it was an integral component, in the strategic development of some conglomerates (*see* CONGLOMERATE STRATEGY). Many such diversification moves occurred by acquisition.

During the 1980s the initial impact of the research on corporate excellence was to indicate that successful firms were those in which some logic occurred in diversification moves. As a result of unsuccessful acquisitions (*see* ACQUISITION STRATEGY), these were either sold or floated off and the proceeds returned to shareholders to avoid predatory attacks on the parent.

In addition, the significant take-up of VALUE-BASED PLANNING focusing on shareholder value encouraged the divestment of businesses contributing negative value. Interestingly, these short-term pressures from the stock market, which only influenced Western companies, were largely absent in Japan, where the KEIRETSU STRUCTURE provided a stability which could actually permit firms to redefine their core business on a regular basis. As a result, Japanese firms and their Keiretsu groups have increased their degree of diversification. Similar patterns of corporate development can also be observed amongst the Korean chaebol (*see* CHAEBOL STRUCTURE) and large businesses owned and/or managed by Chinese in the Pacific Rim.

Bibliography

Peters, T. & Waterman, R. (1982). *In search of excellence.* New York: Harper & Row.

DEREK F. CHANNON

core competences Core competences are " . . .a set of differentiated skills, complementary assets, and routines that provide the basis for a firm's competitive capacities and sustainable advantage in a particular business" (Teece et al., 1990). They are " . . .the specific tangible and intangible assets of the firm assembled into integrated clusters, which span individuals and groups to enable distinctive activities to be performed" (Winterschied, 1994).

The concept of core competences is associated with the resource-based view of the firm Rather than emphasizing (as in traditional approaches to strategy) products and markets, and focusing competitive analysis on product portfolios, the resource-based approach regards firms as bundles of resources which can be configured to provide firm-specific advantages. Prahalad & Hamel (1990) characterize the difference of approach as between a "portfolio of competences versus a portfolio of businesses". The resource-based model is able to address a number of issues which mainstream strategic analysis has found difficult. Amongst these issues are diversification (see Mahoney & Pandian, 1992), and the changes in competitive environment that most firms are experiencing (globalization, deregulation, technological change, and quality), which mean that traditional sources of competitive advantage are being eroded (Hamel & Prahalad, 1994).

The term "core competences" is most closely associated with the work of Hamel & Prahalad. Other terms which are used include intangible resources (Hall, 1992), strategic capabilities (Stalk & Shulman, 1992), strategic assets (Dierickx & Cool, 1989; Amit & Schoemaker, 1993), firm resources (Barney, 1991), core capabilities (Leonard-Barton, 1992), and distinctive competences (Andrews, 1971).

Core competences are typically characterized as:

- unique to the firm
- sustainable because they are hard to imitate or to substitute
- conferring some kind of functionality to the customer (in the case of products and some services) or to the provider (in the case of other services)
- partly the product of learning and, hence, as incorporating tacit as well as explicit knowledge
- generic because they are incorporated into a number of products and/or processes

Recognition of the potential significance of core competences for competitive advantage was stimulated by research such as that by Rumelt (1974), which showed that of nine potential diversification strategies, the two which were most successful were those which were built on an existing skill or resource base within the firm.

Hamel & Prahalad have distinguished between three types of competences: market access, integrity-related, and functionally related. Market access competencies bring the firm into contact with its customers; integrity-related competences enable the firm to do things to a higher quality, better and/or faster than its competitors; and functionally related competences confer distinctive customer benefits.

Within the literature and debate on the subject, there is a division between what Klavans (1994) has characterized as technological and institutional views of competences. The former focuses on "objective" capabilities, such as Honda's knowledge of engine design; while the latter focus on, for example, managerial processes for organizational learning. Leonard-Barton (1992) goes further than this. She defines what she describes as a core capability, as a knowledge set which has four dimensions: employees' knowledge and skills; knowledge and skills embodied into technical systems; managerial systems which enable the creation of knowledge; and the values and norms associated with the knowledge and its creation. She argues that this fourth dimension is often ignored. In so arguing, she shares the view of, amongst others, Child (1972), that the identification of core competences is, at some level, a political process.

The concept has proved to be attractive both to industrialists and to business strategists. At a time when companies are increasingly homogeneous in terms of technologies, regulatory environments, and location, the suggestion that competitive advantage can be won through the configuration and application of corporate level resources has great appeal. Writing in 1992, the *Economist* Intelligence Unit identified the following uses for the concept:

- to guide diversification through the identification of basic strengths
- to drive revitalization through the identification of core business areas
- to guard competitiveness through an earlier recognition of key skills (many firms realize what they have lost through outsourcing or divestment only when it is too late)
- to provide a focus and justification for R&D in the development and maintenance of core competences
- to inform the selection of strategic alliances which build on complementary core competences
- to balance Strategic Business Unit (SBU) objectives with company objectives

This relationship between the center and SBUs is a critical issue in the management of core competences. By definition, core competences exist beyond individual SBUs. They are underlying strengths which inform, support, and differentiate the firm's business across its SBUs. Since they are not the only source of competitive advantage, there is the potential for conflict and tension between SBU objectives and corporate objectives. To deploy core competences effectively requires, at some level, cross-SBU consensus on objectives and practice. For many firms who have followed the path of increasing SBU autonomy, achieving such consensus is a major challenge in the management and/or exploitation of core competences. Yet without such a consensus firms cannot exploit, maintain, and protect their competences.

Other challenges relate to the identification, development, and maintenance of core competences. There are significant difficulties involved in the identification of core competences. At one level, firms all too easily proclaim one or more core competences. This proclamation is usually the result of internal reflection rather than external comparisons, and can lead to firms attempting to protect an advantage which they subsequently find that all their competitors share. A second difficulty is the scope of core competences. One of the most widely cited examples of a competence is Honda's expertise in engines. But, what exactly does this expertise consist of? The issue in identification is the level of specificity which should be employed. Is it sufficient to say Honda has a core competence in engine design, or should the identification of a core competence try to delve deeper into what it is about Honda's engine design that provides them with advantage; or, perhaps more significantly, what it is about the way in which they manage their engine design expertise that provides the advantage? This issue of scope is an obstacle for many firms in the identification of their competences. Prahalad & Hamel (1990) recommend three tests to help identify core competencies. A core competence should: first, provide potential access to a wide range of markets; second, make a significant contribution to the perceived customer benefits of the end product; and, third, be difficult for competitors to imitate.

This leads to the challenges of development. Acquisitions, alliances, and licensing may all play a critical role. In turn, this raises issues about the capacity of the organization to learn, but the process of learning is one of the least discussed elements of core competence management. Competences take time to develop (Dierickx & Cool, 1989) which necessitates a longer-term and committed approach to strategic direction-setting. Such an approach is often difficult in the current turbulent environment. Firms need to engage in long-term visioning about where they might want to be in 10–20 years' time, and about the competences which they will need to deliver this vision (Hamel & Prahalad, 1994).

The key issue in the maintenance of core competencies is who "owns" them within the firm. Given that they cross SBUs, who is responsible for their continued development and use? They are all too easily lost through being taken for granted, outsourced, or starved of development resources. A related issue is their longevity: core competences do not last for ever. Firms need to review their competency portfolio on an ongoing basis in order to maintain and retain only those which continue to provide advantage.

See also **Strategic core competences**

Bibliography

Amit, R. & Schoemaker, P. J. H. (1993). Strategic assets and organisational rent. *Strategic Management Journal*, **14**, 33–46.
Andrews, K. R. (1971). *The concept of corporate strategy*. Homewood, IL: Irwin.
Barney, J. B. (1991). Firm resources and sustained competitive advantage. *Journal of Management*, **17**, 99–120.

Child, J. L. (1972). Organisational structure, environment and performance: the role of strategic choice. *Sociology*, **6**, 1–22.
Dierickx, I. & Cool, K. (1989). Asset stock accumulation and sustainability of competitive advantage. *Management Science*, 35, 1504–14.
Economist Intelligence Unit (1992). *Building core competences in a global economy*. Research report no. 1-12. New York: *Economist* Intelligence Unit.
Hall, R. (1992). The strategic analysis of intangible resources. *Strategic Management Journal*, **13**, 135–44.
Hamel, G. & Prahalad, C. K. (1994). *Competing for the future*. Cambridge, MA: Harvard Business School Press.
Klavans, R. (1994). The measurement of a competitor's core competence. In G. Hamel & A. Heene (eds), *Competence-based competition*. Chichester: John Wiley.
Leonard-Barton, D. (1992). Core capabilities and core rigidities: a paradox in managing new product development. *Strategic Management Journal*, **13**, 111–25.
Mahoney, J. T. & Pandian, J. R. (1992). The resource-based view within the conversation of strategic management. *Strategic Management Journal*, 13, 363–80.
Prahalad, C. K. & Hamel, G. (1990). The core competence of the corporation. *Harvard Business Review*, **68**, 79–91.
Rumelt, R. P. (1974). *Strategy, structure and economic performance*. Cambridge, MA: Harvard University Press.
Stalk, G., Evans, P. & Shulman, L. (1992). Competing on capabilities: the new rules of corporate strategy. *Harvard Business Review*, **70**, 57–69.
Teece, D. J., Pisano, G. & Shuen, A. (1990). *Firm capabilities, resources and the concept of strategy*. Consortium on Competitiveness and Co-operation Working Party no. 90-9. Berkeley, CA: Center for Research in Management, University of California, Berkeley.
Winterschied, B. C. (1994). Building capability from within: the insiders' view of core competence. In G. Hamel & A. Heene (eds), *Competence-based competition*. Chichester: John Wiley.

DOROTHY GRIFFITHS

core process   Such a process is defined as a set of linked activities that take an input and transform it to create an output which is of value to the customers of the process. The concept of horizontal activity flows forms the basis for business process re-engineering. Traditional business was organized by functional departments that might include production, procurement, logistics, sales, marketing, accounts, and technology. Each department undertook elements of work which was then passed on to another department, often with responsibilities passing upwards within each department before responsibility was passed to the next, and then coming down into the lower levels of the business for operational action. This upward *and* downward activity led to inefficiencies, slow speed, and possibly poor levels of customer satisfaction. The contrast between the business system and the core process business method is illustrated in figure 1.

To eliminate the inefficiencies of this vertical up and down movement, to reduce time within the corporation, and to reduce costs by removing unnecessary organizational layers, the concept of viewing the corporation as a series of horizontal flows has been conceived in the West. It has become exceptionally fashionable in recent years, in the guise of re-engineering, business process re-design, transformation, and core process re-design and has led companies to adopt the cross-functional form of organization. In many cases, adopting the concept has led to dramatic breakthroughs in cost, time, and quality. There are also high levels of failure

for a variety of reasons (*see* RE-ENGINEERING DISADVANTAGES).

The concept of core processes is the key to the introduction of re-engineering. There are many processes within the corporation, but only a small number will be critical or "core." These may vary somewhat between organizations but, usually, in re-engineering projects the corporation reorganizes around three to five critical processes. Those selected within the individual corporation will be focused on one or more of the critical strategic factors that determine competitive success. Stated in terms of time, quality of product and/or service, and cost, they should become faster in time-to-market, and yield improved on-time delivery and reduced administrative costs. For manufacturing companies, core processes will often include:

- product design and development
- procurement
- logistics
- manufacture
- despatch and shipment

Each core process will usually involve a number of key activities which cut across the traditional functional vertical activities of the corporation.

CORE PROCESS

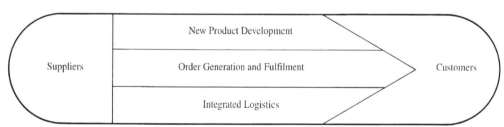

BUSINESS SYSTEM

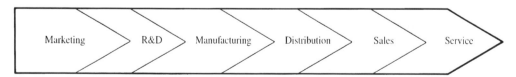

Figure 1 The core process versus business system approach.
Source: Kaplan & Murdock (1991).

For example, the integrated logistics core process for a consumer goods company includes forecasting, purchasing, manufacturing, and distribution to the wholesaler through the retailer to the ultimate consumer. Some may be similar across industries, such as new product development where time-to-market might be critical. Others may be industry-specific.

The achievement of breakthrough performance gains requires the introduction of a disciplined and phased approach. McKinsey and Company advocates a five-phase approach, as set out below.

Phase 1: Identifying Processes

Core process redesign requires corporations to re-think their value chains and re-evaluate their organizational structures. The identification and definition of core processes is therefore an initial and critical activity, requiring creativity and effort. McKinsey have identified a number of principles that are useful in defining core processes:

- A core process should address major strategic directions and problems in terms of competitive position, and should be readily recognizable to customers and suppliers.

- All major processes and information flows affecting throughput time, total cost, and quality should be included. This involves capturing major interdependencies and identifying any unnecessary functions and systems that can be eliminated.

- The focus should be defined at high enough levels such that re-design can yield "breakthrough" improvements.

- The core process view of the corporation seeks to optimize the interdependent activities and functions within a core process. Some functions such as manufacturing may form part of more than one core process.

- The same core processes may not be core for every company.

Phase 2: Defining Performance Requirements

Each core process should address one or two objectives of competitive success which should be defined in terms of key performance requirements. These will usually be strategic rather than merely financial, covering areas such as time, quality, service, and new product success rates. These key performance indicators also need to be projected forward and any gap between current and required performance clearly identified. This requires evaluating these gaps by BENCHMARKING against the best.

Phase 3: Pinpointing Problems

When performance gaps have been identified, a detailed diagnostic study needs to be undertaken to seek out the causes and so identify opportunities for change. This involves a detailed PROCESS MAPPING and information flows, and an analysis of the existing information and technical systems architecture. An understanding of the existing systems architecture is essential, since improvements in core processes almost invariably involve heavy investment in information technology. However, few corporations can consider changing their key information processing in one go; nor would this be practicable. Prioritization of any changes is therefore essential.

The detailed mapping will identify a large number of process and systems problems, the causes of which contribute to performance gaps. These problems, too, need to be prioritized and addressed. Many of these problems may seem small, but cumulatively they add up.

Phase 4: Developing a Vision

This phase has the twin objectives of developing a long-term re-design vision and a set of specific change initiatives. It begins by identifying options and creating a master plan. After the options have been reviewed, a set of specific long-term and short-term initiatives are selected that address all the key elements of work processes information systems and organization design.

Phase 5: Making It Happen

Once specific initiatives have been defined, a detailed roll-out needs to be developed to ensure that improvement opportunities are achieved. Many initiatives are usually involved in this process. To minimize risk many of these will need to be tested by experimentation. This will involve many individuals throughout the business or corporation. To reduce fears and to encourage change, it is essential to adequately communicate about the initiatives and to achieve a number of "quick wins." These both stimulate longer-term initiatives and also provide the performance gains to pay for the change process. The sequencing of change is essential. Launching initiatives in waves helps to reduce risk and allows the organization to add skills and capabilities. Further progress against key initiatives can be monitored against planned time frames, costs, and estimated benefits.

Bibliography

Kaplan, R. B. & Murdock, L. (1991). Core process redesign. *McKinsey Quarterly*, no. 2, 27–43.

Johansson, H. J., McHugh, P., Pendlebury, A. J. & Wheeler, W. A. III (1993). *Business process reengineering*. Chichester: John Wiley.

McManus, J. J. (1994). *An implementation guide on how to reengineer your business*. Cheltenham, UK: Stanley Thornes.

DEREK F. CHANNON

corporate governance This term refers to the process whereby the boards of corporations lead them. While the term itself has become internationally accepted, the actual systems of corporate governance operated in different countries vary substantially. Interest in the concept has been heightened by a realization that corporate governance may have an important bearing on the relative competitive position of different countries. While for many observers the concept is concerned primarily with the legal framework affecting corporations, it is also imperative to understand that governance is also importantly concerned with people.

In particular, the roles played by the chief executive officer and/or the chairman in some cases in establishing the corporate vision and implementing strategy is critically important. The influence of these key individuals is a key determinant in establishing corporate strategy, culture, and direction. Major shifts in the strategy of corporations, while being influenced by environmental and competitive forces, usually only occurs after a change in one or both of these senior officers.

The system of governance in different countries has been identified as being along a series of continua such as the following:

individual – collegiate
confrontation – cooperation
selfish – sense of social obligation
legalistic – bound by honor and obligation
short-term, impatient – long-term, patient
rigid, hierarchical – flexible

In the USA the system tends to be legalistic, short-term, and confrontational. In Germany and Japan the systems tend more to the right. The Japanese, for instance tend to think of business in military terms, with long-term struggles in which heavy casualties occur being acceptable. The German approach places emphasis on social as well as economic objectives. France and the USA tend to go for individualism in executive management, while the German and the Japanese operate collegiately with the power of the chief executive officer, while important, not usually operating without board consensus. German and Japanese management also enjoy the possibility of taking a long-term view as a result of their being generally protected from unwanted takeover bids, because a significant percentage of their shares are held in friendly hands by members of the same industrial grouping or housebanks. By contrast, U.S. companies tend to be subject to short-term pressures for performance as a result of significant institutional shareholder expectations and an investment banking industry which actively encourages takeover bids. In France the situation is more similar to the German and Japanese position, while the UK mirrors the USA.

The second key principle of corporate governance is that the executive management of the corporation should be accountable for its actions. While shareholders, especially in the USA, have been encouraged to take a more active role in the management of companies, in reality institutional shareholders have tended to be relatively passive until recent years, and this remains the case in most other markets.

As a result, the monitoring of executive accountability tends to fall on nonexecutive directors. These are full members of the board, theoretically appointed to add value to the board's decision-making process and, as such, they need to work closely with the executive.

The use of nonexecutive directors differs widely around the world. In the UK nonexecutive directors have the same legal obligations as executive directors. Recent recommendations by the Cadbury Committee argued that the role of nonexecutive directors be enhanced, but there has also been counter-argument that this should be avoided if it appears to threaten the drive and efficiency of the corporation. Moreover, some nonexecutive directors who also perform executive duties in other companies would find it difficult to actually attend sufficient board meetings to make an appropriate contribution because they accept multiple board appointments. Moreover, much criticism has been advanced in the UK about interlinking board memberships between different companies, which could create conflicts of interest. This charge has surfaced in particular with regard to the payment of salaries and bonuses of senior executive officers, since although nonexecutive directors tend to control remuneration committees, cross appointments between companies frequently occur.

The U.S. unitary board system has a pronounced supervisory role with the majority of the board being outside members. Day-to day management is exercised by a formal executive committee. This reports to the board, which focuses on strategic management and supervision. Every quoted company must contain outside directors so as to man an audit committee required by each of the three stock exchanges. In many companies, nonexecutives make up the majority of boards. While the principle of the unitary board and audit committees can work well, it is still dependent upon the character, experiences and ability of the members. In some cases the CEO tends to have undue influence over nonexecutive appointments, which even the extensive use of nominating committees has not resolved.

By contrast to the U.S. system, a two-tier board system is mandatory in Germany and some other European Union countries. This system consists of a supervisory board and a management board. Supervisory boards are required for all public companies (AGs) and are optional for private companies (GmbHs). One third of the members of such boards must be elected by employees, with this proportion rising to 50 per cent for companies with more than 2000 employees.

The function of the supervisory board is to monitor, supervise, and advise the management board. This includes appointing and removing the members of the managing board, deciding on managing board members service contracts, and approving the annual accounts. Supervisory board members may not sit on the managing board, and are required to act in the interests of the company as a whole rather than the constituencies they represent.

The supervisory board concept has, however, been criticized for being a far from perfect monitoring system. First, in many companies it meets infrequently. Second, the flow of information from the managing board tends often to be inadequate. Third, the average German supervisory board member also sits on a number of boards and hence cannot devote substantial time to each company.

Nevertheless, the flow of information between financial advisers in Germany and Japan and reporting of the true state of affairs is much superior to the position in the USA and UK, where these relationships are maintained at arms length. Hence in Germany and Japan the major banks operate as an additional safeguard. Furthermore, in Japan most major companies belong to the leading keiretsu groups, the lead companies of which also provide a supervisory role via organizational features such as the Presidents' Councils.

One result of the leveraged buyout movement in the USA was the emergence of new financial entities which retained a monitoring and even interventionist role in companies after such buyouts. These companies, while financially oriented, were usually not true banks or industrial holding companies, but took the form of supervisory shareholders until the companies acquired had improved to the point at which they could be refloated or the component parts sold off.

The concept of corporate governance thus varies widely around the world, based on different, historic corporate development systems. With the growing development of global industries and the emergence of economic blocs, some pressures for the development of common systems can be expected, but this would seem a long way off.

Bibliography

Charkham, J. P. (1995). Corporate governance: lessons from abroad. In Sir William Nicoll, D. Norburn & R. Schoenberg (eds.). *Perspectives on European Business*. London: Whurr.

Price Waterhouse (1995). *Effective Corporate Governance*. London: Price Waterhouse.

Useem, M. Bowman, E. Irvine, C. W. & Wyatt, J. (1993). U.S. institutional investors look at corporate governance in the 1990s. *European Management Journal*, 11 (2), 175–89.

DEREK F. CHANNON

corporate transformation   The high failure rate of Business Process Reengineering (BPR) projects has led to the development of a more subtle approach which has been called a biological model of corporate transformation, identifying the corporation as essentially an organic evolving entity. The model consists of four broad categories of activity leading to transformation and, as developed by Gemini Consulting, corporate transformation is defined as "the orchestrated redesign of the genetic architecture of the corporation, achieved by working simultaneously – although at different speeds – along the four dimensions of Reframing, Restructuring, Revitalisation and Renewal". These four dimensions are seen as a biological process as follows:

- *Reframing* is seen as shifting the company's perception of what it is and what it can achieve and is designed to open the corporation's mind set and allow it to refocus.

- *Restructuring* deals with the body of the corporation and addresses competitive fitness. This activity is most akin to the BPR approach and involves similar techniques.

- *Revitalization* endeavors to link the revised corporate body to its environment, and is considered to be the factor which most clearly differentiates transformation from the harshness perceived of reengineering. The intention is not to obliterate activities but, rather, to change them positively to encourage revitalized performance.

- *Renewal* is concerned with the "people" side of transformation and with the spirit of the

company. It is concerned with investment in skills and purpose to allow the company to self-regenerate with new confidence and enthusiasm rather than the often morale-sapping impact of reengineering projects, which are a major cause of failure. This activity is perhaps the most difficult to achieve, and is seen by many critics of reengineering change to be the point at which many consultants, brought in as change agents, leave their clients.

Gemini believes that 12 corporate "chromosomes" comprise the bio corporate genome, three for each of the four Rs. While each chromosome can be considered independently they are all integrated into a total system. The chief executive officer and the executive leadership are seen as the genetic architects of the corporation and are thus not expected to be involved in operational detail.

The Reframing Chromosomes

(1) *Achieve mobilization.* This activity is the process of bringing together the mental energy required to initiate the transformation process, and involves moving motivation and commitment from the individual to the team and ultimately to the total corporation.

(2) *Create the vision.* The development of a corporate vision is essential to provide a shared mental framework which stretches the future dimensions of the corporation and in human terms provides a common sense of purpose which people can identify with. The role of the CEO in establishing such a vision is crucial.

(3) *Building a measurement system.* Once the corporation is mobilized and provided with a vision, new measurement systems which allow management to monitor progress towards the future will usually be required. While often quantified, such measures will usually emphasize the strategic progress rather than the financial history. In human terms, the system should also create an identifiable sense of commitment (*see* BALANCED SCORE CARD).

The Restructuring Chromosomes

(4) *Construct an economic model.* This involves the systematic top-down disaggregation of a corporation in financial terms from shareholder VALUE-BASED PLANNING to ACTIVITY-BASED

COSTING and service level assessment. It provides a detailed view of how and where value is created or cost allowed in the bio analogy of the cardiovascular system for resources to be deployed where they are needed, and redistributed from where they are not needed.

(5) *Align the physical infrastructure.* This element is analogous to the corporate skeletal system and consists of the appropriate alignment of the resources of the corporation's assets, such as plants, warehouses, transportation, equipment, and the like. While these are relatively fixed, there is also a need for continuous monitoring and, on occasion, change as when a bone is fractured, to allow for strategic healing.

(6) *Redesign the work architecture.* The work of the corporation is achieved via a complex network of processes which is identified as the work architecture. These need to be correctly configured and aligned and this process can be linked to reengineering.

The Revitalization Systems

(7) *Achieve a market focus.* To Gemini, revitalization implies growth. To achieve this, customer focus provides the starting point, as developing new and perhaps undiscovered benefits that the corporation can offer to its customers leads to business growth. For the corporation, market focus provides the senses in the biological analogy.

(8) *Invent new business.* Growth can also occur as the result of the development of new businesses. These can emerge from the cross-fertilization of capabilities from within the corporation or by the introduction of activities from outside via mergers and acquisitions. STRATEGIC ALLIANCES, joint ventures (*see* JOINT VENTURE STRATEGY) and the like. The biological analogy of this concept can be seen as the reproductive system.

(9) *Change the rules through information technology.* The strategic use of information technology can produce new ways to compete by redefining the rules of the game in many traditional industries. Biologically, the use of such technology is analogous to the nervous system.

The Renewal Systems

(10) *Create a reward structure.* An appropriate reward structure is seen as a major motivating force on human behavior. When the motivation system is wrongly aligned with desired behavior it can also act as a serious demotivator and encourage undesired behavior.

(11) *Build individual learning.* Corporate transformation can only successfully take place when the skills and learning of many individuals are also transformed. Individual learning promotes self-actualization of the people who constitute the corporation.

(12) *Develop the Organization.* Corporations are seen as needing to organize for continuous learning, enabling them to constantly adapt to an ever changing environment in which the pace of change is often accelerating. Organizational development thus allows the corporation to evolve and fosters a sense of community amongst individuals.

Conclusion

The corporate transformation process has been applied in many corporations around the world. Such transformations often involve modifying the behavior of many thousands of people, often on a global basis. Such transformations take time, often involving a number of years, but the end result is expected to produce transformed corporations capable of continuous adaptation to permit successful evolution.

Bibliography

Gouillard, F. J. & Kelly, J. N. (1995). Transforming the Corporation. New York: McGraw-Hill.

DEREK F. CHANNON

cross-functional management structure Many Japanese companies introduced cross-functional management structures during the 1960s when they recognized, first, that inter-departmental communication and cooperation were poor and departmental group dynamics were not aligned toward corporate strategy and, second, for a specific function such as quality management, departmental responsibilities were usually unclear and the department lacked the authorization to act. In 1962, therefore, Toyota recognized that it was necessary to introduce a

Table 1 Organization and administration of cross-functional management committee meetings.

Items	Kacru Ishikawa	Toyota Motor Corporation	Komatsu Ltd
Organization	Cross-functional committee	Quality function and cost function committees	Quality assurance function committee (as example)
Reporting role	Report to board of executive committee	Report to board of executive committee	Report to TQC promotion committee
Responsibilities	Responsible for dealing with cross-functional matters in all departments, assigning responsibilities, and establishing system rules and audits	Same level of responsibility as board of directors or board of managing directors; serves as a practical decision-making body	Responsible for improvement of the quality assurance system – which includes all processes from product planning to sales and service – and for upgrading the level of quality assurance
Areas of work		Planning, auditing, coordinating, and recommending	
Composition	Committee chairman: executive with the rank of senior vice president or executive vice president who is in charge of functions	Chairman: generally a senior vice president of a department to which a particular function is closely linked	Committee: quality assurance managing executives
	Committee members: about five executives with the rank of director or higher, one or two executives from other areas, and a facilitator	Members: executives of functionally related departments	Committee members: about five related executives
	Staff support office: each department concerned	Facilitators: about ten executives with the rank of vice president or senior vice president who report directly to the chairman	Staff support office: quality assurance department

Additional items	[Example] quality assurance
	1 Monthly status of quality assurance and investigation of claims status
	2 Establishment and revision of departmental assignments concerning areas of cross-function responsibilities
		(1) Establishment of objectives; (2) plans and policies to achieve targeted objectives; (3) plans concerning new products, equipment, manufacturing, and sales; (4) important bottom-up items; (5) measures to eliminate barriers to implementation; (6) action necessary as a result of checking; (7) checking performance results of corporate policy and the plan for subsequent year; (8) other necessary items for cross-functional management	In order to carry out its objectives, the committee reviews and makes recommendations to the TQC committee on the following:
			1 Plan concerning corporate quality assurance
			2 Concerning quality assurance
			  a. Improvement plan for the system and the improvement programme
			  b. System improment items and departments responsible

Meeting frequency	Regular and monthly	Once a month, as a rule	Once every other month, as a rule

Source: Kozo Koura (1993).

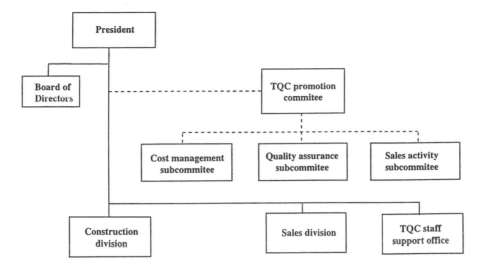

Uchino Construction

Company receiving 1985 Deming Prize,
small medium sizes company category

Figure 1 A simple cross-functional structure.
Source: Kozo Koura (1993).

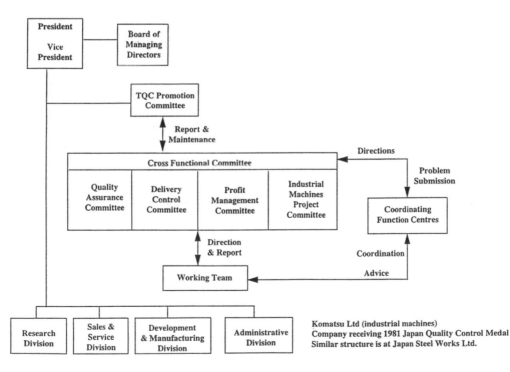

Figure 2 A general cross-functional organization.
Source: Kozo Koura (1993).

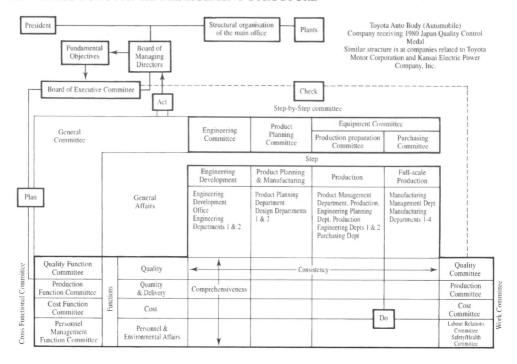

Figure 3 An advanced cross-functional structure.
Source: Kozo Koura (1993).

cross-functional management structure as part of its TQC (Total Quality Control) program.

The first step in cross-functional management is to select a method of analyzing cross-functions that is consistent with overall strategy. At Toyota Motor, functions were divided into four groups; overall planning, objective functions, means functions, and service functions. By contrast, Toyota Auto Body, a related concern, recognized two functions; primary functions and step-by-step management. Other Japanese concerns adopted similar concepts, as shown in table 1, while the term "cross-functional management" became widespread in Japan during the 1980s. Most companies viewed quality assurance, cost (or profit) management, delivery control, and personnel management as primary functions, while new product development was seen as an auxiliary function. However, not all functions were given the same priority and significance. Normally, primary functions did not change; while auxiliary functions, which also often included sales management and occasionally purchasing and

safety, might change according to conditions and corporate needs.

Top management identified the organizational structure clearly and specifically in order to promote cross-functional management. Groups of functions by implementation format were used to categorize cross-functional forms into four categories (type O to type III) according to the size and structural complexity of the concerns involved. The existence of departments having primary responsibility for each and every function was a prerequisite. A slightly less complex methodology has grouped the structures of corporations receiving the Deming prize into three classes; simple, general, and advanced.

A simple structure is illustrated in figure 1. In it, the TQC promotion committee promotes cross-functional management. This structure is found in smaller concerns with up to around ten executives and a limited labor force, with the TQC committee operating through a series of smaller focused subcommittees.

The general structure is found in larger corporations and is shown in figure 2. The structure of a leading construction company, Hazama-Gumi, is illustrated. The main office and branch office each have their own TQC committee which, in turn, has three subordinate functional committees covering quality assurance, awarded contract management, and profit management. The central office also has two additional committees covering subcontracting management and technology development. In many companies a variant of this structure involves the TQC promotion committee operating with a series of substructure cross-functional committees. For example, in Komatsu these consist of quality assurance, delivery control, profit management, and industrial machines project committees.

The advanced structure was first established by the Toyota Motor Corporation and has been widely adopted by other companies within the Toyota Group. In an assembly business without other divisions, each and every function of quality, cost delivery, and personnel management is applied horizontally to each step of the process; product planning design, test production, production preparation, full scale production, sales, and service. (See figure 3.)

In this example, the general committee and the cross-functional committee service the company executive committees. Each functional committee is composed of the executives concerned and responsible primarily for the "plan" stage of the PDCA CYCLE. Each department in charge of each step is responsible for implementation ("do"). Major issues emerging between the "plan" and "do" stages are reviewed by the cross-functional committee. The "step-by-step" committee is composed of executives in charge of each step, and also includes executives and senior managers of the departments concerned. This group also coordinates targeted items for each function with action items, and checks the assurance status of the development process. The work committee for senior managers is convened by an executive who is responsible for a given function. This committee is in charge of deploying corporate functional policy and is responsible for coordination and checking during the deployment stages.

The cross-functional committee within Japanese corporations is primarily responsible for the establishment, maintenance, and improvement of cross-functional management in the areas of quality, cost, profit, and delivery. It also has other responsibilities concerned with improvement. These include cross-functional management in other functions; creating and promoting long-term and annual cross-functional management plans; company-wide horizontal deployment of the results of cross-functional management; and planning and implementation of cross-functional audits.

The serious way in which Japanese companies address the issue of cross-functional coordination compares with conventional Western structures that emphasize vertical, hierarchical arrangements. The use of the HORIZONTAL STRUCTURE is a relatively very recent phenomenon in the West and is usually implemented as an element in the introduction of corporate re-engineering projects (*see* RE-ENGINEERING DISADVANTAGES).

The effects of cross-functional management structures include the following:

- accelerated decision making and implementation of quality assurance, cost/profit management, and delivery control policies
- greater awareness of cross-functional management issues at all levels of the organization and improved departmental cooperation and relationships
- that as a result of cross-functional treatment of issues, no extra departments or sections are required
- that employee suggestions are implemented more easily
- that departmental executives adopt a perspective more tuned to corporate needs, rather than to narrow departmental interests

Bibliography

Kozo Koura (1993). Administrative aspects and key points of cross-functional management.

Kenji Kurogane *Cross functional management*. Tokyo: Asian Productivity Organisation.

Masao Kogure (1986). Cross-functional management. *Quality Control*, 37 special issue, 253–9.

Shiggeru Aoki (1981). Cross functional management for top management. *Quality Control* 32 (2), 92–8; 32 (3), 66–71; 32 (4), 65–9.

DEREK F. CHANNON

cross-subsidization   Cross-subsidization refers to using profits earned in one product market to support activities in another. It may be carried out on government instructions, such as for social reasons (the cost of postage, for example, may be set to be uniform nationwide, with the cities' traffic subsidizing rural areas), or it may be for commercial motives, using the strategy to enable a firm to compete in a market in which it would otherwise find it difficult to survive, or to otherwise enhance the combined revenue earning potential of the two product markets, particularly if these involve COMPLEMENTARY PRODUCTS.

Types

There are three main cross-subsidization strategy variants, all of which price one of the goods (the base good) low to ensure purchase of the other, and then price the other (more profitable) good high, to more than recoup lost revenue. The three strategies are: loss leadership (predominantly used in retailing, whereby the base good is priced low to attract the price-sensitive customer to the outlet, while other goods that the customer would like to buy once he is in the outlet are priced at more profitable levels); the razor and blade strategy (whereby the base product is priced low in order to lock the buyer into making subsequent purchases of the more profitably priced complementary products); and the trade-up strategy (whereby the base product is priced very competitively, and the buyer is expected to subsequently move up the range and buy items which are more profitable).

Preconditions

For a cross-subsidization strategy to work even with buyers who are able to see through the mechanisms, a number of conditions must hold. First, the demand for the base good must be sufficiently price-sensitive to attract the customer in the first place. Then, demand for the profitable good must not be as price-sensitive, so that this is purchased at the high price and its supply must be restricted so that the firm does not end up supplying only the unprofitable good. Finally, a strong link must exist between the two, so that purchase of the base good leads to (repeated) purchase of the profitable good as well. This link typically deteriorates with time,

and as products mature, cross-subsidization becomes less relevant. This is because the profitable good may become more widely available, or because SUBSTITUTE PRODUCTS are developed.

Implications for Strategy

As a result of the necessity for the above conditions to hold, for a company to be able to exploit the cross-subsidization potential between two products, an effort must be made to create barriers to entry (*see* BARRIERS TO ENTRY AND EXIT) into the market for the profitable good and to strengthen the connection between the base and the profitable good (e.g., by raising the SWITCHING COSTS involved). It is not important, however, to erect barriers in the market for the base good, and as long as the above conditions hold, that market may even be left to other suppliers.

Turning to pricing, the increasing difficulty that the firm will face over time in continuing to profit from the sale of goods in this way implies that prices may well need to be adjusted so that, over the long term, the profit margins for the two goods become comparable.

Bibliography

Laffont, J. J. & Tirole, J. (1990). The regulation of multiproduct firms. *Journal of Public Economics*, XLIII, 1–36.
Porter, M. E. (1985). *Competitive advantage: creating and sustaining superior performance.* New York: The Free Press.

STEPHANOS AVGEROPOULOS

customer profitability matrix   Prices are often determined not on the basis of average production costs; in reality, different customer segments may have very different costs. Careful segmentation of the customer base can reveal that such variations in the cost to serve may vary by as much as 30 per cent.

Unfortunately, normal accounting cost systems do not reveal the different costs associated with servicing different customer groups. ACTIVITY-BASED COSTING systems are much better at revealing the true costs to serve. In drawing up the customer profitability matrix illustrated in figure 1, it is important to allocate indirect costs, which are not often considered, to the maximum extent, in the following categories:

- *Presale costs.* Differences occur in the buying process for different customer segments. These costs might include location, the need for customization, and other presale costs.
- *Production costs.* Customization, differences in packaging, timing, set-up time, fast delivery, holding inventory, and the like can cause significant cost differences between customer segments.
- *Distribution costs.* Customer location and the mode of shipment can vary significantly between customers. These costs can be relatively easily identified, but such analysis is rarely undertaken.
- *Aftersale service costs.* Costs include training, installation, repair, and maintenance costs. Many such costs are covered by warranty cover and customer claims need to be carefully analyzed to establish after-sale costs.

Having undertaken such detailed cost analysis, the actual prices charged to different customer segments, including all discounts, special offers, and the like, need to be assessed, together with the volume consumed over time in terms of value (not merely volume).

The prices and costs are then plotted on the customer profitability matrix as shown. Net price is shown on the vertical axis and cost on the horizontal. The size of each circle represents the value of each customer segment. Very large customers may be identified individually. The

cross-lines represent average price and cost, while the diagonal line shows the break even point at which price equals cost.

The resulting matrix shows which customer segments have high costs in relation to the prices they pay. They can be assigned to one of the four quadrants as follows:

- *Carriage trade.* High cost, high net price. Customers in this segment are willing to pay a high price for superior service. A classic example is private banking.
- *Bargain basement.* The low-cost, low net price position is less related to either service or quality. Using the above analogy, this would refer to life-line banking.
- *Passive.* Low cost, high price; less related to quality or service, and not very price-sensitive either. Buying behavior is low in price-sensitivity.
- *Aggressive.* High cost, low price. Such businesses enjoy high quality and service together with low price. Strong negotiators and technological leaders are often found in this category.

The matrix is then interrogated to develop strategies which help to maximize profitability. For example, Citibank in New York re-segmented its check handling business. The company found that a small number of checks represented a high level of value. These were segmented away from the volume element of check handling and processed separately, at lower cost but providing a superior level of customer service.

Strategically, a company can define itself on the basis of the type of customer it seeks to service. For example, a "Pile it high, sell it cheap" retailer such as Kwik Save would be located in the bottom left sector, while a specialist, high-price, high-cost competitor such as Harrods would operate in the top right box. Transition from one quadrant to another may well be extremely difficult and may take a long time.

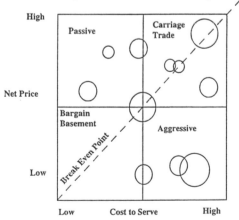

Figure 1 The customer profitability matrix.
Source: Shapiro et al. (1987).

Bibliography

Shapiro, Rangan, Moriarty & Ross (1987). Manage customers for profits (not just sales). *Harvard Business Review*.

DEREK F. CHANNON

D

delayering This is the process of reducing the number of layers in the vertical management hierarchy. The concept became widely known and adopted following its introduction and development in the US General Electric Company, when the incoming Chief Executive, Dr. Jack Welch, set about reducing the ranks of hierarchy between his office and the workplace. At the same time he eliminated many of the staff functions which had developed at GE, creating a strategic management focused line function.

In companies which re-engineer (*see* RE-ENGINEERING DISADVANTAGES) to an ACTIVITY-BASED COSTING system of management with a HORIZONTAL STRUCTURE, the elimination of at least one layer of middle management is usually common. Companies successfully implementing such systems make use of information technology driven management information systems which allow senior management to gain on-line real-time access to operations. As a result, decision making can be speeded up, middle management does not act as an information filter, and top management can become interventionist in line operations.

Bibliography

Channon, D. F. (1995). Direct Line Insurance. In C. Baden-Fuller & M. Pitt (eds), *Strategic Innovation: an international casebook on strategic management.* London: Routledge.

Tichy, N. & Sherman, S. (1993). *Control your destiny or someone else will.* New York: Doubleday.

DEREK F. CHANNON

deregulation This is the abolishment or considerable weakening of an existing regulatory regime (*see* REGULATION) to increase the responsiveness of a previously regulated industry to its input and/or output markets and lead to more competition.

Deregulation can take place within any one country or part thereof (such as the deregulation of the US airline industry or of London buses), across larger geographic areas (such as the telecommunications industry in Europe), or on a global basis.

Causes and Timing

Deregulation can be the result of two main developments. First, it may become desirable because of the growing inefficiencies that regulation can impose by artificially isolating markets that the growth of multinationals and the GLOBALIZATION of the marketplace tend to integrate. Second, it may become desirable when technological innovations make regulatory limitations obsolete; for instance, by means of fundamentally transforming cost structures or, again, redefining the boundaries of industries.

The need for deregulation, therefore, typically emerges as a result of largely external influences, although government action is usually required to permit and enact the required changes. As far as the incentives for government itself are concerned, this not only has to take into account social and efficiency considerations and the interests of consumers, but also the interests of producers, who may well have developed close political ties while regulated. According to the balance between these factors, government involvement can either be responsive (in which case it acts upon requests by powerful interest groups adversely affected by regulation, such as innovative producers or overcharged consumers), or proactive (in which case it acts before any powerful interest group expresses any desire for deregulation, this sometimes being observed in cases in which deregulation forms part of a larger government initiative, such as PRIVATIZATION). Historically, banking is one of the industries that has been deregulated as a result of innovations, whereas public utilities have been deregulated as a result of political initiative.

The Impact of Deregulation

Impact on market structure and level of competition.   Deregulation has a profound impact on a firm's competitive environment. Because it reduces barriers to entry (*see* BARRIERS TO ENTRY AND EXIT), allows firms to go into related fields, and encourages new firms to develop, it increases the number of firms in the previously regulated market, and enhances competition in that market. The new firms may well bring with them cost cutting technologies, additional capacity, and hence the ability to cut prices. At the same time, unbundling gives customers greater flexibility to make product/service and price/performance trade-offs, so their level of knowledge increases and they become more price sensitive.

An additional factor which makes the environment more competitive is that, in their effort to match new entrants, established competitors imitate new offerings without full knowledge of their own costs, thereby leading to deep price cuts.

A McKinsey study on the post-deregulation US airline, financial services, telephone, trucking, and railroad industries made some detailed observations as to the implications of these changes (Bleeke, 1991). According to the study, therefore, an industry changes immediately after deregulation when a number of new companies enter the market. Prices and profitability fall rapidly, the most attractive segments often become the least profitable, the variation in profitability between the best and worst performers widens, and many entrants go out of business or merge with stronger competitors. Waves of mergers and acquisitions initially consolidate weak competitors and subsequently combine the strong, and many companies are forced to abandon many areas of activity, largely because of the increasing cost of competing in any single one of them. During this period, the overall market grows, despite any failures, and

flexibility is key to survival, particularly with respect to pricing, so that all potential sources of profit are exploited. Similarly, the organization's resources need to be conserved, and large expenditures need to be considered twice, even if they are intended to lead to the introduction of cost cutting technology.

Some five years after deregulation, the industry stabilizes and the competitive environment changes again. The weakest competitors have all gone, larger companies have learned how to compete with new rivals, and the price gap between new entrants and existing companies diminishes as the latter's cost cutting efforts have taken effect. At this stage, the deregulated market can be assumed to have completed the phase of post-deregulation reorganization and should be considered just like any competitive industry.

Impact on the use of technology and the variety of output.   Regulated industries face little competition, and they find it relatively easy to pass on increased costs to customers. This means that they need not worry so much about cost cutting, although some recently developed regulatory regimes have shown the capability to successfully control costs (see the relevant discussion in REGULATION). The use of technology in regulated industries, therefore, is predominantly applied to providing higher levels of service. As deregulation puts heavy emphasis on cost cutting, however, cost cutting technologies are brought into the industry.

Similarly, unbundling and the removal of constraints on price and product competition lead to a broader range of offerings and affords the customer a full range of product/service and price/performance tradeoffs. Lower quality at lower prices becomes an option, therefore, but when deregulation is not complete and some monopolistic elements remain (e.g., because of natural monopolies), the danger of lower quality for higher profits remains or even increases as the oversight of the regulatory authority ceases to exist.

Impact on culture, skills, and the strategic process
Turning to the organizations themselves, culture is one of the predominant variables that need to change with deregulation. The traditional attitude of regulated organizations is to accept the guidance of the regulatory authorities

and so to be reactive rather than proactive. By contrast, many of the new competitors entering deregulated industry deliberately seek to gain competitive advantage by circumventing existing regulatory barriers (as these are weakened during the process of deregulation), and this makes proactive strategy development advisable for the incumbent companies as well. This typically demands a complete and time-consuming change in organizational culture.

In addition, while regulation requires an emphasis on political and negotiation skills to deal with the regulator, the post-deregulation market environment requires heavier emphasis on planning, marketing, and financial skills.

As a result, therefore, previously regulated companies typically go through a transitory period of weakness upon deregulation, during which the new skills are developed or brought in and assimilated.

Impact on strategic outcome

Diversification. Turning to the strategy innovations of the deregulated firms, these are often influenced by the kind of relationship that the firm previously enjoyed with its regulator. If this was cosy, and if the firm had focused all its activities around the regulator, diversification will follow into other markets with equal or better profit potential (the reason why the firm would have avoided such diversification while regulated is that the regulator would have been unable to act to the firm's advantage in unrelated industries. Similarly, if deregulation implies that the regulator adopts a change agent role, to reduce the amount of help that it used to provide to the regulated firms, then the increasing divergence between the interests of the regulator and the regulated industry would again be expected to lead the firm into markets over which the regulator has no control.

In addition to product market diversification, geographic diversification also takes place with deregulation, for the same reasons. Moreover, this can be due to the fact that the regulated firm is now free to go abroad (and has the incentives to do so), or it may be that a particular deregulation is coordinated internationally (e.g., European deregulation in telecommunications).

Alliances and acquisitions. Where deregulation opens up new markets, either by means of the combination of technologies or by allowing companies to enter foreign markets, alliances, joint ventures, and acquisitions are often pursued as a means of acquiring missing skills or rapidly building market share.

Successful post-deregulation strategies. As most of the above industry-wide changes have been observed to take place in every deregulated industry, it is reasonable to expect that a number of generic responses to deregulation will exist. Indeed, three studies (Bleeke, 1983, 1991; Channon, 1988) have identified several such strategies, and the indicative rationalization of their findings which follows is only intended to act as an introduction to the illuminating studies themselves.

In essence, the studies have observed that the industry is too volatile during the first five years of deregulation for any particular strategy to be successful, even if a company prepared early enough so that it could have such a strategy in place. Instead, as has already been mentioned, flexibility and opportunism are necessary, while working toward positioning the company for the time when the initial five year period expires. At the end of that period, most successful companies are found to have positioned themselves in one of the following ways.

1. *Broad-based distribution strategies.* Firms that adopt strategies of this kind market a wide range of products over wide geographic areas, nationwide or globally. Each market can often only accommodate a small number of such competitors although, in the early stages of deregulation, many companies contend for such a positioning. Essential requirements for success as a broad-based distributor include: (i) the integration of operations and marketing across the entire area served (as loose regional affiliations are inadequate for achieving the broad service and information coverage required, and for the purposes of unified marketing); (ii) the availability of cost information that allows price adjustment according to the sensitivity of specific segments, as competition dictates (*see* ELASTICITY); and (iii) the development of

a full service perspective, as regulations permit.

2. *Cost-focused strategies.* The second strategy is of low-cost production of a narrow range of products. Again, because of ECONOMIES OF SCALE and the like, there is only space for few low-cost producers at equilibrium. While, therefore, this is a strategy much favored by new entrants immediately after deregulation (because they may have cost advantages over incumbents), many subsequently migrate to adopt specialty or segment-focused strategies, leaving behind them, ironically, a much less profitable industry. Migration may be initiated by a realization that their own costs are rising, it can be because yet lower cost competitors enter the market, or because they have attacked incumbents or broad-based competitors in their key markets who, in turn, being more powerful, have waged costly price wars against them. Success as a low-cost provider requires paramount emphasis on cost reduction, often brought about as much by streamlining and the use of technology as by the identification of innovative methods to eliminate entire stages of the value chain (e.g., by the use of direct mail to substitute retail selling). The lack of structural costs gives entrants a strong advantage over incumbents, as does their lack of established commitments, particularly in customer relations based service businesses, which allows them to select the segments they wish to serve, and to price competitively in those segments knowing that, if established firms followed suit, they would be cannibalizing the profitability of their existing operations. In addition, marketing is based on price, with minimal or no service offered.

3. *Segment-focused strategies.* The third strategy provides premium or expensive services at premium prices. There are a number of segment-focused strategy variants. Some have appeared later on in the deregulation process (as technology permitted), and some are found more in some industries than in others. In principle, segment-focused strategies require companies to be able to identify the right segment(s). In addition, the establishment of a close

relationship with customers (e.g., by the means of customer databases), bundling, and increasing product complexity and added features can be helpful in reducing customers' price sensitivity and providing opportunities to cross-sell additional products. Each of the segment-focused strategies is now discussed individually.

- *Speciality (niche) strategies.* A niche positioning (focusing upon either product or geography) can be chosen by companies too small to attempt national or global strategies. Niche competitors sometimes turn out to be broad-based competitors that have retrenched back to their core skills, so they are often well equipped to hold on to their markets, particularly if their niche is customer/product oriented rather than geographically defined. Niche strategies are relatively high-risk and high-return, by virtue of their specialization and their focus on some particular product or geographic area. Innovative segmentation and the development and marketing of products for these segments is necessary for the successful implementation of these strategies.

- *Composite service strategies.* The composite service strategy was first observed in the financial services industry, in which some firms rebundled products and services in innovative ways, striving for synergies. In this category, one should also place firms which provide information to customers so that these can make a more informed choice as to the product they require after deregulation has opened the way to a multitude of product/service and price/performance tradeoffs. The success of such strategies is often associated with the ability to create added value by such rebundling. An established customer base, the credibility to offer the services in question, an alternative delivery system, and a low-cost structure relative to traditional suppliers of similar services (although the rebundlers are themselves not necessarily price cutters) are also associated with success.

- *Global service strategies.* The global service strategy is pursued by firms that sell high value added services to selected multinational

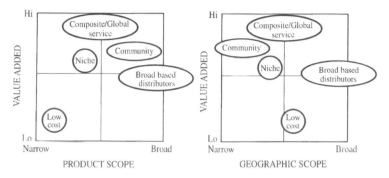

Figure 1 Strategies under deregulation.

and other large customers. The strategy requires sophisticated integrated delivery systems, coupled with the provision of a considerable level of personalized service. There are relatively few customers for such firms, and the amount of business required to make them profitable means that only a handful of global service firms can populate each industry worldwide.

• *Community strategies.* The final segment-focused strategy aims for the provision of a broad range of products to largely undifferentiated customers in small, protected geographic markets. A high level of service is provided to achieve customer loyalty, and a premium is charged for it. The markets in which these firms operate are too small to be tempting for larger competitors. Broad-based distributors and low-cost producers find it uneconomic to reach the small customer bases, and specialty companies are kept away by virtue of the local market being unsophisticated and offering little scope for segmentation. Customer loyalty provides an additional layer of protection. Overall, community firms can earn healthy profits, particularly if some regulation remains in place, provided that they do not try to expand into areas which are also served by larger firms. The strategies remain vulnerable in the long term, however, and community firms are threatened if some development allows more open entry into their markets. Having said that, community firms are sometimes found cooperating with potential predators, e.g. by buying from larger specialist concerns prevented from developing national strategies.

Finally, competition and price reductions in adjacent markets can adversely influence community firms, which may be obliged to lower prices even though they face no direct challenge. In order to succeed, community firms require a very high market share. In addition, they must price selectively, according to the level of competition which is faced in each product line, they must stress personal service, watch costs and productivity and avoid complacency, and perhaps develop ties with larger firms. Growth comes from entry into other community markets, particularly those vacated by larger competitors.

4. *Shared utility strategies.* Finally, shared utilities are firms that specialize in activities which are expensive for the smaller firms, yet essential for their competitive survival (e.g., the provision of financial information). They undertake these activities on behalf of the smaller firms and, as economies of scale are achieved by virtue of the size of the combined activities, they provide these services at a cost that is very advantageous to the buyer firms. As with community firms, market share is very important, so there is only space for very few shared utilities in each industry. Their existence makes it possible for many small firms to populate a market which would otherwise be oligopolistic, so they can enhance competition in an industry and earn good profits by doing so. Common elements of success in shared utilities include the ability to identify the appropriate activities (which cannot be activities core to the value chains of the

prospective customers), and the ability to be effective and cheap in undertaking them. Servicing some key players and becoming the industry standard is also important at the early stages, and this can determine whether or not the service will catch on.

Choice of post-deregulation strategy.   From this brief description of the most commonly encountered post-deregulation strategies, it should be possible to select a shortlist of appropriate strategies for any particular firm.

It should also be evident, however, that the choice is fairly deterministic, both for incumbents and new entrants, at least for the early years after deregulation. Morover, given the few strategies that incumbents can choose from, it is possible that more will strive to pursue a certain strategy than the market will accommodate. In this sense, regulated markets which were made up of few large firms may have an easier transition, although the accumulation of market power also tends to make such firms inflexible, and it is harder for them to adjust to the competitive environment.

Impact on structure.   Turning to organizational structure, diversification and a newly competitive environment both result in a strong trend toward organizational restructuring, this mainly involving divisionalization and the setting up of a series of customer-oriented marketing units to deal with the increased range of services and products offered.

In addition, particularly where deregulation takes place in conjunction with privatization and involves the setting up of a competitive market starting from a single organization, the incumbent organization may have to be split into a number of competing enterprises, horizontally or vertically; or, alternately, third parties may be given the right to establish new companies and compete.

Overall impact on performance.   Having already discussed the effect that deregulation has on prices (and the ways in which this can be moderated), the impact on performance should follow. Overall, however, it is not possible to evaluate the likely impact of deregulation on any particular firm without consideration of the actions which any such firm takes to prepare for and react to deregulation. In the long term,

performance may either increase or fall, because while regulation is expected to assure a reasonable stream of profits for all, deregulation opens the way to both very low and much higher levels of profits.

In the short term, the profits of established competitors are very often under threat, and profitable national monopolies are likely to face a difficult time adjusting to their new environment, particularly if all regulatory protection is removed at once. Initially, profits tend to fall, until reorganization and change of culture for competition are complete. At this point, a longer-term danger exists if the organization overlooks important environmental changes (*see* BLIND SPOTS), and this may well determine whether it survives in the competitive environment. If it adjusts, a whole new range of opportunities for considerably higher turnover are open to it, both nationally and internationally. Otherwise, if it remains largely unchanged in its culture and organization, it is likely to perish. A third possibility that is sometimes observed is that an organization appears to be adjusting well but, for a number of reasons, makes the wrong choices in the product market. This can also compromise performance.

Bibliography

Bleeke, J. A. (1983). Deregulation: riding the rapids. *McKinsey Quarterly* (Summer), 26–44.
Bleeke, J. A. (1990). Strategic choices for newly open markets. *Harvard Business Review*, **68** (5), September–October, 158–66. Reprinted in *McKinsey Quarterly* (1991), no. 1, 75–89.
Channon, D. F. (1986). *Global banking strategy*. Chichester: John Wiley. See chapter 9.
Mahimi, A. & Turcq, D. (1993). The three faces of European deregulation. *McKinsey Quarterly*, no. 3, 35–50.
Mahon, J. F. & Murray, E. A. Jr. (1981). Deregulation and strategic transformation. *Journal of Contemporary Business*, 9 (2), 123–38.

STEPHANOS AVGEROPOULOS

directional policy matrix   The directional policy matrix (DPM) was developed as a portfolio planning tool within the Royal Dutch Shell Group. Businesses were mapped on a three by three matrix identifying business sector prospects and the company's competitive capabilities, as illustrated in figure 1. The position of

Business Sector Prospects

		Unattractive	Average	Attractive
Company's Competitive Capabilities	Weak	Disinvest	Phased Withdrawal	Double or Quit
	Average	Phased Withdrawal	Custodial	Avis or Try Harder
	Strong	Cash Generation	Growth	Leader

Figure 1 The Shell directional policy matrix.
Source: Royal Dutch Shell Group.

each business was identified using a number of variables in a manner similar to the General Electric COMPETITIVE POSITION – MARKET ATTRACTIVENESS MATRIX.

The detailed techniques used by Shell were developed specifically for the petrochemical industry, but the model was generally applicable to any diversified enterprise. While any particular geographic area could be defined, for the majority of petrochemicals it was found useful to consider economic blocs as markets, as there was generally greater movement of chemicals within these blocs rather than between them. The time scale for investment was chosen as the effective forecasting horizon. This was based on business growth rate and the lead time for new capacity installation.

Shell uses four main criteria for assessing business sector prospects:

1. *Market growth rate.* Sectors with high growth are not always the most profitable, but growth is a necessary condition for growth of sector profits. Such conditions might vary according to industry:

Sector growth rate per year	Market growth rating
0–3 per cent	* Minimum
3–5 per cent	**
5–7 per cent	*** Average
7–10 per cent	****
10 per cent and over	***** Maximum

2. *Market quality.* A number of criteria are used to assess sector quality. These include questions such as:

- Does the sector have a record of high, stable profitability?

- Is the product resistant to commodity pricing?

- Is the technology freely available or restricted?

- Are suppliers few or many?

- Is the market dominated by a few major customers?

- Does the product have high added value when converted by the customer?

- Is the product one with high switching costs?

- Is the product free from risk of substitution?

A sector in which most of the above are answered with a yes gains a four- or five-star rating.

3. *Industry feedstock situation.* In the chemical industry, feedstock availability is a critical factor which often conditions expansion. However, shortage of feedstock availability for competitions is treated as a positive factor, as it reduces competitive pressures.

4. *Environmental aspects.* Sector prospects are influenced by the extent of restrictions on production, transportation, and marketing. Such influences need to be taken into account in sector prospects. This is especially true as environmental law evolves

and, in the developed economies, increasingly mirrors US law.

Company competitive capabilities. Shell assesses the relative strength of a chemical business's competitive capabilities using the three criteria listed below. These are usually assessed at the present time, although future positions that may be achievable as a result of the implementation of strategies can also be plotted.

1. *Market position.* Market share is the main criteria used to assess market position. Star ratings are awarded as follows:

   ***** Leader. A company which has high relative market share, the precise size of which is decided on a case-by-case basis.
   **** Major producers. The position in which there is no single leader but rather between two and four strong competitors operate; this is a common condition in the chemical industry.
   *** A second division competitor with a strong but not dominant market share.
   ** A low-share competitor with weak R&D.
   * A negligible competitor.

2. *Production capability.* This criterion is a combination of process economic, hardware capacity, location and number of plants, and access to feedstock. Star ratings are awarded on the basis of questions such as the following:

   - *Process economies.* Does the producer use a modern production process? Is the process owned or licensed? Is R&D capability adequate to maintain or improve process technology?

   - *Hardware.* Is capacity now or in the future adequate to support the share position? Does the producer have distributed plant to guard against breakdowns, strikes, and the like? Are delivery mechanisms competitive?

   - *Feedstock.* Is feedstock availability adequate? Does the business enjoy a feedstock cost advantage?

3. *Product research and development.* For performance products, R&D capability is assessed as a blend of product range, quality development record, and technical service competence. A star rating from one to five

is then assigned. No rating is made for commodity products. The star ratings are then converted to numerical values, with one star being awarded a zero and five stars a four. In its simpler form, all of the variables are given equal weighting; while in more advanced models the individual variables are weighted. The results are then plotted on the DPM. Each cell suggests an alternate strategy as follows:

- *Leader.* Businesses in this cell tend to be high-share concerns, with low costs and a superior technical position. While such businesses are usually profitable, cashflows may be marginal due to growth and the need for continuous investment. Such businesses must be supported as a priority.

- *Try harder.* Products in this cell need to have investment with a view to driving them into leader positions. Unless such investment is made, such a position becomes a liability.

- *Double or quit.* A small number of businesses can be adequately supported to convert them into the leadership positions of tomorrow.

- *Growth.* Products tend to fall in this sector when there are only between two and four key competitors (four-star position) supported by appropriate production capability and R&D strength. Such businesses tend to be profitable and approximately cash neutral.

- *Custodial.* Typically, custodial positions tend to occur when there are a relatively large number of competitors and the company concerned is relatively weak. For such businesses, the major objective is to maximize cash generation without the commitment of additional resources.

Businesses in the left-hand column of the DPM tend to exhibit below average growth combined with poor market quality and/or weaknesses in the industry feedstock position and environmental outlook.

- *Cash generation.* This position implies a strong competitive capability in a slow growth market. While profitable, such

Table 1 Classification of business sectors in order of priority.

Criteria	• Matrix position
	• Profit record
	• Other product-related criteria
	• Judgement
Category I	Hardcore of good quality business consistently generating good profits; e.g., engineering thermoplastics.
Category II	Strong company position. Reasonable to good sector prospects. Variable profit record; e.g., chlorinated solvents.
Category III	Promising product sectors new to company, .e.g., new chemical business.
Category IV	Reasonable to modest sector prospects in which the company is a minor factor. Variable profit record, e.g., chemical solvents.
Category V	Businesses with unfavorable prospects in which the company has a significant stake; e.g., detergent alkylate.

Source: Robinson et al. (1978).

businesses do not enjoy new attractive investment opportunities and therefore are managed to maximize cash generation.

• *Phased withdrawal.* Businesses with an average to weak position in a low-growth sector, while not generating excessive cash, nevertheless remain profitable. As a result, the recommended strategy is to aim for a phased withdrawal rather than rapid exit. Such a strategy should aim to maximize residual shareholder value for the business.

• *Disinvest.* Businesses in this sector are usually already making losses. Such businesses should be sold or closed. Ironically, MBO's have been a significant source of such disposals, with the incoming owner/ managers able to generate significant improvements in performance. It is important for management to accept that such businesses are losers: there is a tendency for too many managers to persevere with such concerns, usually with continuing losses, rather than accepting an exit strategy.

Table 2 Nonproduct strategic options.

Category 1	Joint venture to make olefins with petroleum company having secure oil feedstocks.
Category 2	Make maximum use of land and infrastructure at existing sites.
Category 3	Develop new major coastal manufacturing site in EC.
Category 4	Develop a foothold in the US market.
Category 5	Reduce dependence upon investment in Europe in order to spread risk. Develop manufacturing presence in, say, Ruritania.

Source: Robinson et al. (1978).

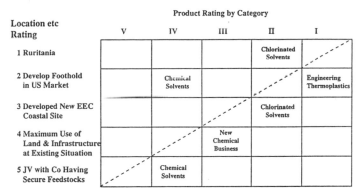

Product Rating by Category

Location etc Rating	V	IV	III	II	I
1 Ruritania				Chlorinated Solvents	
2 Develop Foothold in US Market		Chemical Solvents			Engineering Thermoplastics
3 Developed New EEC Coastal Site				Chlorinated Solvents	
4 Maximum Use of Land & Infrastructure at Existing Situation			New Chemical Business		
5 JV with Co Having Secure Feedstocks		Chemical Solvents			

Figure 2 The second order directional policy matrix.
Source: Royal Dutch Shell Group.

The Second Order Matrix

Shell have also developed a second order DPM which enables management to combine two parameters for investment decisions. This system relates the product strategy criteria with the company's priorities in other areas; notably, location and feedstock security.

A classification of the strategic positions identified in the DPM is illustrated in table 1. New ventures and double or quit businesses are only considered after those with proven profitability or cash generation capacity have been allocated the resources required to achieve their optimal potential.

In table 2 is shown a list of nonproduct market strategic options. These are normally developed at the corporate level, at which top management has a clear vision of preferred positions.

The two criteria options are contained in figure 2, which shows a second order DPM. In this system businesses can occur more than once when they satisfy different nonproduct market priorities. This matrix provides a convenient method of displaying alternate strategic priorities from which decisions can be determined.

Bibliography

Robinson, S. J. Q., Hichens, R. E. & Wade, D. P. (1978). Planning a chemical company's profits: Royal Dutch Shell Group of Companies, the Directional Policy Matrix – tool for strategic planning. *Long Range Planning*, no. 3, 8–15.

Royal Dutch Shell Company (1975). *The directional policy matrix: a new guide to corporate planning.* London: Royal Dutch Shell.

DEREK F. CHANNON

diversification Most companies begin as single business concerns (*see* SINGLE BUSINESS STRATEGY) serving a local regional market. In the early years of corporate development, most companies operate with a limited product range. While the initial market offers scope, expansion may still come from market and/or geographic growth. The great majority of companies either choose, or are forced, to limit their growth aspirations.

Those corporations which choose, or are presented with opportunities, to develop tend to do so by diversification as and when their original strategies mature. The evolution of strategic development has led to the development of a number of models, based especially on the work of Chandler. On the basis of his observations, Scott produced an early model of corporate growth, shown in figure 1. In this model, companies evolved from the single business phase to an integrated structure and finally to a related, or unrelated, diversified strategy which, as indicated by Chandler, was managed by a multidivisional structure. In refinements of this stages of corporate growth

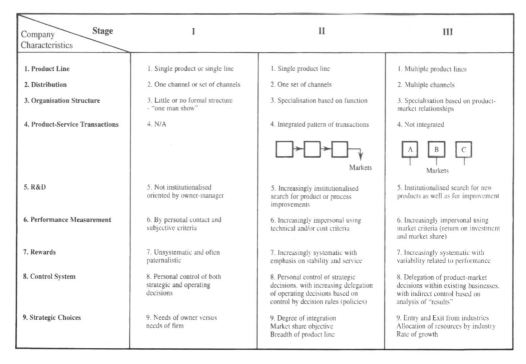

Company Characteristics \ Stage	I	II	III
1. Product Line	1. Single product or single line	1. Single product line	1. Multiple product lines
2. Distribution	2. One channel or set of channels	2. One set of channels	2. Multiple channels
3. Organisation Structure	3. Little or no formal structure - "one man show"	3. Specialisation based on function	3. Specialisation based on product-market relationships
4. Product-Service Transactions	4. N/A	4. Integrated pattern of transactions	4. Not integrated
5. R&D	5. Not institutionalised oriented by owner-manager	5. Increasingly institutionalised search for product or process improvements	5. Institutionalised search for new products as well as for improvement
6. Performance Measurement	6. By personal contact and subjective criteria	6. Increasingly impersonal using technical and/or cost criteria	6. Increasingly impersonal using market criteria (return on investment and market share)
7. Rewards	7. Unsystematic and often paternalistic	7. Increasingly systematic with emphasis on stability and service	7. Increasingly systematic with variability related to performance
8. Control System	8. Personal control of both strategic and operating decisions	8. Personal control of strategic decisions, with increasing delegation of operating decisions based on control by decision rules (policies)	8. Delegation of product-market decisions within existing businesses, with indirect control based on analysis of "results"
9. Strategic Choices	9. Needs of owner versus needs of firm	9. Degree of integration / Market share objective / Breadth of product line	9. Entry and Exit from industries / Allocation of resources by industry / Rate of growth

Figure 1   Three stages of organizational development.
Source: Scott (1971, p. 7).

model, the product market/geographic diversification strategies amongst large corporations, initially in the USA, and in manufacturing industry were examined. This was later extended to cover other major developed country economies and to embrace service industries and, more recently, combinations of service and manufacturing concerns, as these developed from the 1970s onward. This research indicated that there were some industries which had difficulty in diversifying substantially, because of their cashflow generating characteristics and the need to invest in all aspects of the business in order to maintain an integrated flow of product. These were concerns that had adopted a DOMINANT BUSINESS STRATEGY, which corresponded with Scott's Stage II corporations. Normally, a major trauma, such as the first oil-price shock for oil companies or the impact of PRIVATIZATION for utilities concerns, was necessary for such firms to have the funds or the will to move to a fully diversified mode, by adopting either a RELATED DIVERSIFIED STRATEGY or a CONGLOMERATE

STRATEGY. The definition of each of these categories is dealt with at length elsewhere; however, financial relatedness tends to be neglected, and moves which embrace this variable tend to be classified as unrelated. Nevertheless, it can be argued that the combination of a cash-generating business such as gambling with investment in hotels represents a clear way to achieve financial SYNERGY.

The strategic evolution of the top 200 British corporations is shown in figure 2. In this sample no differentiation has been made between service and manufacturing concerns; state-owned enterprises have been included, as have service industries without "turnover" measures. Historically, most such research has used classifications such as "Fortune 500", which was traditionally biased toward manufacturing, to identify the sample for evaluation.

The evolutionary trend has clearly been from undiversified strategies to more diversified concerns. Until 1980 the number of single business companies declined steadily, from 34 per cent in 1950 to only 2 per cent in 1980. This

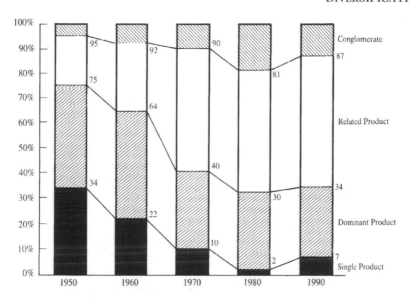

Figure 2 Diversification in the top 200 UK companies, 1950–1990.
Sources: Channon (1973), Times 1000, and ARs 1980–1990.

attrition occurred as a result of companies diversifying or being acquired by more diversified corporations. Those enterprises remaining in the category were those involved in highly successful industries, such as high-share food retailers, or those protected from stock market pressures by enjoying mutual ownership, such as some building societies and life insurance concerns. During the late 1980s, the number of single business concerns increased. This was a function of the process of privatization, which created a number of large new firms in the utilities industry, particularly in water and electricity supply. Interestingly, these newly created public companies were, in most cases, seeking to diversify by geography and partially by vertical integration.

Many firms diversify initially by limited moves through an ACQUISITION STRATEGY into new activities to become dominant business concerns (*see* DOMINANT BUSINESS STRATEGY). For most, this is a transitory step toward full diversification. There remains, however, a stable core of dominant business concerns which lack either the financial resources or the product market/technological skills to break out from the position. Such firms tend to be involved in high capital intensity, low differ-

entiation businesses, in which free cashflows are inadequate to provide the funds to move into new markets.

Most firms that diversify do so by acquisition, by purchasing businesses in areas which appear to be related to the original CORE COMPETENCIES of the firm. However, this strategy is often flawed by the failure to clearly identify relatedness, by inexperience in acquisition (and in particular post-acquisition) procedures, and by a lack of attention by top management, as reflected in the board structure, to achieving the expected synergy. Nevertheless, by 1990 the number of related diversified corporations amongst the top 200 British firms had increased from 20 per cent in 1950 to a level of 53 per cent.

The number of large British firms which could be classified as conglomerates in 1990 (*see* CONGLOMERATE STRATEGY) showed a reduction from the 19 per cent identified in 1980. The number of unrelated diversified concerns had grown to this level consistently from 1950 onward. Although the trend observed in the UK was not as marked as in the USA, the pattern was similar. During the 1980s, the reduction in the number of conglomerate strategies came about because some companies reduced their product market scope, there were acquisitions and break-ups of highly diversified concerns, and the make-up of the top 200 companies was influenced by the addition of the substantial number of newly privatized concerns.

Overall, based on the UK experience, and supported by research in other developed economies (albeit over a lesser period of time, and less concerned with service businesses), there is clear evidence that enterprises grow, at least in part, by diversification by product and/ or geography.

The process of diversification has largely occurred through acquisition, especially in the West. In recent times, stock market and external pressures have led some companies to reduce their product market scope by DIVEST-MENT, although others have continued to diversify. In the absence of similar pressures, Asian corporations seem to have successfully continued to diversify. Despite the evolutionary trend toward diversification, there is strong evidence that many of those using such moves are unsuccessful. The reasons for this include the following:

- *Lack of integration capacity.* Many diversifiers do not possess the managerial skills to successfully integrate new activities.

- *Lack of board attention.* In many companies, especially those breaking out from dominant business positions, little attention is paid at board level to new business ventures.

- *Misunderstandings about relatedness.* Many moves into apparently related industries turn out not to be; for example, brewing companies might have diversified into hotels as a way of selling more beer, without recognizing that sales of alcohol were a small component in successful hotel operation.

- *Inexperience with acquisitions.* Most diversifications occur as a result of acquisitions. Unfortunately, the majority of companies available for purchase tend to suffer from some weakness, which usually needs correction. This is turn requires a skillful post-acquisition TURNAROUND STRATEGY, which companies diversifying themselves out of relative weakness rarely possess. As a result,

acquisitions may well not generate the performance that was expected.

- *Clash of corporate cultures.* Each organization has a unique culture. It is imperative that the disparate cultures of organizations attempting to merge are sufficiently compatible to avoid dysfunctional organization side-effects.

- *Incorrect market identification.* Not necessarily the same as problems with relatedness, this error may occur in particular with unrelated diversification moves in which apparently attractive entries are made into markets that turn out to be much less attractive. For example, many manufacturing firms in mature markets attempted to enter the financial services market, often with disastrous consequences.

- *Difficulties of synergy release.* It has been shown that while synergy is relatively easy to identify in theory, it is extremely difficult to release in practice, with the possible exception of financial synergy.

- *Move too small.* Many firms embarking on diversification moves for the first time tend to adopt a timid approach, making only a relatively small move. Apart from not achieving competitive advantage in the industry sector into which the firm diversifies, small moves also suffer from a lack of board attention, and difficulties of integration.

- *Inadequate functional skills.* These can be related to several of the other reasons for failure. If the diversifying firm lacks the critical success factor core skills, these must be rapidly imported or the move may well fail.

- *Imposition of wrong style of management.* Diversification often involves entry into a new industry, in which the style of management may be quite different from that of CORE BUSINESSES. Top management often fails to recognize such differences, and endeavors to introduce a culture, values, and control systems which, while relevant to the core business, are wholly inappropriate to the diversification.

Overall, diversification by product and by geography seems to be a natural process of evolution. The parameters that define the boundaries are not yet clearly delineated. Interestingly, while Chandler puts forward the proposition that structure follows strategy, the ultimate degree of diversification which can be achieved by the firm may be driven by structure. Is the KEIRETSU STRUCTURE espoused by major Japanese and Korean entities superior to the SBU structure used by Western corporations, in which failing units are candidates for divestment, superior or not? Time may tell.

Bibliography

Chandler, A. D. (1962). *Strategy and structure.* Cambridge, MA: MIT Press.

Channon, D. F. (1973). *Strategy and structure of British enterprise.* Cambridge, MA: Harvard Division of Research.

Channon, D. F. (1978). *The service industries: strategy, structure and financial performance.* London: Macmillan.

Rumelt, R. (1974). *Strategy structure and financial performance.* Cambridge, MA: Harvard Division of Research.

Scott, B. R. (1971). Stages of corporate development. Unpublished paper, Harvard Business School.

Wrigley, L. (1971). Divisional autonomy and diversification. Unpublished doctoral dissertation, Harvard Business School.

DEREK F. CHANNON

divestment   In the late 1980s, divestment strategies became more common as a result of stock market pressures being applied to highly diversified corporations. Such firms, which had largely expanded by acquisition into unrelated product markets, were seen by acquisitive predators as candidates for break-up, as the sale of the constituent businesses would produce a substantial surplus over the market capitalization plus a bid premium. The activities of predators were also supported by stock market arbitrageurs, some commercial banks, and fund managers. In addition, bids for such companies could be orchestrated by specialist investment bankers, who would bid for such companies with a view to subsequently breaking them up. These pressures also led a number of companies to break up their own businesses to avoid the attention of predators. Again, commercial and investment banks, management consultants, and other market operators might initiate such break-ups.

Other reasons for divestment include: differences in cultural fit (for example, moves by pharmaceutical or tobacco companies into cosmetics); failure of businesses to fit with revised parent company strategies introduced by new leaders (for example, US General Electric transformed its portfolio of activities during the 1980s following the appointment of a new Chief Executive in 1981); businesses being divested or liquidated if they make a negative contribution to shareholder value following the adoption of a VALUE-BASED PLANNING system; and, finally, businesses which are identified as having weak portfolio positions.

Divestiture can result from the sale or liquidation of an existing business. The first of these policies was preferred, as the parent could hopefully rid itself of any liability for the divested activity. Such a move might take place by an outright sale to a third party, for whom the activity might be beneficial by, for example, increasing market share, adding new complementary products, improving distribution access, and importing new technologies. Selling such a business to existing management, usually via a LEVERAGED BUY-OUT STRATEGY was also often an attractive alternative. Liquidation was the most messy and usually least preferred method of business disposal. Such a move could result in hardships for displaced employees, expensive plant closures, image problems for the corporate parent, and potential litigation from injured parties.

While there has been some increase in divestiture as a result of stock market pressures, overall many corporations have increased their level of diversification during the 1980s and early 1990s, although they may well have substantially adjusted their portfolio of businesses by a mix of sales and purchases.

Bibliography

Bowman, C. & Asch, D. (1987). *Strategic management.* Basingstoke, Hampshire: Macmillan Education.

Rowe, A.J., Mason, R. O., Dickel, K. E., Mann, R. B. & Mockler, R. J. (1994). *Strategic management,* 4th edn. Reading, MA: Addison-Wesley. See pp. 439-40.

Thompson, A. A. & Strickland, A. J. (1993). *Strategic management*. Homewood, IL: Irwin. See pp. 178–81.

Toy, S. (1985). Splitting up. *Business Week* 50–5.

DEREK F. CHANNON

divisional structure   In his classic study of the evolution of large-scale US corporate enterprise, Chandler (1962) observed that as large corporations evolved they became more complex. He reported, for example, that the natural development of the railroads made it impossible to centralize all decision making. Decentralization was essential because communication systems were inadequate for information to be passed in time for the center to influence or make decisions.

Chandler noted that there was a natural tendency for some firms to diversify: he explored in depth the evolution of four major US corporations, The Du Pont Corporation, Standard Oil (later Exxon), General Motors, and Sears Roebuck, and observed how in the late 1920s a new organizational form developed in these concerns. Led by the Du Pont Company, these firms all found that the growing complexity of the organization made a FUNCTIONAL STRUCTURE inefficient and unwieldy. As a result, these firms developed a divisional form of organization in which operations were subdivided into a series of multifunctional units. The role of the central office changed to one of supervision and coordination of the organizational units, which were operationally autonomous, and the establishment of overall strategy. While this structure, shown in figure 1, became the key organizational form for diversified companies and was spread around the world by US corporations, and especially by US consultants McKinsey and Company, the Mitsubishi ZAIBATSU STRUCTURE in Japan had developed in a very similar fashion some 15 years earlier.

The new structure broke the organization up in a way which provided divisional management with all the ingredients to operate as a complete business which could be measured in terms of

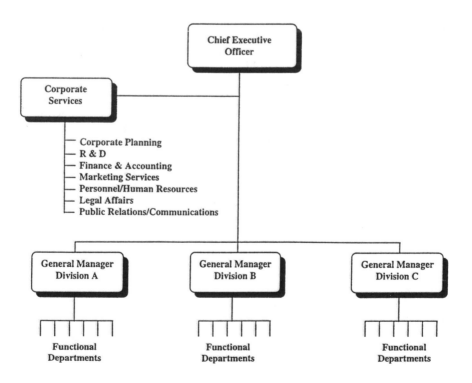

Figure 1 The multidivisional form of organizational structure.

profit performance. It made it easier for central management to establish investment policy, apply rewards and sanctions based on performance, and establish alternative strategies for different divisions; perhaps most of all, it helped to develop a cadre of general managers, which facilitated the strategy of further diversification. Functionally organized companies seriously lacked in their capability to diversify because, apart from the CEO, they did not develop such general managers. The central office could also develop a sophisticated service function, especially in finance and planning.

In the postwar period the divisional structure spread rapidly throughout US industry, and as many of these firms began to move overseas, particularly into the developed countries of Europe, it gave them a dramatic advantage by comparison to the functional or holding company structures more normal in Europe. Servan Schreiber (1969) described this as the "American challenge" and noted that it was the divisional form of organization that was the secret of the success of American corporations in penetrating European markets.

Throughout the 1970s in manufacturing industry around the world, the divisional form of organization became widely accepted in diversified corporations. As observed by Chandler (1962), in related product diversified and geographically diversified corporations the divisions were supported by a large central office, with sophisticated staff units charged with insuring interdivisional coordination where necessary; for example, insuring efficient management of interdependency for products such as feedstocks and the like, coordinating corporation-wide services in specialist areas such as computing, and providing an overall perspective via strategic planning and finance. Some central management of human resources and legal and external affairs was also normal.

The role of the board in the divisional organization was to set and monitor strategy, to measure and evaluate the performance of the divisions, to assign resources, to establish management information and control systems, to design and implement reward and sanction systems, and to make key appointments. The constitution of the board consisted usually of the chairman and chief executive, together with executives concerned with finance, often plan-

ning and human resources management, plus nonexecutive directors. In many, but not all, divisional structures, the general managers of major divisions were also included as members of the board.

In the late 1960s, the development of conglomerate businesses (see CONGLOMERATE STRATEGY) challenged the concept of the large central office. The new conglomerates operated a wide range of unrelated businesses, organized as product divisions, but the central office of such corporations was very small. The primary functions of the central office in these corporations were the establishment of overall strategy, acquisition search and purchase, post-acquisition rationalization, and tight financial monitoring of divisional performance. Some also had a number of general operating managers attached to the center who were capable of evaluating the operating activities of divisions placed under their control. The rationale for this small central office system was that there was deliberately no SYNERGY, other than financial, between the operating divisions; hence there was no need for central interdivisional coordination, R&D, and the like. This system appeared to be very successful for many years, especially when the overall technology requirements of the corporation were limited. However, failure occurred at Litton Industries when a number of major technological projects went out of control simultaneously. This caused a serious loss of stock market confidence in conglomerates, although in reality the financial performance of the group, when well managed, remained superior to that of related diversified businesses.

In the 1980s and 1990s, superior information technology and the trend toward DELAYERING has extended the concept of the small central office to most forms of diversified corporations while, despite some moves back to CORE BUSINESSES, many conglomerates remain.

The choice as to whether a geographic or product division system was adopted was a function of the degree of product complexity. As product diversity increased there was a clear move toward the adoption of a product division system. Industries such as food, where strong local needs made the establishment of uniform product and marketing strategies difficult, were somewhat of an exception. Geographic divisions were common in such cases: production and products themselves were therefore localized and the need to establish centralized product divisional management had less value. By the late 1970s, most large diversified firms in the USA and UK had found and adopted the multidivisional form, and a substantial number were endeavoring to operate this in conjunction with a portfolio system of management, the most commonly used of which was the GROWTH SHARE MATRIX. The same trend was found amongst the major corporations of other leading European countries; however, the degree of penetration of the divisional form was less developed and holding companies were still common, in part due to the complex shareholding patterns found in many European groups. These made it difficult to establish a common central office to set strategy for quasi-independent subsidiaries, in which minority shareholdings might hold considerable influence.

In the late 1970s, it also became recognized that the make-up of a division itself might be suboptimal. For example, in large divisions some activities might be growing rapidly while the main activities might be in decline. Since the corporate strategic resource allocation objectives and performance measurement tended to be established at the divisional level, such a growth business might be treated as a CINDERELLA BUSINESS. At the US General Electric Company, therefore, it became recognized that the division did not necessarily represent the appropriate breakdown of the corporation. Hence, from the development of the PIMS program, and in conjunction with McKinsey and Company, the SBU STRUCTURE was developed. The SBU then became the lowest level planning unit in General Electric. A large division could therefore consist of several SBUs, each of which might be assigned a different strategic objective, performance measure, and dedicated resources, irrespective of the overall expected performance of the division itself. With this structure it was also possible to transfer some of the historic central staff functions to the divisional level and so reduce the size of the central office.

The divisional form was also important in the development of international strategy. As well as increasing the degree of product diversity, many corporations had developed international opera-

tions. The early multinationals tended to emerge from the European colonial powers, who established overseas operations in their colonies. British companies, for example, set up operations in the old Empire, French, and Dutch companies similarly. These concerns operated essentially as stand-alone units, since communications were inadequate to permit any central office control over operations. There was also no coordinated R&D, and the industries concerned tended to be either low-technology, such as food, or to involve the gathering of raw materials such as oil. The HOLDING COMPANY STRUCTURE was therefore the norm for such corporations, with central office control usually being exercised by the annual visit of a senior main board director.

After World War II, by contrast, major US corporations began to develop their overseas activities. Unlike the early Europeans, the US corporations moved to penetrate the developed economies, and especially Western Europe. Moreover, it was the technology-led concerns in computing, chemicals, and the like which decided to go multinational. These firms were amongst the earliest to adopt the divisional form of organization.

In the early stages of internationalization, such firms normally established a separate international division. Exports from all domestic product divisions passed through such an export division. As international activities developed, however, it became normal not only to establish overseas sales organizations but also to set up production facilities. In the early phases of this process the establishment of geographic divisions tended to be common. Further development of overseas production facilities, coupled with growing product complexity, caused tension between overseas geographic divisions and domestic product-based divisions. As a result, there was pressure to ensure coordination between all similar product activities and to develop worldwide product research facilities. The possibility of interplant cross-border product and feed stock interchange therefore led to the movement toward the creation of worldwide product divisions. The boundaries between these three divisional variants were mapped by Stopford & Wells (1972) and are shown in figure 2.

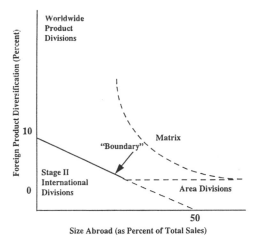

Figure 2 Size abroad, as a percentage of total size.
Source: J. Stopford (1980), p. 108.

From the early 1970s, there was also a growing trend in some industries to move to truly global rather than regionally oriented strategies. Products and components could be produced in one region and shipped around the world for assembly before being sold in a third region. This trend to complexity in both product and geography led to the development of an even more complex organizational form, the MATRIX STRUCTURE, which usually divided the corporation into a combination of both geographic and product divisions. In this structure, multiple reporting relationships were common, in which country executives reported to both area and product divisions.

The divisional organizational form has been an extremely important structural development in the management of the modern corporation. While the structure has continued to evolve, the basic premise remains, and its widespread adoption around the world has been a major element in the development of the strategy and structure of the diversified enterprise.

Bibliography

Chandler, A. D. (1962). *Strategy and structure.* Cambridge, MA: MIT Press.
Channon, D. F. (1973). *The strategy and structure of British enterprise.* Cambridge, MA: Harvard Division of Research.
Dyas, G. P. & Thanheiser, H. T. (1976). *The emerging European enterprise.* London: Macmillan.
Rumelt, R. P. (1974). *Strategy, structure and economic performance.* Cambridge, MA: Harvard University Press.
Schreiber, J. J. S. (1969). *The American challenge.* New York: Aran Books.
Stopford, J. (1980). *Growth and organisational change in the multinational firm.* Arno Press.
Stopford, J. & Wells, L. T. (1972). *Management and the multinational enterprise.* London: Longman.
Williamson, O. E. (1985). *The economic institutions of capitalism.* New York: The Free Press.

DEREK F. CHANNON

dog businesses Such businesses are defined as those in which the growth rate is slow and the relative market share is low compared to the leading competitor. Because of this low share such businesses are often expected to have a higher cost structure than industry leaders. Moreover, to gain share in a mature environment is difficult and extremely expensive. The recommended strategy for such weak businesses is therefore seen as DIVESTMENT or rapid harvesting. While this may be so, care should be taken to insure that the cashflow prospects are as poor as the GROWTH SHARE MATRIX model suggests. Often, low capital intensity dog businesses can be fruitful cash generators, and harvesting can often be extended.

DIVESTMENT is the practice of selling businesses which appear not to fit with prevailing strategy. This was a recommended strategy for dog businesses. In addition, during the late 1970s and early 1980s acquisition strategies (*see* ACQUISITION STRATEGY) were popular and a further wave of predatory purchases occurred, often fueled by commercial and investment banks. In addition, unlike earlier such movements in the 1960s, such purchases became increasingly cross-border as the major world capital markets globalized. In the late 1980s and early 1990s this practice became less popular, as some of the emerging conglomerates themselves came under attack (*see* CONGLOMERATE STRATEGY), forcing divestments to reduce stock market vulnerability, increase shareholder value, and encourage the retreat to CORE BUSINESSES. Many corporations did indeed sell activities which were considered noncore; for example, BAT disposed of its retail businesses to avoid an unwanted predator attack, ICI split in two with the flotation of its pharmaceutical business, and Sears Roebuck and Xerox spun off their financial services businesses. Other companies such as Hanson Trust, BTR, US General Electric Company, and the like increased their overall degree of DIVERSIFICATION while also selling many businesses which did fit financially and/or strategically into their overall corporate strategy.

See also **Growth share matrix**

DEREK F. CHANNON

dominant business strategy   Such businesses were defined empirically by Wrigley and others as those in which at least 70 per cent of sales were accounted for by one key business. Dominant business corporations tended to be of several types. First, they were identifiable as being in an unstable transitory phase between single businesses and fully diversified enterprises. Second, they had developed naturally one key business which was so large that diversification to a more diversified classification was difficult: such concerns included the oil companies, which despite their efforts found it difficult to find other activities which matched the main business. Third, there were companies which were trapped as dominant businesses: these businesses, including steel and other metal producers, tended to be high in capital intensity so that their cashflow generating capacity was inadequate to both support the existing business and provide funds for diversification. Fourth, there were concerns in which one business had grown so rapidly that they had moved from a related diversified strategic position back to a dominant business position: IBM, in which for a period mainframe computers dominated, provides an example.

It had proved very difficult for many dominant businesses to diversify successfully. Despite having many of the strategic management skills at the center, such firms tended to operate as integrated Stage II businesses. As a result, they lacked the general management skills needed to manage a multibusiness corporation. Moreover, in the case of concerns such as oil companies, the size and scale of the main activity was such as to leave attempted diversifications without champions at board level, because of the tendency for such firms

to attempt to impose the corporate culture of the core business on diversifications, irrespective of whether or not this was appropriate.

The definition of the dominant business firm was subsequently refined by Rumelt (1974) to provide a measure of the degree of relatedness and vertical integration involved with a strategy. While the primary definition remained, four subdivisions of the dominant business form were identified:

- *Dominant–vertical.* These are vertically integrated firms that produce and sell a variety of end products, no one of which contributes more than 95 per cent of sales.

- *Dominant–constrained.* These are nonvertical dominant business firms that have diversified by building on some particular strength, skills, or resource associated with the original dominant activity. In such firms the preponderance of diversified activities are all related one to another and to the dominant business.

- *Dominant–linked.* These are nonvertical dominant business firms that have diversified by building on several different strengths, skills, or resources or by building on new strengths, skills, or resources as they are acquired. In such firms the preponderance of the diversified activities are not directly related to the dominant business but each is somehow related to another of the firm's activities.

- *Dominant–unrelated.* These are nonvertical dominant business firms in which the preponderance of the diversified activities are unrelated to the dominant business.

Bibliography

Channon, D. F. (1973). *The strategy and structure of British enterprise.* Cambridge, MA: Harvard Division of Research.

Rumelt, R. P. (1974). *Strategy, structure and economic performance.* Cambridge, MA: Harvard Division of Research.

Scott, B. L. (1970). Stages of corporate development. Unpublished paper, Harvard Business School.

Wrigley, L. (1970). Divisional autonomy and diversification. Unpublished doctoral dissertation, Harvard Business School.

DEREK F. CHANNON

downsizing Ironically seldom discussed in the context of re-engineering and indeed denied, but nevertheless a common consequence, downsizing refers to a head count reduction which usually occurs as a result of attempts to achieve radical shifts in productivity. These transformations have tended to result in head count cuts of around 25 per cent against initial stretch targets of 40 per cent. In particular, downsizing has occurred with white collar workers as a result of improved information technology, this having led to savage reduction in corporate staff (*see* DELAYERING). Over 85 per cent of Fortune 1000 firms downsized between 1987 and 1991, with more than 50 per cent downsizing in 1990 alone, when almost a million American managers lost their jobs. Similar trends have also occurred in Europe. Only in Japan has the philosophy of permanent employment been largely maintained, although even there pressures have been mounting, recruitment has been sharply cut back, excess workers have been transferred to subsidiaries or suppliers, and firms have been forced to diversify in efforts to maintain employment.

Nevertheless, downsizing is not necessarily a reactive and negative phenomenon but, rather, can be part of the process of "right sizing," whereby the head count employed is appropriate for the firm to gain or maintain competitive advantage. This is the outcome of the Japanese KAIZEN practice in which costs are continuously reduced and the workforce is actually redeployed to new activities.

Unfortunately, however, when a firm suffers a serious decline in profits, downsizing occurs as a first response cost cutting device. It is often not necessarily the most appropriate response; but it occurs because the firm has failed to monitor changes in its external environment and is faced with unexpected cost pressures, resulting from poor quality, inflexibility, obsolescent strategies, failure to develop new products, technology bypasses, and failure to monitor the appropriate competitors. The workforce therefore tends to suffer as a result of managerial failures rather than through any fault of its own. Furthermore, the downsizing exercise itself does not address the underlying causes of strategic failure; and, moreover, the reduction in morale caused by downsizing, the probable future resistance to change, and the loss of faith

in management can in the long term far outweigh the short-term reduction in cost. The actual process can also prove costly, notably in those countries in which social legislation makes redundancy terms especially expensive.

It is important therefore to gain employee commitment, rather than compliance, to the need for continuous cost reduction. Japanese companies have achieved this by their policy of permanent employment. While kaizen policies are common, the response of the Japanese workforce to endaka, the rapid appreciation of the yen, has been to double efforts to cut costs; for example, by dramatically increasing employee suggestions.

There are also alternatives to downsizing. As in Japan, most Western companies stop hiring. Many encourage early retirement, do not replace leavers, and the like. Other strategies might include outsourcing, job sharing, restricted overtime, short-time working, and switches to part-time working. Salary cuts are used infrequently (but not for top management in Japan).

When downsizing becomes inevitable, it is important that it is done effectively. A number of conclusions on how this should be achieved have been identified:

- couple productive restructuring with downsizing, either concurrently or in immediate sequence

- continue top down and bottom up downsizing

- pay special attention to both employees who lose their jobs and those who do not

- insure that adequate advance notice is provided and involve the workforce in the process

- downsize not only inside the firm but within the firm's external network

- keep your head – and your heart and soul – during a crisis

- insure that early warning systems are in place to avoid future BLIND SPOTS

- create and sustain an information-porous organization

- use competitive BENCHMARKING to insure that you do not suddenly wake up to find that you are no longer competitive

Bibliography

Cameron, K. S., Freeman, S. J. & Mishra, A. K. (1991). Best practices in white collar downsizing managing contradictions. *Academy of Management Executive*, 57–73.

Collins, R. S., Oliff, M. D. & Vollman, T. E. (1991). *Manufacturing restructuring: lessons for management.* Manufacturing 2000 Executive, Report No. 2. Lausanne: IMD.

Henkoff, R. (1990). Cost cutting, how to do it right. *Fortune*, 26–33.

Vollman, T. & Brazas, M. (1993). Downsizing. *European Management Journal*, 11, 18–28.

DEREK F. CHANNON

Driving Force® By the mid-1970s, Kepner-Tregoe, the worldwide consulting and training company, had become a leader in rational decision making and problem solving, techniques which it had developed some 15 years previously. This was based on the original research conducted by Drs Kepner and Tregoe at the Rand Corporation. Until then, its decision making methodology had been fundamentally used for operational decisions. However, at the behest of the Davos Symposium, research was conducted into whether the application of these techniques to strategic issues could be made at the highest levels in organizations: the fundamental difference being that, frequently, considerably more judgement and less data are available in the strategic arena than when making day-to-day operational decisions and thus they were that much harder.

This research led to the discovery of the power of the Driving Force®, which has been refined over time so that, in the past 20 years, over 500 major worldwide corporations have benefitted from its application in providing clarity of strategic thinking and more effective strategic decision making.

Before exploring these ideas, however, some definitions are required. "Strategy" is a much used and abused word, and means different things to different people and organizations. Kepner-Tregoe has found that the following definition has stood the test of time. Strategy is "the *framework* within which *choices* about the future *nature* and *direction* of an organization can be made." By "framework" is meant the boundaries or parameters which indicate what is within its compass. The choices that need to be made are fundamentally about what products and services will and will not be offered, what customers and end users will and will not be served, and what geographies will and will not be addressed. The *nature* of an organization is that which is its very essence or – to use today's more familiar term – core.

Thus a company such as McDonald's has, as its nature, "fast foods" for which it is instantly recognizable. More narrowly, one might associate it simply with hamburgers. "Coca Cola" is synonymous with soft drinks and, more particularly, with one specific brand. The term "direction" is concerned with where an organization is heading, which may or may not lead to a change in its nature. Thus British American Tobacco transformed itself from an organization fundamentally associated with tobacco and related products to an industrial conglomerate, the make-up of which – somewhat like Hanson Plc – is now of a wide variety of disparate products with nothing in common except, conceivably, financial hurdle rates which must be passed. Conglomerates or diversified corporations have a nature which is undefinable at a corporate level except through financial criteria.

Given this definition of strategy, the key question to be asked is how an organization determines what its strategic future will be. For Kepner-Tregoe, the answer has been to use the Driving Force® concept, the discussion of which is at the heart of this section. The term "Driving Force®" has become common currency in recent years, and it would probably surprise many people to learn that it is a registered trademark of Kepner-Tregoe, and has been so for a decade and a half.

Driving Force®, is defined as "the primary determinant of the products and services that an organization will and will not offer and the customers and marketplaces it will and will not serve." The term "primary" is vital here. Of course there are many influences on these key decisions, but when an organization is confronted with limited resources, opposing claims on them, investment decisions, and the search for and consolidation of its competitive advantage, it is the Driving Force® that will make the difference.

The uses and benefits of the Driving Force® concept will be described later, but it is now appropriate to examine what the Driving Forces® themselves are. At Kepner-Tregoe, it is believed that there are eight. These eight are slightly modified from their original concept – on the basis of much experience – and have been reduced from the original nine.

The one that has been dropped is "Size/Growth" since, in the first ten years of using these ideas with clients, only two organizations were found to have this Driving Force®, and it was seen as a very temporary one anyway. The classic example from the 1980s of an organization that might have been driven by size and growth was Saatchi & Saatchi, which had as its stated aim the desire to become the world's largest advertising agency. While this situation was achieved, it was not necessarily the source of Saatchi & Saatchi's competitive advantage, nor a sustainable long-term strategy. The eight Driving Forces® are as follows:

- Products and Services Offered
- Markets Served
- Low-cost Production
- Operations Capability
- Technology
- Method of Sale/Distribution
- Natural Resources
- Return/Profit

Each Driving Force® has a number of characteristics: namely the focus they provide, the competitive advantage that they offer, the SYNERGY that is created around them, and the clarity of communication internally and externally that is facilitated by their adoption. How an organization itself determines which one should be its future Driving Force® is a major strategic decision making operation, undertaken over many months by boards of directors who often face more than one viable alternative.

Products and Services Offered

An organization pursuing a Products and Services Offered Driving Force® will meet a basic and enduring need in the marketplace by offering a limited range of related products and/or services which the customer perceives to provide benefits that are not received or available from alternative suppliers – and for which the buyer is willing to pay a premium price, if necessary, for the supplier to provide these benefits. A Products and Services Offered organization will have a clear and narrow definition of this basic need, and will be familiar with the specific requirements of customers who have that tightly defined and enduring need.

The primary competitive advantage that the organization will exploit is its ability to meet customer requirements in the design and modification of its products, supporting services, delivery, and pricing, all of which enable the organization to differentiate its products in ways that the customers value as superior when compared with alternate offerings. Its only motive to sell really new products is if they directly result in more sales of their core products, as in the case of Volkswagen–Audi when they offered car insurance.

The Products and Services Offered organization may deliver products and services at a competitive, but not necessarily the lowest, cost. Since the competitive advantage is based on perceived value rather than cost, it will usually attempt to gain a premium price for the features and benefits of its differentiated products and services.

Possible examples include ICI Decorative Paints (Dulux) and Rover Cars.

Markets Served

An organization pursuing a Markets Served Driving Force® has an especially strong relationship or franchise with a specific well defined group, or groups, of customers or end users who share many common characteristics and needs. It understands these customers' needs and buying patterns. Through this close relationship, the organization identifies an increasingly broad range of needs that it can fulfill for the core customer group.

The primary competitive advantage of a market served organization is that it understands its customers needs better than its rival; is able to meet those needs in a superior way; and generates fierce customer loyalty and identity with the organization. This organization must also have the capabilities to develop new and different products and services ("new" meaning new and different for this organization) that meet different needs than those currently being served.

Through its familiarity with customers and their needs, the organization may differentiate its products and/or services if value and quality as perceived by the customer are more important than low cost. Alternately, it may concentrate on providing products and/or services at the lowest cost if its customers' primary buying motives require this competitive advantage. This organization will, therefore, frequently outsource its products and/or services from lower-cost producers, provided that it can insure its favorable image and name, or even license its name to manufacturers.

Possible examples include Marks & Spencer, who added food and financial services to the same customer base as had been built up within their clothes retailing operation; and Dunhill and LVMH, both of which are in the luxury goods market, with customers who have very high disposable incomes and an "image" to create and who are loyal and long lasting.

Low-cost Production

An organization pursuing a Low-cost Production Driving Force® has a set of production capabilities able to produce products or services at the lowest cost relative to competitive offerings. This type of organization will maintain and increase its cost advantage over its competitors through advanced process technology and cost-conscious management of its production. It will use its knowledge of advances in process technology or production methods to stay ahead of competitors and to avoid obsolescence of its production capabilities.

Because of the nature of the production capabilities, economies of scale are important. The organization guided by Low-cost Production will produce standard products consistent with its capabilities, maintaining steady and high production levels or insuring ready availability of large volumes. Its product range will be limited.

Possible examples include the International Paper Company and food companies producing "own label" products for other food manufacturers and/or retailers.

Operations Capability

An organization pursuing an Operations Capability Driving Force® has a set of capabilities – physical, human, and technical – often very specialized, which, when used in a variety of combinations, produces a wide range of products or services. The organization's competitive advantage stems from these capabilities and the ability to use them flexibly, allocating the appropriate mix of capabilities to deliver specific products or services to precise orders – and specifically from their customers. This organization will seek optimum use of its capabilities by controling capacity in response to demand or seeking innovative ways in which to generate and package products or services.

Organizations may concentrate on highly flexible uses of production capabilities in a "job shop" setting or may build on unique combinations of technical operations capabilities. In either case, products or services are often generated in relatively small numbers, or are single projects unique to individual customers. The features and benefits of the products or services will be set by the customer's specification and the nature of the organization's capabilities. Turnaround time and low costs are important competitive factors, particularly for a "job shop" environment.

Possible examples include "quick print" companies.

Technology

An organization pursuing a Technology Driving Force® builds its strategic vision around a body of knowledge, or a set of technological capabilities. It has the people and the physical resources to develop this basic technology, and to apply it in innovative ways in order to satisfy existing, emerging, or completely new needs.

The technology organization's competitive advantage rests in the unique quality or quantity of this technological expertise, and the ability to generate a wide range of applications of this technology. It will strive to stay at the forefront of its chosen technology, changing the boundaries within which it operates as the technology advances. It will be considered as a leader in its chosen field.

The organization with a Technology Driving Force may choose to retain control over its technological capability by producing products or services emanating from the technology base. However, some Technology-driven organizations keep their focus on the technology base and then license aspects or applications of the technology to others for product development and production (or set up joint ventures). When competitors gain advances in technology, the firm's Driving Force® must change.

Possible examples include Xerox (in its early days) and Genentech (in the field of biotechnology).

Method of Sale/Distribution

An organization pursuing a Method of Sale/Distribution Driving Force® has a set or system of logistics, distribution, and sales capabilities – and the physical, human, and systems resources necessary to fully exploit them – in order to provide a variety of products or services in a wide market using this competitive advantage. These distribution and sales capabilities may be unique in their quality, quantity, or position compared with those of competitors. They may provide the organization with an opportunity to price its products at a premium. Alternately, the organization may build on its ability to exploit distribution and sales capabilities similar to those of its competitors at a lower cost.

To gain maximum advantage from its existing distribution and sales capabilities or system, an organization may choose to handle compatible products which are not its own. The organization may also seek to develop or acquire other distribution or sales channels or systems which are similar in nature to its current capabilities. The specific content and scope of its capabilities may change over time so that the organization sustains a competitive advantage in its uniqueness.

Possible examples include Avon Cosmetics, McDonald's, and post offices.

Natural Resources

An organization pursuing a Natural Resources Driving Force® owns or controls a significant natural resource (or more than one). It often, but not necessarily, possesses the capability to process that natural resource into usable forms. The organization's competitive advantage rests in the quality, cost of exploitation, quantity, location, or form of the natural resources

themselves. The organization will, therefore, seek to maintain its advantage in one or more of these areas, adding to the natural resource ownership or control as necessary. It may also seek ownership or control of other similar natural resources that may be used as substitutes.

A Natural Resources driven organization may itself produce a variety of products or services from the resource, or may license product development and production to other organizations (possibly through joint ventures). It may simply sell the raw material to third party manufacturers. It will seek to insure that these products or applications have added value for the customer or end user. Regardless of the current way in which this organization converts that natural resource to products, its primary strategy will be to control the resource for future exploitation.

Possible examples include Shell Oil Company and De Beers Diamonds.

Return/Profit

An organization pursuing a Return/Profit Driving Force®, builds its strategic vision around the skills involved in managing a portfolio of diverse businesses. This type of organization often acts as a holding company, and has interests in several businesses. It manages its portfolio of businesses from a financial perspective, its objectives being to maximize return/profit within a certain set of risk guidelines and financial hurdle rates. Typically, organizations with a Return/Profit Driving Force® will acquire businesses rather than develop new products or customers groups. They will quickly dispose of those businesses that do not attain their financial goals.

The organization's primary competitive advantage rests in the ability to manage diverse businesses. The businesses within a Return/Profit organization may have no particular product and market constraints or synergy, other than pre-set profit targets, and will be managed with high levels of financial skill and control. Each of the businesses within the Return/Profit type of organization will have its own Driving Force® and vision, which is based upon the sustainable competitive advantage of that business. There will be little or no

	PRODUCTS/SERVICES		
	Current	Modified	New
MARKETS Current	1	4	7
MARKETS Extended	2	5	8
MARKETS New	3	6	9

OR

	PRODUCTS/SERVICES		
	Current	Modified	New
MARKETS Current	1	2	3
MARKETS Extended	4	5	6
MARKETS New	7	8	9

Figure 1.

Products/services offered
priorities/direction

Markets served priorities/
direction

strategic dependence between the businesses in the holding company's profile.

Possible examples include Hanson Plc, which has interests in tobacco, coal, batteries, bricks, and electricity supply, and BTR.

Summary

The uses and benefits of the Driving Force® are as follows:

1. To provide the means of creating strategic clarity.
2. To allow an organization to identify its source of competitive advantage and build on it.
3. To enable an organization to chart its way through the thrust for new business as encapsulated in the business priority matrix shown in figure 1, or any other logical path as determined by the chosen Driving Force®,. Each Driving Force® will result in a different sequence of the thrust for new business, and will provide guidance to insure that organizations avoid going in too many directions at once.
4. To use the criteria developed in selecting the right Driving Force® in key decisions, particularly in those screening whether or not to enter new customer and market sectors as well as to research, develop, purchase, and market new products or services.
5. To use it as the arbiter for scarce resource allocation. Thus, for example, an organization driven by its method of distribution is more likely to put new money into improving its logistics and networks than

one which is driven by technology which would, not unnaturally, give priority to R&D.

6. To use it for the analysis of competitor's actions.
7. To gain an insight into what are the key capabilities and core competencies required for an organization to succeed in meeting the objectives inherent in its own Driving Force®.
8. To structure organizations and thus insure that strategic alignment can be achieved.

The Driving Force® concept has many advantages over other methods of strategic analysis and decision making. For example, the Porter method, focusing as it does on the low-cost commodity versus differentiated/value added spectrum, is too simplistic; and the GROWTH SHARE MATRIX model focuses too heavily on the financial aspects of an organization's future strategy. In summary, it is an exceptionally powerful tool to help organizations determine the right future for them, and to illustrate what needs to be done to effectively implement a chosen strategy.

Bibliography

Tregoe, B. & Zimmerman, J. W. (1980). *Top Management Strategy.* New York: Simon & Schuster.
Tregoe, B. & Zimmerman, J. W. *et al.* (1989). *Vision in action.* New York: Simon and Schuster. See pp. 45–65 and 209–14.

MIKE FREEDMAN

E

economies of scale Costs per unit of output may be reduced for technological and organizational reasons as a result of producing a large output per unit of time rather than a small one. They may also be reduced by producing in a large organization which administers many lines of production. The first kind of cost reduction is referred to as economies of scale, and has implications for horizontal growth and integration, while the second is called ECONOMIES OF SCOPE, and has to do with DIVERSIFICATION. Cost reduction that is a result of growth in cumulative output is said to be the result of EXPERIENCE AND LEARNING EFFECTS. These effects are interlinked in practice, but merit individual treatment for analytical purposes.

Concepts and Definitions

An organization is said to be enjoying economies of scale if its marginal cost is falling as its output per unit of time increases. The minimum output at which the major economies of scale can be achieved is called the minimum efficient scale. Economies of scale act as a powerful competitive tool and also a barrier to entry (*see* BARRIERS TO ENTRY AND EXIT) for firms planning to enter the industry at lower volumes.

Types

Economies of scale can be internal or external. Internal economies can be categorized as plant or organizational, according to the level at which they are generated.

Plant economies relate to the costs of both plant construction and operation. They can arise as a result of: (i) the specialization of productive assets (as the scale of production increases, workers can acquire increased proficiency through the repetition of tasks, and special purpose equipment can be used to undertake limited sets of operations more efficiently than general purpose equipment can, and also reduce the need for regular setting up); (ii) the use of larger machines (which are typically more efficient and have lower unit costs than smaller machines, as the productive capacity of equipment tends to rise faster than its cost); (iii) because of the container principle (the cost of container-type capital equipment such as blast furnaces, oil tankers, pipes, vats, etc. is typically a function of surface area, which rises more slowly than volume); (iv) the more effective use of by-products (which are produced in more substantial quantities); (v) the removal of indivisibility related waste in the use of personnel and equipment (where, for low levels of output, whole units of assets such as maintenance teams or delivery vehicles need to be maintained despite the fact that they may only be necessary for brief periods); and, finally, (vi) simply because large numbers may provide regularity in the place of unpredictability.

Organizational economies can also be achieved by: (i) specialization (in this case of plants, administrative personnel, etc.); (ii) the use of first-rate managers (as a larger organization may be better placed to recruit them, make use of their skills, and provide scope for their promotion); (iii) power with suppliers and buyers (*see* FIVE FORCES MODEL); (iv) economies in advertising; (v) the cost of capital (which falls with size and lower risk); (vi) capacity for innovation (because research teams and equipment are only divisible down to a certain point, it may be that only larger firms can afford the laboratories and equipment necessary while, at the same time, they can spread their research efforts on a variety of projects, reducing the risk of failure); and, finally, (vii) further economies can often be achieved through rationalizing after the acquisition of another firm.

Turning to external economies, these relate to benefits which are also experienced beyond the boundaries of the organization in ways other than through cost reduction. These may include improved infrastructure (road, railways, docks, and airport development), the location of ancilliary industries such as those supplying the required inputs in convenient proximity to the firm, or the development of skills, aptitudes, and loyalties in the local population.

Needless to say, the above examples are only sources of potential economies, and they require effort in order to be realized. An approximate estimate of the extent of available cost reductions can be obtained by looking at the overall costs of similar establishments (plants and firms) of different capacities, by observing which sizes of establishments tend to survive over time and which do not, or – in the case of firm level economies – by using simple engineering estimates of the costs of production at alternate levels of output.

Implications for Strategy

As economies of scale lead to lower costs, production at a scale which enables them to become available is generally desirable.

In addition to their ability to increase profits through cost reduction, economies of scale may also act in an entry deterrent capacity, because they force aspiring entrants to accept a cost disadvantage, or come in on a large scale, with all the risks and costs that this entails (these risks also being augmented by the fear that retaliation may well be forthcoming, as it may not be possible to accommodate a large new entrant as easily as a smaller one).

Having said that, blind efforts to increase output in order to reduce costs may well be the wrong strategy, particularly if the firm does not ensure that it is indeed able to find markets for the additional output, or if it fails to notice that its market would prefer some differentiation in the products (which typically reduces the ability to exploit economies of scale), as opposed to straightforward cost reduction.

Moreover, in the development of a strategy based on economies of scale, it is important to consider all elements of the value chain, and all functions. An entirely new product, for ex-

ample, may well be considered to benefit from economies of scale even if it is sold at very small quantities, if the organization which markets it has already put in place a considerable distribution operation which can handle the product, and which already enjoys economies of scale. The extent to which distribution accounted for the total cost of the new product would then have to be examined to see how safe that market is from potential imitators.

Diseconomies of Scale

As with economies of scale, diseconomies relate to marginal cost changes for given levels of output. Theoretically, diseconomies begin to appear at low levels of output, but in practice they only become significant at higher levels, where they begin to erode any benefits from economies until, ultimately, they make production uneconomic. The combined effect of economies and diseconomies of scale, therefore, shapes the marginal cost curve in a U-like form, which in practice frequently has an elongated horizontal segment in the middle.

As with economies of scale, there are internal and external diseconomies. Internal diseconomies may arise as a result of: (i) coordination and administration complexity (which necessitates an ever growing ratio of administrative to productive personnel and, ultimately, leads to a situation in which the highly interrelated processes involved are liable to great disruption if there are hold-ups in any one part of the organization); (ii) transaction costs, such as those related to transportation when markets or employees are geographically scattered; (iii) morale problems (as a result of excessively specialized, tedious, and repetitive jobs, or if employees feel that they are an insignificant part of the organization); (iv) labor relations difficulties (resulting from the consequent bureaucratization and the need to maintain a large number of differentiated positions and levels); and, finally, (v) other less direct and less observable costs, such as losses arising from delayed or faulty decisions or distorted managerial incentives.

Similarly, sources of external diseconomies typically include the increasing cost of inputs such as office space, which rises in the city, for example, as firms congregate in search of the external economies otherwise to be gained.

In principle, diseconomies of scale are more significant at the organizational level, as any plant level diseconomies may be avoided by building several factories of the optimal size.

The most significant role of diseconomies of scale is that they limit the scope for the exploitation of economies of scale. As a result, they place a limit on the maximum size that a firm can economically reach, and therefore make it optimal for any market to be populated by a number of competitors. At the exceptional extreme, at which diseconomies do not become significant before the market is exhausted, a natural monopoly is said to exist.

Bibliography

Pratten, C. & Dean, R. M. (1965). *The economies of large scale production in British industry.* Cambridge: Cambridge University Press.
Scherer, F. M. (1974). Economies of scale and industrial organisation. In H. Goldsmith, H. Mann and J. Weston (eds), *Industrial concentration.* Boston: Little, Brown.
Silberston, Z. A. (1972). Economies of scale in theory and practice. *Economic Journal,* **82** Supplement, 369–91.
Stigler, G. (1958). The economics of scale. *Journal of Law and Economics,* **1**, (October), 54–71.
Townsend, H. (1968). *Scale, innovation, merger and monopoly: an introduction to industrial economics.* Oxford: Pergamon Press. See chapters 1–6.

STEPHANOS AVGEROPOULOS

economies of scope   In contrast to ECONOMIES OF SCALE, economies of scope refer to increased variety in operations, not higher volume of output. Economies of scope therefore emerge where unit costs fall because of synergies arising from the production of more than one product. These can be the result of shared distribution, advertising, purchasing, and similar activities. Together with CROSS-SUBSIDIZATION, economies of scope allow the monopolization of a perfectly competitive industry.

Economies of scope can therefore be an active component of strategy development when the application of centralized management leads to lower costs. Ironically, some financially oriented acquisitive conglomerates may be relatively more successful in achieving such economies than many related diversified concerns. Indeed, diseconomies of scope can also readily occur when endless diversification adds to managerial bureaucracy or when a failure occurs in strategy implementation, such as when like concerns fail to integrate. This is especially common when moves aimed at achieving STRATEGIC FIT fall down, usually on cultural and/or organizational grounds.

Bibliography

Thompson, A. A. & Strickland, A. J. J. (1993). *Strategic management: concepts and cases,* (7th edn), Homewood, IL: Irwin. See pp. 171–2.

DEREK F. CHANNON

efficiency   There are many kinds of efficiency; namely, allocative efficiency, productive (technical) efficiency, x-efficiency, and y-efficiency. The above terms are discussed in more detail below. Pareto efficiency is discussed elsewhere (*see* PARETO ANALYSIS).

Allocative Efficiency

This refers to the efficient allocation of resources between the production of different products (by different firms), and is said to be achieved when an output mix is produced which is regarded as "socially desirable." Allocative efficiency is, therefore, more of a macroeconomic concern and less relevant for the individual firm, although it can also be used to consider matters such as the appropriate ratio of human to mechanical capital and the like.

In contrast with x-inefficiency, which places society inside its production possibility boundary, allocative inefficiency places society at the wrong point on the boundary. In the simplest economic models, allocative efficiency can be achieved when prices equal the marginal cost of production. Inefficiency usually occurs as a result of distorted signals in a market economy, which themselves can be the result of EXTERNALITIES or anti-competitive behavior.

The measurement of allocative efficiency requires marginal cost information, which is often not available. This means that the effort to measure allocative efficiency is often not made, particularly as the incentives for the individual firm to do so are limited. The absence of competition or potential competition, however, is typically associated with high levels of allocative inefficiency.

Productive Efficiency

A firm is said to be productively efficient when it employs the least cost combination of input factors to produce a given output (see x-efficiency).

An economy is said to be productively efficient if two conditions are fulfilled; namely, that each firm is on its relevant cost curve (i.e., it is x-efficient), and that all firms have the same level of marginal cost (i.e., the marginal cost of producing the last unit of output is the the same for every firm in the industry).

x-Efficiency

This term, coined by Professor Harvey Leibenstein, refers to departures from the lowest cost method of producing some given level of output, and describes the effects of individuals being selectively rational and making decisions that involve less than complete concern for all constraints and opportunities; that is, agents who do not constantly act as maximizers.

There are three main components of x-efficiency; namely, intra-plant motivational efficiency, external motivational efficiency, and nonmarket input efficiency.

There are also four main sources of x-inefficiency. The first has to do with incomplete contracts for labor (one form of x-inefficiency, for example, is the result of a poor agency relationship (*see* AGENCY THEORY), and a significant component of organizational slack can include overstaffing and spending on prestige buildings and equipment). The second is relevant when not all factors of production are marketed, which includes motivational matters (it considers, for example, inefficient behavior as a result of employee attitudes to effort, and to the search for, and utilization of, new information – an example might be when employees are too hungry or unmotivated to concentrate on their tasks). The third source of x-inefficiency centers on a production function which is not completely specified or known. Finally, x-inefficiency may be the result of tacit cooperation between competing firms as a result of interdependence and uncertainty, or of imitation, and in this case the extent of x-inefficiency

is assumed to increase with market power, for reasons that include a relaxation in cost controls.

x-Efficiency can be affected, among other things, by factors such as the exploitation of any ECONOMIES OF SCALE that may be available.

As a result of x-inefficiency, higher costs lead to reduced competitiveness. Leibenstein (1966) found that "x-inefficiency exists, and that improvement in x-efficiency is a significant source of increased output."

y-Efficiency

This term was coined by Michael Beesley (1973). In contrast to x-efficiency, y-efficiency refers to the revenue side of a firm's activities. A firm is said to be y-inefficient if it fails to expand its markets (e.g., through efficient market research and promotion) to the extent required for profit maximization.

Like x-inefficiency, y-inefficiency is sometimes assumed to be nurtured by the lack of competitive pressures on the firm, which lead to insufficient incentives to develop new markets.

Considerations of y-efficiency have implications for the scale and scope of a firm's activities (see, for example, DIVERSIFICATION).

Bibliography

Beesley, M. E. (1973). Mergers and economic welfare. In *Mergers: take-overs and the structure of industry*, Reading no. 10. London: Institute of Economic Affairs.

Leibenstein, H. (1966). Allocative efficiency vs. x-efficiency. *American Economic Review*, **56** (3), 392–415.

Leibenstein, H. (1975). Aspects of the x-efficiency theorem of the firm. *Bell Journal of Economics*, **6** (2), 580–606.

STEPHANOS AVGEROPOULOS

---

elasticity Elasticities are simple measures that indicate the change in one quantity as a result of a change in another, *ceteris paribus*.

Early work on demand measurement and price elasticity looked at agricultural products. These studies were useful because of the large price variations observed, which were caused by fluctuating crop yields combined with competitive market conditions, and which troubled farmers and the general population alike. They were made possible precisely because of these

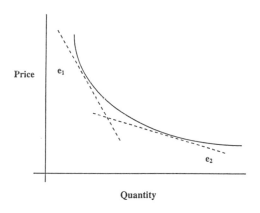

Figure 1 Price elasticity and the demand curve.

reasons; that is, because of widely fluctuating prices and quantities.

There are a variety of elasticities, and a new one can be defined for any two variables where one affects the other. Frequently used elasticities consider how the demand or supply functions are affected by their individual determinants. The price elasticity of demand can be calculated, for example, to indicate the sensitivity in the demand for a product to variations in its price. In general, demand elasticities tend to rise as quantity held rises. If one has no shoes, for example, the demand for the first pair will be quite insensitive to price; when one already has a few pairs, however, one is expected to become more price-sensitive (for the same level of income, and funds to spend on shoes). Elasticity, therefore, changes according to the point on the demand curve at which one lies: here the number of shoes already owned (see figure 1).

Types of Elasticity

Strictly speaking, elasticity can be measured at any point on the relevant curve and specifies the change in one variable which would result from an infinitesimal change in another. This is called the point elasticity, and it is used when one is dealing with curves expressed using mathematical functions.

In practice, however, where the relevant function may not be fully specified, elasticities are measured using discrete data (e.g., by varying the price by, say, 5 per cent and observing the change in the quantity demanded). In this case, ranges – rather than points – are more useful. Arc elasticity, therefore, is defined in order to measure the relative responsiveness of one variable to a discrete change in another. One can consider, for example, the arc price elasticity of demand.

Finally, there are cross-elasticities, where the responsiveness of a relevant quantity for one product is measured for a change in a quantity relating to a second product. For example, the cross advertising elasticity of demand for product A with reference to product B will indicate how advertising expenditure for product B affects the demand for product A.

In the following discussion, some of the elasticities that are more frequently encountered in practice will be considered.

Elasticities of Demand

Elasticities of demand can be considered with reference to any of the variables in the demand function. Typically, these include price, advertising, income, and price expectations. Demand is said to be elastic when elasticity is greater than 1, and inelastic when it is below 1. In the (theoretically encountered) extremes, a perfectly elastic demand is associated with an horizontal demand curve, and a perfectly inelastic demand with a vertical curve. By (confusing) convention, the absolute value of demand elasticities is sometimes reported.

Price elasticity of demand. This is probably the most widely used elasticity. The mathematical formula for the arc price elasticity of demand is as follows:

$$E_p = \frac{\Delta Q/Q}{\Delta P/P} = \frac{\Delta Q}{\Delta P} \cdot \frac{P}{Q}$$

where P is price and Q is quantity. If Δ is replaced throughout by the partial differential operator (∂), then the formula for the point price elasticity is obtained:

$$E_p = \frac{\partial Q/Q}{\partial P/P} = \frac{\partial Q}{\partial P} \cdot \frac{P}{Q}$$

By convention, products with elastic demand (products the price elasticity of which is greater than 1) are said to be luxuries, while products with inelastic demand (those with elasticities below 1) are said to be necessities.

A number of factors are associated with higher price elasticity. One important determinant is the extent to which a product is a luxury, as necessities have demand which is less elastic than luxuries (status symbols may well have a higher value for some people the more expensive they get, but this does not affect the shape of the downward-sloping demand curve, as there would always be enough other people who would be willing to purchase the good if its price fell further). Another factor is the availability of SUBSTITUTE PRODUCTS, as buyers of products for which no good substitutes exist tend to have fewer options than to buy the specific product. A third factor is the proportion of the buyer's income spent on the product; goods and services that account for only a small proportion of total expenditure tend to have more inelastic demands. The information available for the purchase is also relevant: the price elasticity of demand will be relatively high for search products, since consumers know exactly what they are purchasing and leap at the chance to buy the product at a lower than normal price (on the contrary, the price elasticity of demand will be relatively inelastic for experience and credence products). Finally, demand is usually more elastic in the long run than in the short run, as consumers take time to adjust their consumption patterns to changes in prices and to find alternatives.

As far as the firm is concerned, in order to maximize revenue it needs to be aware of the demand curves that it is facing and of the elasticities of its buyers. An increase in the price (P) of a product that faces inelastic demand will raise total revenue, while an increase in the price of a product that faces elastic demand will reduce total revenue. The relationship between marginal revenue (MR) and price elasticity (E_p) can be expressed as follows:

$$MR = P(1 + \frac{1}{E_p})$$

This expression is derived from the definitions of the two quantities. Total revenue is maximized where marginal revenue is zero, which is where elasticity is equal to unity.

Cross-price elasticity of demand. This is given by:

$$E_{XY} = \frac{\Delta Q_X / Q_X}{\Delta P_Y / P_Y} = \frac{\Delta Q_X}{\Delta P_Y} \cdot \frac{P_Y}{Q_X}$$

Cross-elasticities are generally not symmetrical; that is, the change in demand for product X caused by a change in the price of product Y may not be equal to the change in demand for product Y generated by a change in the price of product X.

Cross-price elasticities have implications for product line pricing, and are useful in determining optimal policies with reference to prices and quantities for various demand levels and/or other considerations such as competitor actions (price changes, for example). Also, if prices are set competitively and are driven by the market, they can be useful in determining demand. Good cross-price elasticity measurements can also be used to indicate whether two products are complements (*see* COMPLEMENTARY PRODUCTS), substitutes (*see* SUBSTITUTE PRODUCTS), or neither.

Advertising elasticity of demand. The advertising elasticity of demand for a product measures the responsiveness of the quantity demanded to a change in the advertising budget for that product.

Such responsiveness can come about primarily in two main ways. First, advertising shifts the product's demand curve to the right by bringing the product to the attention of more people and increasing people's desire for the product; and, second, it makes the demand for the product less price elastic by such means as enhanced brand loyalty.

A positive relationship between advertising and the quantity demanded is expected, but the responsiveness of sales to advertising is also expected to decline as advertising expenditure continues to rise. The advertising elasticity of demand for experience and credence goods is relatively high, because consumers may be persuaded to try these products by advertisements that emphasize attributes such as the product's brand name.

As far as the usefulness of that elasticity for the firm is concerned, it can help to determine the optimal advertising level. Dorfman & Steiner (1954) first showed that the profit maximizing ratio of advertising expenditure to sales revenue (the advertising to sales ratio) is given by the ratio of advertising elasticity to price elasticity. In essence, this means that the higher the advertising elasticity, and the lower the price elasticity, the higher will be the profit maximizing advertising budget as a proportion of sales revenue.

Cross advertising elasticity of demand. This measures the responsiveness of the sales of product X to a change in the advertising effort directed at another product Y. It is negative between substitutes and positive between complements.

Income elasticity of demand. The income electricity of demand may be defined as the change in quantity demanded divided by the change in consumer income, *ceteris paribus*.

Three laws of economics are relevant to a discussion of this elasticity. First, the income effect stipulates that when the price of some commodity falls, the real income of the consumer rises, so he or she is likely to purchase more goods. Second, the substitution effect suggests that a fall in the price of a good makes it less expensive in relation to other goods, leading the rational consumer to switch some portion of his or her total expenditure from the relatively lower priced items to the relatively higher priced ones. Finally, Engel's law suggests that the percentage of income spent on food (necessities) decreases as income increases.

By convention, goods with a positive income elasticity of demand are called normal goods (demand for them increases as income increases), and those with a negative elasticity are called inferior goods (demand for them falls as income increases, through a negative income effect).

The income elasticity of demand is a function of whether the good is a necessity or a luxury, whether the good is inferior (in which case a negative income effect applies), and also the level of income itself (as poor people respond differently than rich people).

A firm can use this elasticity to plan for capacity according to its forecasts for economic growth. If the income elasticity for its product is positive (normal good), then demand for the product will grow more rapidly as the economy grows (as consumer income rises), and it will fall

more rapidly than consumer income when the economy is recessing. Demand for an inferior good, on the other hand, will fall as GNP rises, and yet increase during economic downturns.

Advertising efforts can become more effective by focusing on those potential customers whose buying patterns are likely to be affected. For example, knowledge of which products will be demanded by people with rising income (such as professionals) and which will not may be the key to better sales. Similarly, elasticities can be used to determine the location of outlets, with normal goods being sold in areas with rising income, while inferior goods are marketed in areas where the standard of living is falling.

(Price) elasticity of price expectations. Finally, the elasticity of price expectations is defined as the change in future prices expected as a result of current price changes. When this exceeds unity, it indicates that buyers expect future prices to rise (or fall) more than current prices have changed.

This elasticity is particularly useful in estimating demand in an inflationary environment. A positive coefficient, particularly if it is greater than unity, suggests that current price increases may shift the demand function to the right, which may result in the same or greater sales at the higher prices while consumers try to beat the expected price increases by building up stocks. Eventually, however, the large inventory accumulated by the consumers, or a competitor's reactions, will tend to lower the elasticity, perhaps even turning it negative, and will result in shifting the demand curve to the left.

Price Elasticity of Supply (Production Elasticity)

Turning to the supply function, the price elasticity of supply is defined as the ratio of the change in output resulting from a change in the amount of some variable input employed in the production of a good. There can be, for example, a labor price elasticity of supply. This is equivalent to the ratio of the marginal to the average product for that input.

In general, the price elasticity of supply depends on how costs respond to output changes, including how easily producers can shift from the production of other commodities. Elasticity typically increases with time, as it becomes easier to switch between the production of other goods.

Bibliography

Dorfman, R. & Steiner, P. (1954). Optimal advertising and product quality. *American Economic Review*, **44**, 826–36.
Naylor, T. H., Vernon, J. M. & Wertz, K. L. (1983). *Managerial economics: corporate economics and strategy*. New York: McGraw-Hill. See pp. 230–2.

STEPHANOS AVGEROPOULOS

electronic data interchange This is the electronic exchange of structured information (invoices, orders, etc.) between different organizations, using a standard format. It is this use of standards that differentiates electronic data interchange (EDI) from traditional computer communications and enables the use of a common, shared network by many organizations, thus avoiding the need for separate links between individual organizations' computer systems, with associated high costs. A key characteristic of EDI is that the information transferred must be directly usable by the recipient's system without manual intervention. This reduces operating costs, administrative errors, and delivery delays.

The widespread use of EDI in industry means that it is no longer a discretionary expenditure. Pressure by large organizations to trade electronically has resulted in the need to conform to EDI networks to retain customers and suppliers. Today, EDI may be viewed as the cost of staying in business (Earl, 1992). The primary business benefits of EDI are clearly operational. However, its potential extends beyond merely impacting the operational level to include possibilities for redefining the boundaries between organizations, increasing competitive edge, and providing new business opportunities. The Tradenet system introduced by the Singapore government is an example of the strategic use of EDI at a national level. Tradenet was introduced to enable ships using the Port of Singapore to reduce turnaround time. It links the Port Authority with government agencies, traders, transport companies, shipping lines, freight forwarders, and airlines, using a common document. On arrival at the port the shipper enters the cargo details into the system and transmits them via the Port Authority to the appropriate government agencies for clearance. The result is that appropriate approvals may be received in 15 minutes, rather than the 2 days taken previously.

The most widely cited benefits of EDI are as follows:

• *New ways of carrying out business.* EDI enables an organization to change the way in which it performs business functions internally and to redefine its relationships with the external environment. For example, by speeding up the ordering process and reducing the time between receiving an order and dispatching the goods, through EDI, a company may change its focus from that of product driven to being more customer centered, with emphasis being placed on the timely provision of goods and services to the client.

• *Internal efficiency gains.* The automated exchange of operational information results in a reduction in paper work and clerical processing. By eliminating manual input, EDI reduces the need for re-keying of data and the opportunity for mistakes. It also cuts the time delays that accompany traditional inter-company communications, resulting in significant cost savings and improved cash-flow. R. J. R. Nabisco estimates that processing and paper purchase order costs the company $70 per order, whereas processing an EDI order costs 93 cents.

• *Control over stock-holding levels.* The provision of timely and accurate information on stocks which are in low supply facilitates "quick response" and JUST IN TIME manufacturing, by reducing stock-holding levels and integrating ordering and inventory management systems.

• *Control over relationships with suppliers.* EDI may be used to strengthen an organization's hold over its suppliers or to share information with them to mutual advantage. On-line access to multiple suppliers provides the opportunity to assess which suppliers have the appropriate stock available and at what price, enabling negotiation of prices and insuring the best deal. The provision of immediate feedback on a range of information, such as quality defects, may also be used to increase the power of the purchaser. Alternately, information may be shared to provide more collaborative structures and practices, enabling suppliers and their customers to align their operations. For example, suppliers may electronically monitor stock at the shop-floor level and deliver new stock when the quantities of the product fall below minimum levels, thus by-passing warehousing requirements. Packaging of goods may be done in a way which correlates with the way in which products are displayed on the shelves, in addition to considering which suppliers have the appropriate stock available and at what price.

- *Improved customer relationships.* The provision of EDI facilities may enhance the image of a company with its customers. Many companies are beginning to insist on EDI trading; for example, the automotive industry. The recent formation of the Organisation for Data Exchange by Tele-Transmission in Europe (ODETTE) links vehicle and component manufacturers in many European countries.

The role of standards has been paramount to the success of EDI. Standards may be agreed at any of a number of levels; international, national, industry sector, or regional. They define trading documents in an agreed format by data items (such as customer name, address, and article number) and by grouping these items in the form of messages (such as invoices). Once all partners have agreed a common standard, this obviates the need for conversion of the documentation by each recipient to meet their internal systems requirements. The basis for an international standard – EDIFACT – has been agreed. However, in addition to EDIFACT there are a number of industry-specific standards. These include SWIFT (Society of Worldwide Inter-bank Financial Telecommunications), which enables banks to send payment instructions to each other in a standardized format. Another, TRADACOMS, is a comprehensive set of EDI standards, covering invoices, orders, delivery notes, and the like. It is the most widely used standard in the UK.

Bibliography

Earl, M. J. (1992). Putting information technology in its place: a polemic for the nineties. *Journal of Information Technology*, 7, 100–8.

BENITA COX

excess capacity A plant or firm is said to have excess capacity when it has production capacity available for use which is more than sufficient to satisfy current demand. This can either be due to market imperfections, or it can be pursued for strategic purposes, to improve a firm's competitive standing.

As far as the former family of causes is concerned, excess capacity is a result of the absence of a market mechanism which balances demand and supply in the short run. The main factors that inhibit perfect alignment of the level of utilization with its determinants include: (i) demand uncertainty (a firm may prefer to sustain some excess capacity rather than be found to be unable to meet demand when this peaks); (ii) the lumpiness and indivisibilities of capacity increases (which cause a sawtooth pattern of utilization unless firms coordinate supply by agreeing time variations in market shares); (iii) unexploited ECONOMIES OF SCALE (which may make it optimal to operate larger plant at less than full capacity rather than smaller plant at full capacity); (iv) the reluctance of firms to reduce their presence in a market, which induces them to accept considerable excess capacity before scrapping equipment (this being the result of the irreversibility of many exiting decisions); (v) the cost of backlogging; and (vi) market concentration (perhaps because of better supply coordination or more scope for reallocation of capacity across products).

Turning to the strategic use of excess capacity, this can serve as a barrier to entry (*see* BARRIERS TO ENTRY AND EXIT) to rivals that plan to enter the industry or increase their share in it. This can be done by SIGNALING that the firm is prepared to counter the efforts of such rivals by raising output and reducing prices: the use of excess capacity makes such threats more credible, particularly if the investment that is made toward it is sunk and irreversible, and if any economies of scale are available. This is because the challenger would then be likely to expect that the excess capacity will, indeed, be used against him (Spence, 1977). Even then, however, there are circumstances in which excess capacity does not serve as a credible threat, and the incumbent may be better off accommodating the entrant (Dixit, 1980).

Evidence shows that, in general, strategic factors are the cause of excess capacity in a minority of industries only, and these predominantly tend to experience high growth and market undifferentiated products. Some survey work has suggested that the cost of responding to competitive threats such as copied products may normally be too high to justify any response and, even when a response is deemed necessary, that the availability of superior strategic weapons such as product differentiation may obviate the need for strategic excess capacity (Driver, 1994).

Bibliography

Baumol, W. J. & Willig, R. D. (1981). Fixed costs, sunk costs, entry barriers and sustainability of monopoly. *Quarterly Journal of Economics*, 405–31.
Dixit, A. K. (1980). The role of investment in entry deterrence. *Economic Journal*, **90** (March), 95–106.
Driver, C. (1994). Excess capacity: theory and evidence using micro-data. Working Paper, Management School, Imperial College.
Gilbert, R. & Lieberman, M. (1987). Investment and coordination in oligopolistic industries. *RAND Journal of Economics*, **18** (2), 17–33.
Spence, M. (1977). Capacity, investment and oligopolistic pricing. *Bell Journal of Economics*, **8**, 534–44.
Sutton, J. (1991). *Sunk costs and market structure: price competition, advertising and the evolution of concentration.* Cambridge, MA: MIT Press.

STEPHANOS AVGEROPOULOS

experience and learning effects Costs per unit of output may be reduced for technological and organizational reasons as a result of producing a large output rather than a small one. If such cost reduction is linked to the level of cumulative output, then the firm is said to be enjoying the experience, or learning, effect (sometimes also referred to as learning by doing (Arrow, 1962), the progress curve, or the

improvement curve). If the cost reduction is linked to the number of units produced per unit of time, then ECONOMIES OF SCALE are involved. ECONOMIES OF SCOPE refer to cost reduction which is the effect of production in a large organization that administers many lines of production. These effects are interlinked in practice, but merit individual treatment for analytic purposes.

The Learning Effect

Cost reduction as a result of growth in cumulative output has been documented at least as early as in 1925, when it was observed in relation to the direct labor costs of aircraft manufacturing. When discussed in the context of direct labor costs, this cost reduction is referred to as the learning effect. Put simply, learning improves labor productivity; that is, the more units employees will produce, the more ways they will find to produce them faster and cheaper. This may be because repetition allows workers to discover improvements and short cuts which increase their efficiency.

The Experience Effect

During the mid-1960s, such cost reductions were also explicitly observed by Bruce Henderson at the Westinghouse Corporation, where he was a consultant. A consensus then emerged that such cost reductions applied not only to the labor portion of manufacturing costs, but also to costs incurred at every stage of what is today called the value chain (*see* VALUE CHAIN ANALYSIS), including marketing and R&D costs, and overhead. Bruce Henderson, together with the Boston Consulting Group (BCG), studied the concept in detail, and ways were found in

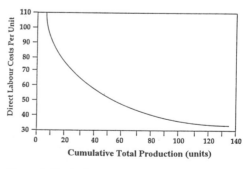

Figure 1 Typical experience curve (linear scales).

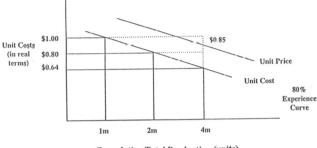

Figure 2 Typical experience curve drawn on logarithmic scales. As cumulative volume grows there is a real decline in product cost — this can lead to cost leadership pricing strategies.

which to utilize it for strategic decision making.

The experience curve specifies that, for every doubling in cumulative output, unit costs of value added net of inflation will fall by a fixed percentage α, typically 20 per cent. This means that the concept can be used to predict costs further down in time. If C_t and C_0 are the costs at times t and 0, respectively, and P_t and P_0 are accumulated volume of production at times t and 0, the following relationship holds:

$$C_t = C_0 \left(\frac{P_t}{P_0} \right)^{-\alpha}$$

The curve is plotted using a grid, with inflation adjusted cost per unit on the vertical axis, and accumulated volume of production, measured in units produced, on the horizontal axis. (See figure 1.) Plotted on logarithmic scales, the experience curve becomes a straight line, as shown in figure 2.

It is worth observing here that the curve can be drawn on a marginal as well as an average basis, as the two only differ by a constant proportion in a straight line. This is convenient, as unit costs are typically measured over a small portion of total production. More importantly, price and profit are concepts best examined marginally. As a consequence, much experience curve calculation is often undertaken on a marginal basis.

For the curve to be meaningful, it is important to define products accurately and consistently. The BCG recommends that these are defined in terms of perceived value to the customer, which implies that the same experi-

ence curve would continue to apply for product innovations which continue to serve the same customer requirements.

Sources of Experience

There are two points which should now be made clear. First, each cost element in an end product (stage in the value chain) has its own experience curve, and it is the aggregation of these curves that makes up the average experience curve for that product. As a result, the curve for the product will tend to be an approximation (see figure 3).

Second, the experience curve concept does not specify any sources of cost reduction. It simply observes the fact of the cost reduction, leaving the rest open to debate. However, factors such as economies of scale, economies of scope, the learning effect, work specialization, new production methods and processes (these are particularly important in capital-intensive industries – *see* INVESTMENT INTENSITY), product standardization (which allows the repetition of tasks inherent in experience building), product redesign and/or substitution effects (as experience is gained with the product, it can be redesigned to conserve material or use cheaper substitute materials, or to allow greater efficiency in manufacture and the like), and changes in the resource mix are among the many potential sources available for exploitation. Moreover, experience may also be gained by sharing value chain activities between a number of products, so that a common

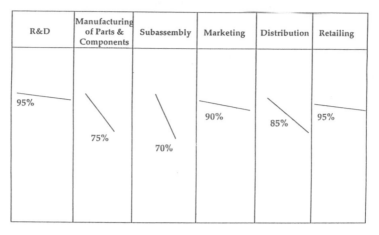

R&D	Manufacturing of Parts & Components	Subassembly	Marketing	Distribution	Retailing
95%	75%	70%	90%	85%	95%

Figure 3 Experience effects differ for different stages in the value added chain.
Source: Hax & Majluf (1984).

experience base is developed, and also in prioritizing value chain activities, such as by finding the optimal balance between R&D and advertising. All of these are more than sufficient to justify the cost reductions observed.

Turning to circumstances which seem to encourage experience building, this is greater (by definition) when production starts – as it doubles from the first unit to the second, and then again to the fourth – but at the thousandth unit, say, another thousand would have to be produced for experience to double once more. Ultimately, when production processes mature, the differences become much smaller.

Also, experience building appears to be greatest in situations where new and advanced technology is involved, and where the capital input dominates the production function, although this is not a matter of consensus. In addition, the lower the employee turnover is, the fewer employee interruptions there are, and the greater the ability of the firm is to transfer knowledge from the production of other similar products, the steeper the curve is.

Experience related cost benefits are not automatic; instead, they can be achieved through constant efforts.

Determination of a Curve's Characteristics

To use the experience curve proactively and to measure a company's own slope and that of competitors', such as for the purposes of

pricing, involves an accurate determination of a number of variables including the moment in time at which experience started to be built up and the volumes involved. In addition, discontinuities such as changes in technology or major product line renovations must be taken into account. Frequently, many calculations regarding competitors' curves cannot be performed directly, and proxies such as market share must be used, perhaps implying that more discontinuities will have to be taken into account.

In addition, as has already been mentioned, it is important for the accurate determination of the curve's characteristics that the entire value chain is considered, and not just the market share of the end product. This is necessary not just because each activity will have its own experience curve, the aggregation of which will determine the firm's overall slope, but also because decisions on the product mix of multiproduct firms may result in the accumulation of different volumes at each stage. Many firms finding themselves displaced from a dominant position have observed, in retrospect, that their definition of dominance was a narrow one.

Implications for Strategy

An appropriate experience effect based strategy for a particular firm depends, among other things, on the firm's current position, the

Competitive Position	Product Life Stage		
	Growth	*Maturity*	*Decline*
Leader (high share)	Reduce prices to discourage new competitive capacity Use own capacity fully	Hold market share by improved quality, increasing sales effort, advertising	Maximise cash flow by reducing investment and advertising, R&D, etc., expenses (market share will decline)
Follower (low share)	Invest to increase market share Concentrate on a segment that can be dominated	Withdraw from the market, or hold share by keeping prices and costs below those of the market leaders	Withdraw from the market

Figure 4 Some implications for product strategy.
Source: Allan & Hammond (1975, p. 9).

product's life cycle stage, the firm's resources relative to competitors, its time horizon, its information about the market, and its current and anticipated cost functions.

The experience concept suggests that, for a firm with a suitably long time horizon, the present value of its profits can be maximized by building up market share as rapidly as possible to attain relative cost advantages.

In order for such a strategy to be successful, the model stipulates that the firm should only attempt to enter a market if it has the capability for leadership, and that the market it attempts to enter is a growing one, as this makes the acquisition of market share easier (competitors may not resent losing relative share as much as absolute share, and they may not even be aware that they are losing relative share if their information about the market is inadequate). Then, once the firm has decided to enter the market, it should do so as rapidly as possible, to prevent other firms from gaining more experience. These concepts have also given rise to the development of the GROWTH SHARE MATRIX, again by the BCG.

A question that arises in a discussion of the experience curve is whether it is possible to attack a competitor that has accumulated considerable experience. Indeed, the cost differential which such a competitor is likely to have achieved makes a head-on attack to achieve similar market share difficult. However, if one looks at the concept more closely, it should become clear that it is not just the market share

of the end product which is important, but that of all of the activities in the value chain. A good distribution organization, for example, perhaps shared by many different products, may well be sufficient to attack a low-cost producer that only produces a single product, or that has neglected his logistics. Similarly, "changing the rules of the game" may be possible using a new technology, or by means of practices such as JUST IN TIME production, total quality management, and the like which, although relatively easy to imitate, can allow the entrant to reduce costs and enter the market on a comparable cost basis.

A related danger faced by companies that rely heavily on the experience effect to retain their leadership is that some experience cannot be constrained within the boundaries of single companies and tends to diffuse into entire industries; for example, through employee mobility or specifications for equipment ordered from outside suppliers. Similarly, some innovations may come from outside the industry, thereby being available to all competitors. In general, therefore, industry-wide learning and imitation may make relative cost advantages estimated on the basis of experience building too optimistic, with all the dangers that this involves.

Implications for Pricing

Assuming that a firm has decided to go down the experience curve, it may use pricing to assist it to do so more rapidly. This can be done by

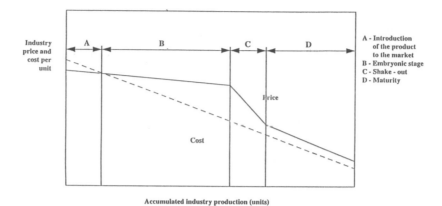

Figure 5 The unstable experience curve effect.
Source: Hax & Majluf (1984).

setting prices on the basis of expected, rather than current, costs, so that the market can be developed and market share built up faster, as the experience of Texas Instruments during the 1970s has shown. This will typically have an adverse impact on current profits, although – if the firm is lucky – its efforts will be facilitated if some of its competitors have a shorter horizon, and are not so insistent on retaining their relative share.

Having said that, it should be observed that the experience effect predicts a path for costs, not prices. In most cases, including Japanese companies, prices tend to follow costs throughout the different stages of the development of a new product in a reasonably competitive market. In a small number of cases typically observed in countries such as the US, however, a very distinct relationship has been observed between the two.

According to this pattern, the firm has three options that can be pursued during the development phase. First, it may set a fairly high price, to impose a monopolistic rent and enjoy a monopolistic profit. Alternately, it may set a price close to costs, to deter potential entrants (*see* SIGNALING), or it may even price below cost, as just discussed. In fact, this latter choice is the most commonly observed pattern nowadays. Soon afterwards, in the phase during which demand is typically greater than supply, costs fall while prices remain firm under a "price umbrella" supported by the market

leader. This is a profitable period for all, and many entrants are lured into the market and build up capacity. The beginning of the third, shakeout, period is marked by the decision by some competitor to reduce prices in order to gain share. Prices then start to tumble, falling faster than costs, and driving marginal producers out of the market. The industry begins to reorganize itself for greater emphasis on efficiency, by means of recombination or otherwise. Market shares change, and sometimes leaders too, and this continues until margins are restored to reasonable, positive levels, which indicates the beginning of the stability phase. The four stages are depicted in figure 5.

Limitations

A factor that limits the applicability of the experience curve concept is the type of product involved. When specialty (as opposed to commodity) products are involved, there may exist opportunities for differentiation that can induce the consumer to pay a premium, thereby making cost a less relevant factor for profitability. The section on Porter's GENERIC STRATEGIES discusses the relative importance of cost reduction and differentiation. Moreover, the experience curve model is not well suited to explain the viability of smaller businesses.

Finally, an important danger in using the experience curve model blindly lies in product and process obsolescence, as these can make the experience curve irrelevant before it can be fully exploited. When striving for cost reduction, therefore, a firm should keep in mind that it may need to maintain a regularly updated product range, as well as flexible production facilities, and both of these are likely to limit the scope for experience building. Too much emphasis on economies may impair the ability of the firm to respond in a flexible way to technological advances, environmental changes, and innovations taking place outside the firm; and, similarly, it may prevent the realization of product differentiation to capture a wider range of customers – often more profitable ones too.

The Experience Curve and the PIMS Project

For a discussion on the experience curve to be complete, the Profit Impact of Market Strategy (PIMS) project needs to be mentioned (*see* PIMS STRUCTURAL DETERMINANTS OF PERFORMANCE). These studies have looked at market share and profitability; and also at variables such as operating expense ratios, relative quality, capital intensity in different market positions, profit margins, and the like. In principle, the PIMS data have confirmed the experience effect data, but PIMS has added a further dimension to the discussion. Therefore, Buzzell *et al.* (1975) and others have found that market leadership not only makes a positive contribution to profitability through lower costs, as the experience effect specifies, but also has a strong association with perceived quality. This enables the market leader (but not any followers) not only to have lower costs, but to charge higher prices too.

Bibliography

Allan, G. B. & Hammond, J. S. (1975). *Note on the use of experience curves in competitive decision making*. Case no. 175-174, Harvard Business School. Boston, MA: Intercollegiate Case Clearing House/Cranfield, UK: Case Clearing House.
Arrow, K. J. (1962). The economic implications of learning by doing. *Review of Economic Studies*, **29** (3), Reprinted 1970 in Perspectives Series. Boston, MA: Boston Consulting Group Inc.
Boston Consulting Group (1982). *Perspectives on experience*. Boston, MA: Boston Consulting Group Inc.
Buzzell, R. D., Gale, B. T. & Sultan, R. G. (1975). Market share – a key to profitability. *Harvard Business Review*, **53** (1), 97-107.
Hax, A. C. & Magilus, N. S. (1984). *Strategic Management: An Integrative Perspective*. New Jersey: Englewood Cliffs.
Henderson, B. D. (1980). *The experience curve revisited*, Perspectives Series Boston, MA: Boston Consulting Group Inc..
Henderson, B. D. (1984). The application and misapplication of the experience curve. *Journal of Business Strategy*, **4** (3), 3-9.
Hirschman, W. B. (1964). Profit from the learning curve. *Harvard Business Review*, **42** (1), 125-39.

STEPHANOS AVGEROPOULOS

externalities The production and/or consumption of some products may give rise to some harmful or beneficial effects that are borne by organizations or people not directly involved in such production or consumption. Such side-effects are called externalities, spillovers, or external costs.

Early works on externalities include Sidgwick (1887) and Marshall (1890). A few years later, Pigou (1920) considered the legal implications of externalities, and determined that where externalities exist in the form of social costs, it is efficient for common law to be applied so as to force the internalization of such externalities. Coase (1937), however, disagreed with this view, claiming that some externalities are sometimes self-correcting, and suggested that holding the party which created the externality liable under common law is not necessarily efficient; instead, efficiency would be best achieved by balancing costs and benefits, in which the role of causality was not decisive.

Types

Externalities can be categorized along a number of dimensions. The first is whether they are negative or positive, according to whether the party which is affected by them benefits or suffers. Second, externalities can be production- or consumption-based, according to their source. Third, there are technological and pecuniary externalities. Technological ones, the most common kind, simply relate to the indirect effect of a consumption or production activity on the consumption or production of a third party. Pecuniary externalities, on the other hand, work through the price system when prices play additional roles other than equating demand and supply, such as when they transmit information in an asymmetric information environment, or when they are affected by some party, in which case this change also affects the welfare of other parties (e.g., one industry's increasing consumption of petroleum affects another industry's welfare through the higher petroleum prices).

Turning to examples of some types of externalities, external costs of production may include oil spills, or the impact of extensive farming on wildlife. External costs of consumption, on the other hand, may include the impact on nonsmokers of smoking in public places, or the effect of a neighbor's decision to plant trees, the roots of which may travel beyond the boundaries of the land on which they are planted and cause damage to nearby properties.

External benefits of production, on the other hand, may come in the form of lower training costs when a worker goes to work for another firm, improvements to regional infrastructure, such as rail facilities, which may result from the needs of one firm but subsequently be used by others, or the growth in peripheral supplier businesses, or technology spillovers, which can often explain the clustering of similar firms in certain geographic areas. Similarly, external benefits of consumption may include the existence of a well maintained garden, which increases the value of neighboring properties, or the installation of a new, quieter air conditioner.

Sources

Externalities arise primarily because of an incomplete definition of property rights in the law. For example, they enable an industry which pollutes its environment through the use of its assets to pass on the costs of cleaning up to the rest of the community.

Consequences

Externalities, which are identified by discrepancies between social and private costs, typically lead to market failure. The most commonly encountered implication of externalities is the misallocation of resources by the market mechanism; that is, allocative inefficiency (*see* EFFICIENCY). This typically comes about in two distinct ways. First, externalities may cause a deviation in the prices of goods from the marginal cost of producing them and,

second, externalities in the form of information spillovers may lead firms to invest at suboptimal levels, if they have reason to believe that they will be unable to recoup the full cost of, say, some R&D investment.

Solutions

A number of solutions exist to reduce the impact of externalities. These include prohibition, directives, or other regulation to eradicate or limit activities that generate externalities. For example, cars may only be permitted to be driven for up to a set number of days per week, or a requirement may be imposed for safety devices such as seat belts to be installed, in order to reduce fatal accidents.

Another method, which is more suited to dealing with production externalities of non-public goods, is forced internalization, whereby the party that generates the externality is forced to deal with it itself, effectively eradicating the externality, which becomes part of the producer's own set of constraints. A company that pollutes a river may be obliged, for example, to acquire or merge with another company which makes heavy use of the polluted water further downstream. A rather less radical method of forcing internalization is by means of financial transactions such as (Pigovian) taxes (or subsidies, as appropriate), or the marketing of externality generation rights; that is, the artificial creation of a market for the externality.

Finally, as has been shown by Coase, it may be possible to reduce the harm caused by externalities if the parties involved cooperate voluntarily. An example may be the situation in which a city that suffers from airborne pollution pays the offending factory to install improved equipment or relocate.

As far as a choice between the above methods is concerned, each is likely to have different enforcement costs and a different probability of evasion, so the specific circumstances will dictate the most appropriate one. In principle, it is more efficient not to eradicate the externality, but to limit it to the point at which the benefit from any further marginal reduction equals the cost of any such reduction.

Bibliography

Arrow, K. (1969). The organisation of economic activity: issues pertinent to the choice of market vs.

non-market allocation. In *The analysis and evaluation of public expenditure: the PPB system*. 91st US Congress, 1st Session, Joint Economic Committee. Washington, DC: US Government Printing Office. See pp. 47–64.

Coase, R. H. (1937). The nature of the form. *Economica*, **4** (November), 386–405.

Coase, R. H. (1960). The problem of social cost. *Journal of Law and Economics*, **3**, 1–44.

Marshall, A. (1890). *Principles of economics*, 8th edn, 1948. London and New York: Macmillan.

Pigou, A. C. (1920). *The economics of welfare*. London: Macmillan. Reprinted 1952. London: Macmillan/New York: St. Martin's Press.

Shapley, L. & Shubik, M. (1969). On the core of an economic system with externalities. *American Economic Review*, **59**, 687–9.

Sidgwick, H. (1887). *Principles of political economy*, 2nd edn. London and New York: Macmillan.

STEPHANOS AVGEROPOULOS

F

first mover advantage The timing of strategic moves may be critical for success as a result of the positive advantages accruing to first movers. Being first has a significant payoff when: (i) it enhances the firm's image and reputation with buyers; (ii) early entry can tie up key raw material sources, new technologies, distribution channels, and the like, so as to shift the cost boundaries of a business or industry; (iii) first time operators build customer loyalty which is hard to dislodge; (iv) it constitutes a pre-emptive strike which is difficult to copy. The use of IT has been a major mechanism for achieving long-term first mover advantages, which have been very difficult to overcome by follower competitors. Examples would include American Hospital Supply's ordering systems for hospitals, the American Airlines flight booking system, Merrill Lynch's Cash Management Account, and Direct Line Insurance's motor insurance operation.

For such success it is necessary to:

- redefine the business to use IT to fundamentally transform the existing way of operating, usually to provide a superior quality of service at a significantly reduced cost

- be first to introduce new systems, including the necessary investment to achieve rapid growth to pre-empt the position of any followers

- exploit first mover advantage to achieve customer loyalty to a brand position, which will remain after competitors attempt to follow

However, being first is no guarantee of success. Indeed, it may involve much greater risk than being an early follower. First mover disadvantages occur when: pioneering is expensive and experience effects are low; technological change is so rapid that early investments rapidly become obsolete; copying is easy and customer loyalty is fickle; and the skills and know-how of first movers are easy to replicate. It is, therefore, extremely important to assess the critical timing for market entry and to insure that adequate resources are available and are deployed to pre-empt early competitive moves.

Bibliography

Porter, M. (1980). *Competitive strategy*. New York: The Free Press. See pp. 232–3.
Thompson, A. J. Jr. & Strickland, A. J. (1993). *Strategic management*. Homewood, IL: Irwin.

DEREK F. CHANNON

five forces model This concept originates in the work of Michael Porter. It is designed to help the analysis of the basic posture of competition in any industry, by taking a broader look at the forces of competition than is usually considered, and bringing together a number of different factors in a convenient model. In essence, the five forces model specifies five main sources of competition; namely, the bargaining power of suppliers and buyers, the threat of potential entry from outside the industry, the threat posed by industries producing substitute goods or services, and, finally, competition from companies currently in the same industry.

The development of a viable strategy, therefore, should first involve the identification and evaluation of all five forces, the nature and importance of which vary from industry to industry and from company to company, and then aim to protect the firm from the resultant dangers. An outline of the model is depicted in

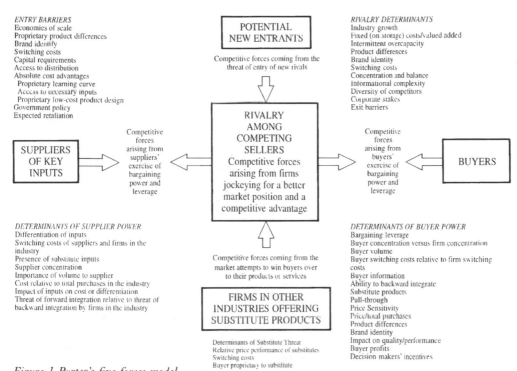

ENTRY BARRIERS
Economies of scale
Proprietary product differences
Brand identify
Switching costs
Capital requirements
Access to distribution
Absolute cost advantages
 Proprietary learning curve
 Access to necessary inputs
 Proprietary low-cost product design
Government policy
Expected retaliation

POTENTIAL
NEW ENTRANTS

Competitive forces coming from the
threat of entry of new rivals

RIVALRY DETERMINANTS
Industry growth
Fixed (on storage) costs/valued added
Intermittent overcapacity
Product differences
Brand identity
Switching costs
Concentration and balance
Informational complexity
Diversity of competitors
Corporate stakes
Exit barriers

SUPPLIERS
OF KEY
INPUTS

Competitive
forces
arising from
suppliers'
exercise of
bargaining
power and
leverage

RIVALRY
AMONG
COMPETING
SELLERS
Competitive forces
arising from firms
jockeying for a better
market position and a
competitive advantage

Competitive
forces
arising from
buyers'
exercise of
bargaining
power and
leverage

BUYERS

DETERMINANTS OF SUPPLIER POWER
Differentiation of inputs
Switching costs of suppliers and firms in the
industry
Presence of substitute inputs
Supplier concentration
Importance of volume to supplier
Cost relative to total purchases in the industry
Impact of inputs on cost or differentiation
Threat of forward integration relative to threat of
backward integration by firms in the industry

Competitive forces coming from the
market attempts to win buyers over
to their products or services

FIRMS IN OTHER
INDUSTRIES OFFERING
SUBSTITUTE PRODUCTS

Determinants of Substitute Threat
Relative price performance of substitutes
Switching costs
Buyer proprietary to substitute

DETERMINANTS OF BUYER POWER
Bargaining leverage
Buyer concentration versus firm concentration
Buyer volume
Buyer switching costs relative to firm switching
costs
Buyer information
Ability to backward integrate
Substitute products
Pull-through
Price Sensitivity
Price/total purchases
Product differences
Brand identity
Impact on quality/performance
Buyer profits
Decision makers' incentives

Figure 1 Porter's five forces model.
Source: derived from Porter (1980) and Porter (1979), reprinted in Mintzberg & Quinn (1991).

figure 1. Subsequently, each of the forces is discussed, in turn.

The Bargaining Power of Suppliers

The main ways in which suppliers can influence combatants in an industry are by raising prices (thereby squeezing profitability), by reducing the quality of the product or service supplied, including delivery schedules etc. (thereby damaging a company's reputation), or even by reducing output to any given company or to the industry as a whole.

Therefore, suppliers may have considerable bargaining power. Whether they constitute a strong or a weak competitive force depends on a number of factors. A supplier group is powerful: (i) if its concentration is high, and more so than the industry it supplies; (ii) if its product is not a standard commodity that is available on the open market from a variety of suppliers, but is unique, or at least differentiated; (iii) if the supplier's product makes up a sizeable fraction of the costs of an industry's product; (iv) if the supplier's product is crucial to the industry's production process; (v) if the supplier can supply the industry more cheaply than the industry can make the input itself; (vi) if the supplier's product significantly affects the quality of the industry's product; (vii) if there are no SUBSTITUTE PRODUCTS; (viii) if there are SWITCHING COSTS that are high enough to prevent the industry from making use of any available substitutes; (ix) if there is a credible threat of the supplier integrating forward into the industry's business; or (x) if the industry is not an important customer of the supplier group (if the industry is an important customer, the supplier's fortunes will be closely tied to the industry, so there will be an incentive to protect it by means of reasonable pricing and quality, and assistance in other activities, such as R&D).

In general, suppliers are more likely to exercise their leverage when market conditions in their own industry are weak.

In addition to controling the above factors, the firm can limit the power of the supplier: (i) by buying from several sources to insure competition – though not too many, so as to remain significant to each buyer; (ii) by dividing orders between suppliers that are themselves in competition; (iii) by occasionally seeking proposals from other suppliers, to collect information and test the market; (iv) by raising the quantities demanded by means of aggregating purchases with sister business units or companies – or by making longer-term agreements, with phased deliveries; or (v) by attempting to understand the supplier's costs.

The Bargaining Power of Buyers

As with suppliers, buyers can become a threat to profitability. They can force prices down, or demand higher quality or more service. To do this, they may decide to play producers against each other, or refuse to buy from any single producer.

Buyers can generally be classified as commercial buyers or consumers. In broad terms, however, their buying behavior is independent of this classification, except that where the commercial buyer is a retailer who can influence consumers' purchasing decisions, his bargaining power is significantly enhanced.

As with suppliers, the extent to which an industry is threatened by its buyer groups is influenced by a number of factors. In principle, a buyer group is powerful: (i) if it is concentrated; (ii) if the products that it purchases from the industry are standard and undifferentiated (enabling the buyers to compare suppliers and sometimes play one against another); (iii) if the quality of the product is not particularly important; (iv) if there are readily available substitutes; (v) if the industry's product does not save the buyer money; (vi) if buyers purchase in large volumes (in which case they are likely to be more skilled in negotiation) and/or purchase a sizeable part of the industry's output (in which case they pose a greater threat if they change to another supplier), particularly if heavy fixed costs characterize the industry; (vii) if the products purchased represent a significant fraction of the buyers' cost, turnover, or income, or form a significant component of their own product (in which case buyers are likely to be more selective); or (viii) if buyers pose a credible threat of integrating backward.

Buyers are more likely to exercise their bargaining power if they earn low profits, as this will create an incentive to lower purchasing costs or otherwise squeeze the industry, or to attempt to share its profits; for example, by backward integration.

In addition to controling the above factors, the firm can limit the power of buyers by targeting and selling to buyers who possess the least power to influence it adversely. In general, a company can only sell profitably in the long term to powerful buyers if it is a low-cost producer or if its product is sufficiently differentiated. If the company lacks both, each sale to a powerful buyer makes the company more vulnerable, and targeting and selling to the weaker buyers only becomes very important.

The Threat of New Entrants

New entrants to an industry often bring with them substantial resources and additional capacity, and they require market share. In all but the most perfectly competitive markets, this can be destabilizing. This is particularly true where organic entry is involved, but the acquisition of a weaker company within the industry by a strong company from outside it may well have the same effect.

The seriousness of this threat depends on how likely it is for a new firm to enter the industry, the difficulty aspiring entrants would face in entering the industry, and the response that they would expect to encounter once they started to compete in that industry. The first of these is largely a function of how promising the industry appears. High industry growth rates indicate future profitability, and high current profits are also inducive. The factors that affect the obstacles to entry are discussed in more detail in the section devoted to BARRIERS TO ENTRY AND EXIT.

The Threat of Substitute Products

The availability of SUBSTITUTE PRODUCTS influences the actions of the firm's customers. The fewer the substitutes, and the greater the difficulty of switching to them (*see* SWITCHING COSTS), the more secure the firm's revenue is.

Rivalry Among Competing Sellers in an Industry

All of the above forces constitute threats that must be dealt with by more or less every company in an industry. In addition, companies have to face each other's competitive initiatives, typically implemented using the traditional tools of product introduction and innovation, pricing, quality, features, services, marketing campaigns, the use of distribution, and the like.

Intense rivalry is related to a number of factors, including: (i) the existence of a large number of competitors that are comparable in size and power, making it more difficult for a winner to emerge and for stability to be reached; (ii) slow industry growth, and hence insufficient business for everyone, which implies that whenever any competitor has expansionary views, fights for market share are likely; (iii) the acquisition of a (weak) existing firm by a strong firm outside the industry, making aggressive share building moves likely; (iv) a lack of product differentiation or high switching costs, obliging all companies to fight for exactly the same market; (v) perishable products, as these put more pressure on firms to achieve rapid sales; (vi) high fixed costs, also creating a strong temptation to cut prices, sometimes secretly, to increase capacity utilization; (vii) capacity indivisibilities; (viii) high exit barriers (*see* BARRIERS TO ENTRY AND EXIT); (ix) the speed with which competitors can respond to any given initiative; as the faster they can do so, the smaller the reward is from any such initiative; (x) competitors dissatisfied with their current standing and eager to improve it by launching destabilizing offensive attacks; and (xi) competitors diverse in terms of resources, styles, strategies, priorities, and personalities, with different ideas of how to compete.

Except where a head-on collision is deemed necessary and beneficial, such as where a large market share is required, companies can defend themselves by building barriers to entry, including differentiation and switching costs. When they choose to venture into new markets, they can avoid being fiercely resisted by selecting fast growing sectors with low fixed costs and by staying clear from markets that cannot accommodate them or those where incumbents have high exit barriers.

When a company's strengths and weaknesses have been identified (*see also* SWOT ANALYSIS), the company must be positioned so that it can exploit, rather than be damaged by, any changes anticipated in environmental factors, such as the product life cycle, industry growth rates, and the like, and then also protected and ready to effectively respond to any initiatives

from other companies. Pursuing offensive strategies without taking these factors into account is risky, and unlikely to remain successful in the long run.

Bibliography

Cowley, P. (1986). Margins and buyer/seller power in capital intensive businesses. PIMS Asso. Ltr no. 40. Cambridge, MA: Strategic Planning Institute (PIMS).

Porter, M. E. (1979). How competitive forces shape strategy. *Harvard Business Review*, **57** (2), 137–45. Reprinted, with deletions, in H. Mintzberg & J. B. Quinn (1991). *The strategy process: concepts, contexts, cases.* (2nd edn), Englewood Cliffs, NJ: Prentice-Hall. See pp. 61–70.

Porter, M. E. (1980). *Competitive strategy: techniques for analyzing industries and competitors.* New York: The Free Press.

Thompson, A. Jr. (1980). Competition as a strategic process. *Antitrust Bulletin*, **25** (4), 777–803.

Thompson, A. J. Jr & Strickland, A. J. (1993). *Strategic Management.* Homewood, IL: Irwin.

Yip, G. (1979). Entry of new competitors: How safe is your industry? PIMS Asso. Ltr no. 17. Cambridge, MA,: Strategic Planning Institute (PIMS).

STEPHANOS AVGEROPOULOS

Five S strategy   *see* 5S STRATEGY

fragmented businesses   In fragmented businesses, there is little or no correlation between size and profitability: examples include restaurants, specialist engineering, and chemical specialties. In such industries, ECONOMIES OF SCALE may well be outweighed by the costs of complexity; and competitive advantage can be achieved by uniqueness independent of size, such as through customer focus, geographic concentration, design, patent protection, and the like. When no specific competitor dominates, factors such as these tend to be more important than relative competitive position. To counter such unique advantages it has been advocated that the creation of specific segments be used to promote standardization of design and geographic coverage, and reductions in uniqueness can be used to reduce or eliminate the strategic advantage of smaller fragmented competitors.

See also **Advantage matrix**

Bibliography

Boston Consulting Group (1974). *Segmentation and strategy*. Boston, MA: Boston Consulting Group.
Boston Consulting Group (1974). *Specialization*, Boston, MA: Boston Consulting Group.
Rowe, A. J., Mason, R. O., Dickel, K. E., Mann, R. B. & Mockler, R. J. (1994). *Strategic management*, 4th edn. Reading, MA: Addison-Wesley. See pp. 119–22.

DEREK F. CHANNON

functional structure   In the single-business firm, the natural way to divide up the various activities is to organize by specialist function, as shown in figure 1, in which is illustrated a typical functional structure for a small to medium manufacturing business. At the top is a board, usually composed of the senior managers of the specialist functions together with a chairman and chief executive. In many companies the personnel and R&D function heads are not included on the board, and operate predominantly in line support roles. Human resources management and R&D are thus often excluded from the formulation of strategy. The board may or may not contain nonexecutive directors. As a result of investor and political pressure, the presence of nonexecutive directors is becoming the norm in public companies. However, in many smaller concerns and those that are privately owned, nonexecutives may still be excluded.

Depending upon the size of the business, the marketing and finance functions may be fully developed or the company may essentially operate a sales function and an accounting function. In smaller concerns, the accounting function may also be responsible for the company secretary and for legal aspects of the preparation of budgets and plans. Medium-term corporate plans, which tend to be financial in orientation, may also be developed.

As such firms grow larger, the functions become more fully developed. Research and development, which in smaller companies often tends to be subordinate to the production function, develops into a full blown function. Finance and accounting tend to become separated. Marketing is introduced and tends to become superordinate to the sales function. A separate company secretary position is often established and a specialist corporate planner is introduced. While such companies may still be essentially single-business, it is common that multisite operations may commence, and the production function may therefore develop to involve several site managers, with an overall production manager located at the primary central site. Similarly, the sales function is often changed by the effort to open new markets, and especially export markets overseas. The introduction of an additional export sales manager is thus also likely as overseas sales expand and distribution is established, usually via the use of agents or distributors in the early stages.

The functional structure is also very effective in managing the single business in the service industry sector. In retailing, for example, a similar structure would be found; although "production" as a function is not normally present, being replaced by a function usually known as "operations." This essentially refers to distribution system management and the management of stores. These are usually grouped geographically and handled by regional managers. Merchandising and buying are other critical functions which essentially replace marketing.

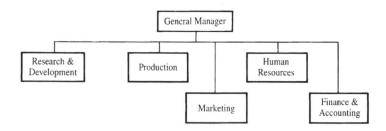

Figure 1 Functional organizational structures.

The functional structure is the logical pattern for dividing up the activities of the business, provided that it is not too complex, either by product or geography. Even when a single-business firm expands geographically, it is possible to retain a form of functional structure in many cases, provided that production is not distributed but remains centralized.

Major problems arise with the functional structure as the firm diversifies by product and/or geography, where the latter also contains production facilities. When these new strategic moves occur, a number of structural variants tend to be invoked, including the introduction of the functional holding company, the holding company (*see* HOLDING COMPANY STRUC-TURE), the area division and the product division (*see* DIVISIONAL STRUCTURE). It is extremely unusual that firms move from a functional to a MATRIX STRUCTURE, an SBU STRUCTURE, or a customer-based structure, these usually being found in large complex organizations.

Apart from problems of handling diversification, problems associated with the functional form include: a failure to develop general management skills; difficulties in functional coordination; potential over-specialization; that profit responsibility is forced to the top; that it may lead to functional empire building; and that there may be a tendency to prevent entrepreneurship and reconfiguration of the value chain.

Bibliography

Chandler, A. D. (1962). *Strategy and structure.* Cambridge, MA: MIT Press.

Channon, D. F. (1973). *The strategy and structure of British enterprise.* Cambridge, MA: Harvard Division of Research.

Thompson, A. A. & Strickland, A. J. J. (1993). *Strategic management: concepts and cases,* (7th edn), Homewood, IL: Irwin. See pp. 223–5.

DEREK F. CHANNON

G

gap analysis The first step in strategic analysis is the establishment of the corporate mission, which can then be translated into a series of quantifiable objectives. These will normally be at least partially financial, but a number are likely to be strategic. The corporate objectives can then be compared with an extrapolated performance for the corporation, generated from the sum of the expectations of the business units.

A comparison of the objectives and the expected business outcomes will usually lead to a performance gap between the two. Gap analysis is concerned with why the gap occurs and the development of measures for reducing or eliminating it. This might be achieved by changing the objectives, or by changing strategy at the level of the businesses. The forecast is initially developed subject to four key assumptions:

1. The corporation's portfolio of businesses remains unchanged.
2. Competitive success strategies in the firm's products and markets will continue to evolve as in the past.
3. The demand and profitability opportunities in the firm's marketplaces will follow historic trends.
4. The corporation's own strategies in the respective businesses will follow their historic pattern of evolution.

The first step in gap analysis is to consider revising the corporate objectives. Should expected outcomes from the businesses exceed aspirations, the objectives can be revised upward. When aspirations substantially exceed possible performance, it may be necessary to revise the objectives downward.

When, after such adjustments, a significant gap still remains, new strategies need to be developed to eliminate the gap. To forecast sales increases likely to result from the introduction of alternative growth strategies for each business, managers can estimate the following measures of market structure:

- industry market potential (IMP)
- relevant industry sales (RIS)
- real market share (RMS)

The IMP is estimated as shown in figure 1. It is assumed, first, that all customers who might reasonably use the product will do so, second, that the product will be used as often as possible and, third, that the product will be used to the fullest extent. The IMP therefore represents the maximum possible unit sales for a particular product. The difference between this value and current sales represents the growth opportunity for each product. The RIS equals the firm's current sales plus competitive gaps, and the RMS equals sales divided by the RIS.

Four components then contribute to the gap between the firm's sales potential and its actual performance, as follows:

- *Product line gap.* Closing this gap involves completing a product line, in either width or depth, and introducing new or improved products.
- *Distribution gap.* This gap can be closed by expanding distribution coverage, intensity, and exposure.
- *Change gap.* Using this strategy, the firm endeavors to encourage nonusers to try the product and to encourage existing users to consume more.

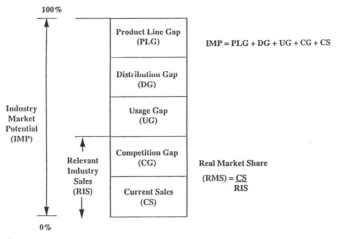

Figure 1 Gap analysis.
Source: Rowe et al. (1994), p. 245.

• *Competitive gap*. This gap can be closed by improving the firm's position through taking extra market share from existing competitors.

If the expected gap cannot be closed by decreasing industry market potential or gaining additional market share, attention may be shifted to assessing the firm's portfolio of businesses with a view to modifying it to add higher-growth activities and/or divesting low-growth businesses.

Bibliography

Ansoff, I. (1987). *Corporate strategy*. Harmondsworth, UK: Penguin.

Drucker, P. (1989). *The new realities*. London: Mandarin. See pp. 202–3.

Rowe, A. J., Mason, R. O., Dickel, K. E., Mann, R. B. & Mockler, R. J. (1994). *Strategic management*, 4th edn. Reading, MA: Addison-Wesley. See pp. 240–6.

Weber, J. A. (1977). Market structure profile and strategic growth opportunities. *California Management Review*, **20** (1)

DEREK F. CHANNON

generic strategies   Several efforts to classify strategy have been made at various times. One of the earliest was Ansoff's (1965) PRODUCT MARKET DIVERSIFICATION MATRIX. This specifies an appropriate strategy for the marketing of new or existing products to new or existing markets, and is described in more detail in the appropriate section. A weakness was that the sustainability of the strategies involved was not addressed.

Porter made this point and, viewing strategy as basically aimed at securing a long-term sustainable advantage in a competitive market, developed another classification of what he called generic strategies.

He suggested that there are three generic strategies to choose from, and each business unit can have its own strategy. According to Porter, a business can strive to supply a product or service more cost-effectively than its competitors (cost leadership), it can strive to add value to the product or service through differentiation and command higher prices (differentiation), or it can narrow its focus to a special product market segment which it can monopolize (focus). Not following any of these strategies characterizes a firm as being "stuck in the middle."

The place of generic strategies in the overall strategy of a firm is indicated in figure 1, which also shows the relationship between Porter's and Ansoff's strategies.

The rationale for the three strategies, and their completeness as an option set, are depicted in figures 2 and 3, respectively. The isoquants, lines of equal return, make it explicit that the same return on investment can be achieved with two different market shares.

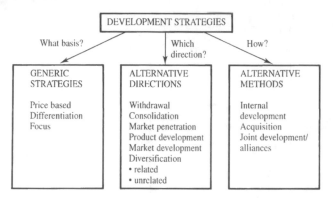

Figure 1 Development strategies.
Source: Johnson & Scholes (1993).

Choice of Strategy and Strategy Characteristics

The choice of generic strategy should be based on the firm's business unit's strengths and weaknesses, and a comparison of those with the strengths and weaknesses of competitors.

Cost leadership. If a firm can become the lowest-cost producer in the industry, then cost leadership may be the most appropriate strategy to pursue.

Cost reduction should be continuous, so that the cost differential with competitors is maintained, and should involve all stages of the value chain. It can be achieved by means of methods such as proprietary access to cheaper inputs or technologies, or by positioning to exploit any experience effects (*see* EXPERIENCE AND LEARN-ING EFFECTS). Typically, these come with market share, so the control of a large share of the market is likely to be necessary. Where there are limited opportunities to build efficient plant, the second, third, or other low-cost producers may also be able to achieve above average performance.

Moreover, because of the reliance on ECONO-MIES OF SCALE and the like, cost leadership is likely to be more sustainable in the long run if relatively stable, no frills products of reasonable quality are involved. For the same reason, cost leadership strategies are more appropriate in relatively stable environments.

The typical staffing and administrative requirements of a cost leader are also distinct. Unskilled personnel can undertake much of the workload, and technocrats such as scientists and

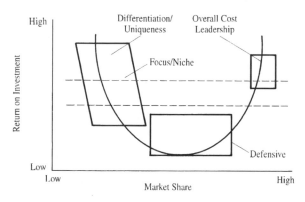

Figure 2 The Porter curve: profitability versus market share of the four generic competitive strategies.
Source: Rowe et al. (1994).

COMPETITIVE ADVANTAGE

		Lower cost	Differentiation
COMPETITIVE SCOPE	Broad target	1 Cost leadership	2 Differentiation
	Narrow target	3A Cost focus	3B Differentiation focus

Figure 3 Three generic strategies.
Source: Porter (1980).

engineers are not required on any large scale, particularly where commodity products are involved. Similarly, cost control is of the utmost importance, and very developed formal systems are often encountered.

Differentiation.   If cost leadership is not a feasible option, but the firm is able to differentiate its products along some attributes which customers value, and the cost of doing so is lower than the extra revenue envisaged, then differentiation may be the appropriate strategy to pursue.

Porter defines differentiation in terms of the ability to charge higher prices, and not on the basis of the product's attributes *per se*. It can be based, therefore, on either product innovation or marketing.

In order to pursue a differentiation (value added) strategy, an accurate picture of the target market will have to be obtained to ensure that there are sufficient ways in which to differentiate the product, and that the marketplace can be subdivided – and is willing to pay for the differentiation. An effort will then have to be made to avoid imitation, and this typically involves a regular redefinition of the basis of differentiation. For the same reason, it would be desirable for the differentiation to be based on a mix of features and activities rather than a simple product feature or service, and for it to involve many parts of the value chain. Added protection from imitation may also be possible by linking into the value chains of suppliers and buyers.

Differentiation, whether innovation- or marketing-based, is more appropriate in dynamic industry environments, in which it can help to avoid, at least in the short run, potentially more costly forms of competition such as price cuts. However, as it often involves new technologies and unforeseen customer and competitor reactions, it also contributes, in turn, to environmental unpredictability.

As far as staffing and administrative requirements are concerned, differentiation requires the employment of experts, and the establishment of mechanisms to facilitate the coordination of these experts, who may work in different functional departments.

Focus.   If it is not possible to access the entire market on the basis of either low cost or differentiation, a defensible niche may still be available to provide above average performance. Marketing to such a niche would again involve a choice between low cost or differentiation but, this time, if the niche is well chosen, the scope of the market would enable the firm to advance on more limited cost and differentiation capabilities.

In principle, a focus strategy exploits the differences in cost behavior in some segments, or the special needs of the buyers in those segments, so it is only available where such segments are poorly served by the broadly targeted competitors and, of course, only sustainable for as long as the niche can be defended.

The difficult point for the focuser is reached when the niche has been exhausted, at which time he may be tempted, out of a false sense of security derived from his success within the narrow scope of the niche, to target the broader market. This can have catastrophic consequences.

"Stuck in the middle."   From the above discussion, it should be evident that each strategy makes its own demands on the organization in terms of skills and administrative structure, and is more appropriate in different sets of circumstances. Nevertheless, a firm pursuing one strategy would act foolishly if it did not act to gain from elements of the other strategies too, as long as this did not detract it from its chosen strategy. A differentiator, for example, should pursue all cost reduction which does not

Table 1   Risks of the generic strategies.

Risks of cost leadership	Risks of differentiation	Risks of focus

Cost leadership is not sustained:
• competitors imitate
• technology changes
• other bases for cost
  leadership erode
	Differentiation is not sustained:
	• competitors imitate
	• bases for differentiation
	  become less important to
	  buyers
		The focus strategy is imitated.
		The target segment becomes
		structurally unattractive:
		• structure erodes
		• demand disappears

Proximity in differentiation
is lost
	Cost proximity is lost	Broadly targeted competitors
		overwhelm the segment:
		• the segment's
		  differences from other
		  segments narrow
		• the advantages of a
		  broad line increase

Cost focusers achieve even lower cost in segments	Differentiation focusers achieve even greater differentiation in segments	New focusers sub-segment the industry

Source: Porter (1980).

sacrifice differentiation, and a cost leader could differentiate until this started to cost a lot.

However, when a firm confuses its primary goal and source of competitive advantage, and pursues both cost reduction and differentiation indiscriminantly (or not at all), then it is said by Porter to be "stuck in the middle." This, he said, is an unenviable strategy because cost leadership and differentiation are inconsistent in principle, and there will typically be a cost leader, differentiator, or focuser that will be able to compete better than the firm stuck in the middle in any one segment of the market. Firms with such a (lack of) strategy, Porter said, typically end up stuck in the middle because they find it difficult to make the necessary choices.

There are a few cases, however, in which cost leadership and differentiation are not mutually inconsistent, at least in the short run. This may occur, for example, when the firm pioneers a proprietary innovation (whether a product, service, or process), which enables it to reduce cost and at the same time differentiate successfully. With the appropriate barriers erected, it may be possible to exploit such an innovation for a considerable period of time. Similarly, cost leadership and differentiation may also be pursued together when costs are largely determined by market share, and control of a

considerable share enables the firm to use the extra margin to differentiate, and still remain the cost leader. The same may be possible if there are interrelationships between industries that a competitor may be able to exploit while others are not.

In any case, the profitability of a "stuck in the middle" company may remain adequate in the medium term in a high-growth environment (as this sustains inefficiencies), in a particularly attractive industry, or if the firm faces similarly stuck in the middle competitors.

Porter's claim that no firm should be stuck in the middle has, however, received attention which is more deep-rooted than that, and a lot of effort has gone into interpreting and questioning this advice. J. S. Sainsbury, the retailer ("Good food costs less at Sainsbury's"), is often cited as proof that a stuck in the middle strategy can be viable and successful (Cronshaw et al., 1990). Gilbert & Strebel (1991) elaborated on the concept and distinguished between one-dimensional and outpacing strategies, and suggested that the latter are designed for being stuck in the middle.

The epicenter of these discussions is that there exists no reason to imply that a low-cost base should necessarily be coupled with lower prices, or that a differentiated product should be

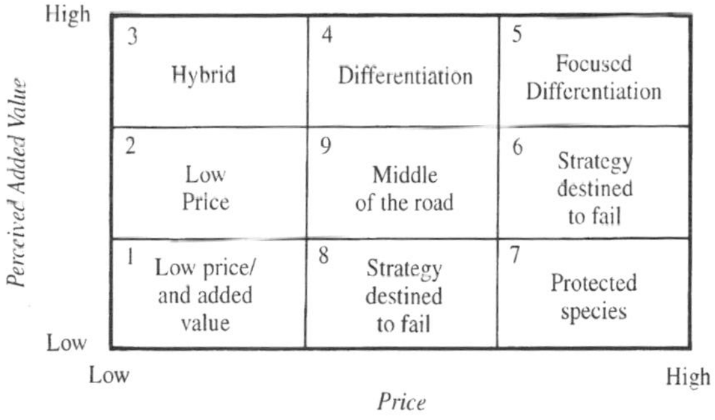

	Strategy	Characteristics, Requirements and Dangers	
1	Low price/low added value	Likely to be segment specific	
2	Low price	Risk of price war and low margins/need to be cost leader	Differentiation
3	Hybrid	Low cost base and reinvestment in low price and differentiation	Differentiation
4	Differentiation		Differentiation
	a) Without price premium	Perceived added value by user, yielding market share benefit	Differentiation
	b) With price premium	Perceived added value sufficient to bear price premium	Differentiation
5	Focused differentiation	Perceived added value to a particular segment, warranting price premium	Differentiation
6	Increased price/standard value	Higher margins if competitors do not follow/risk of losing market share	Likely Failure
7	Increased price/low value	Only feasible in monopoly situation	Likely Failure
8	Low value/standard price	Loss of market share	Likely Failure
9	Medium price/medium value added	Potential for squeeze from above and below	Likely Failure

Figure 4 Competitive strategy options.
Source: derived from Johnson & Scholes (1993), p. 211, fig. 3.

coupled with premium prices. The low-cost base could simply be used to earn higher margins or, indeed, a differentiated product could be priced low enough to achieve a higher volume of sales (pricing differentiated products low enough to gain entry into a new market is only a temporary strategy which can lead to no competitive advantage, so it is of no relevance here). The underlying cause that leads to the overlap has been identified by Mathur (1986, 1988), who observed that whereas differentiation is an output concept, cost leadership is relevant to both inputs and outputs.

Finally, some of the most common dangers to sustainability that are inherent in each of the strategies are shown in table 1. In addition, there is a further danger specific to the diversified firm (*see* DIVERSIFICATION). When this pursues an assortment of generic strategies through its distinct business units (either to target different segments of the same market, or entirely different markets, a situation which does not signify a "stuck in the middle" condition), there is a danger that top management will have developed a preference for a particular strategy, and that it will attempt to impose this on all business units. This is to be avoided.

Other Generic Strategies

Porter's model is a simple and intuitive one. It is possible, however, to elaborate on his classification and develop several other assortments of generic strategies, although the marginal contribution to understanding that each addition makes falls rapidly. Johnson & Scholes (1993), for example, define Porter's strategies in terms of the relationship between perceived value added and price, as shown in figure 4.

Bibliography

Cronshaw, M. J., Davis, E. & Kay, J. (1990). On being stuck in the middle – good food costs less at Sainsbury's. *Proceedings of the British Academy of Management Annual Conference, Glasgow.*

Gilbert, X. & Strebel, P. (1991). Developing competitive advantage. In H. Mintzberg & J. B. Quinn (eds), *The strategy process: concepts, contexts, cases*, (2nd edn), Englewood Cliffs, NJ: Prentice-Hall. See pp. 82–93.

Johnson, J. & Scholes, K. (1993). *Exploring corporate strategy*, (3rd edn). Englewood Cliffs, NJ: Prentice-Hall.

Mathur, S. S. (1986). Strategy: framing business intentions. *Journal of General Management*, 12 (1), 77–97.

Mathur, S. S. (1988). How firms compete: a new classification of generic strategies. *Journal of General Management*, 14 (1), 30–57.

Mintzberg, H. (1988). Generic strategies: toward a comprehensive framework. In *Advances in strategic management*, 5, 1–67. Greenwich, CT: JAI Press. Reprinted, in abbreviated form, in H. Mintzberg & J. B. Quinn (eds) (1991), *The strategy process: concepts, contexts, cases*, (2nd edn). Englewood Cliffs, NJ: Prentice-Hall. See pp. 70–82.

Porter, M. E. (1980). *Competitive strategy: techniques for analyzing industries and competitors*. New York: The Free Press.

Porter, M. E. (1985). *Competitive advantage: creating and sustaining superior performance*. New York: The Free Press. See pp. 11–26.

Rowe, A. J., Mason, R. O., Dickel, K. E., Mann, R. B. & Mockler, R. J. (1994). *Strategic management: a methodological approach*. 4th edn. Reading, MA: Addison-Wesley. See pp. 134–44.

STEPHANOS AVGEROPOULOS

globalization The development of international strategy forms a natural part in the evolution of many corporations, as does product market diversification. The main reasons tend to be to exploit perceived market opportunities, superior competitive positions as the result of lower costs, investment incentives, market access and the like, and access to raw materials or other critical resources. In addition, overseas development may occur as a result of fluctuation in exchange rates, lower overseas cost structures, host country government policies, and the pattern of international competition. For some industries – such as automobiles, aerospace, personal computers, and pharmaceuticals – this has led to radical transformations of the industries on a global basis.

The early development of international strategy tends to begin with the establishment of export organizations using local agents or dedicated sales teams. With success may come the establishment of assembly operations and overseas production complexes. Such activities tend to be managed by the creation of an export division. Further overseas development by multi product line businesses normally results in the creation of worldwide product division systems in which geographic responsibility may be most concerned with local integration, legal, and tax considerations, rather than operational management. Ultimately, matrix structures may develop, incorporating product and geographic responsibilities.

International patterns of competition can thus be categorized in a number of different ways:

(1) Licensing foreign corporations to use the corporation's technology and/or distribute products and services.
(2) Operating as a domestic-based corporation and exporting overseas via agents/distributors or dedicated organizations.
(3) Adopting a multi-country strategy whereby strategy varies from country to country to fit local specific needs and where economies of scale are less important. Such industries have tended to include food, breweries and retailing, although in some cases global strategies have developed or are emerging for brands such as McDonalds, Coca Cola, Fosters Lager, and Marks and Spencer.
(4) Operating a global low cost strategy by attempting to become a key low cost supplier to buyers around the world. Such industries might include oil, chemicals, automobiles, and computer chips.
(5) Adopting a global differentiation strategy to create products differentiated from competitors but with a consistent image. Such strategies can be found in Citibank in global electronic funds transfer, Sony in consumer electronics, and General Electric in industrial diamonds.
(6) Adopting a global focus strategy by attempting to service a specific niche in many strategically important countries, such as Citibank in global retail banking, Caterpillar in earth-moving equipment, and Boeing in aerospace.

The choice as to which strategy to adopt is dependent upon the characteristics of the specific industry that the firm is engaged in, and has been changing over time as a result of:

• increasing similarities between national markets as a result of greater international travel, greater information exchange, more similarities in lifestyles, media coverage and the internationalization of corporate strategies

- the emergence of substantial economies of scale and the effect on unit costs in manufacturing, marketing, and R&D

- economic policies which permit and may require worldwide presence, with the creation of trading blocs such as the European Union and NAFTA

McKinsey and Company has identified a number of factors favouring globalization, therefore, which can be classified as follows:

- demand factors: homogeneous requirements for customers operating worldwide (such as machine tools and plant construction); uniform technical standards (for instance, chemicals and metals); homogeneous demand from consumers (as in consumer electronics, automobiles, and cameras).

- supply factors: significant economies of scale, purchasing, manufacturing, distribution, and R&D; advantages in access to strategic resources; opportunities for clear product/service differentiation.

- economic factors: low/no customs barriers; free movement of capital; favorable fiscal regimes.

Bibliography

Henzler, H. & Hall, W. (1986), *McKinsey Quarterly*, Winter 52-68.

Thomson, A. A. Jnr & Strickland, A, J. (1995), *Strategic Management Concepts and Cases.* 8th edition, 158-169. Irwin, Homewood, Illinois.

Porter, M. E. (1990), The Competitive Advantage of Nations. 53-57. Free Press. New York.

Bolt, J. F. (1988), Global Competitors: Some Criteria for Success. 34-41. *Business Horizons*, **31**, No. 1 Jan-Feb.

DEREK F. CHANNON

growth share matrix Derived from the early work of the Boston Consulting Group in the 1960s on experience curves, the growth share matrix became, and remains, the most widely used portfolio model for influencing investment and cash management policy in

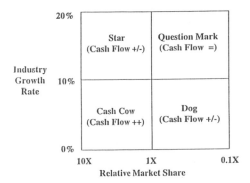

Figure 1 The Boston Consulting Group growth share matrix.

diversified corporations. The matrix is illustrated in figure 1. The horizontal axis is drawn to a logarithmic scale and identifies the relative market share of each of the businesses within the company's portfolio. In this system relative market share is defined as that of the company's business divided by that of its largest single competitor. By definition, therefore, only one company within a defined market can have a relative share greater than one. The vertical axis depicts the industry growth rate in real terms, with the impact of inflation removed.

Businesses are mapped on to the matrix, with the size of each business being reflected by the area of the circle used to depict it. The relative position of each business within the four quadrants indicates the expected cashflow to be generated and suggests an investment strategy. The cut line on the vertical axis is set at 10 per cent real growth, while the relative share cut line is set usually at the 1.0x level.

A business in the bottom left quadrant is a CASH COW. A high market share coupled with slow real growth is expected to generate surplus cash as a result of high profitability due to lower cost. Moreover, future investment needs of such businesses are limited as growth has declined.

Those in the top left quadrant are STAR BUSINESSES with high relative share and high growth. While such businesses are profitable, they are largely cash neutral, since profits need to be continuously reinvested while the growth rate remains high in order to maintain market position.

Businesses in the top right quadrant enjoy high growth but low relative share. The

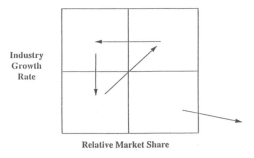

Figure 2 The growth share matrix cashflow sequence for success.

objective for a few such QUESTION MARK BUSINESSES is to take the surplus cashflow from the cash cows in order to invest heavily while the growth rate is high, to convert them into future stars.

Those in the bottom right quadrant are said to be DOG BUSINESSES. These concerns have low relative share and low growth. They are expected to suffer a cost disadvantage as a result of their low share. However, it is anticipated that to convert such businesses into cash cows would take disproportionate effort in a mature market, where share gain would have to be obtained from established high share rivals. Such businesses are therefore candidates for harvesting, exit, or disposal.

The underlying concept of the growth share matrix is the belief that, for the average business, there is an 80 per cent experience effect (*see* EXPERIENCE AND LEARNING EFFECTS) and that relative market share can be used as a relatively easily measured surrogate for cumulative production volume.

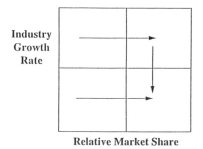

Figure 3 The growth share matrix sequence for disaster.

Businesses with a high relative market share should therefore enjoy a significant cost advantage compared with competitors:

	64%	80%	100%	120%	165%
relative cost					
relative market share	4x	2x	1x	0.5x	0.25x

Similarly, real growth rate is seen as a surrogate for market attractiveness, with high and low real growth equating to high and low attractiveness, respectively. The rationale for this stems from the concept of the product life cycle.

The growth share model can be used in a variety of different ways. First, it permits the company to map its businesses in a way that enables management to rapidly visualize the position of its total portfolio. As a result the strategic dynamics for the total corporation can be planned for its future development. The ideal sequence for development is depicted in figure 2. Surplus cash is syphoned off from cash cows and redeployed, first to any star businesses requiring it, and then to a carefully selected number of question marks with a view to building these into the stars of the future. Dog businesses, unless strong in cash generation, should be divested or closed. Good cash generating dog businesses are due to low capital intensity and are candidates for harvesting rather than divestment.

By contrast, the sequence for disaster, illustrated in figure 3, indicates a failure to invest in star businesses due to a lack of positive cashflow businesses. As a result, stars lose share to become question marks which, in turn, are converted into dogs as markets mature.

It can be argued that the graphic presentation of the matrix represents a static snapshot of the business portfolio. This criticism has been addressed by the development of the share momentum graph illustrated in figure 4.

This graph is developed over a relevant time period (say, five years) and, by plotting the position of each business unit in terms of the two dimensions of total market growth versus growth in sales for the business, the businesses that have been gaining or losing share can be readily observed. Those businesses falling below the diagonal have been losing share, while those above it have been gaining share. The chart is a useful quick indication to management as to

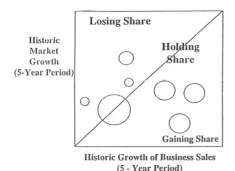

Figure 4 The share momentum graph.

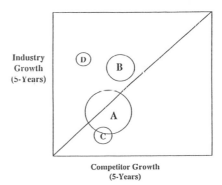

Figure 6 The industry share momentum matrix.

which businesses are succeeding or failing relative to the market; it also offers a useful correction in situations in which management may believe that it is performing well in achieving growth in a business, whereas in reality it may be losing share.

The growth share matrix can also be a useful tool in evaluating competitive dynamics. This is illustrated in figures 5 and 6.

The relative market position of major competitors is illustrated in figure 5. The vertical cut line is in this case set at the industry overall growth rate level. Those competitors above the cut line are growing faster than the market average, while those below it are losing share. A consequence of this analysis is that different competitors may classify businesses in different ways. Competitor A, with the largest market share, is clearly operating as a cash cow, but is also trading market share for cash by growing at less than the market, allowing competitors B and D to see their businesses as question marks and therefore investment opportunities. Only competitor C recognizes that its business is a dog.

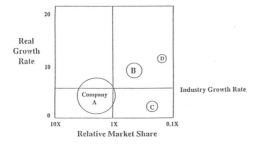

Figure 5 The industry growth share matrix.

Taking the same industry over time, as shown in figure 6, clearly indicates that competitor B has been growing faster than competitor A, as well as faster than the market as a whole.

In addition to analysis at the level of the industry as a whole, further refinements of growth share analysis are to analyze businesses by product and by technology. For example, the 1978 product portfolio of Eastman Kodak is illustrated in figure 7. The figure shows that many of the company's activities are concerned with thin film coatings, yielding ECONOMIES OF SCOPE and shared experience in this area of technology. As a result, product groups that might otherwise have been classified as dogs may well make a contribution to Kodak's overall position in a core technology. A similar analysis might well have been concerned with activities rather than technology. Share momentum charts can also be developed that reflect product-based portfolios over time.

The growth share matrix has therefore provided an extremely useful multifunctional management tool for both diagnosing the position of the multibusiness and multiproduct firm and for understanding industrial and competitive dynamics.

However, the technique is also subject to a number of criticisms, which include the following:

1. Growth share matrix positioning implies that relative market share can be used as a surrogate for cost. There is therefore a fundamental assumption that, on average, an 80 per cent experience effect underlies

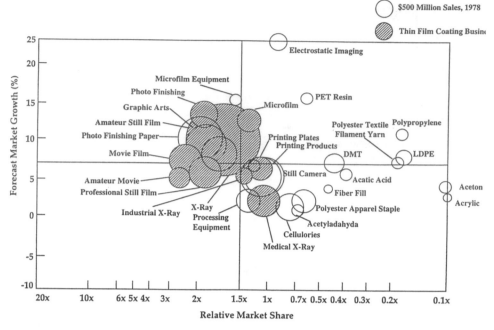

Figure 7 The growth/share matrix for Eastman Kodak, 1978.
Source: Bogue & Buffa (1986).

market share. Evidence from the PIMS program suggests that the actual cost advantage derived from higher and lower relative shares is substantially less than this.

2. Detailed experience analysis is rarely undertaken, due to the cost and the lack of appropriate data. Moreover, the impact of shared experience from technology, activities, and the like may not be adequately incorporated.

3. The model assumes that only the two variables of relative market share and industry growth rate are necessary to establish the strategic position of a business. Evidence from the PIMS program and actual practice clearly indicates that these variables alone, while important, can be readily outweighed by other factors such as relative investment intensity, productivity, and the like.

4. In calculating relative market share it is assumed that "market" has been accurately defined. This need not be the case, especially in situations in which market boundaries are in a state of flux as a result of geographic, product, or customer segment changes.

Bibliography

Bogue, M. C. & Buffa, E. S. (1986). *Corporate strategic analysis.* New York: The Free Press. See chapters 2 and 5.

Hax, A. L. & Majluf, N. S. (1984). *Strategic management.* Englewood Cliffs, NJ: Prentice-Hall. See chapter 7.

Henderson, B. D. (1973). *The experience curve reviewed, IV. The growth share matrix of the product portfolio. Perspectives no. 135.* Boston, MA: Boston Consulting Group.

Lewis, W. W. (1977). *Planning by exception.* Washington, DC: Strategic Planning Associates.

DEREK F. CHANNON

H

holding company structure The conventional holding company structure, illustrated in figure 1, is usually found in companies which have attempted to expand or diversify by acquisition. In its classical form, the central office plays no role in the strategy of the constituent member companies within the holding company and, indeed, there may also be no central financial control. In the 1970s such companies were common as an original strategy began to mature or be subjected to excessive pressure. As a consequence, almost invariably after the appointment of a new chairman or chief executive officer, such firms attempted to break out from the mature/decline strategic position by diversifying rapidly through acquisition (*see* ACQUISITION STRATEGY), or by eliminating competition by buying them up. As the holding companies lacked the appropriate post-acquisition capabilities of integrating the new subsidiaries, they were allowed to manage themselves. A classic example would have been the development of GKN, a leading British manufacturer of screws, which expanded and at the same time attempted to eliminate competition by purchasing major competitors. There was no central

control and, as a result, within the group the subsidiaries continued to compete with one another, so eliminating the expected benefits. The central office in this structure was virtually nonexistent, consisting only of the chairman and a secretary.

The board structure of such holding companies tends to be made up of CEOs of a number of the subsidiary companies, operating under a chairman who might be a nonexecutive, or at least unable to intervene in the operations of the subsidiaries. In the absence of any formalized strategic plans, subsidiaries tend to pursue their own strategies, and are interested in preserving their autonomy rather than being subject to strict financial and strategic control from the central office. When a holding company is established, board membership may well change, and functional specialist directors of the original core company leave the board. This process is necessary in order to change the functional bias of the executive board members, who might otherwise concentrate on the original business to the detriment of new diversifications. However, where the original core business is especially large as, for example, in oil,

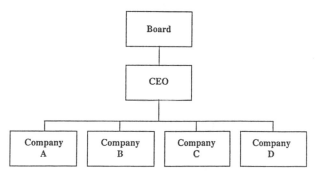

Figure 1 A holding company structure.

Figure 2 A functional holding company structure.

banking, and tobacco, this change in board emphasis is especially hard to achieve.

A further form of the holding company structure is also current, in that some corporations exist in which, again, no attempt is made to influence the strategy of subsidiaries, although they are subject to tight financial control. Hanson Trust, for example, could be classified as a holding company. The difference between this form and the historic pattern is the sophisticated financial control systems, the central office strategic capabilities in acquisition search, post-acquisition rationalization, and the imposition of tight financial controls. Thus while no product market strategy is immediately apparent and the break-up and disposal of acquired companies is undertaken, the financial characteristics of the residual activities form part of an ongoing strategy. In the case of Hanson, therefore, disposals help to recover the financing of an acquisition, leaving the residual businesses to generate a high rate of return on a relatively limited capital outlay. The residual businesses also tend to be cash generators, allowing the build up of a cash war chest to finance the next acquisition. This type of holding company, while apparently having no synergistic product market strategy, does have SYNERGY within a financial portfolio concept.

The traditional holding company strategy tends to be basically unstable. Without control there is a natural tendency for subsidiaries to undertake actions which may lead to financial imbalance. Acquisitions may not be adequately integrated or rationalized, and strategic moves may be undertaken which, while increasing corporate size, may also lead to reduced profitability. As a result, most of these holding companies have eventually been acquired by the

second type, or have reorganized by adopting a DIVISIONAL STRUCTURE as consultants are brought in to establish greater control.

Functional Holding Company

The functional holding company structure is an intermediate variant that is often used in the early stages of diversification away from the single business stage (*see* SINGLE BUSINESS STRATEGY). Diversification in the early stages normally occurs through acquisition (*see* ACQUISITION STRATEGY) and a new subsidiary is usually grafted on to an existing functional structure, as shown in figure 2.

The constitution of the board of the new enterprise is usually modified to add the CEO – but not the functional directors – of the acquired company. The chairman and nonexecutive directors of acquired companies are often dismissed. The same is true of the CEO if the bid is contested.

This structure is rarely stable. First, in making a diversification, the acquiring company often underestimates the STRATEGIC FIT between itself and the acquiree. Second, the board culture still strongly reflects that of the parent, and board meetings tend to emphasize the affairs of the parent rather than those of the acquiree, even if the new arrival makes a substantial contribution to overall profitability. Third, the constitution of the board is predominantly made up of functional specialists – not general managers. As a result, it is common that the CEO of the acquired company may resign out of frustration. A serious common mistake then is for the parent company to install one of its own senior managers as the new CEO of the acquiree. Performance suffers further, and this tends to be compounded if further

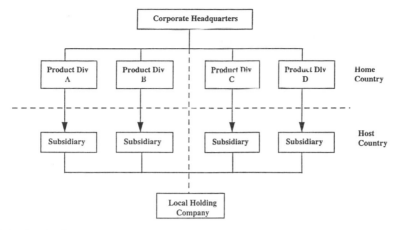

Figure 3 A local umbrella company structure.
Source: Channon & Jalland (1979).

acquisitions are undertaken which lead to the establishment of a holding company structure.

Research indicates that, as DIVERSIFICATION develops, one of the two traditional holding company structures is introduced. However, while corporate sales overall tend to expand sharply, profitability declines after a relatively short time. While the initial bout of diversification occurs after a change in the chairman and/or the chief executive, the failure of the diversification moves to produce improved profitability leads to a second change of leadership, which is often introduced from outside the company in order to establish a shift in corporate culture. This is often initiated by board changes and by the introduction of external consultants to rationalize and reorganize the business and to introduce a new structure. In the 1970s and 1980s this tended to mean the introduction of a DIVISIONAL STRUCTURE and/or an SBU STRUCTURE. In the 1990s even more fundamental changes are taking place in strategy/structure revisions, especially in industries in which changes induced by information technology are transforming cost structures. Here the process of re-engineering (*see* VALUE-DRIVEN RE-ENGINEERING) is tending to convert conventional vertical organizational linkages toward customer quality driven horizontal linkages.

Holding company structures may also be widely used for legal and fiscal reasons, which may or may not have organizational management implications. For example, an intermediate holding company might be used to avoid withholding taxes on dividends paid to shareholders resident outside the domicile of particular corporations. Thus Swiss corporations might operate with Panama-based holding companies which receive dividends from some of their overseas subsidiaries that can be distributed to shareholders without withholding.

Similarly, local umbrella holding companies, as shown in figure 3, are often required by multinationals to legally coordinate the individual interests of product divisions. Such a holding company can: (i) present a unified corporate face to local government and markets; (ii) provide a communication channel for details regarding existing and future operations necessary for business unit coordination; (iii) provide an overall corporate perspective on local opportunities; (iv) achieve tax optimization; (v) ensure consistent personnel policies; and (vi) consolidate divisional funds to permit more local borrowing and to provide easier management control for centralized cash and foreign exchange management.

Bibliography

Channon, D. F. (1973). *The strategy and structure of British enterprise.* Cambridge, MA: Harvard Division of Research.

Channon, D. F. & Jalland, M. (1979). *Multinational strategic planning.* New York: Amacon.

Goold, M. & Campbell, A. (1987). *Strategies and styles: the role of the centre in managing diversified companies.* Oxford and Cambridge, MA: Basil Blackwell.

Rumelt, R. P. (1974). *Strategy, structure and economic performance.* Cambridge, MA: Harvard Division of Research.

DEREK F. CHANNON

horizontal structure   In traditional vertical organizations, work is divided into functions, then departments, and finally tasks. The primary building block of performance is the individual, with the chain of command rising through the function, and the manager's job is concerned with assigning individuals to tasks and then measuring, controling, evaluating, rewarding, and sanctioning performance.

This structure has come under increasing pressure in today's rapidly changing environment, in which time and cost pressures are forcing reconsideration of the vertical structure and a move toward horizontal structures, organized around the CORE PROCESS.

In the horizontal form of organization, work is primarily structured around a small number of core processes or work flows, as shown in figure 1 (*see* VALUE-DRIVEN RE-ENGINEERING; CORE PROCESS). These link the activities of employees to the needs of suppliers and customers, so as to improve the performance of all three. Work, and the management of work, are performed by teams rather than individuals. While still hierarchical, the new structure tends to be flatter than traditional functional systems.

The processes of evolution, decision making, and resource allocation shift toward continuous performance improvement. Information and training occur on a "just in time" basis rather than "need to know," while career progression occurs within the process rather than the function, making individuals generalists rather than specialists. While individual rewards may be made, compensation also relates to team performance.

A number of key principles have been identified at the center of horizontal organizations. These include the following.

1. Organize Around the Process, not the Task

In a horizontally structured corporation, the focus of performance can be shifted by organizing the flow of work around company-wide processes. This involves selecting a number of key performance indicators, (KPIs), quantitative but not necessarily financial measures, based on customer needs, and tying them to work flows. To achieve this, the corporation's activities need to be subdivided into around

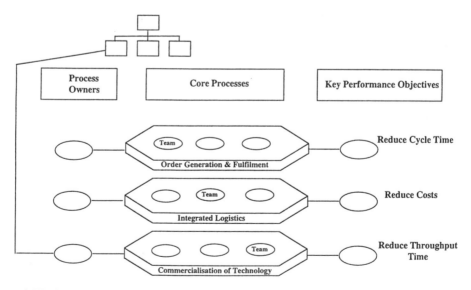

Figure 1 The horizontal organizational structure.
Source: Ostroff & Smith (1992).

three to five "core processes." These might include order generation through to fulfillment, new product development, integrated logistics management, and branch management. The redesign of these processes can produce major one-off gains and then lay the basis for the introduction of continuous improvement strategies.

The structure for such a change involves the creation of a cross-functional team based upon the workflow, not on the individual task (*see* CROSS-FUNCTIONAL MANAGEMENT STRUCTURE). These work flows are then linked to others, both upstream and downstream. Organizing mechanisms for the structure include:

- the appointment of a leader, or team of leaders, to "own" and guide each core process

- assigning, to everyone involved in the process, objectives related to continuous improvement against "end of process" performance measures

- establishing measurement systems for each process, to integrate overall performance objectives with those of all work flows within the process

- reaching explicit agreement on the new staff requirements between upstream and downstream activities

- creating process-wide forums to review, revise, and syndicate performance objectives

2. Flatten the Hierarchy by Minimizing the Subdivision of Work Flows and Non Value Added Activities

In horizontal organizations, hierarchy is still seen as necessary, although ideally core processes can be "owned" by a single team. In reality, effective teams rarely exceed 20–30 people, far fewer than the thousands involved in core processes in large corporations. As a result, some hierarchy is needed, although one or two layers of functional hierarchical structures are normally eliminated.

The mechanism of DELAYERING is used to combine related but formerly fragmented tasks, eliminating activities that do not add value or contribute to the achievement of performance objectives, and to reduce as far as possible the number of activity areas into which each core process is divided. While horizontal organizations are almost invariably flatter than vertical structures, this is not the key objective of restructuring; rather, this is to reshape the organization so that every element contributes directly to the achievement of the KPIs.

3. Assign Ownership of Processes and Process Performance

Leadership is still important in horizontal organizations. Thus teams or individuals are assigned "ownership" of each core process and are responsible for achieving performance objectives. Such individuals and/or teams are often responsible for the activities of thousands of employees engaged in the core process.

4. Link Performance Objectives and Evaluation to Customer Satisfaction

The primary driver in horizontal organizations may well be customer satisfaction rather than justifiability or shareholder value. These latter two terms might well be derived variables of the former.

Vertical organizations tend to drive for financial results and focus attention on the bottom line contribution of each function. In horizontal organizations, by contrast, the primary measure may well be customer satisfaction. This is measured in a variety of ways, many of which are nonfinancial, such as relative market share, growth rate, and market penetration, in the sense in which these are measures of relative competitive position.

As teams develop a clear understanding of how to manage a core process, they often find it useful to evaluate activity areas from the perspective of the external customer. In this way they use customer satisfaction measures to drive all the internal measures of performance.

5. Make Teams, not Individuals, the Principal Building Blocks of Organizational Performance and Design

Managers who organize around work flows treat teams, not individuals, as the key organizational building blocks. Teams regularly outperform individuals due to their greater skill base, broader perspective, and ability to solve complex problems. Moreover, many people find working in teams more rewarding than operating alone.

However, real teams need to be organised and motivated! As individuals they may offer a superior mix of skills, but unless these are orchestrated the result may actually be dysfunctional. For horizontal organizations to be successful, therefore, organization by teams is necessary, but leadership and orchestration of these skills is essential for them to be complementary.

6. Combine Managerial and Nonmanagerial Activities as Often as Possible

When teams are organized horizontally around work flows, it is important to make such teams as self-managing or empowered as possible. The premise behind this concept is that those who participate in the process know it best and, if so motivated, have the most to contribute to improving its productivity. Moreover, as problems develop, decisions can be made quickly and action can be taken in real time without interrupting critical work flows.

By contrast, in vertical organizations the benefits of self-management are constrained to within the function, where actions may ironically cause decreased efficiency in subsequent dependent functions. Moreover, lower hierarchical level personnel may lack the authority to make changes, which need to be approved at senior levels within the organization. When such moves threaten the existing power system, changes may well be resisted.

Horizontal structures combine rather than separate managerial and nonmanagerial activities wherever possible. Teams must therefore be empowered to exercise training and information processing, and be motivated to evaluate and change when, how, where, when, and with whom they interact, and in so doing become the real managers of the process.

7. Treat Multiple Competencies as the Rule, Not the Exception

In horizontal structures, the more skills that individuals bring to the team, the greater is the team's ability to manage the core process for which it is responsible. By contrast, in vertical organizations the trend is toward task specialisation to maximize efficiency. This does not mean that horizontal structures can afford to ignore functional specialist skills; therefore they also need to embrace such skills when they are identified as essential.

However, specialist skills are often illusory and may be used to reinforce the existing structure. It is therefore necessary to identify carefully what specialist skills are needed and which can be discarded. Often, this is a political decision rather than an operational one.

8. Inform and Train Personnel on a "Just in Time to Perform" Basis, Not on a "Need to Know" Basis

In vertical organizations, information has often been used as a source of power rather than to improve the performance of a function or relationships between functions. Information has tended to flow on an "up–over–down–back" basis, leading to time delays, and dispersed – and perhaps contradictory – decision making. Despite training and attempts at improved coordination and cooperation in many corporations, interfunctional coordination is far from optimal.

In horizontal organizations, information is ideally made available on a "just in time to perform" basis, and is provided to those responsible for implementation. Moreover, the reward structure is linked to achievement of the core process activity rather than the function; hence it behoves the participants within the process to maximize rather than hinder efficiency.

9. Maximize Supplier and Customer Contact

In horizontal structures, corporations aim to bring their employees into direct, regular contact with suppliers and customers. Such contact increases their insight into the total value added process within an industry. Done well, this provides opportunities for building supplier and customer loyalty and to improve cost efficiency. Managers sometimes resist this vertical integration because it reduces their power and influence over the business process. Evidence suggests, however, that overcoming such resistance provides an important means of strengthening customer-driven performance.

10. Reward the Development of Motivational Skills and Team Performance, Not Just Individual Performance

In horizontal organizations, synchronizing the reward and sanction systems is important for successful implementation. The emphasis on developing the role of the individual within the core process team is very different from the narrow, individualistic competitive approach in the vertical functional system.

For teams to be effective, members must accept mutual accountability on agreed purposes and objectives. Within this structure some individual rewards are permissible; however, the competitive pressure imposed under the functional system, which may lead to sub-optimal behavior, can be dampened. To maximize their rewards, team members must partially sacrifice their own position for the good of the team.

Conclusions

It is not easy to find the correct balance between vertical and horizontal structures. However, it is important to recognize that such a structural transformation may well be necessary, and will need to overcome the existing power structure for successful implementation. Horizontal structures are a natural consequence of re-engineering strategies and, while accepted by top management, may well meet serious resistance in the ranks of middle management who may be "delayered" in the process of change (*see* RE-ENGINEERING DISADVANTAGES).

Bibliography

Kaplan, R. B. & Murdock, L. (1991). Core process redesign. *McKinsey Quarterly*, no. 2, 27–43.
Ostroff, F. & Smith, D. (1992). The horizontal organisation. *McKinsey Quarterly*, no. 1, 148–68.

DEREK F. CHANNON

hot desking   A growing number of companies are redefining the way in which office work is undertaken. These companies believe there is no longer a need for many of their staff to have an individual desk. This phenomenon has been termed "hot-desking" because each desk can be used by more than one person. It is part of a wider redefinition of the workplace as a result of new technology, customer needs, and drives to reduce nonproductive labor and the cost of premises.

The logic of the new approach is based on the fact that for sales, consultancy, and other activities involving face-to-face contact with external organizations and individuals, some 70 per cent of working time is spent outside the office. The maintenance of full scale accommodation means extra building/space costs and unnecessary "status" costs, and actually encourages attendance in the office rather than out in the field. These cost variants can be dramatic. In corporate banking, for example, making the relationship person's office a car, equipped with a laptop computer, fax machine, and telecommunications links, standardizing reporting formats, and eliminating the need for most dedicated secretarial back-up can save up to 300 basis points – a dramatic saving in markets in which margins are often measured in unit basis points.

Crucial to the changes, however, is the need to install efficient support systems to service the mobile employee. Calls need to be channeled to mobile telephones or stacked; faxes need to be stored and easily retrievable on a screen or as hard copy, and similar considerations apply for electronic mail. However, the impact of office "downsizing" goes well beyond cost reduction. Many companies have dramatically reduced their use of paper, and filing systems have become electronic, further reducing space needs. Essential documents can be stored in secure, low-cost, off-site warehouses. In addition, many companies are encouraging their employees to work from home, as PCs also permit video conferencing, and this trend is likely to accelerate over the coming years. Indeed, new residential complexes are being developed to cater for some workers.

The trend toward hot desking and accompanying change in work patterns and space utilization costs has become well accepted in corporations such as computer firms, accountancy practices, consultancy companies, and the like. The impact on overhead cost structures can be dramatic; in Japan, savings in overheads have been a most important category of cost reduction in recent times.

Bibliography

Becker, F. & Steels, F. (1995). *Workplace by design.* San Francisco: Jossey–Bass.

DEREK F. CHANNON

information systems, strategic use of Recent years have seen a change in the role of information systems (IS) from that of support for business operations to a potential weapon to gain strategic advantage. Whereas in the past the value of information systems was seen as resulting from their ability to automate routine processes and transactions, it is now recognized that through their potential to inform and innovate, organizations who adopt and use information systems wisely can gain both a short- and long-term competitive edge.

A well-known example is the introduction by American Airlines of SABRE, a computerized reservation system which has both changed the basis of competition in the airline industry and served as a source of competitive advantage for the airline itself. SABRE was the first on-line reservation system to be developed, and was used by 48 per cent of travel agents in the USA. Its function was primarily to list flight availability, fares, and times, but it also provided a whole range of further information, such as baggage tracking and control, hotel reservations, and crew scheduling. In addition to listing its own flights, the system also listed flights offered by rival airlines. However, American's own flights were displayed first, thus making it more likely that the travel agent would book a passenger on American Airlines than on another airline. So effective was this strategy that other airlines felt the system to be providing American Airlines with an unfair advantage and anti-trust suits followed. The result of these actions was to permit American Airlines to charge other carriers for use of its system. By charging $1.75 for every reservation made through SABRE, of $400 mllion pretax profits on $5.3 billion sales revenue made in 1984, SABRE earned $170 million pretax profits on $338 million reservation revenues.

Examples such as the success of SABRE have encouraged organizations to consider whether there is a potential for them to harness the power of systems to leap-frog the competition, develop new markets, and increase profitability. The approach being adopted by these companies is to try to align the technology investments more closely with the company's business goals. In some instances this requires a complete re-thinking of the business, the processes, and the particular employee skills required, as well as gaining an understanding of the potential of the new technology. A central issue is how organizations identify the factors that will enable them to maximize the technological potential. In recent years a number of characteristics associated with the strategic use of information systems have been highlighted (Ward, 1992), the most pertinent of which are as follows:

The ability of the system to link an organization more closely to its customers or suppliers. Organizations who are successful with IS are those who link their systems together along the value chain most effectively and integrate the information into the organization's value adding process (Porter & Miller, 1985). Consider, for example, the Economost system developed by the McKesson Corporation. McKesson is a wholesale distributor of drugs to independent pharmaceutical outlets. It provided its customers with portable data-collection devices to check and control inventory, automatically process orders, and schedule shipments. Order data was transmitted to McKesson's computer and assembled orders were packed and delivered in a sequence that reflected the arrangement in which the merchandise was packed on the shelves in the customer's store. If a customer ordered their merchandise from another supplier this upset the inventory control system, thus creating additional work and incurring cost. McKesson also provided a claims service for customers of the drug stores. Many of the customers had their prescription purchases covered by medical insurance programs. McKesson provided a plastic identification card for these customers, so that when purchasing prescription drugs they were required to pay only a nominal amount toward the price of the prescription. The remainder of the payment was claimed through McKesson. Because this service was free it encouraged customers to return to the same drugstore. Over a ten-year period following the introduction of Economost, sales increased at McKesson from $900 million to $5 billion. Automation enabled the company to reduce warehouse staff from 130 to 54, eliminate 500 clerical jobs, and reduce merchandise buyers from 140 to 12. The average order size increased from $4,000 per month to $12,000 per month.

The ability of the system to provide information that enables strategic decisions to be made – to know where, when, and how to obtain critical information. Benetton, the largest purchaser of wool in the world, avoids stockpiling by obtaining information on demand for its products from the point of sale systems in its franchised outlets.

The ability of the system to enable an organization to develop new products. Merrill Lynch used information systems to provide a cash management account which combined separate financial products such as cheques, charge cards, and brokerage services into a single product, with the customer's idle funds being immediately transferred into interest-bearing accounts. While Merrill Lynch provided the brokerage facilities, they collaborated with Banc One to provide the necessary banking facilities. Within the first year of its introduction the cash management account attracted $1 billion in assets. Within six years there were 400,000 new accounts in place and the managed assets totaled $85 billion.

As in other areas, the strategic advantages gained by information systems are typically short-lived. What is today's competitive advantage becomes tomorrow's competitive necessity, and continuing enhancements and upgrading of systems is required to stay ahead. However, as companies move toward implementing global strategies the need for information systems development increases. Information itself is a key resource that requires effective support and full-time management. The companies that will succeed in the increasingly global markets will be those whose information systems investments enable access to relevant information in timely and accurate ways.

Bibliography

Porter, M. E. & Miller, V. E. (1985). How information gives you competitive advantage. *Harvard Business Review*, **63** (4) (July–August), 149–60.
Ward, J., Griffiths, P. & Whitmore, P. (1992). *Strategic planning for information systems.* Chichester: John Wiley.

BENITA COX

information technology, strategic impact of When information technology (IT) determines the basis upon which a company competes in an industry, affects its relationship with customers and suppliers, or alters the fundamental nature and structure of a business or the industry within which it operates, it has a strategic impact. Some of the ways in which IT has had a strategic impact are explored below.

IT has long been viewed as a valuable asset. The main difference in the 1970s was it merely "fitted" into an organization. It was used to automate routine transaction processes and tasks, formerly carried out by armies of clerks. By substituting labor, IT helped to reduce the cost of operations, while at the same time it improved organizational efficiency. The information that it provided was mainly used for decision making at an operational level. Its strategic impact was limited (mainly to back office operations).

In the 1980s, following advances in processing power, speed, and accuracy, alongside significant improvements in price performance,

IT began to be integrated into organizations much more extensively. Companies started to use IT to reshape themselves and manage their businesses differently, to take advantage of cheaper resources and improve overall performance (Gross & Coy, 1995). This is when companies really began to harness the power of technology and use it to build competitive advantage.

Subsequently, throughout the 1990s, IT has continued to play an increasingly important role, to the extent that many companies now question whether they can compete effectively without it (Gross & Coy, 1995). IT has become so powerful that whole business strategies are formulated around it. A company's technology can determine the markets in which it competes and the products that it makes, as well as its services offering.

IT is being integrated throughout the activities of a business, both vertically and horizontally, to allow companies to process information about their operations, customers, suppliers, and competitors. Combined with economic and demographic data, this information is viewed as a strategic resource that is used to support strategic decisions about a business and formulate competitive strategies. IT is no longer just used to automate business processes – it is being used to transform them.

Companies are using IT to radically redesign their underlying business processes. They are restructuring their organizations and streamlining operations, to increase internal efficiency and produce greater value at lower cost. The integration of warehouses with production and distribution helps to manage stock levels and organize product lines to be delivered to customers more efficiently.

Better use and management of information allows companies to respond more quickly to changes in demand for their products and to cut down on wastage. IT helps to reduce time and costs incurred in business processes, right across the value chain. It serves as a means of providing a lower-cost method of delivering a better level of service to customers.

Personal computers on managers' desks are being linked to management information systems (MISs), cutting across functional business boundaries to give broader access to data files, to empower people to make decisions about the business more quickly and act promptly. The coalescence of telecommunications, on-line information services, and end-user software means that large amounts of data can be passed quickly and easily and relatively cheaply between people, offices, and different countries.

The use of IT allows whole layers of management to be removed from the organizational hierarchy. These layers are no longer perceived to add value to the business. Whereas people's main function was seen to be acting as "human relays," simply passing information between management layers (Drucker, 1988), IT brings together people who would otherwise communicate through an intermediary. It allows managers to access information, from remote areas of the business, for themselves. The net impact has been a significant reduction in head count and a flatter organizational structure (see DELAYERING).

Inter-organizational links with customers and suppliers help to extend the concepts of improved operational efficiency and functional effectiveness, beyond the boundaries of a single firm, to include transactions between different organizations. Companies can pass information beyond their corporate boundaries 'to business partners, and new channels of distribution can be created to provide further operational efficiencies and revenue enhancements. The time and cost incurred in business processes can be reduced right across the value chain.

Many companies have embarked upon IT partnerships, using ELECTRONIC DATA INTERCHANGE (EDI) link up with suppliers and customers and to communicate with them down the telephone line. They can shop electronically for the cheapest suppliers and search for stock availability. Data networks can be set up by suppliers to service customers and form customer–supplier partnerships. On-line global data interchange with key customers provides a virtually instantaneous means of placing status inquiries for new orders. With the development of global electronic information systems, companies can link up with hundreds of key customers internationally.

Companies are making use of electronic linkages to establish combined marketing programs, using common customer databases and offering joint purchasing incentives. Airlines, hotels, car rentals, and bank credit cards, for example, are being woven into a single combined electronic marketing effort, spearheaded by information networks (Konsynski & McFarlan, 1987). Marketing alliances have been formed among banks, grocery chains, and food companies. Participant companies gain access both to new customers and territories and, like airline reservation systems, to ECONOMIES OF SCALE through cost sharing (Konsynski & McFarlan, 1987).

Information partnerships create opportunities for scale and cross-selling between companies. They can make small companies look, feel, and act big, and allow them to reach customers once considered beyond their reach. They can make large companies look small and close, and allow them to target niche markets and provide a new basis of differentiation (Konsynski & McFarlan, 1987).

IT serves to extend geographic business boundaries and enlarge the target market. This has resulted in accelerating cross-border flows of goods and materials. Companies have developed sophisticated international electronic mail and conferencing procedures, in which support staff around the world have direct access to each other. Global sources of knowledge can be tapped into quickly, barriers of time zones removed, and overall response time to problems sharply reduced.

Business processes become independent of geography, facilitating the geographic transfer of work from areas of high-cost labor to areas of low-cost labor. Data may be input in one country and transmitted to another, electronically. The trend within manufacturing is to migrate to low-wage nations (Gross & Coy, 1995), coordinating production via a communications network.

Technology is transforming a wide spectrum of industries, bringing down barriers to entry, changing industry infrastructure, and upsetting the traditional "food" chain. IT has transformed the structure of organization, the type of work carried out, and where it is undertaken. New technologies assure that this trend will continue. Firms are becoming increasingly dependent upon their IT, and the IT activity is now strategic to every company.

Bibliography

Drucker, P. (1988). The coming of the new organisation. *Harvard Business Review*, **68**, 56–61.

Gross, N. & Coy, P. (1995). The technology paradox, how companies can thrive as prices dive. *Business Week*, 3398-728, (March 6), 36–44.

Konsynski, B. & McFarlan, W. (1987). Information partnerships – shared data, shared scale. *Harvard Business Review* (September–October), Reprint No. 90506.

KAYE LOVERIDGE

investment intensity   Over the long term many capital-intensive businesses, especially those involved in basic industries, achieve wholly inadequate rates of return on the capital they employ. Around the world examples abound in what are becoming known as S.C.R.A.P INDUSTRIES sectors, to which list could readily be added many businesses involved in construction materials such as flat glass; agricultural commodities such as palm oil or wheat; extractive industries such as tin, coal, and soda ash; and many fields of transportation, typified by the malaise in passenger airlines around the globe.

That these sectors have experienced periods of attractive return or that certain competitors manage to break out is not in question. What remains observable, however, is that over the long term the typical level of performance for the majority is totally inadequate.

The extent to which capital-intensive businesses underperform the norm in the Profit Impact of Market Strategy (PIMS) database (*see* PIMS STRUCTURAL DETERMINANTS OF PERFORMANCE) is explored in order to develop the reasons for that underperformance.

Defining Investment Intensity

Capital or "investment intensity" is defined as:

> the net book value of plant and equipment plus working capital (i.e. total assets less current liabilities) expressed as a percentage of sales revenue or as a percentage of the value added generated by the business (where value added is defined as net sales revenue less all outside suppliers inputs).

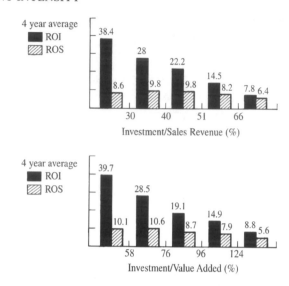

Figure 1   Investment intensity is a severe drag on profitability.

In many instances, to obtain a balanced view on the underlying investment intensity of a business, both measures of investment intensity need to be employed. A business that has a low investment/sales ratio because it turns its asset base frequently may at the same time have a high investment/value added ratio because its value added is low.

The Impact of Investment Intensity

What, then, is the typical profit performance of investment intensive businesses as when compared to the business universe? To answer this question the 3,000 plus businesses in the PIMS database were divided into five equal groups on the basis of their average four year level of investment/sales revenue and investment/value added and their profit performance observed in terms of pre-tax, pre-interest return on investment (R.O.I), and return on sales (R.O.S.) as shown in figure 1.

It can be seen that, whichever measure of investment intensity is employed, R.O.I. performance declines steeply as investment intensity rises. Businesses in the lower quintile of the distributions achieve approximately five times the R.O.I. of their investment intensive counterparts. When R.O.S. is considered the perfor-

mance fall-off is again quite marked for the upper quintile of the distributions.

When taken at face value, the investment intensity finding is not only of great, importance for the business community but controversial in nature. Put simply, if profitability is the key concern, the argument runs that resources should be channelled away from investment intensive businesses unless significant outperformance of the norm can be achieved.

Why do Investment Intensive Businesses Underperform?

What lies behind the investment intensity finding? Is the effect more illusory than real? Several plausible nonbehavioral reasons can be put forward: the relationship is largely definitional; it reflects a managerial focus on R.O.S. or absolute return; it captures the profit penalties of poor asset utilization or investing in new assets. Moreover, the relationship is exaggerated because it makes no allowance for investment grants, tax allowances or the like. Each hypothesis is examined in turn before considering possible behavioral explanators of the finding.

A definitional relationship. When the investment level in a business increases it simultaneously increases the denominator of the R.O.I. ratio, hence dragging down the value of the

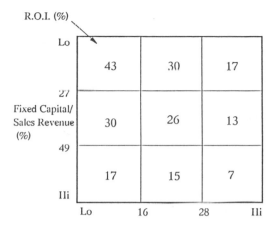

R.O.I. (%)

Working Capital/Sales Revenue (%)

Figure 2   Both fixed and working capital drag on profitability.

ratio. That there is more than a definitional relationship to the investment intensity effect is demonstrated if we examine R.O.S. in figure 1. If a business is to hold R.O.I. as investment intensity increases, R.O.S. should also increase smoothly. In practice, R.O.S. is at best flat and in fact starts to tail off at higher levels of investment intensity. Moreover, "return" has been taken pre-tax, pre-interest, with no financial charge made on the amount of investment used in the business. If even a modest capital charge rate is applied to a business's returns to reflect its investment use, the relationships in figure 1 would start to turn sharply down. If businesses with high levels of investment are not able to achieve profit margins sufficient to offset the higher level of investment that they need to sustain their sales, there must be more than just a definitial relationship at work.

Inappropriate managerial focus. It can be argued that management may be focusing on R.O.S. or the absolute level of return achieved in the business irrespective of the heavier investment burden required to generate the sales. If this mind-set is in place it should be recognized that an adequate return on capital employed does not result. The more likely explanation is that management find they cannot extract adequate returns over time because of the destructive nature of competition that

typically accompanies high levels of investment intensity.

Poor utilization of investment. If a business is suffering from poor levels of capacity utilization, its investment intensity will rise and the finding may be capturing little more than businesses which are ineffectual users of their investment base. To check for this possibility the average level of capacity utilization was tracked as investment intensity increased. As can be seen in table 1, no discernable differences were apparent.

This, of course, is not to argue that high capacity utilization levels do not have a major benefit for investment intensive businesses. When we examine the upper third of the PIMS database in terms of fixed capital intensity, businesses with utilization levels above 84 per cent achieve on average an R.O.I. of 19 per cent, as opposed to an R.O.I. of only 8 per cent for those with utilization levels below 70 per cent. Given this profit trap, it is readily apparent why management may adopt a defense of throughput mentality, even if margin has to be sacrificed and ultimately the return becomes inadequate to reflect the increased investment in the business.

Composition of the investment base. Is the investment intensity effect primarily due to the fixed capital or the working capital tied up in

Table 1 Capacity utilization levels associated with investment intensity.

	Values on PIMS database quintiles				
	Lower quintile		Mean		Upper quintile
Investment/sales revenue (%)	21	35	45	58	90
Capacity utilization (%)	75	75	76	76	75
Investment/value added (%)	44	67	86	109	163
Capacity utilization (%)	74	75	77	77	75

Table 2 The nature of the investment base.

	Values on PIMS database quintiles				
	Lower quintile		Mean		Upper quintile
Gross book value of plant and equipment/sales (%)	12	26	37	52	97
Newness of plant and equipment (net book/gross book) (%)	57	54	53	53	53
GBV replacement cost (%)	193	199	196	192	196

a business, or a function of both? It is shown in figure 2 that both drag on R.O.I. in a similar manner.

The clear profit trap at 7 per cent R.O.I. is for businesses with high levels in each investment component. The double drag on profitability is mitigated when operating with low levels of one or the other.

The age of fixed assets may distort an investment measure taken at net book value. New fixed assets, especially if added at high replacement costs, would temporarily increase the ratio. No evidence of this effect is found in table 2.

In part, such effects will be smoothed because all analysis is based on four year averages. Moreover, there may be a case that new fixed investment could in fact reduce the overall investment ratio by generating a disproportionate amount of sales or value added.

Overstatement. The magnitude of the investment intensity problem may be overstated because of the measurement of "return" and "investment" employed here. Return has been taken pre-tax, pre-interest, hence making no allowance for tax breaks which encourage investment, and hence the after tax return may be more favorable, notwithstanding interest charges. Investment in a business may be a harsh yardstick if part of that investment has been provided by grants or subsidies.

As PIMS data does not capture after-tax return or isolate the proportion of investment "given" to a business, no analysis to this end was performed. For this reason the investment intensity finding may or may not be overstated. The observation remains that as the investment used in a business increases, profitability declines. Managements who run businesses on the basis of tax breaks or investment allowances rather than on their intrinsic worth tread a dangerous path running the risk of building on castles of sand.

The Behavioral Explanation. The previous discussion shows that while there are definitional elements to the investment intensity finding, there remains a significant element of the finding which is to be explained by behavioral factors.

With high levels of investment in a business, costs often become more fixed in nature with a high break-even resulting. The high levels of investment also raise exit costs. In this situation the key managerial task is to keep assets productive and highly utilized at adequate price levels. When marketplace occupancy levels sink below the break-even level, either because of too much capacity addition or because of a weakening in demand, the business becomes highly vulnerable to outside pressures in attempting to keep its investment working – it becomes a "buyers' market." Quite often under these conditions management has little alternative but to weaken on price to defend volume. Competitors faced with the same situation have little option but to match such moves, and profits spiral downward for all participants.

The problem is perhaps most acute, but not limited to, the base S.C.R.A.P. industry settings, which are often caught by the twin pincers of heightened investment intensity and reduced ability to differentiate. The situation comes about in low growth markets, with technology played out and the ability to innovate and differentiate reducing. In order to become more cost competitive, managerial attention switches from product to process R&D. The change in emphasis further reduces the abillity to differentiate, while process R&D. invariably leads to a substitution of capital for labor. The twin pincers close; more investment intensive with a higher break-even without the ability to differentiate increases managements propensity to weaken on price. In their desperation to meet the new break-even, business is taken on the basis of contribution, with competitors readily able to respond on price. Destructive competition ensues and profitless prosperity results.

Once trapped it may be difficult to escape: the supply–demand imbalance may be long enduring; exit barriers are high; and competitors entrenched. Trying to escape the worst forms of price-based competition by seeking to differentiate the offer in some way is in the majority of cases no more than a comforting illusion. The incremental nature of innovation provides few opportunities to break out. Those that are found often require investment and cannot be "ring-fenced" from imitation – any edges achieved only give a short breathing space before being matched by competitors. If escape by price addition does not improve the margin equation, the hope is that a sustainable cost reduction on the back of a better technology will. With the technology largely played out, such leapfrogging is rare. Even where a step-wise technological advance is made it remains difficult to keep it proprietary – the cost savings pass on to the market.

The management of an investment intensive business also need to be mindful of the potential double profit penalty that can result when incurring substantial discretionary expenditure in their efforts to escape. Businesses in the upper third of the PIMS database in terms of investment intensity that incur heavy R&D. (over 5.9 per cent of sales revenue) or marketing (over 14.9 per cent of sales revenue) expenditure achieve on average only a 4 per cent R.O.I. The danger is that such high levels of expenditure are incurred but do not lead to a sustainable improvement in cost, price or investment behavior which can be kept proprietary over the long term.

Overview

The investment intensity phenomenon is real and damaging to business. It cannot be explained away as merely a definitional relationship. Heavy investment naturally leads to added anxieties about maintaining throughput. Faced with internal, market, and competitive pressures, management sacrifices margin and destructive forms of competition ensue. Once trapped, it is difficult to escape. Attempts to improve operating performance and market place position are difficult to sustain against able competitors in unfavorable market circumstances. The danger also remains that, in their efforts to escape the investment intensity trap, management compound their difficulties by their actions.

It should be recognized that while increased investment intensity damages a business, in many cases management have little choice but to do the "wrong thing" to stay competitive. When faced with this dilemma, management should not assume that increased investment will automatically improve profitability – rather, the reverse. Any increase in investment intensity that does not result in a major long-term advantage will exacerbate the problem. With heightened exit barriers the business is locked into a more unfavorable situation and management desperation increases.

The authors would like to acknowledge the assistance of John Hillier of the Strategic Planning Institute in researching the PIMS database.

Bibliography

Schoeffler, S., Buzzell, R. D., & Heany, D. F. (1974), Impact of strategic planning on profit performance. *Harvard Business Review*, **52**, 137–45.

KEVIN JAGIELLO and GORDON MANDRY

J

joint venture strategy Joint ventures may well prove to be a useful, and indeed necessary, way to enter some new markets, especially for multinational firms. In some markets which restrict inward investment, joint ventures may be the only way to achieve market access. Within joint ventures, clear equity positions are usually taken by the participants; such holdings can vary substantially in size, although it is usually important to establish clear lines of management decision making control in order to achieve success.

A lesser form of participation, which may or may not involve equity participation, involves STRATEGIC ALLIANCES. Joint ventures do tend to have a relatively high failure rate. Nevertheless, they also enjoy a number of specific advantages.

Advantages of Joint Ventures

First, for the smaller organization with insufficient finance and/or specialist management skills, the joint venture can prove an effective method of obtaining the necessary resources to enter a new market. This can be especially true in attractive developing country markets, where local contacts, access to distribution, and political requirements may make a joint venture the preferred, or even legally required, solution.

Second, joint ventures can be used to reduce political friction and local nationalist prejudice against foreign-owned corporations. Moreover, political rules may discriminate against subsidiaries that are fully foreign-owned, and in favor of local firms, through the placing of government contracts or through discriminating taxes and restrictions against foreign firms importing key materials, machinery, and components. With the development of trading blocs such as the European Union and NAFTA, intergovern-mental negotiations have seen the introduction of tariff walls to protect the participants. As a result, despite the development of GATT, the use of joint ventures to gain access to trading bloc markets has increased, especially by firms from the Pacific Rim.

Third, joint ventures may provide specialist knowledge of local markets, entry to required channels of distribution, and access to supplies of raw materials, government contracts, and local production facilities. Japanese companies have actively exploited joint ventures for these purposes. Triad alliances have thus often led to Japanese manufacturers linking with European and/or North American manufacturers to provide badge engineered products, which have enhanced the global volume production of the Japanese suppliers and gained them access to Western developed country markets without political friction. Similarly, after the first oil-price shock, the Japanese moved swiftly to use joint ventures in order to gain access to secure supplies of oil. As a result, while Western oil companies supplied some 80 per cent of Japan's oil imports in 1973, by 1995 this had been reduced to around 25 per cent, the balance being supplied via Japanese corporations operating via joint ventures.

Fourth, in a growing number of countries, joint ventures with host governments have become increasingly important. These may be formed directly with state-owned enterprises or directed toward national champions. Such ventures are common in the extractive and defense industries, where the foreign partner is expected to provide the necessary technology to aid the developing country partner.

Fifth, there has been growth in the creation of temporary consortium companies and alliances, to undertake particular projects which are considered to be too large for individual companies to handle alone. Such cooperations include new major defense initiatives, major civil engineering projects, new global technological ventures, and the like.

Finally, exchange controls may prevent a company from exporting capital and thus make the funding of new overseas subsidiaries difficult. The supply of know-how may therefore be used to enable a company to obtain an equity stake in a joint venture, where the local partner may have access to the required funds.

Disadvantages of Joint Ventures

Despite the advantages of joint ventures, there remain substantial dangers that need to be carefully considered before embarking on a joint venture strategy.

The first major problem is that joint ventures are very difficult to integrate into a global strategy that involves substantial cross-border trading. In such circumstances, there are almost inevitably problems concerning inward and outward transfer pricing and the sourcing of exports, in particular, in favor of wholly owned subsidiaries in other countries.

Second, the trend toward an integrated system of global cash management, via a central treasury, may lead to conflict with local partners when the corporate headquarters endeavors to impose limits or even guidelines on cash and working capital usage, foreign exchange management, and the amount, and means, of paying remittable profits. As a result, many multinationals that generate joint ventures may do so outside a policy of global strategy integration, making use of such operations to service restricted geographic territories or countries in which wholly owned subsidiaries are not permitted.

A third serious problem occurs when the objectives of the partners are, or become, incompatible. For example, the MNC may have a very different attitude to risk than its local partner, and may be prepared to accept short-term losses in order to build market share, to take on higher levels of debt, or to spend more on advertising. Similarly, the objectives of the participants may well change over time, especially when wholly owned subsidiary alternatives may occur for the MNC with access to the joint venture market.

Fourth, problems occur with regard to management structures and staffing of joint ventures. This is especially true in countries in which nepotism is common and in which jobs have to be found for members of the partner's families, or when employment is given to family members of local politicians or other locals in positions of influence. From the perspective of MNCs, seconded personnel may also be subject to conflicts of interest, in which the best actions for the joint venture might conflict with the strategy and objectives of the MNC shareholder.

Finally, many joint ventures fail because of a conflict in tax interests between the partners. Many of these could actually be overcome if they were thought through in advance; however, such problems are rarely foreseen. One common problem occurs as a result of start-up losses. Due to past write-offs, accelerated depreciation, and the like, it is common for capital-intensive businesses to report operating losses in their first few years. It is therefore possibly more attractive for the local partner if these losses can be used to offset against other locally derived profits. To obtain such tax advantages, however, certain minimum levels of shareholdings may be necessary, and this may be in conflict with the aspirations of an MNC partner. The precise nature of the shareholding structure of joint ventures therefore needs to be considered at the formation stage in order to maximize fiscal efficiency and avoid this form of conflict.

The Joint Venture Agreement

Because of the potential difficulties that can occur with joint ventures, they should be formulated carefully and the Articles of Association only drawn up after consideration of the objectives and strategies of the participants, both at the time of formation and as they might reasonably be expected to evolve in the future. Furthermore, such an agreement should set out, in clear language, the rights and obligations of the participants, taking care that differences in interpretation due to translation are not introduced when more than one language is used. The country of jurisdiction under which any disputes would be settled also needs to be clearly stated. The joint venture agreement should then cover the following points:

- the legal nature of the joint venture and the terms under which it can be dissolved

- the constitution of the board of directors and the voting power of the partners

- the managerial rights and responsibilities of the partners

- the constitution of the management and appointment of the managerial staff

- the conditions under which the capital can be increased

- constraints on the transfer of shares or subscription rights to nonpartners

- the responsibilities of each of the partners in respect of assets, finance, personnel, R&D, and the like

- the financial rights of the partners with respect to dividends and royalties

- the rights of the partners with respect to the use of licenses, know-how, and trademarks in third countries

- limitations, if any, on sales of the joint venture's products to certain countries or regions

- an arbitration clause indicating how disputes between partners are to be resolved

- the conditions under which the Articles of the joint venture agreement may be changed

- consideration of how the joint venture can be terminated

Bibliography

Channon, D. F. & Jalland, M. (1979). *Multinational strategic planning.* London: Amacom/Macmillan. See pp. 200–6.

Farok, Contractor & Lorange, P. (1988). Why should firms cooperate? In Farok, C. & Lorange, P. (eds). *Cooperative strategies in international business.* Lexington, MA: Lexington Books.

Harrigan, K. R. (1985). *Strategies for joint ventures.* Lexington, MA: D. C. Heath.

DEREK F. CHANNON

just in time   In the face of substantially superior productivity and lower cost, as a result of low market share and high experience effect costs, Japanese car producers sought ways to gain competitive advantage against their major US competitors. On a visit to the USA in the 1950s, the production director of Toyota Motors, Mr. Taichi Ohno, observed the replenishment pattern of shelves in US supermarkets, which were only refilled when they became empty. As a result, stocks could be significantly reduced, provided that deliveries of replenishments arrived at the moment of stockout. From this observation, the concept of "just in time" (JIT) production was born which, together with increasing labor productivity, resulted in Toyota ultimately gaining competitive advantage over the company's American rivals. The system developed at Toyota was also rapidly copied by other Japanese car makers, and by producers in many other indigenous industries.

The key to JIT is to produce (or deliver) the right items in the quantity required by subsequent production processes (or customers) at the time needed. As a result, buffer stocks of work in progress (WIP) and the like can be eliminated. The system also seeks to coordinate the final assembly activity to coincide with customer demand and so eliminate the need for finished goods stocks. While market share has been identified as an important factor in business unit profitability, other variables – notably fixed and working capital intensity – have been determined to also be powerful determinants of profitability such that they can eliminate the potential advantage of superior share. Thus Toyota, in competing against General Motors, used lower capital intensity brought about by JIT production systems as a key variable to establish competitive advantage.

However, the total JIT system involves more than simply inventory management. Rather, it is a comprehensive strategy to create competitor advantage via production. This is achieved as follows.

Inventory Management

A key element in JIT production is the reduction or elimination of WIP, so as to reduce the finished goods inventory. The result of successful implementation of such a strategy is a substantial reduction in capital intensity, which results in a major improvement in return on equity. JIT exposes problems in identifying ways in which inventory can be reduced, and

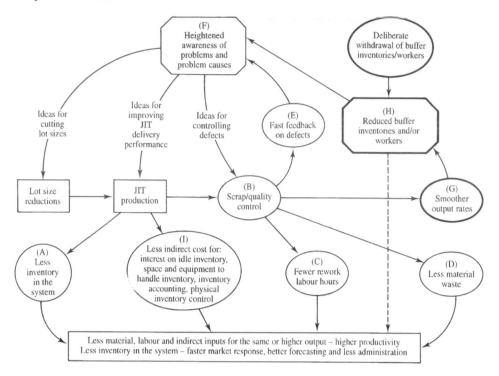

Figure 1 The effects of JIT production.
Source: Schonberger (1982).

Japanese corporations aim for lot sizes that are considerably less than one day's supply. Moreover, small lot sizes reduce cycle inventory which, in turn, helps to cut lead times. While these reductions in WIP and stocks of finished goods reduce operating costs, potential problems with suppliers increase the element of risk. Hence a critical ingredient in JIT production systems involves the development of a close interdependency with important suppliers.

Competitive Priorities

Low cost and consistent quality are the two production priorities that are emphasized most. As a result, Japanese producers seek to provide products such as automobiles with high-level specifications as standard, rather than slowing production lines by providing customized products.

Positioning Strategy

Under JIT, a product focus is selected to achieve high-volume, low-cost production. The workforce and capital equipment are organized around product flows which, in turn, are arranged to conform to work operations.

Process Design

The use of small lot sizes adds substantially to cost. This problem is especially important in fabrication industries. A solution is to design the process to minimize set-up costs. Indeed, the implications of extra capital cost to carry excess capacity versus extra operating costs need to be carefully evaluated.

A further solution is to reduce set-up frequency. Thus Japanese manufacturers may well be prepared to give away features on their products in order to reduce the cost of changeovers, rather than adopting a product line that has a number of variable features that require different production runs.

If costs are to be constrained, the workforce also needs to be flexible; thus helping to absorb shocks in production which are not dampened by inventory buffers. This may require significant investment in education and training.

A product focus also helps to reduce set-up frequency and corresponding costs. This can be a significant ingredient in establishing the overall cost structure. When volume is insufficient to insure a revenue stream, technology may be used to reduce costs by producing components with common features on a common, small volume production line. Changeover costs from one component to another are therefore reduced. A final method of reducing set-up costs is to use an approach in which one worker operates several machines, each of which advances the production process by one step at a time. The Japanese also make considerable use of automation to reduce costs; they have installed around 6–8 times the number of robots per head compared with other industrialized countries. The Japanese workforce is also trained to be flexible and, with enterprise unions, does not suffer from the restrictive practices found in some countries.

Workforce Management

In the Japanese system, decisions normally undertaken in the West by management are influenced by the workforce. Virtually everyone is engaged in quality circles, which form one element in job enlargement. While the workforce is normally concerned with continuous operational improvements and management with planning investment improvements, inevitably the two spheres overlap. In some companies, meetings to discern methods of cost reduction actually take place on a daily basis. Workers are also rotated, with the best being trained as generalists rather than lesser performers. Decision making in such an environment also tends to take place by consensus, rather than the confrontation that often occurs in the West. The status difference between all workers is also reduced, as are salary differentials.

Excess Capacity

As well as reducing inventory to the absolute minimum, Japanese concerns also attempt to eliminate excess capacity, which is seen as a form of waste.

Supplier Management

Close relationships are forged between manufacturers and component suppliers. These too are expected to drive for continuous productivity gains and thereby reduced costs, to minimize stocks through the application of JIT systems, and to locate close to a manufacturer's plant. Any necessary buffer stock is the responsibility of the supplier. Similarly, suppliers take responsibility for component quality, so obviating the need for inward goods quality checks. In return, manufacturers maintain close relationships with suppliers and a steady level of production output.

Production Scheduling

To reduce disruptions that might hinder inventory reduction, components are standardized as much as possible, even though final products may appear to be customized. Component standardization increases volumes, which provides experience gains as well as reducing inventory. Second, production schedules are standardized and lot sizes for final products are very small. Daily output for a month tends to be the same, and only then is adjusted for forecast errors and inventory imbalances.

Product Quality

Quality is seen as being everyone's concern and is paramount to the management of a JIT system. Workers are all given the opportunity to stop the production line at the first sign of a quality defect, while machines operate autonomation, or jikoda, whereby the machine will automatically stop if it begins to produce output outside specification. Under the line stop system, supervisors and/or engineers rush to the trouble spot to correct the problem. While, in the early stages of production set-up, this slows down production, ultimately the line speeds up, re-work is minimized, quality is established, and productivity is improved.

Much control is established by correct plant layout rather than by sophisticated computerized control systems. For example, Japanese factories make considerable use of visual controls such as "Andon" or lantern lights which help to expose abnormal conditions, buzzers, video cameras, and "line of sight" to rapidly identify and relay information.

Production Control Boards

Throughout Japanese factories, the performance of work groups is made readily accessible through the extensive use of visual displays of performance, such as statistical control charts. These measure performance against agreed targets and are completed by workers themselves. In most Western concerns, the collection of control data tends to be undertaken by accounting functions for management and the workforce is not kept fully informed about their performance.

Bibliography

Krajewski, L. J. & Ritzman, L. P. (1987). *Operations management*. Reading, MA: Addison-Wesley.

Schonberger, R. J. (1982). *Japanese manufacturing techniques*. New York: The Free Press.

Suzaki, K. (1985). Comparative study of JIT/TQC activities in Japanese and Western companies. *First World Congress of Production and Inventory Control, Vienna.*

Suzaki, K. (1987). *The new manufacturing challenge.* New York: The Free Press.

DEREK F. CHANNON

K

kaizen The Japanese term "kaizen" means "continuous improvement" and is an all embracing concept covering JUST IN TIME, TOTAL QUALITY CONTROL, and KANBAN. It applies at all levels in Japanese corporations. A kaizen program can be subdivided into three areas based on complexity and hierarchical level, namely:

• management-oriented kaizen

• group-oriented kaizen

• individual-oriented kaizen

Management-oriented Kaizen

Under the Japanese system, continuous improvement is considered to be an activity that involves everyone. Managers are expected to devote half their time to seeking ways to improve their job, and those of the personnel for whom they are responsible. Sometimes these tasks become blurred, as blue collar workers also come up with ways of changing production processes as part of their own kaizen programs, whereas this task is technically the responsibility of management.

The kaizen projects undertaken by management involve problem solving expertise and professional and engineering knowledge. Particular use is made of the "Seven Statistical Tools." These are used by managers, but are also displayed within the factory and at the level of the work group. These tools (some of which are described in greater detail elsewhere) are as follows:

1. *Pareto diagrams.* These classify problems according to cause and phenomenon, normally with 80 per cent of cost being accounted for by 20 per cent of factors.

2. *Cause and effect diagrams.* Also called "fishbone diagrams," these are used to analyze the characteristics of a process and the factors that determine them.

3. *Histograms.* These display the data from measurements concerning the frequency of an activity, a process, and the like.

4. *Control charts.* Two types in use; they detect abnormal trends with the help of line graphs. Sample data is plotted to evaluate process situations and trends.

5. *Scatter diagrams.* Data concerning two variables are plotted to demonstrate the relationship between them.

6. *Graphs.* These depict quantitative data in readily recognizable visual form: a variety of graphic displays are used. Graphic displays are widely used in Japanese culture, compared with Western reliance on numerical tabulations.

7. *Checksheets.* These are designed to tabulate the outcome through routine checking of a situation.

These statistical tools are used by all levels within the organization, are prominantly displayed throughout working areas, and all personnel are trained to use them.

Opportunities for improvement are to be found everywhere. However, kaizen is also the application of detail – each contribution may be small, but the cumulative effect is dramatic. In particular, kaizen is concerned with WASTE ELIMINATION, JUST IN TIME, and TQC. Management-oriented kaizen may also involve group activities: *ad hoc* and temporary organizational units, such as kaizen teams, project groups, and task forces, may be created to undertake a specific task, and then dispersed upon its completion.

Group-oriented Kaizen

In group work, kaizen is achieved via quality circles and other small group activities that use statistical techniques to solve problems. It also involves workers operating the full PDCA CYCLE and requires the groups to identify problems, analyze them, implement and test new practices, and establish new working standards. Groups are rewarded not so much with money, but with prestige. Group achievements are communicated throughout the organization, partially via cross-functional structures (*see* CROSS-FUNCTIONAL MANAGEMENT STRUCTURE): groups engaged in one business activity, and evaluating tasks similar to those of other groups, are expected to learn from one another in order to maximize productivity.

At all levels in the Japanese corporation, these small groups are no longer informal but, rather, have become an integral component of continuous improvement. The advantages of this practice are seen as follows:

- the setting of group objectives and working toward their achievement reinforces the sense of team working

- members share and coordinate their respective roles better

- labor–management communication is improved

- morale is improved

- workers acquire more skills and develop cooperative attitudes

- the group becomes self-sustaining and solves problems that are normally considered the province of management

- labor–management relations are significantly improved

Individual-oriented Kaizen

At this level, kaizen involves the individual identifying ways of improving the productivity of the job. In particular, individuals contribute via the use of suggestion schemes. While in the West such schemes tend to be poorly supported, in Japan targets are now set for the number of suggestions to be contributed by work groups and individuals. As a result, in large corporations the number of suggestions

can amount to many millions, and each year the number increases. When sharp appreciation of the yen has taken place, as in 1987 and 1994–5, the number of suggestions has increased dramatically – in part because workers were hired under the assumption of permanent employment – in an attempt to maintain relative competitive advantage. The main areas for suggestions in the Japanese system have been identified as follows:

- improvements in one's own work

- savings in energy, materials, and other resources

- improvements in the working environment

- improvements in jigs and tools

- improvements in office working practices

- improvements in product quality

- ideas for new products

- customer services and customer relations

- other

Kaizen policies are the norm in Japanese corporations. While sharp increases in the exchange rate make Japanese practices less competitive from time to time, the positive response of the workforce as a result of kaizen programs attempts to rapidly restore the Japanese productivity advantage. The low level of fear of forced redundancy has a significant impact on workers who, basically, may well suggest ideas which – if implemented – might actually eliminate their own jobs.

Bibliography

Cooper, R. (1994). *Sumitomo Electric Industries Ltd: the kaizen program*, Case 9-195-078. Cambridge, MA: Harvard Business School.
Masaaki Imai (1986). *Kaizen*. New York: McGraw-Hill.

DEREK F. CHANNON

kanban   Literally translated, kanban means "visible record." More generally, it is taken to mean "card." The system was developed by Mr. Taichi Ohno of Toyota Motors, the founder of JUST IN TIME, and based on the practice, within

US supermarket groups, to replenish stocks within stores only when they were approaching stockout.

In the kanban system developed at Toyota, every component or part has its own special container designed to hold a specific number of parts, preferably a small quantity. Each container has two kanban cards, which identify the part number and container capacity, amongst other information. The first of these, the production kanban, serves the work center producing the part; while the other, called a conveyance kanban, serves the user receiving center. Each container moves from the production area and its stock point to the using work station and its stock point and back, with one kanban being replaced during the traffic flow.

Within the kanban system, the work section using a component effectively pulls through the next consignment in the following sequence:

1. The consuming work group picks up components as required.
2. The kanban cards are placed in a box.
3. These are sent to a warehouse or to a previous process. As components are picked up to re-supply the using group, most cards are exchanged for the production cards attached to the components.
4. As the exchange takes place, production cards are collected in another kanban box.
5. The selected components are brought back to the user unit with move cards attached to them.
6. The production cards are brought back to the component manufacturing unit, where only the amount indicated by the production cards will be produced.
7. When production is completed, the production cards are attached to those goods produced.
8. Goods are transferred to the warehouse, thus ending the cycle.

Level/mixed production scheduling helps to smooth the flow throughout the factory. When kanban is introduced and a downstream process experiences fluctuating demand, all the upstream processes need to have adequate and flexible capacity to absorb such fluctuations. As a result, smoothing out any such fluctuations becomes an element in kanban management, functioning as a tool for fine tuning of production while linking all of the processes in a chain. For successful implementation, a number of factors need to be taken into account:

- the sales/marketing function and production need to collaborate to determine the production schedule for final assembly to insure level/mixed production
- a kanban route through the factory needs to be carefully established
- to develop a steady flow and level/mixed production, usage of kanban should be tied to small lot production and frequent changeover
- for seasonal or promotional items, or in the start-up phase of a new product, where substantial take-up volume fluctuations may occur, coordination with the sales/marketing function becomes essential
- the entire kanban system needs to be updated when long-term changes in demand occur
- a reliable rational production system is essential for the successful use of a kanban system

In using the kanban system, a number of specific rules apply:

- workers from a downstream process should obtain parts from the upstream process according to the information described on the kanban move card
- workers in the production process should produce parts according to the information on the kanban production card
- if there is no kanban card, there is no production and no transfer of components
- the kanban card must always be attached to the parts container unless it is in transit
- workers should insure that 100 per cent of the parts produced are of the required quality; otherwise, the production line should be halted until defects are corrected
- the number of kanban cards should be gradually reduced in order better to link processes and to eliminate waste

Limitations of Kanban

Kanban is feasible in almost any plant that produces goods in whole units, but not in process industries. It is beneficial in the following circumstances:

- kanban should be an element of JIT systems

- the parts included in the kanban system should be used every day; companies using the system generally apply it to the high-use parts but replenish low-use items by means of conventional Western techniques

- very expensive or large items should not be included in kanban; such items are expensive to store and carry and should be regulated carefully

Bibliography

Kiyoshi, S. (1987). *The new manufacturing challenge.* New York: The Free Press.

Schonberger, R. J. (1982). *Japanese manufacturing techniques.* New York: The Free Press.

DEREK F. CHANNON

keiretsu structure   This is a specific structural form found in Japan. It occurs essentially in both horizontal and vertical forms, although groupings are also found in production and distribution. There are six main horizontal keiretsu; Mitsubishi, Mitsui, Sumitomo, Sanwa, Fuji, and Dai Ichi Kangyo. The first three of these are industrial groups which are based on leading prewar Japanese ZAIBATSU STRUCTURE; family-based industrial groups, the origins of which date back to Japan's initial industrialization. Originally each zaibatsu had a central holding company which set strategy. After World War II, the holding companies were eliminated, but the post-occupation Japanese government later allowed the industrial groups to reform, led by Mitsubishi. By the end of the 1950s, the historic zaibatsu-based groups had created Presidents' Councils as coordinating vehicles, and the groups had integrated, in part by taking cross-shareholdings in one another, as a protective device against possible hostile takeover bids. The other three major keiretsu groups developed during the 1960s, each based on the nucleus of one of the major city banks (strictly, the Dai Ichi Kangyo group is based on the merger of two groups, following the creation of the Dai Ichi Kangyo bank from the merger of the Dai Ichi and Nippon Kangyo banks). A further industrial group also exists, centered on the Industrial Bank of Japan (IBJ). However, the participants in this group, which includes most major Japanese corporations, do not have the same relationship with the bank and are also members of one of the other horizontal groups. A horizontal keiretsu group is illustrated in figure 1. There are several characteristics of these industrial groups that make them different than Western structures.

First, they all contain financial service companies which can provide finance to other members when necessary: each contains a commercial bank, a trust bank, and a life insurance company. Historically, the commercial bank took in short-term deposits and lent short- to medium-term. In recent times, and especially outside Japan, these organizations have mirrored their Western competitors and added investment banking services. The trust bank took in long-term funds and would lend long. Similarly, the life insurance company would also provide long-term loan funds. While the internal financial concerns do not provide all of the funds needed within an industrial group, and there is a restriction of a maximum of 5 per cent of total shares in any company that can be held by a bank, they do provide a special, formal relationship between the industrial members and the financial sector, quite unlike the position in Western structures.

Second, each group contains at least one trading company, known as the SOGA SHOSHA. These act as trading companies, intelligence gatherers, financiers, and project coordinators in a way that can support other group members. In turn, the other group members form a cross-section of the economy: thus there will be a chemical company, a metal manufacturer, a heavy engineering concern, and the like

Third, the cross-shareholdings between group members make it virtually impossible for external institutions to subject group members to predatory acquisition threats (*see* ACQUISITION STRATEGY). The linkages between a number of Mitsubishi Group companies are shown in figure 2. Shares in the trading company Mitsubishi Corporation are held by member companies such as Mitsubishi Bank, Tokio Marine and Fire Insurance, and Mitsubishi Heavy Industries. In all, about one-third of the company's shares are held by other

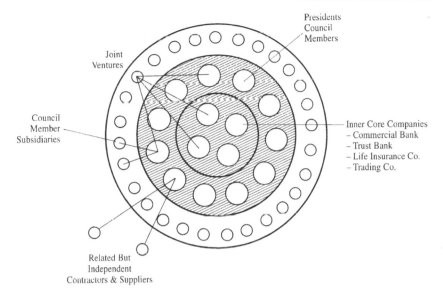

Presidents
Council
Members

Joint
Ventures

Council
Member
Subsidiaries

Inner Core Companies
– Commercial Bank
– Trust Bank
– Life Insurance Co.
– Trading Co.

Related But
Independent
Contractors & Suppliers

Figure 1 A Japanese horizontal keiretsu group.

Mitsubishi Group concerns. In turn, the trading company owns shares in other Mitsubishi companies.

By contrast to Western core business strategies, keiretsu groups have tended to continue to increase their level of diversification. Where new business areas develop, such as ocean mining, it would be quite natural for a keiretsu to enter the industry by forming a separate jointly owned subsidiary to exploit such a market opportunity; again, as in the case of fusion technologies, bringing together the elements of such a technology from across the group to create a new subsidiary.

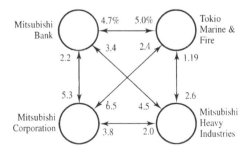

Figure 2 Japanese industrial group cross-shareholdings.
Source: Dodwell Marketing Consultants (1992).

Fourth, in the case of economic adversity in a particular member company, other group members will rally to its support, the financial members providing monetary assistance, while other group members might provide employment on a "loan" basis. In addition, personnel may be assigned to subsidiaries or affiliates. Usually, the major group companies send their managers to lower order companies as senior officers or directors. The bank in particular will often send a senior executive, as CEO, to any group member in financial difficulty. The average rates of directors sent by group members among the six major groups in 1990 were around 60 per cent, with the highest rate being 97 per cent for Mitsubishi and the lowest 41 per cent for Mitsui. In addition to appointments from within, the leading group companies also employ senior retiring government civil servants (this process is known as *amakudari* or "the descent from heaven").

Fifth, while each group will have many hundreds of members, there is a leading group of companies within the structure which form the Presidents' Council, or Shacho-Kai. The number of companies represented in such a structural element varies substantially, depending upon the roots of the keiretsu. Ideally, such a council should contain one representative

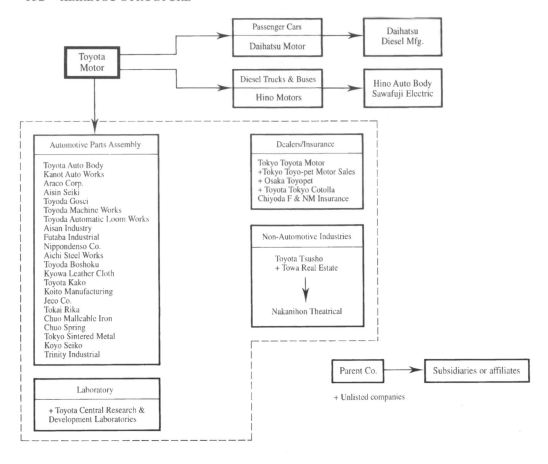

Figure 3 A vertical keiretsu group – the Toyota Motor Group.
Source: Dodwell Marketing Consultants, 1992.

from each industry. In the Mitsubishi Group this is approximately the case; but in the Dai Ichi Kangyo Group this is not so, as this group results from the merger of two major groups, each of which had its own set of companies. The councils meet regularly, on a specific day in each month. While the Presidents' Councils do not set specific group strategy, they do review external factors which affect member companies. The leader of the Presidents' Council in each individual group tends to come from one of a limited number of core companies, which varies between groups. In addition, other regular meetings occur between group member companies at vice-presidential level, and between specialists in planning and public relations.

Vertical keiretsu are groups in which there is a vertical relationship between a core company and its supplying subsidiaries or associates. Typical examples would be the Toyota, Nippon Steel, and Matsushita Groups. The structure of the Toyota Group, which consists of the automobile manufacturer, its sales unit, and its suppliers, is shown in figure 3. While some of the subsidiaries are wholly owned, others are not; but Toyota may have a shareholding and an extremely close relationship. Such groups emphasize industries in which the parent companies are involved. Subsidiaries and affiliates are usually controled by shareholdings and/ or the appointment of the CEO and/or other directors.

Keiretsu groups also occur in Japan within the service industry sector; such as the Seibu–Saison Group, which incorporates financial services, department stores, food retailers, entertainment, restaurants, hotels, and transportation.

The keiretsu form of organization found so extensively in Japan is unique to that country, and is a key element of the ability of Japanese companies to take a longer-term view. It contrasts with the stock market pressures experienced by Western companies, which have forced them to modify strategy in many cases and adopt structures which emphasize short-term profitability. The nearest equivalent to the keiretsu is probably the CHAEBOL STRUCTURE of Korea.

Bibliography

Chen, M. (1995). *Asian management systems*. London: Routledge.

Dodwell Marketing Consultants (1994). *Japanese industrial groups*. Tokyo: Dodwell Marketing Consultants.

Tokyo Business Today (1989). Intimate links with Japan's corporate groups. *Tokyo Business Today*, January, 14–19.

DEREK F. CHANNON

L

Lanchester strategy Although it is less well known than their adoption and adaptation of the quality management theories of Duran and Deming, a number of Japanese companies have evolved a concept of strategic marketing based on the ideas of F. W. Lanchester, who developed a theory of military fire power.

On the basis of World War I battles, Lanchester proposed that the outcome of military combat depended not only on unquantifiable factors such as surprise or luck but also upon factors which could be formulated in a precise mathematical form. He therefore developed two differential equations known as the linear law and the square law. The first of these applied in battles that consisted of the sum of a series of man-to-man duels, in which the total size of each army was essentially irrelevant, and the rate of change of an army over time was negatively related to the weapon efficiency of the opposing force. Thus if army m, with a force of m and a weapon efficiency of b, fought army n of size n and weapon efficiency a, then army m would win when:

$$\frac{m_0}{n_0} > \frac{a}{b}$$

where the subscript zero refers to "zero time."

On a modern battlefield, however, Lanchester argued that a concentration of fire power was possible and that direct man-to-man conflict was therefore replaced. Thus, casualties suffered by one army were related to both the armed efficiency and size of the opposing force. In these circumstances, army m would win if:

$$\frac{m_0^2}{n_0^2} > \frac{a}{b}$$

This was Lanchester's square law.

These concepts were subsequently expanded to include more complex situations, and it was shown that the principles appeared to be useful predictors of casualties during the American capture of Japanese-held islands in the Pacific during World War II.

Japanese consultants have made use of Lanchester's principles to provide insights into business competition. It was proposed by Onada (1979) that a battle between two armies was comparable to the competitive struggle between a market leader and its competitors. In this struggle military strength was equated with MARKET SHARE; tactical military forces (front line troops) became the strength and capability of the sales force; strategic forces (equivalent to the airforce) were pricing, advertising, and product development; and the rate of reinforcement was equivalent to the rate at which each side "captured" potential customers. The potential or uncommitted customers represented the pool of "reserves" on which a company could draw to increase its fighting strength or market share.

The theory required acceptance of the assumption that the rate at which a company could "capture" customers from the uncommitted pool was proportional to its existing market share. Thus, if two companies with shares of 20 per cent and 10 per cent respectively made the same marketing efforts as before, then the ratio at which they captured customers would be 2 : 1.

Target conditions were then established for a number of situations. In the first of these, Onada calculated that a market leader would be in a strong position to defend his position against all competitors with a market share greater than 42 per cent. This was identified as the "premium" position, in which the market

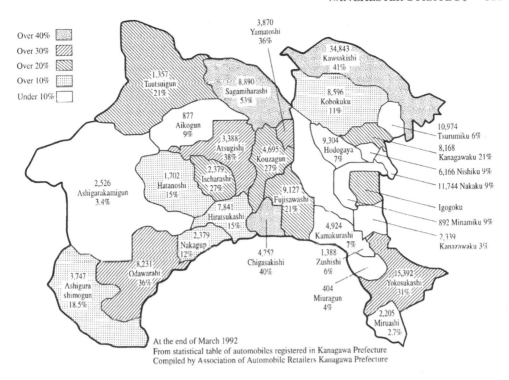

Legend:
- Over 40%
- Over 30%
- Over 20%
- Over 10%
- Under 10%

3,870 Yumatoshi 36%

34,843 Kawsakishi 41%

1,357 Tuutsuigun 21%

8,890 Sagamiharashi 53%

8,596 Kobokuku 11%

877 Aikogun 9%

3,388 Atsugishi 38%

4,695 Kouzagun 27%

9,304 Hodogaya 7%

10,974 Tsurumiku 6%

8,168 Kanagawaku 21%

6,166 Nishiku 9%

11,744 Nakaku 9%

2,526 Ashigarakamigun 3.4%

1,702 Hatanoshi 15%

2,379 Ischarashi 27%

9,127 Fujisawashi 21%

Igogoku

892 Minamiku 9%

7,841 Hiratsukashi 15%

4,924 Kamakurashi 7%

2,339 Kanazawaku 3%

2,379 Nakagun 12%

4,252 Chigasakishi 40%

1,388 Zushishi 6%

15,392 Yokosukashi 31%

3,747 Ashigura shimogun 18.5%

8,231 Odawarahi 36%

404 Miuragun 4%

2,205 Miruashi 2.7%

At the end of March 1992
From statistical table of automobiles registered in Kanagawa Prefecture
Compiled by Association of Automobile Retailers Kanagawa Prefecture

Figure 1 Using Lanchester theory for market domination: the ratio of market share by cities and countries.
Source: Nagashima, S. (1992). *100 management charts.* Tokyo: Asian Productivity Organisation.

share leader could afford to devote more attention to strategic marketing (advertising, pricing, etc.) than to tactical marketing.

Two other target positions were also established at the 74 per cent and 26 per cent levels of market share. A market leader with only a 26 per cent share was vulnerable, while one with a 74 per cent share was considered to be very safe. These two conditions were defined as "polyopoly" and "monopoly" respectively.

The derivation of these market share targets led to a number of propositions about market leadership and the stability of market structures:

- in monopoly and premium markets, the leader is safer than in other markets, and these market share patterns will tend to be stable

- to maintain position, market leaders in monopoly and premium markets need to outperform competitors in strategic marketing

- in polyopoly markets, market leadership will change more frequently, because no competitor will easily gain significant advantage

In addition to these three market conditions, two further conditions, duopoly and oligopoly markets, were defined. These were explained by introducing the concept of the "shooting range." The limits of competition were identified at equilibrium as 74 per cent and 26 per cent respectively. If the competition was between two companies the shooting range was therefore 3 : 1. Outside this range no "saddle" point exists and the competitive power of a smaller company cannot affect the position of a larger one. In a market in which many competitors attack each other, Lanchester's square law was said to operate, and the shooting range was defined as the square root of 3, or approximately 1.7.

Some analysis of these Japanese concepts has been undertaken using the PIMS database; this did not support the stability of the monopoly and premium structures. Nevertheless, the concepts have been widely accepted and used within Japan, and by Japanese companies, in attacking global markets. In this respect, the use of Lanchester's concepts has not been to optimize stable positions but as a *modus operandi* of attack, utilizing concentration of force with a view to eliminating entrenched leaders. An illustration of a Lanchester strategy for market domination in Kanagawa Prefecture, Japan, is shown in figure 1.

While the concept is not well appreciated in the West, it bears some resemblance to the Boston Consulting Group's concept of the RULE OF THREE AND FOUR and McKinsey and Company's concept of the micromarket, in which unless one firm can gain an adequate share of market it should contemplate strategic withdrawal.

Bibliography

Campbell, N. C. G. & Roberts, K. J. (1986). Lanchester market strategies. *Strategic Management Journal*, (May–June).

Onada, T. (1979). *Science to win the competition: the development of Lanchester's strategic models*. Tokyo: Kaihatsu-sha (in Japanese).

Taoka, N. (1977). *The Lanchester laws*. Tokyo: Biginesusha. (in Japanese).

Taoka, N. (1982). *Practical applications of Lanchester strategy*. Tokyo: Biginesusha (in Japanese).

DEREK F. CHANNON

leveraged buy-out strategy   Leveraged buy-outs (LBOs) occur when the management of a company purchase it from existing shareholders and effectively become the owners. The target is typically a public company or a subsidiary of one which is taken private, with a significant portion of the cash purchase price being financed by debt. This debt is secured not by the credit status of the purchaser but by the assets of the target company. The debt used has usually been high-yield securities of substandard investment grade quality, commonly referred to as "junk bonds." During the late 1980s and early 1990s in the USA, and to some extent in Western Europe, LBOs were very popular, and some

financial institutions specialized in the issuance of junk bonds. With the arrival of the credit crunch of the mid-1990s and a number of highly visible failures amongst LBOs and investment banks, the movement lost ground. However, with returning liquidity in the banking system, there are signs of a new surge of interest in the mid-1990s.

An important criterion for an LBO is a gap between the existing market value of the firm and the value determined by a reappraisal of the assets or by the capitalization of expected cashflows. Moreover, after an LBO the incoming management are often able to achieve dramatic savings in the business's operating costs.

LBOs tend to be mature businesses with a demonstrable record of stable consistent earnings, a significant market share, and experienced in place management. Manufacturing and retailing businesses are attractive because they also contain a basis for asset secured loans or stable income streams for unsecured or subordinated debt. Low capital intensive service businesses are less popular because of their narrow asset bases.

LBOs are said to be attractive to all those involved. Typically, the target concern's top management approaches an investment banker with an LBO proposal. In some cases, specialist banks may take the initiative. The bankers then package an LBO deal, usually involving commercial bankers, insurance and finance companies, pension funds, and the like. The final deal will provide the incumbent management with the opportunity to purchase a stake in the common stock that is much greater than they would be able to obtain on the basis of their individual resources, provided that they can successfully secure the debt. Usually, however, the management group's resources still only provide a small percentage of the initial investment.

This equity gap has led to the creation of a new form of financing known as mezzanine-level finance. Such lenders are often limited partnerships with wealthy investors, venture capitalists and pension funds as limited partners, supported by an investment banking firm acting as a general partner. In addition to investing in common equity, mezzanine lenders also hold securities senior to management equity but subordinate to secured debt. Most mezzanine financiers are short- to medium-term investors who expect to resell their share of the equity a few years after purchase to realize a substantial capital gain.

LBOs are far from risk-free. First, an LBO offer may serve to attract more bidders, although this is not a problem if the primary objective is to achieve the best value for existing shareholders. Second, and more important, is the risk of insolvency. Since revolving bank lending is a primary means of financing LBOs, they are very sensitive to increases in interest rates as a result of their highly leveraged position.

The risk of diversification is also a potential problem. LBO firms tend to be relatively undiversified and from mature industries. The process of diversification, especially from a SINGLE BUSINESS STRATEGY or a DOMINANT BUSINESS STRATEGY, suffers a high failure rate. Furthermore, as LBOs revert to private status, results reporting becomes much less transparent than with publicly owned concerns, increasing the risk to lenders.

Bibliography

Diamond, S. C. (Ed.). (1985). *Leveraged buyouts*. Homewood, IL: Dow Jones Irwin.

Law, W. A. (1988). Leveraged buyouts. In J. P. Williamson (Ed.), *Investment banking handbook*. New York: John Wiley.

Shaked, M. A. (1986). *Takeover madness*. New York: John Wiley. See chapter 3.

DEREK F. CHANNON

life cycle strategy An alternative to the "growth share" and "market attractiveness competitive position" portfolio models was developed by Arthur D. Little Inc. (hereafter, ADL) based on the concept of the life cycle as illustrated in figure 1. As with the other portfolio models, the ADL approach first identifies the life cycle position of a business as a descriptor of industry characteristics. Second, the competitive strength of a business is represented by six categories (dominant, strong, favorable, tenable, weak, and nonviable). The combination of these two variables is illustrated in figure 2 as a six by four matrix, on which the position of each business unit suggests a number of logical strategic alternatives, as shown. In using this

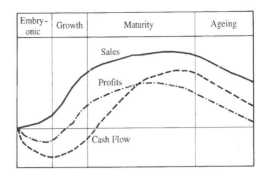

Figure 1   Yearly sales, cashflow, and profits through the industry life cycle stages.
Source: Arthur D. Little Inc.

system the corporation is first segmented into a series of relatively independent business units. Second, the life cycle position of each business is carefully assessed (note that the product life cycle need not necessarily be the same as the business life cycle). Third, the competitive position of each business is carefully assessed.

The label "strategy center" was assigned by ADL to each business that others had defined as a strategic business unit (*see* SBU STRUCTURE). To reach their conclusions on strategy centers, ADL defined them in terms of competitors, prices, customers, quality/style, substitutability, and divestment or liquidation. The first four of these indicate that a strategy center contains a specific set of products for which it faces a specific set of customers and competitors which are also affected by price, quality and style change. Moreover, all products within a strategy center should be close substitutes for one another. A strategy center could also probably survive as an independent business if divested.

The position of a business within its industry life cycle is determined by eight factors. These descriptions are market growth rate, market growth potential, breadth of product lines, number of competitors, distribution of market share among competitors, customer loyalty, barriers to entry, and technology, as illustrated in table 1. Strategy centers do not usually fall into a single life cycle phase for every descriptor, and some judgement therefore needs to be made as to the overall life cycle position of a business. Embryonic businesses are usually characterized by high growth, rapid

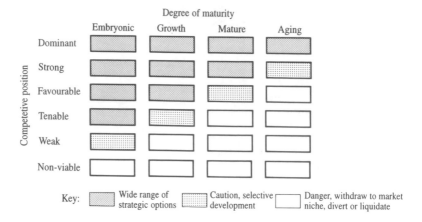

Figure 2   The life cycle portfolio matrix
Arthur D. Little Inc.

technological change, pursuit of a rapidly widening range of customers, fragmented and changing shares of market, and new competitor entries. By contrast, a mature industry is characterized by stability in known customers, technology, and market shares, with well established and identifiable competitors. Interestingly, it is sometimes possible, usually as a result of technological change, to convert mature or emerging industries back into embryonic industries. For example, in motor insurance, Direct Line Insurance has transformed the industry over only eight years by selling policies direct and achieving a growth rate of *c*.70 per cent per annum against the background of a relatively static growth rate for the industry as a whole. Most industries, however, work through the life cycle on a steady basis.

The competitive position of a business is assessed by ADL via a series of qualitative factors rather than the use of quantitative factors such as relative market share. Five categories of competitive position are identified: dominant, strong, favorable, tenable, and weak. The sixth position – nonviable – demands immediate or rapid exit. A dominant position is rare, and comes about because a competitor has managed to establish a quasi-monopoly or has achieved technological dominance. Such positions could be claimed by IBM in computers and Kodak in color film. However, both positions have come under attack in recent years. IBM has failed to

dominate the personal computer market which, because of technological advances, has become an increasing threat to IBM's core mainframe computer business. Similarly, Kodak has begun to face a major threat from electronic digital imaging in its core business of amateur color film, a silver halide based "wet" process activity. A "strong" business, by contrast, enjoys a definite advantage over competitors, usually with a relative market share of greater than 1.5 times. "Favorable" means that a business usually enjoys a unique characteristic; for example, dominance of a specific niche, access to dedicated raw materials, or a special relationship with an important distribution channel. A tenable position means that the firm has the facilities to remain within a market but has no distinctive competence. Nevertheless, the position is such that survival is not a serious issue. Finally, a weak position is not tenable in the long term. Such businesses should either be developed to a more acceptable position or exited.

For portfolio balance using the life cycle model, the firm needs a balanced mix of activities, with mature businesses generating a positive cashflow that can be used to support embryonic or growth operations. Success is also determined by having as many businesses as possible in dominant or favorable positions.

Once the portfolio of businesses has been determined, ADL has developed three further aids to assist managers of strategy centers in

Table 1   Factors affecting the stage of the industry life cycle for a strategy center.

Descriptors	Stages of industry (maturity)			
	Embryonic	Growth	Mature	Ageing
Growth rate				
Industry potential				
Product line				
Number of competitors				
Market share stability				
Purchasing patterns				
Ease of entry				
Technology				
OVERALL				

Source: Arthur D. Little, Inc.

formulating strategy. The first of these concepts was labeled by ADL as *families of thrusts*. The consultants agreed that there were four families of activities which covered the spectrum of business development. These were "natural development," "selective development," "prove viability," and "withdrawal." The fit of each of these families is indicated in figure 3. A "natural development" position is likely to represent a position at industry maturity with a strong, competitive position which, as a result, justifies strong support to maintain or enhance the strategic position. A "selective development" strategy implies concentration of resources into attractive industry segments or where the firm has destructive competitive advantage. "Prove viability" status requires management to come up with a strategy that enhances strategic position or exit. "Withdrawal" clearly suggests exit, the speed of which needs to be clarified to avoid undue haste.

Having identified the family of strategic thrust that is most appropriate for a specific business, management is now challenged to select a specific strategic thrust for the business.

For example, the following thrusts have been applied to the natural development family:

- *Start-up* could be applied in an embryonic stage business to achieve a high share position while the market growth is high.

- *Growth with industry* applies when the firm is content with its industry position and seeks to maintain market share. This position prevails under dominant or strong conditions and at industry maturity.

- *Gain position gradually* is a stance that is applicable when a modest share increase is required to consolidate industry position.

- *Gain position aggressively* is similar to the double or quit position or question mark business. The firm seeks to aggressively build share in an attractive industry while the growth rate remains high.

- *Defend position* applies when the firm already enjoys a dominant or strong position. As part of a defensive strategy, spending should be at whatever level is necessary to maintain the existing position. The relative cost of defense tends to be much lower for industry leaders

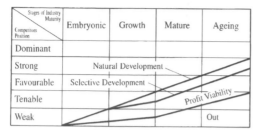

Figure 3 Natural strategic thrusts.
Source: Arthur D. Little, Inc.

Table 2 Grouping of generic strategies by main areas of concern.

Marketing strategies

F	Export/same product
I	Initial market penetration
L	Market penetration
O	New products/new markets
P	New products/same markets
T	Same product/new markets
II	*Integration strategies*
A	Backward integration
G	Forward integration
III	*Go overseas strategies*
B	Development of overseas business
C	Development of overseas production facilities
J	Licensing abroad
IV	*Logistic strategies*
D	Distribution rationalization
E	Excess capacity
M	Market rationalization
Q	Production rationalization
R	Product line rationalization
V	*Efficiency strategies*
N	Methods and functions efficiency
V	Technological efficiency
W	Traditional cost cutting efficiency
VI	*Market strategies*
H	Hesitation
K	Little jewel
S	Pure survival
U	Maintenance
X	Unit abandonment

Source: Arthur D. Little, Inc. (1974)

than for attackers, due to ECONOMIES OF SCALE and ECONOMIES OF SCOPE.

- *Harvest* is relevant at all stages of the life cycle. The key factor for consideration is the speed of harvest. From a strong position, harvesting may be slow, with the cashflows generated being deployed more effectively in newer businesses. Rapid harvesting occurs from positions of strategic weakness and may imply strategies of sale or closure.

The third concept developed by ADL is that of generic strategy (not to be confused with Porter's concept, which is discussed elsewhere). ADL conceived 24 generic strategies, which were then grouped into a series of subcategories as shown in table 2. The three concepts of families, strategic thrusts, and generic strategies were then linked into an overall matrix to demonstrate strategic position.

In the ADL methodology, the position of a business in the life cycle impacts upon its financial performance. A tool used by ADL to assess this is the ronagraph which is illustrated in figure 4. This shows, on the vertical axis, the return on net assets (RONA) generated by each business in the corporate portfolio and, on the horizontal axis, the internal deployment of cashflows. At 100 per cent all cash generated is redeployed within the business, which thus becomes cash neutral. Above 100 per cent the business becomes a cash user, while below 100 per cent a business is a cash generator. In addition, a negative value implies a divestment strategy. On the ronagraph each business unit is represented by a circle, the area of which is proportional to the net investment attached to the business.

In addition to RONA, a number of other indicators are also expected to reflect industry maturity. These include profit after tax, net assets, net working capital/sales, fixed costs/sales, variable costs/sales, profit after tax/sales, and net cashflow/sales.

The final step in the ADL methodology consists of assessing the level of risk associated with a business unit strategy. This involved a substantial level of subjectivity, but ADL have

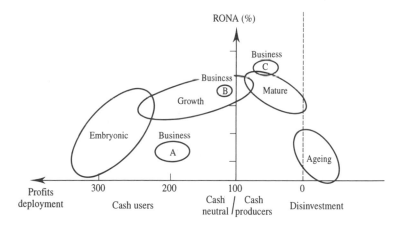

Figure 4   A typical ronagraph
Source: Arthur D. Little Inc.

identified a number of factors which contribute to such risk, including the following:

- *Maturity and competitive position* – derived from the position of the business within the life cycle matrix. The greatest risk occurs for embryonic businesses with a weak market position, and the lowest for a business with a dominant position in a mature industry.
- *Industry* – some are much less predictable than others at the same stage of maturity.
- *Strategy* – aggressive strategies tend to be inherently more risky.
- *Assumptions* – future predictions enjoy varying degrees of probability and hence greater or lesser degrees of risk.
- *Past performance* – while the past is no necessary predictor of the future, stable historic records tend to be less risky than no records or inconsistent ones.
- *Management* – historic management performance counts, although this can be subject to change by events such as mid-life crisis, illness, and the like.
- *Performance improvement* – the gap between actual and predicted performance is also important. Dramatic improvements tend to be much more risky than gradual extensions of existing performance.

While the ADL model is a useful addition to the range of portfolio models, like the others it needs to be used with care. Criticisms of the approach include, first, the usefulness of the life cycle approach, which has been challenged by many as to its validity. Second, where a life cycle can be accepted, the stages of each position vary widely in terms of time. Third, industry activity does not necessary evolve into a well behaved S-curve. Markets can be rejuvenated and maturity can become growth through changes in fundamental industry characteristics. Firms can also fundamentally transform life cycle positions by innovation and repositioning. Finally, the nature of competition varies greatly from industry to industry. Thus fragmented industries may concentrate, while others go in the other direction. Automobiles, for example, have concentrated; while personal computers have moved from fragmentation to concentration and back to fragmentation in the short time interval of around 20 years. Nevertheless, used wisely, the life cycle portfolio model provides a useful addition to the development of the strategic management tool kit.

Bibliography

Arthur D. Little Inc. (1974). *A system for managing diversity.* Cambridge, MA: Arthur D. Little Inc. December.

Arthur D. Little Inc. (1980). *A management system for the 1980s.* San Francisco: Arthur D. Little Inc.

Hax, A. C. & Majluf, N. (1984). *Strategic management.* Englewood Cliffs, NJ: Prentice-Hall. See pp. 182–206.

DEREK F. CHANNON

M

manufacturing strategy   Key decisions in this area fall into two categories:

- *Structure*: relating to the size and shape of the manufacturing facilities. Decisions in this area concern major investment decisions, the "hardware" of manufacturing strategy.
- *Infrastructure*: decisions relating to the systems and organization of running the manufacturing function. The combined effect of decisions in this area can be just as difficult and long-term to change as decisions in the structural area.

A framework for developing a manufacturing strategy is shown in table 1.

Order-winning Criteria

Hill (1985) did much to develop this concept. Order-winning criteria (OWC) relate to column 3 in table 1.

Products gain advantage in the marketplace as a result of features which are better than those of the competition. The identification of such features (OWC) by marketing helps to set objectives that other business functions should meet. The responsibility for meeting such OWC is not always that of manufacturing alone. Some examples of OWC are described below.

Price.   If marketing can define target prices, then other functions are given an objective:

costs = price − profit.

Apart from controling material overhead and labor costs, manufacturing can also plan for reduced costs by process innovation. Designing the product and its delivery system for low-cost manufacture and control can provide further payoffs.

Product quality and reliability.   This OWC has been used by Japanese manufacturers of many different product ranges to win orders from Western competitors. Price and design aspects are little different. Sony is still cautious about publicizing the fact that its color televisions are made in San Diego rather than in Japan.

Delivery speed.   Orders may be won by an ability to respond to customer requirements more quickly than the competition. Lead time reduction in make-to-order businesses (and in others) is often a major strategy objective.

Delivery speed in make-to-stock businesses is often achieved at the expense of high finished product inventories. Customer service and corporate objectives can, however, be enhanced by reduced throughput times and greater manufacturing flexibility.

Delivery reliability.   A company's reputation, and therefore its ability to win orders, can be greatly enhanced by consistently delivering the products by the date specified by the customer. Manufacturing considerations include capacity planning, scheduling, and inventory control.

Product range and color range.   In some markets, orders are won because the product range (and/or color range) are broader than those of the competition. Increased product range rapidly increases the complexity of the manufacturing task; but if it is necessary, then plans must be developed to achieve this objective more economically than in other businesses.

Design leadership.   As a result of design innovation, the company's products may win orders because they perform better, or perhaps because they are the only products capable of performing a needed function. Manufacturing's role here is to support such design leadership by

Table 1 Framework for developing manufacturing strategy.

Business objectives	Marketing strategy	How do products win orders in the marketplace?	Manufacturing strategy	
			Structure	Infrastructure
Sales	Products: • launches • enhancements • terminations	Price Quality	Capacity: • amount • timing • type	Workforce: • skills • rewards • security
Profitability	• range	Delivery: • speed • reliability	Facilities: • size • location • focus	Organization: • structure • control systems
Return on capital employed	Volumes			
	Level of customization	Color range		
Other financial measures		Product range	Process choice	Quality
	Market segments	JIT capability	Vertical integration: • direction • extent • balance	Production and materials control: • sourcing • systems
		Existing supplier		
		Design leadership		New product development Performance measurement systems

Source: after Hill, and Hayes and Wheelwright (1985).

developing new in-house production processes and skills.

Qualifying criteria. Any of the above OWC can change to something which is subtly different: qualifying criteria. These simply qualify the product to be in the marketplace at all. For example, manufacturers of 750 kV transformers who have not supplied working installations in their own countries will not qualify for export tenders, even if they claim to have design technology. Similarly, it is pointless to attempt to enter the toiletries market seriously without a wide product range. Qualifying criteria enable a product to enter or stay in a market; competitive products already possess such criteria.

If price is not the major order-winning criterion, then this does not mean that a company may charge what it likes. Price exploitation must be kept within limits; otherwise, a qualifying criterion may become an order-losing criterion. An important task for marketing is to identify criteria that are order-losing sensitive.

Regular reviews of the manufacturing strategy help to insure its relevance to corporate needs and to the strategic direction. Here, manufacturing strategy decision categories are checked regularly against each other and tested against "How do products win orders. . . ?". At each reiteration, the manufacturing strategy is more comprehensive and better understood. This process often identifies a demand for improvements in the company's marketing strategy!

Taking stock. In table 1 it is proposed that manufacturing strategy can be developed in logical steps. Once business objectives and the marketing strategy (columns 1 and 2) have been developed, then the following further action is needed:

- Marketing analyses OWC and qualifying criteria for each product family.

- A detailed profile is produced to identify current key manufacturing and design capabilities. This should cover each product family, and relate to each division or facility of the company. It will cover aspects such as special skills and capacity for each product line.

Using the manufacturing/design profile, it is possible to conduct a review against marketing requirements in detail. Further valuable information would include:

- an assessment of current and future competitors worldwide, and their capability to manufacture products

- an assessment of potential improvements in process technology

From the marketing review and such additional considerations, a target manufacturing position relative to the competition should be identified as part of the business plan. The constraints in terms of manufacturing structure and infrastructure also need to be assessed.

Implementing manufacturing strategy. Having determined the manufacturing contribution to the business strategy, that position should be formalized through specific goals, such as the following:

- reduce the lead time for product A from four weeks to two weeks by the end of 1996

- increase the inventory turnover from 2 × to 5 × over the next two years

These objectives will be supported by a plan of how they will be achieved, as shown in table 1. The plan will cover the major elements of manufacturing strategy shown in table 2. It will

Table 2   Manufacturing strategy presentation.

1. Corporate strategy
2. Product strategy
3. Market priorities

  - now

  - future

4. The plant:

  - general layout and process flow

  - management control data

  - human resources
    - special risks
    - reward systems

  - inventory

  - production and material control systems

  - quality

  - process automation opportunities

  Plant profile:

  - capacity by product family

  - focus

  - vertical integration

5. Review of how well manufacturing supports current and future needs
6. Team meetings

  - action plan development

7. Team presentations
8. Summary comments and guidelines for follow on assignments (accountability, target dates)

be a formal document, circulated to the key contributors. Action will include:

- creating management awareness and commitment

- prioritizing the tasks and assigning responsibilities

- training employees

The manufacturing strategy will be reviewed regularly (say, every six months). Major changes will only be made if fundamental business factors have altered.

Bibliography

Garvin, D. A. (1988). *Managing quality*. New York: The Free Press.

Hayes, R. W. & Wheelwright, S. C. (1984). *Restoring our competitive edge – competing through manufacturing*. New York: John Wiley.

Hill, T. (1985). *Manufacturing strategy*. London: Macmillan.

ALAN HARRISON

market share   Widely believed to be a critical factor in the determination of competitive position, many firms focus on the achievement of market share gain as a critical strategic factor. However, great care must be exercised in the pursuit of market share. In the Boston Consulting Group model, the GROWTH SHARE MATRIX relative market share is used as a surrogate for cumulative production volume, a critical term in experience effect analysis (*see* EXPERIENCE AND LEARNING EFFECTS). It is assumed that the higher the level of market share is, the more a firm will have produced of a particular product. The firm with the highest relative share should therefore enjoy a lower cost than its smaller rivals (assuming that all firms are on the same experience curve). As defined in the BCG model, relative market share is the share of the firm subdivided by that of the largest single competitor. By definition, therefore, only one firm within a market can enjoy a relative share greater than one. The widespread awareness and adoption of this model has contributed to the belief in the importance of market share. Note, however, that the model refers to *relative share*, not absolute share.

The PIMS model makes use of two market share terms; namely, absolute share and relative share. The PIMS definition of relative share is also different: it is the share of the business under analysis divided by the sum of the shares of the three largest competitors. The PIMS model's use of absolute share also avoids the problem with use of the BCG model in that it has little meaning in fragmented industries. The PIMS model also argues that market share, although a significant variable in the determina-tion of profitability, is actually a derived variable and that relative product quality is its driver. PIMS clearly supports the BCG contention that market share is an important determinant of business profitability. In the PIMS model, however, it is but one of a large number of variables. Moreover, for the variable to be of value, clear market identification is essential. While PIMS uses two market share terms in its analysis, it also emphasizes product quality, productivity, and capital intensity. As a result, making use of these latter variables it is possible to eliminate the advantage of high market share. Japanese competitors have been especially successful at utilizing these variables as a way of countering the volume advantage of US-based competitors in industries, such as machine tools, automobiles, and electronics.

A major problem with the use of market share is its difficulty in measurement. First, it is essential to define exactly what the market is before a firm's share can be measured. This is actually extremely difficult in practice. The PIMS model expends great effort in defining the SERVED MARKET of a business. This is usually some combination of product, customer, and geography that a business chooses to serve. Serious problems of definition can, however, still occur. Moreover, market boundaries can and do shift. For example, in the early 1980s the US General Electric company believed itself to be in a strong market share position in the USA in product areas such as consumer electronics and appliances. While this was true, these markets were in the process of globalizing, and if a global market definition had been adopted GE's position would have been recognized as much weaker. In some industries such as retailing, the correct market share is also extremely difficult to select. This could, for example, refer to national position, regional position, or that immediately surrounding an individual store.

While market share is therefore seen to be important, great care must be exercised in its definition and usage as a strategic variable. Nevertheless, different levels of market share have been shown to suggest alternate operating strategies. Businesses can thus be defined as high, medium, and low market share concerns.

Dependent upon the position of a business, different strategies are suggested.

Strategies for High-share Competitors

While high market share does often generate lower costs in high experience effect markets, this may not always be the case. For example, although Kodak enjoys a worldwide volume advantage over Fuji Film, the latter is the lower-cost producer. Nevertheless, industry leaders are often able to maintain their position, especially when they control activities such as distribution and promotion. Three contrasting strategic positions have been identified for industry leaders:

1. *Stay on the offensive.* Under this strategy, the best offense is the best defense. Leadership and competitive advantage is sustained by achieving FIRST MOVER ADVANTAGE through continuous innovation and improvement. This forces competitors to adopt follow-on strategies. It also provides the possibility of locking up distribution channels and increasing customer switching costs.
2. *Fortify and defend.* This strategy attempts to build barriers to entry for competitors (*see* BARRIERS TO ENTRY AND EXIT). The range of possible specific actions includes:

- raising the cost structure of competitors, as a result of increased promotion, customer service, and R&D

- introducing alternative brands to match competitor product attributes

- increasing customer switching costs

- broadening the product line to maximize store shelf space, to reduce competitor distribution capacity, and to fill niche positions

- introducing fighting brands to maximize price range offering

- adding capacity ahead of the market to try to deter capacity investment, especially by smaller competitors

- driving for experience gains as a result of greater cumulative production volume

- patenting alternate technologies

- signing up exclusivity deals with key suppliers and distributors

This strategy is best for companies with a strong dominance position that are not subject to monopolies legislation. Such a business may well be a CASH COW but can be maintained with a long-term future by continuous adequate investment to maintain position. The critical danger from this strategy is the risk of flanking attacks which endeavor to shift the grounds on which the business is founded.

3. *Follow the leader.* This strategy forces small-share competitors to conform to policies established by the industry leader. Clear signals are established for weaker competitors by: rapid responses to price attacks; heavy promotion spend when challengers threaten; special deals for customers and/or distributors; pressure applied to distributors to reduce competition shelf space availability; and the poaching of key competitor personnel from competitors attacking the leader. On occasion, such behavior can breach ethical standards, and care must be taken to insure that grounds for legal attack by smaller competitors are not provided. The "dirty tricks" campaign by British Airways against Virgin is a classic recent example, in which the industry leader, exasperated by the success of its smaller rival, adopted illegal tactics to try to limit Virgin's progress.

Strategies for Medium-share Competitors

Most product markets tend to be at least oligopolistic. Many have multiple competitors. As a result, most competitors are not industry leaders but, rather, medium-share concerns. Despite their medium-share positions, such businesses may operate a number of wholly viable strategies that are profitable and attractive. Some such companies operate as fierce challengers to industry leaders, while others appear content to accept their subordinate position. Those firms keen to strengthen their strategic position are recommended to adopt the indirect approach rather than engage in head-on confrontation.

In industries in which a substantial experience effect prevails, low-share competitors need to achieve similar cost positions by tactics such as lower capital intensity, higher productivity, use of debt leverage, and superior product quality. Alternately, such firms should aim to achieve differentiation by technological leadership, alternate distribution systems, re-segmentation of the market, and reconfiguration of the value chain. Where ECONOMIES OF SCALE or experience effects are more limited, the strategic options open to medium-share firms are greater and include the following:

1. *Vacant niche.* Such a strategy involves focusing on customer segments that have been neglected by industry leaders. Ideally, such niches should be sufficiently large to justify specialization in product development, distribution, and the like, and to provide profitable opportunities. Such niches might include health foods in the food industry, feeder and commuter airlines, specialist magazines, and investment and insurance products targeted at the middle aged.

2. *Specialist.* This strategy focuses on supplying the needs of specific market segments. Competitive advantage is gained through the differentiation achieved by specialization. Examples include Apple Computers in desktop publishing, Hewlett Packard in specialist calculators, and Baxters in speciality soups.

3. *Superior quality.* This strategy combines segment and/or product differentiation coupled with "superior" quality, where quality is based on customer perception. Customers are then prepared to pay higher prices for such product offerings. Examples include specialist foods from Marks and Spencer, Chivas Regal Whisky, Smirnoff Vodka, Wedgwood china, and branded perfumes.

4. *Passive follower.* Many medium-ranking competitors are content to maintain follower positions behind established industry leaders. Their strategies do not seek confrontation but react to the leader's moves rather than initiating attack policies. Under such stable market conditions – especially as growth slows, but does not drift into decline – medium-ranking competitors are able to maintain satisfactory levels of profitability.

5. *Growth via acquisition.* One strategy to rapidly strengthen market position is by the acquisition of or merger with competitors (*see* ACQUISITION STRATEGY). Such moves may rapidly create high-share positions and reap economies of scale. Industries which have undergone such restructuring include pharmaceuticals, brewing, airlines, heavy chemicals, accountancy, global media, and the like. The dangers in such a strategy stem largely from problems of integration, especially in supposed mergers, where potential clashes between the cultures of new partners may result in dysfunctional behavior.

Despite their nonleadership position, medium-ranked businesses often enjoy attractive profits and established market positions. In the food and drink product sectors for example, food distributors offer at least two branded products, not least to maintain pressure on industry leaders. In many industrial and other consumer product areas, this is also the case. The handicap of lower market size can thus be circumvented by: segment-focused strategies in which price confrontation is avoided; superior technical and quality positions; lower costs, through reduced capital intensity and superior productivity; strategies which reinforce differences from the industry leader; and a focus on alternative distribution strategies and differentiation in advertising and promotion.

Strategies for Low-share Businesses

A number of strategic options are open to businesses with low-share positions. When a low-share position is coupled with low growth or a high cost of product development, unless the parent company can afford to attack and gain share by market means or acquisition, harvesting or rapid exit strategies seem to be recommended.

When it is possible, harvesting maximizes the cash that can be extracted from such a business. Under such a strategy, all unnecessary expenditure is cut, R&D is minimized, and new investment is limited to the maintenance of operations, provided that shareholder value is not destroyed. Prices are raised or maintained rather than cut in a tradeoff of market share for cashflow. A number of indicators have been identified of when a harvesting strategy seems most appropriate:

- in industries with unattractive long-term prospects

- when growing share would be too expensive and insufficiently profitable

- when market share defense is too expensive

- when share is not dependent on the maintenance of competitive effort

- when resources can be deployed elsewhere to improve shareholder value

- when the business is not critical to core activities

- when the business does not add special features to the corporation's overall portfolio

Bibliography

Buzzell, R. D., Gale, B. T. & Sutton, R. G. (1975). Market share – a key to profitability. *Harvard Business Review*, **53**, 97–108.
Buzzell, R. D. & Gale, B. T. (1987). *The PIMS principles*. New York: The Free Press. See chapter 9.
Hammermesh, R. B., Anderson, M. J. & Harris, J. E. (1978). Strategies for low market share businesses. *Harvard Business Review*, **56**, 95–103.
Kotler, P. (1978). Harvesting strategies for weak products. *Business Horizons*, **21** (5).
Kotler, P. (1978). *Marketing management*. Englewood Cliffs, NJ: Prentice-Hall. See pp. 397–412.
Porter, M. E. (1985). *Competitive advantage: creating and sustaining superior performance*. New York: The Free Press. See chapter 15.
Thompson, A. & Strickland A. J. (1993). *Strategic management*, 7th edn. New York: Irwin. See pp. 226–68.
Woo, C. Y. & Cooper, A. C. (1982). The surprising case for low market share. *Harvard Business Review*, **60**, 106–13.

DEREK F. CHANNON

matrix structure Often found in complex multinationals, matrix structures involve a combination of geography and product, as illustrated in figure 1.

In multinational corporations that have multiple product lines, country organizations will normally have a manager, and may operate production units and certain sales and marketing teams for the corporation's product groups sold in that country. However, product divisions, to which geographic management will be subordinate, will tend to set strategy for each worldwide product division as a whole. Reporting relationships are therefore complex, with many executives reporting to more than one central unit.

Country managers report primarily to the area management and are responsible overall for the activities of the corporation within a specific country. They will also usually act as the corporation's representative for external affairs within a country. Each country may be treated as a profit center, but under some matrix systems and for a variety of reasons (for example, tax treatment, location of high-cost facilities or services, and the like), the maximization of profitability by country may well be subordinate to regional or global product and profit considerations. In multinational corporations the management of international tax is especially important, as is management of the exchange rate risk.

Below the country manager level, operations tend to be divided by product group. The management of such groups have dual reporting relationships to the country manager and to their own product divisions. In many matrix structures the latter relationship overrides the former, again increasing the difficulty of assessing country units on a pure profit basis. In the banking industry, for example, the use of worldwide account teams to service key global customers may well result in the sacrifice of profitability in one country in order to provide a superior customer service worldwide. Similarly, banks relinquish profits on scarce risk lending capacity in difficult countries in order to provide such capacity to selected worldwide key account customers at lower rates.

In general, the importance of the geographic component of matrix structures has diminished over time, and in some companies the position of an overall country manager has disappeared, with each main product division operating as a global business in its own right. Matrix structures are complex and difficult to manage. There is frequent rivalry between the perceived interests of geographic units and product groups. The general trend, however, has been

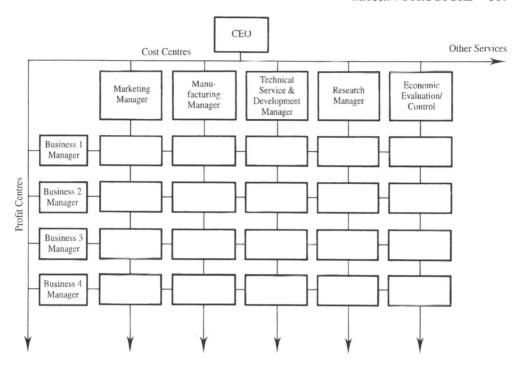

Figure 1 The form of a matrix organization.

that the greater the degree of overseas product diversity, the more likely it has been that product considerations take precedence.

A specific problem that has affected corporations operating multinational matrix structures has been the dominance of headquarters operations staffed predominantly by home country nationals in attempting to set the strategies of overseas subsidiaries. Where domestic product groups have attempted to set global strategy, there has often tended to be a lack of knowledge of overseas conditions, and policies have often been established on the basis of domestic conditions. This is especially true of US multinationals, but also applies to MNCs from other countries – most recently to the emerging Japanese MNCs. While, clearly, the US domestic market is usually paramount, the failure to appreciate international conditions and to allow non-US nationals sufficiently strong geographic inputs into policy making has often led to the growth of overseas competition that has proved damaging. The contrast with Japanese corporations in this respect is marked. Japanese corporations very carefully examine local mar-

kets and design strategies to meet local product needs and minimize political friction, although foreigners have not been significantly accepted by these corporations.

The Japanese have also structurally attempted to coordinate not merely by product and geography but also by function. In this, production especially is coordinated on a worldwide basis and cross-functional product divisional teams endeavor to insure that any interdivisional rivalries are minimized, while gains made in one division are transferred rapidly to others. This elimination of rivalries leads to cooperation in the production of hybrid products, using fusion technology to cut across divisional boundaries. Marketing is less coordinated on a worldwide basis and localized marketing strategies may well be used. By contrast, in many Western companies operating a DIVISIONAL STRUCTURE and/or an SBU STRUCTURE, the boundaries between divisions or SBUs may well make such cooperation difficult, especially when reward structures are based on unit rather than corporate performance. In such circumstances sharing profits or accepting costs from another unit may apparently diminish unit performance despite actually or potentially improving overall corporate results.

Bibliography

Bartlett, C. A., Bartlett, A. & Sumantra, G. (1990). Matrix management not a structure, a frame of mind. *Harvard Business Review*, **68** (4), 138–45.

Davis, S. M. & Lawrence, P. R. (1978). Problems of matrix organisations. *Harvard Business Review*, **56** (3), 131–42.

Galbraith, J. R. (1971). Matrix organisational designs. *Business Horizons*, **15** (1), 29–40.

DEREK F. CHANNON

MBWA (management by walking about)

This style of management is identified with corporate excellence. Leaders adopting MBWA do not wholly rely upon bureaucratic reporting systems but see for themselves, in one way or another, how the corporation actually works by personally meeting staff and customers.

These informal channels involve talking to customers and suppliers, listening to junior employees, and making regular on-site visits. This enables the leadership to avoid receiving filtered and sterilized information which otherwise may come through the conventional reporting procedures.

There are many examples of organizations in which MBWA has proved to be successful:

- Marks and Spencer directors regularly pay surprise visits to stores to observe operations at first hand and to meet customers.

- Apple Computer directors regularly man customer complaints telephones to gauge customer reactions at first hand.

- Japanese companies provide expenses for regular superior–subordinate beer nights, to allow criticisms to be voiced without fear.

- McDonalds founder Ray Kroc regularly visited store units and did his own personal inspection on Q.S.C. and V. (Quality, Service, Cleanliness, and Value).

- At Hewlett-Packard there are weekly "beer busts" in each division, attended by both

executives and employees, to create a regular opportunity to improve communications.

Such managers maintain their "feel" for a business which otherwise might disappear with increases in size, which bring with them increased bureaucracy and isolation.

Bibliography

Peters, T. J. & Peters, N. (1985). *A passion for excellence*. New York: Random House. See chapters 2, 3, and 19.

Thompson, A. & Strickland A. J. (1993). *Strategic management*, 7th edn. New York: Irwin. See pp. 226–68.

DEREK F. CHANNON

McKinsey 7S model

While, historically, a relationship was established between strategy and structure, the concept has been broadened by McKinsey and Company to encompass a framework linking strategy and a number of other critical variables. It has been argued that the strategy–structure model is an inadequate description of critical elements in the successful implementation of strategy, and that a successful "fit" between those elements and corporate strategy is essential to insure successful implementation. The McKinsey model is illustrated in figure 1.

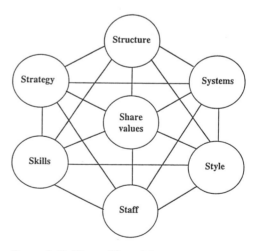

Figure 1 McKinsey 7S model.
Source: Waterman et al. (1980).

McKinsey and Company believe that there are seven broad areas which need to be integrated to achieve overall successful strategy implementation. Apart from strategy itself and formal organizational structure, the other variables that they have identified are as follows: shared values, attitudes, and philosophy; staffing and the people orientation of the corporation; administrative systems; practices and procedures used to administer the organization, including the reward and sanction systems; organizational skills, capabilities, and core competencies; and the management style of the corporation as set by its leadership. This model is called by McKinsey the 7S framework.

Structure

In the McKinsey model, it is argued that while formal structure is important, dividing up the organizational task is not the critical structural problem: rather, it is developing the ability to focus on those dimensions that are currently important to the evolution of the corporation, and being ready to refocus as critical dimensions shift.

Systems

By systems, McKinsey and Company mean the procedures, formal and informal, which make the organization work. It is important to understand how the organisation actually works: it is often reliant on informal rather than formal systems.

Style

Although it is often underestimated, management style, and especially that of the CEO, is an important determinant in what is strategically possible for the corporation.

Staff

In the McKinsey model, the nature of the people factor is broadened and redefined. Consideration of people as a pool of resources, who need to be nurtured, developed, guarded, and allocated, is seen to turn this dimension into a variable that needs to be given close attention by top management.

Skills

Given a chosen strategy, this variable enables the corporation to evaluate its capabilities realistically in the light of the critical factors required for success. One particular problem may actually be in weeding out old skills, which can be a significant block to necessary change and can prevent the development of new skills.

Shared values

At the core of the model are superordinate goals and shared values around which the organization pivots. These values define the organization's key beliefs and aspirations and form the core of its corporate culture. Corporations needing to change their values endeavor to undergo dramatic transformations which involve fundamental reappraisals of all aspects of activities. Sometimes such changes are introduced as re-engineering projects (*see* RE-ENGINEERING DISADVANTAGES; VALUE-DRIVEN RE-ENGINEEERING). A major reason for the high failure rate of these projects is their lack of success in implanting new shared values that can embrace the radical changes required to achieve the dramatic stretch targets set by such programs.

Bibliography

Waterman, R. (1982). The seven elements of strategic fit. *Journal of Business Strategy*, no. 3, 68–72.
Waterman, R., Peters, T. & Phillips, J. (1980). Structure is not organisation. *The McKinsey Quarterly*, summer, 2–20.

DEREK F. CHANNON

mission   The "mission" of a company is an important element in establishing the strategy of the organization. Establishing the mission itself is usually a difficult and demanding task. Top management tends to agonize for long periods of time over the development of a mission statement: the process involves negotiation and compromise, but is usually leadership led – and depends upon a critical input from the CEO. Surprisingly, perhaps, despite all the effort expended, many mission statements tend to seem full of platitudes and motherhood statements.

Mission statements need to be communicated throughout the organization. Top management must also demonstrate their importance by "living" them as an example. In this way a

clear mission statement can become an important inspiration to employees and can lead to
commitment and loyalty to the corporation.
Once established, missions are difficult to
change, as they become critical ingredients in
the corporate culture. For example, IBM has
attempted to change its mission several times,
but the critical elements established by the
company's founder, Thomas Watson, still
encourage the IBM sales function to attempt
to achieve "quota" by the year end, rather than
seeking to provide customers with "solutions",
or to promote nonmainframe sales.

Good mission statements tend to be simple
and easy to understand at all levels of the
organization. They stimulate enthusiasm and
commitment amongst employees; they are
challenging; they are short and easily absorbed
and accepted; and they are frequently repeated.
For example, in the US General Electric
Company, the mission for each business is to
"be number one or two in the world or sell it,
close it or fix it." Such a statement is readily
understood and memorable.

Many Japanese companies have long emphasized a corporate mission or philosophy. Each
strategic plan, lasting on average three years, has
a clearly identifiable name which is well known
throughout the organization. The key ingredients of such plans are fully communicated
throughout the organization, and employees
take on the corporate mission and values until
such time as the strategy is changed.

A well developed mission statement helps top
management in a number of ways. First, it
crystallizes top management's own view of the
long-term strategic position of the firm. Second,
it helps to insure that the behavior of lower-
order personnel is directed toward achievement
of the corporate mission. Third, it conveys a
message to external stakeholders, such as
financial institutions that may influence their
investment strategies. Fourth, it insures organizational confidence, in that top management
knows where it wishes to drive the corporation.
Fifth, it provides a pathway for establishing
longer-term strategy.

Bibliography

Thompson, A. A. & Strickland, A. J. (1993). *Strategic management*, 7th edn. Homewood, IL: Irwin. See pp. 24–7.

DEREK F. CHANNON

N

Nemoto's principles of leadership In its efforts to embrace Total Quality Management (TQM), Toyota Motor has adopted a number of principles of leadership developed by its managing director, Masao Nemoto. In attempting to introduce quality management and JIT production, he found that many managers adopted styles that conflicted with these objectives. He therefore devised a series of leadership principles, which have now become known as the "Sayings of Nemoto." The principles, set out below, apply especially to senior management who wish to get their associates to adopt TQM methods.

1. *Strive for continuous improvement (see* KAIZEN). Managers should seek ways to continuously improve the work of their employees on a gradual rather than a radical basis and in an atmosphere in which improvement is nonthreatening.
2. *Coordinate between divisions.* Managers of specific divisions, departments, business units, and the like should cooperate rather than compete and must share responsibility. Nemoto goes on to say: "One of the most important functions of a division manager is to import coordination between his own division and other divisions. If you cannot handle this task, please go to work for an American company." In Toyota, much cross-divisional coordination is built in through the use of a CROSS-FUNCTIONAL MANAGEMENT STRUCTURE.
3. *Let everyone speak.* This move guides supervisors of quality circles at Toyota, insuring full participation and learning by all the circle members. It has also been generalized to all meetings and throughout the annual planning process. It is assumed that everyone has a useful contribution to make, that the group can take ownership of any decision, and that top management can make plans that will command the support of all those required to implement them. The concept of employee empowerment has recently been embraced in the West, under re-engineering programs (*see* RE-ENGINEERING DISADVANTAGES; VALUE-DRIVEN RE-ENGINEERING).
4. *Do not scold.* The concept of withholding criticism, or of *not* enforcing power dominance based on executive office, is alien to most managers. At Toyota the policy is for superiors to avoid criticizing and threatening when mistakes are made. In this way, the fear of reporting mistakes is removed and thus corrective action may be taken immediately. An example of this is the "line stop" system, in which all line employees are encouraged to stop the production line when a mistake occurs. In early production runs, therefore, progress tends to be slow, but eventually errors and mistakes are eliminated as a result of management action, allowing dramatic improvements in both productivity and quality.
5. *Make sure that others understand your work.* At Toyota, managers are expected to develop their presentation and communication skills and to teach their associates and subordinates about their activities in order to improve collaboration. In many Western concerns, information is seen as a source of power and is jealously guarded, leading to rivalry and inefficiency.
6. *Rotate the best employees.* As with many Japanese companies, Toyota job rotates its managers to create generalists as distinct from specialists. In the West there is a

strong tendency for business unit managers to keep their best employees, in order to maintain efficiency; while in Toyota the opposite is the case, the company arguing that it gains most in the long run by training its best employees.

7. *A command without a deadline is not a command.* Tasks without an attached deadline are much less likely to be completed. At Toyota, therefore, employees are instructed to ignore reports that are not accompanied by such a time horizon.

8. *Rehearsal is an ideal occasion for training.* Mr Nemoto encouraged managers to focus on the rehearsal of reports and presentations, not just the final event. He argued that such occasions provided an excellent opportunity for increasing skills and improving understanding, because the setting was informal and relaxed.

9. *Inspection is a failure unless top management takes action.* It is argued that management must be seen to prescribe specifications whenever a problem is reported, in order to demonstrate that the observations of problems and their reporting is seen to be an item of importance. Failure to take action diminishes the perceived importance of the process.

10. *Ask subordinates "What can I do for you?"* This process is known at Toyota as "creating an opportunity to be heard at the top." If top management is seen to be willing to help employees with problems, they will be more enthusiastic, more committed, and will take management objectives more seriously.

Bibliography

Masao Nemoto (1987). *Total quality control for management: strategies and tactics from Toyota and Toyota Gosei,* (translated by David Lu). Englewood Cliffs, NJ: Prentice-Hall. See chapter 1.

DEREK F. CHANNON

nonfinancial performance indicators These are measures of performance that do not appear in the company accounts. Although they are called "nonfinancial," this does not mean they have no financial impact. Moreover, it is argued that these are measures that drive financial performance, while financial measures themselves are focused on outcome.

Sales figures, for example, may depend upon a company's ability to deliver their products on time, to meet customer specifications. Similarly, the success of new product development may depend upon a company's ability to get a product to market before competitors. With ever-decreasing product cycles, time and delivery performance are clearly important nonfinancial measures that need to be monitored.

Traditional, financial performance accounting measures, such as return on investment and earnings per share, have been criticized for giving misleading signals, with regard to continuous improvement and innovation. These are activities that today's competitive environment demand (Kaplan & Norton, 1992). It is now important to look beyond a company's financial record, at a broader range of measures. While financial measures worked well in the past, they are out of step with the skills and competencies that companies are trying to master today (Kaplan & Norton, 1992).

As the quality movement gained momentum in the 1980s, it stimulated the development of an array of techniques, as companies saw that quality could be used as a strategic weapon to differentiate themselves from their competitors. They committed substantial resources to developing new measures, such as defect rates, response times, and delivery commitments, to evaluate the performance of their products, services and operations (Eccles, 1991).

According to Eccles, companies need to design their performance measures from scratch. They should begin by asking "Given our strategy, what are the most important measures of performance?" If their strategy is to compete on quality, quality metrics will be needed to support them. Companies need to ask "How do these measures relate to one another?" Defect rate, for example, is a quality measure that is presumed to affect customer satisfaction. Most importantly: "What measures truly predict long-term financial success in our business?" Customer satisfaction? If so, it needs to be measured. Basically, if it matters, the message is to measure it.

In the 1980s, companies that failed to notice a decline in customer satisfaction and the quality of their products, saw their strong financial records deteriorate (Eccles, 1991). While many companies can honestly say they have been carrying out surveys of customer satisfaction for years, it is also true that these surveys were rarely examined at board level. Where companies describe their strategies in terms of customer service, innovation, or the quality of their products and capabilities of their people, nonfinancial measures need to reflect these strategic priorities and be monitored by the board.

In the UK, Bass Brewers Limited developed and implemented some new performance measures in 1993, to reflect their new way of working. They included a broader range of measures to summarize the overall state of health of the company, outside of finance. While quality and customer service, for example, had always been important to the company and had received attention, it was not measured as ratios. These measures are now submitted to the board and have become almost as important as financial statements.

In the past, while quality at Bass was measured throughout the brewing process, the aim was to get the brew right, to meet quality specifications, at the end of the brewing process. There were limits within which the condition of the beer could fall and, as long as the final package fell within those limits eventually, it would pass the quality test. Where beer had to be re-filtered, an extra cost was generated, and so Bass began to look at quality on a "right first time" basis and to measure how often they got it right first time. This is an example of a quality measure that has cost implications. The principle of getting it right first time, eliminating waste and rework, has become much more important to Bass, along with the need to reduce costs in the business.

Current management accounting theory began to be widely criticized following the publication of Johnson & Kaplan's *Relevance lost, the rise and fall of management accounting* (1987). The theme throughout this book is that performance measurement needs to be customer- and market-oriented, to measure external needs, not just internal requirements. It should support the organization's strategy, which needs to be customer-driven.

At the beginning of 1992, IBM UK Limited changed their performance measurement system, to focus on internal and external measures that they felt were important. Their business goals today are driven by five key measures: customer satisfaction, shareholder value, world class quality on the Baldridge scale, employee morale, and a robust balance sheet. These measures represent the interests of their main stakeholders; their customers, their shareholders, their employees, and government.

IBM realize that they have to be customer-driven, that unless they achieve their drive for customer satisfaction and world class quality, they can forget their other measures. A customer service mentality is regarded by IBM as their number one critical success factor. They realize that getting their products to market quickly, working together in teams, and developing a service-based culture will be critical to their success in the future. They believe that performance measurement is fundamental to making their new organizational structure work.

However, measures of customer satisfaction are only important in so far as they ultimately end up as cashflow. Customer satisfaction, for example, may be maximized if a company gives its products away, but of course the company will go out of business. The appropriate balance has to be found, one that attempts to maximize customer satisfaction while at the same time minimizing the cost of providing it.

Following the takeover of United Distillers, by Guinness, in 1986, the company grew faster than it had ever grown before. Their success is largely attributed to the singlemindedness of the Guinness personnel, who quickly agreed that their objective was to make a profit and focused on making their brands more profitable. United Distillers believe that a company has to determine its criteria for success; then it can measure its success on the basis of whether it meets its performance objectives. However, success has to be measured in a commercial sense. At UD, success means making money, because, as they emphasize, if they do not make money they run the risk of being taken over by a company such as Hanson and asset stripped.

While, in the past, the production workers were considered to be the most important, UD brought in more marketing personnel, with an understanding of brands, and they carried out a large amount of qualitative research, to find out what their customers wanted. Thus the company shifted away from being producer-focused, to become more customer-focused.

By being more responsive to their customers' needs and gaining a better understanding of their brand activities, UD was able to hold on to market share, even at a time of changing consumer tastes, increased awareness of health and fitness and changes in fashion and mixing of spirits and they were very successful. They quadrupled the profits of many of their brands and increased overall profit by 28 per cent. This is an example of where responsiveness to customers – not accounting costs – was necessary for competitive excellence in long-term profitability.

Being responsive to customers involves being flexible, reducing lead times, and removing constraints from the business (Johnson, 1992). Nonfinancial performance indicators form part of a broader set of measures, and help to motivate improvements in critical areas of the business to determine the overall health of a company.

Measures that include the quality of a firm's products, the level of service to customers, and the customers' satisfaction with that service, help – together with a range of other measures – to predict a company's long-term performance and strength in the marketplace. The use of a balanced set of measures can motivate break-through improvements in critical areas such as product, process, customer, and market development (Kaplan & Norton, 1993). These factors are crucial to a company's success in the marketplace.

Performance measures need to be grounded in strategic objectives and competitive demands (Kaplan & Norton, 1993). Today, performance measurement is an integral part of the management system. It is no longer the sole responsibility of the accounting function, but the responsibility of everyone in the company.

Bibliography

Eccles, R. (1991). The performance measurement manifesto. *Harvard Business Review*, **69**, 131–7.
Kaplan, R. & Norton, D. (1992). The balanced scorecard – measures that drive performance. *Harvard Business Review* (January–February), 71–9.
Kaplan, R. & Norton, D. (1993). Putting the balanced scorecard to work. *Harvard Business Review*, **71**, 134–47.
Johnson, H. (1992). *Relevance regained, from top-down control to bottom-up empowerment*. New York: The Free Press.
Johnson, H. & Kaplan, R. (1987). *Relevance lost, the rise and fall of management accounting*. Boston, MA: Harvard Business School Press.
Singleton-Green, B. (1993). If it matters, measure it! *Accountancy* (May), 52–3.

KAYE LOVERIDGE

O

organizational culture The interest in organizational culture during the 1980s – to practitioners and researchers alike – was stimulated by two factors. The first of these was the impact of Japanese enterprises in international markets, and the search to identify a possible link between national culture and organizational performance. The second factor was the perceived failure of the "hard S's" – systems, structure, and strategy – to deliver a competitive advantage, and the belief that this elusive success was more a matter of delivering the "soft S's," such as staff, style, and shared values. However, the early attempts to prescribe a specific culture and manipulate cultural change met with little success, and have led to a reappraisal of what the concept of "culture" involves.

Smircich (1983) provides a useful framework for reappraising the concept. She classifies the perspectives of culture as falling into two broad camps. In the first perspective culture is seen as a "product," something an organization "has." In such an approach, organizational culture is deemed to be as capable of classification and manipulation (usually by management). By contrast, in the second perspective organizational culture is regarded as more of a "process," something an organization "is." According to this perspective, "culture" is much more difficult to pin down and pigeon-hole, and does not lend itself to manipulation.

Culture as a "Product"

This perspective generates a spectrum of definitions, ranging from those that emphasize the surface indicators to those that try to tap some deeper meaning. The surface manifestations include definitions such as "how things get done around here," or culture as a "stock of values, beliefs, and norms widely subscribed to by those who work in an organization." In this vein, an influential approach has been Handy's division of cultures into four types: power, role, task, and person (Handy, 1978). Deeper definitions refer more to culture as "mental processes or mindsets characteristic of organizational members."

Hofstede (1990) defines culture as the "software of the mind." His work, conducted in over 50 countries, has concentrated on unearthing national cultural differences and determining how these influence organizational life. He claims that organizations have to confront two central problems: how to distribute power and how to manage uncertainty. He then identifies five value dimensions which, he claims, discriminate between national groups, and which influence the way in which people perceive that an organization should be managed to meet these two key problems. The dimensions are as follows:

- power distance, i.e., the extent to which people accept that power is distributed unequally

- uncertainty avoidance, i.e., the extent to which people feel uncomfortable with uncertainty and ambiguity

- individualism/collectivism, i.e., the extent to which there is a preference for belonging to tightly knit collectives rather than a more loosely knit society

- masculinity/feminity, i.e., the extent to which gender roles are clearly distinct (masculine end of the spectrum) as opposed to those where they overlap (feminine end of the spectrum)

- Confucian dynamism, i.e., the extent to which long-termism or short-termism tends to predominate

Hofstede's work is only based on employees of one organization. Furthermore, the extent to which one country can be said to have an homogeneous culture is .problematic. Nevertheless, Hofstede's work has been highly influential. It attempts to explain why differing national cultural mind-sets will cause difficulties when a manager from one country goes to work abroad. Difficulties can also be predicted when two organizations from countries with different cultural mind-sets attempt to merge. Adler's work (1991) on differing national negotiating styles is also useful for gaining an understanding of cultural differences between nations. It is interesting to speculate whether globalization will increase the need to understand national cultural differences (as multinationals seek to manage diverse workforces) or whether the need will decrease as globalization brings about an homogenization of national cultures.

In terms of the desire to "learn from Japan," it is possible to identify specific cultural values in Japanese society which might influence economic performance, such as the importance attached to reciprocity between those of different status. However, there are successful organizations in other parts of the world in which these conventions are flouted. Indeed, even within Japan, there is a range of organizational practices as to how employees are treated. It is also difficult to disentangle the effects of culture on performance from other factors, such as industrial structure, manufacturing practices, and the role of the state (Dawson, 1992). The evidence on the attempts to introduce Japanese practices in other countries is also mixed (for the UK experience, see Oliver & Hunter, 1994).

The "culture as a product" perspective has also focused on the role of comparative organizational cultures within a country. Here an attempt has been made to provide a rigorous test as to what sort of a culture will lead to high performance. Denison (1991) argues that the four specific variables that influence performance are involvement, consistency, adaptability, and mission. Denison notes how these variables are, to some extent, contradictory: for example, consistency in terms of having agree-

ment can sometimes inhibit adaptability. It is also important that a culture is appropriate to its environment, so it is unlikely that there is one universal culture that suits all environments. On the other hand, environments change much more rapidly than organizational cultures, which can take many years to develop. Kotter & Heskett (1992) claim that cultures in which there is a strong consensus that key stakeholders should be valued, leadership at all levels is seen as important, and the culture underpins an appropriate strategy, can serve as valid generalizations, but these claims have yet to be put to the test. Brown (1994) carries a useful summary of both this issue and of the literature on models of organizational cultural change, of which Schein's model (1985) is the best-known.

Culture as a Process

Smircich's other perspective sees culture as a root metaphor for understanding organizations. This perspective makes it difficult to define culture. Organizations do not so much *have* cultures; it is more that they *are* cultures. This has implications for those who wish to try to change a culture.

The "culture as root metaphor" concept sees culture as something that is collectively enacted, where all who experience a culture at first hand become part of its generation and reproduction. To assume that one group (usually management) can unilaterally modify a culture is thus to mistake its essential properties. This is not to deny that culture changes – indeed, its enactment is a continuous process – but it usually changes in unintended ways. It is important also to recognize that collective enactment does not mean harmony and agreement; the power to enact is not equally shared amongst all groups.

The concept also has implications for those who wish to research cultures: the researcher inevitably becomes part of the enactment process (Weick, 1983). Trying to fix a culture and establish typologies is just an interpretation, one more part of the enactment process. As Martin (1993, p. 13) puts it: "Culture is not reified – out there – to be accurately observed."

However, this does not mean that the concept of "culture" is valueless except as a stick to beat those who see it as a product. Morgan (1986) argues that culture can be a powerful metaphor for enabling thought about organizations, drawing attention to the importance of patterns of subjective meaning, of images, and of values in organizational life.

Conclusion

The life cycle of organizational culture mirrors that of many other alleged managerial panaceas, running through the stages of initial enthusiasm, followed by a critical backlash, and ending up with a more widely based consensus on the limited applicability of the concept, which often highlights the complexity of management as a discipline.

Culture as a "product" has already gone through this cycle. It soon became clear that "culture" is not something that can easily be manipulated. Indeed, culture as a "process" seems a more powerful perspective in that it recognizes that culture depends upon human interaction – it is continuously being produced and re(created). To believe that one group can unilaterally change an existing culture according to some blueprint is mistaken. Culture does change – but often slowly and in unpredictable ways. Managers who wish to establish a blueprint might be better advised to go for a greenfield site and then carefully control recruitment and selection (Wickens, 1987). There is also the danger of thinking of culture as a monolithic entity to which all organizational members subscribe. Martin (1993) terms such a view "integrationist" and contrasts it with a "differentiation" focus, which stresses the importance of subcultures and the potential for conflict between these subcultures.

Even if a particular culture could be established by managerial fiat, the links between culture and organizational performance are not well-established. Assuming that cultures can be measured and pigeon-holed, there is no clear evidence that one particular type of culture is always associated with success – indeed, some of the features which are claimed to be linked with success are themselves contradictory. Furthermore, the sheer complexity of the factors involved in organizational performance makes it difficult to pin-point the exact contribution made by culture alone.

Bibliography

Adler, N. (1991). *International dimensions of organisational behaviour*. Boston, MA: PWS-Kant.

Brown, A. (1994). *Organisational culture*. London: Pitman.

Dawson, S. (1992). *Analysing organisations*, (2nd edn), London: Macmillan.

Denison, D. (1991). *Corporate culture and organisational effectiveness*. New York: John Wiley.

Handy, C. (1978). *The gods of management*. Harmondsworth, UK: Penguin.

Hofstede, G. (1990). *Cultures and organisations: software of the mind*. Maidenhead, UK: McGraw-Hill.

Kotter, J. P. & Heskett, J. L. (1992). *Corporate culture and performance*. New York: The Free Press.

Martin, J. (1993). *Cultures in organisations*. Oxford: Oxford University Press.

Morgan, G. (1986). *Images of organisations*, Sage.

Oliver, N. & Hunter, G. (1994). The financial impact of Japanese production methods in UK companies. Paper no. 24. Cambridge, UK: Judge Institute of Management Studies.

Schein, E. H. (1985). *Organisational culture and leadership*. London: Jossey–Bass.

Smircich, L. (1983). Concepts of culture and organisational analysis. *Administrative Science Quarterly*, **28**, 339–58.

Weick, K. (1983). Enactment processes in organisations. In B. Staw & G. Salancik (eds), *New directions in organisational behaviour*. Malabar, FL: Robert E. Krieger.

Wickens, P. (1987). *The road to Nissan: flexibility, quality, teamwork*. London: Macmillan.

MICHAEL BROCKLEHURST

organizational life cycle While it is possible to identify the formal structure of a corporation, at any moment in time this picture is static. In reality, organizations actually evolve, and the pattern of their progress has been observed by many researchers, leading to a number of similar models of evolution which may be termed organizational life cycles. Two such models are illustrated in figures 1 and 2.

Initially, firms tend to be created by individual entrepreneurs or groups. Such firms tend to operate a relatively undiversified product market strategy. Most decisions are taken by the owner–entrepreneur and such firms cannot usually afford professional management skills in most functions. As a result, the organizational structure is informal and there is a lack of professional standards. Most small firms do not progress beyond this stage: this is often by design, in addition to the fact that they do not

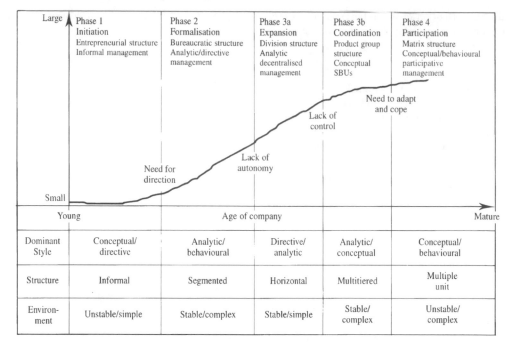

	Phase 1 Initiation Entrepreneurial structure Informal management	Phase 2 Formalisation Bureaucratic structure Analytic/directive management	Phase 3a Expansion Division structure Analytic decentralised management	Phase 3b Coordination Product group structure Conceptual SBUs	Phase 4 Participation Matrix structure Conceptual/behavioural participative management
Dominant Style	Conceptual/ directive	Analytic/ behavioural	Directive/ analytic	Analytic/ conceptual	Conceptual/ behavioural
Structure	Informal	Segmented	Horizontal	Multitiered	Multiple unit
Environ- ment	Unstable/simple	Stable/complex	Stable/simple	Stable/ complex	Unstable/ complex

Figure 1 Match of management with organizational life cycle.
Source: Rowe et al. (1994).

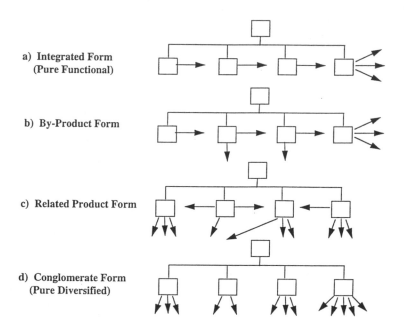

a) **Integrated Form**
    (Pure Functional)

b) **By-Product Form**

c) **Related Product Form**

d) **Conglomerate Form**
    (Pure Diversified)

Figure 2 Stages in the transition to the pure diversified form.
Source: Mintzberg (1989).

enjoy strategies that are capable of substantial growth. In such firms it is also difficult for founding entrepreneurs to give up decision making authority to others, and this also tends to block growth prospects. Board structures in such concerns tend to be dominated by the founder and his or her family, and since such concerns are usually privately owned, few have nonexecutive board members.

For those firms which do grow, however, size usually adds some complexity although, as long as the historic product market strategy remains viable, diversification is limited. Nevertheless, size makes some delegation of decision making necessary and professional management is usually added to create a FUNCTIONAL STRUC-TURE. Decisions, while usually still dominated by the founding entrepreneur until his or her death, involve functional specialists operating under direction.

The first major corporate crisis usually occurs with the death or retirement of the founder; unless, of course, he or she is unable to prevent the firm from entering an operational crisis, which also usually results in the removal of the founder. The organizational structure then tends to become a centralized bureaucracy and continues to pursue the original strategy established by the founder, but it lacks the original streak of imagination shown in the creation of the firm.

Eventually, the original strategy tends to mature and – often after the appointment of a new leader – the firm searches for new areas of activity into which to diversify. Such strategic moves usually occur through acquisition, and by this stage many such firms may well have become public companies. Most firms attempt to diversify into product market areas perceived by management to be related to the historic core activities. Unfortunately, this often turns out not to be the case, and many such DIVERSIFI-CATION moves fail to achieve the expectations of the acquirer.

The organizational changes that accompany such strategic moves tend to result in the adoption of a HOLDING COMPANY STRUCTURE. Initially, a functional holding company system is usually introduced, with the board consisting of the original functional executives together with the CEO of any newly acquired concern. While such diversification moves may well lead to significant increases in corporate sales, profits usually do not grow commensurately. As a result, a further crisis may well develop and the share price may decline, often leading to a change in either the chairman or the chief executive, or both.

At this point it is common for management consultants to be brought in to help the company introduce a divisional or business unit structure (see SBU STRUCTURE), together with suitable management information planning and control systems: the firm is ill equipped to introduce these on its own. The new structure also assists in the development of a cadre of general managers capable of continuing the strategy of diversification. A particular problem occurs with diversification away from a DOMI-NANT BUSINESS STRATEGY position, especially where the main business is significantly larger than the diversification moves. In these circum-stances the main focus of the board remains centered on the functions of the traditional core business or on geographic areas of operation.

While most diversification strategies move from a single or dominant business to related diversified areas, some firms adopt a CON-GLOMERATE STRATEGY. While both strategies involve divisional or business unit structures, historically, conglomerate businesses operated with a very small central office, while related diversified concerns tended to have larger central offices, which were required to coordi-nate activities between operating units. Improved information technology, re-engineer-ing, and the like have tended to result in reductions in the size and scope of the central office of all diversified concerns.

Concurrently with higher levels of product market diversification, many larger firms have also adopted multinational strategies, or envir-onmental and technological factors have required the integration of cross-functional activities. In such firms, a form of MATRIX STRUCTURE has therefore tended to be adopted.

Different leadership styles also tend to be needed at the different stages of the organiza-tional life cycle. In the initial phase, the successful executive is entrepreneurial and creative, usually with a strong dominant per-sonality. Many such individuals tend to come from socially depressed backgrounds and have ethnic origins that involve Jewish, Muslim, or Asian ethics.

In phase 2 (see figure 1) the successful executive focuses on pursuing growth with the original strategy, while introducing a formal functional structure coupled with appropriate financial controls and rudimentary planning systems. The management style tends to be analytic, but to lack the imagination necessary to evolve new strategies.

At the start of phase 3, a new chairman and/or chief executive is charged with breaking out of the historic strategy, usually through acquisition. This is generally accomplished by forceful leadership, with tight centralized control. As a result, the new strategy often fails to achieve its objectives; newly acquired executives find it difficult to work under such a leadership style, and the acquiring firm lacks the appropriate information and control systems to manage a diversified enterprise. As a result, a further leadership change often occurs, to introduce a style embracing a combination of analytic and behavioral skills. Such a leader has a broad strategic vision, a capacity to deal with complex situations, and the ability to achieve results by operating through other managers.

In phase 4, the best leadership style tends to be a combination of analytic, conceptual, and behavioral skills, together with a clear vision for the future direction of the corporation. Such leaders are capable of dealing with high uncertainty, coping with rapid change in the environment and technology, and delegating responsibility across a complex matrix structure.

Bibliography

Channon, D. F. (1973). *The strategy and structure of British enterprise.* Cambridge, MA: Harvard Division of Research.

Galbraith, J. R. & Kaganjian, R. K. (1986). *Strategy implementation.* Los Angeles: West.

Greiner, L. E. (1972). Evolution and revolution as organisations grow. *Harvard Business Review,* **56** (August–September).

Hansen, A. H. (1985). CEO management style and the stages of development in new ventures. Unpublished paper Sasem, OR: Atkinson Graduate School of Management.

Mintzberg, H. (1979). *The structuring of organisations.* Englewood Cliffs, NJ: Prentice-Hall.

Mintzberg, H. (1989). *Mintzberg on management.* New York: The Free Press.

Rowe, A.J., Mason, R. O., Dickel, K. F., Mann, R. B. & Mockler, R. J. (1994). *Strategic management,* 4th edn. Reading, MA: Addison-Wesley. See chapter 11.

Scott, B. R. (1971). The stages of corporate development, part 1. Unpublished paper. Boston, MA: Harvard Business School.

DEREK F. CHANNON

outsourcing This occurs when a firm contracts with an outside organization for it to undertake specific activities which, historically, were undertaken by the firm itself. Some activities, such as cleaning and maintenance, have long been contracted out by many organizations; increasingly, however, activities which many might claim are strategic are being outsourced.

In particular, the areas of data processing and information technology management are being outsourced. Electronic Data Systems in particular have grown rapidly, and industry sales reached nearly $50 billion in 1994. The financial services industry has been a major user of outsourcing, with companies such as Banc One and American Express undertaking processing activities for many other organizations. Furthermore, in the UK for example, many government functions, including revenue collection, are being outsourced to private corporations.

Apart from providing specialist service at lower cost, outsourcing helps to reduce capital intensity in a business. Amstrad, for example, was able to grow at over 70 per cent per annum compound because it outsourced all its assembly and component production to Far Eastern manufacturers, concerning itself basically with the design of its range of consumer electronics products and computers. The company did, however, maintain quality control by regularly inspecting supplier plants. On a larger scale, Marks and Spencer also manufactures nothing but rigorously lays down specifications against which its suppliers must produce. This reduced capital intensity can help to improve profitability and, in particular, shareholder value.

However, overuse can lead to potential technological dependency. Canon, for example, supplies some 80 per cent of the engines for laser beam printers. As a result, Western suppliers have become dependent upon the supply of a strategic component from a company which may eventually turn out to be a fierce competitor. Akio Morita of Sony thus described the effect of outsourcing as the "hollowing of American industry where the US is abandoning its status as an industrial power."

The key advantages of outsourcing include the following:

- reduced capital intensity

- transformation of fixed costs to variable costs

- reduced costs due to supplier economies of scale

- that it encourages a focus on customer needs and product development rather than manufacturing

- benefits obtained from supplier innovations

- that it focuses resources on high value added activities (in any manufacturing market value chain, some 40–50 per cent of value added occurs at the distribution end)

It is a most effective strategy when:

- process technology is unavailable

- competitors have superior technology

- suppliers enjoy superior efficiency and quality

- capital for investment is scarce and expensive

- there are enough suppliers to ensure security of competitive supply

The critical assumptions made by companies adopting outsourcing strategies are as follows:

- a strong market position is a critical strategic success factor

- a brand name is sufficient to negate the need for manufacturing capacity

- manufacturing can be separated from design

- manufacturing knowledge is not critical to an understanding of the market

Bibliography

Bettis, R., Bradley, S. & Hamel, G. (1992). Outsourcing and industrial decline. *Academy of Management Executive*, 6 (1), 7–22.

Rowe, A. J., Mason, R. O., Dickel, K. E., Mann, R. B. & Mockler, R. J. (1994). *Strategic management*, 4th edn. Reading, MA: Addison-Wesley. See pp. 345–6.

Welch, J. P. & Ranganath, N. (1992). Strategic sourcing: a progressive approach to the make or buy decision. *Academy of Management Executive*, 6 (11), 23–41.

DEREK F. CHANNON

P

Pareto analysis A number of criteria exist for evaluating the desirability of alternate economic and social states, and the desirability of a change from one such state to another. One such criterion was developed by the nineteenth-century economist Vilfredo Pareto, and states that "in order for a maximum welfare position to be reached then the 'ophelimity' (utility) of some should not increase to the detriment of others."

Pareto efficiency, then, will be achieved when it is not possible to make anyone better off without making someone else worse off. From this perspective, perfect competition transactions (given no externalities) are Pareto efficient, as no-one would voluntarily enter such a transaction if their welfare would be reduced by so doing.

In practice, this is a very strict criterion with limited use. Even if it was possible for the person benefitting from a transaction to fully compensate the one who was losing out, such compensation might never be paid. A less restrictive criterion was, therefore, developed by Hicks and Kaldor, stating that a transaction is desirable if it leads to a potential Pareto improvement; that is, if the gainers could in principle fully compensate the losers and still have a net gain, even though in practice they do not pay compensation at all.

In many industries, the Pareto effect is commonly found along many dimensions. This is illustrated in figure 1 (p. 185). It follows from the observation, for example, that 20 per cent of products will account for 80 per cent of sales. This is illustrated on what is sometimes called an ABC analysis chart. It shows all of the expenses as bar graphs, arranged in order of size. Its purpose is to group relatively large-cost

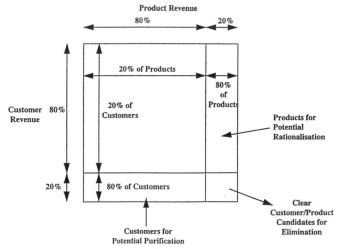

Figure 2   The customer/product Pareto matrix.
Source: Channon (1986).

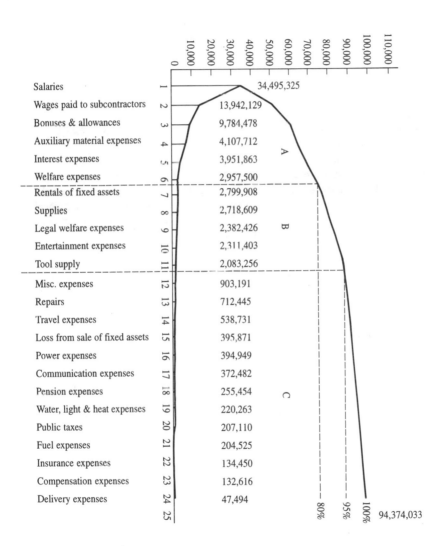

Figure 1 Pareto analysis of production cost, manufacturing expenses and expenditure
Source: Nagashima (1992)

items so as to highlight them for management and control. Group A expenses account for 80 per cent of total expenses, group B for 15 per cent, and group C for the residual 5 per cent. Usually the number of cost categories tends to be in inverse number to their importance. Such a chart enables management to focus attention on critical costs rather than devoting disproportionate service time to less significant factors.

The Pareto effect also applies to many other dimensions, such as customers, sales force, critical machinery, and the like. Combining more than one significant variable, rather than using each variable alone, can therefore produce a useful guide to strategy. This is illustrated in figure 2 (p. 184).

In many businesses there is a strong tendency to add new products and customers while failing to eliminate those which are obsolete or unprofitable. When faced with the need for rationalization of unattractive products and/or customers, the sales function in most businesses is extremely reluctant to undertake such actions. This is so despite the fact that, at worst, 20 per cent of customers and products may well account for the majority of costs in areas such

as stocks, production costs, computer facilities, and administration. Conducting Pareto analysis of a business along the major strategic dimensions is therefore a significant exercise, and one that needs to be undertaken periodically to insure that inefficiencies are not repeated.

For further discussion of the Pareto principle, see Baumol (1977).

Bibliography

Baumol, W. J. (1977). *Economic theory and operations analysis*, (4th edn), Englewood Cliffs, NJ: Prentice-Hall. See chapter 21.
Channon, D. F. (1986). *Bank strategic management and marketing*. Chichester: John Wiley.
Nagashima, S. (1992). *100 management charts*. Tokyo: Asian Productivity Organisation. See pp. 36–7.

DEREK F. CHANNON

PDCA cycle   On his visits to Japan, William E. Deming, the US quality expert, introduced the concept of a continuously rotating wheel, to emphasize the necessity of constant interaction between research, design, production, and sales

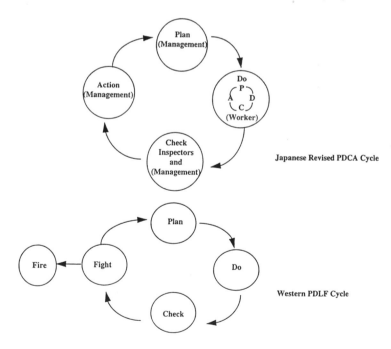

Figure 1   Japanese and Western PDCA cycles.
Source: Masaaki Imai(1986).

Table 1   The PDCA cycle

Design	PLAN	Product design corresponded to the planning phase of management action
Production	DO	Production was seen as corresponding to "doing" the product being worked upon
Sales	CHECK	Sales figures confirmed whether or not the customer was satisfied
Research	ACTION	Action refers to implementation of improvement

as a way of continuous improvement in quality that satisfied customers. This concept became known as the Deming wheel.

While Deming stressed the importance of continuous interaction between the above-mentioned four aspects of the business, Japanese companies extended his concept to cover all phases of management, and the four stages of the Deming wheel came to be identified as four phases of management action as shown in figure 1.

The PDCA cycle is illustrated in table 1, and is a series of activities carried out during continuous improvement (KAIZEN) programs. It commences with an evaluation of the present position, which leads to the development of an improvement plan. When finalized, this is then implemented. The results of implementation are checked to see whether the results expected of the original plan have actually been achieved. When such a plan has been successful, standardization is introduced to insure that the improvement is institutionalized. The cycle itself – like that proposed by Deming – is continuously moving and constantly improving in "quality," which in Japan embraces cost and design, as well as the Western concept of quality. In many Western concerns, due to the adversarial nature of labor relations, the cycle could be classified as PDCF, where F might relate to firing of management and workers for a quiet solution.

Initially, the PDCA cycle tended to be hierarchical, with the checking function being undertaken by supervisors who checked the actions of workers. Action was implemented by managers on the basis of the results established by supervisors in the checking phase. In the West such a cycle takes on an adversarial nature, with "action" tending to mean firing or labor

reduction. As a result, many workers resist the process of continuous change. In Japan, the process has tended to become an "SDCA" cycle, where the "S" denotes standardization. Only after a standard has been established and stabilized should the PDCA cycle be continued, with a view to improving the established standards. Management should have both the SDCA and PDCA cycles working together simultaneously. By turning through the PDCA cycle, managers and workers alike are constantly challenged to improve the business.

Bibliography

Masaaki Imai (1986). *Kaizen*. New York: McGraw-Hill. See pp. 60–5.

DEREK F. CHANNON

PEST analysis   A number of major variables lie well outside the control of the organization: PEST analysis is a broad-brush instrument that can be used in attempts to define and measure their effects. PEST is an acronym of the four categories of change factor: Political, Economic, Social, and Technological. It is therefore essentially an environmental checklist of those external elements which both influence and constrain the attraction of industry profitability. Often used in conjunction with Porter's FIVE FORCES MODEL, it has become a powerful tool for reducing the parameters of risk.

Political Change and Intervention

In most Western countries, political legislators are expressly forbidden to benefit commercially from their legal enactment, despite overt infringements of this principle seen currently in Italy and France. How, then, should the business world influence and forecast likely political intervention? Consider the following situations:

Regional. Will a change of government in the UK, from Conservative to Labour, increase financial support for business start-ups in Northern Ireland?

National. Will the Clinton administration in the US intervene in the investment terms of the Ford Motor Company's decision as to where to site the new Jaguar plant?

International. Given the explosion of Sino–Western joint ventures within Southern China, who will succeed Diang Xiaping as Premier, and will the social market policy be reversed?

Each of these potential situations requires careful evaluation to determine strategic risk and opportunity. Who will be the decision makers? Who will be the key influencers? How can the top manager reduce the lead time from early warning to strategic modification?

Dependency on the Economic Cycle

Demand for every product or service is to some degree dependent upon the economic cycle. Is demand within any product/market segment a leader or a laggard relative to GNP momentum? Some show increased demand during the first phases of the economic cycle downturn; for example, gourmet convenience food. Some, such as two-star restaurant bookings, show the reverse. Relative to the economic cycle, what fiscal and monetary mechanisms are likely to be chosen by central government? Specifically, how will this affect disposable income expenditure patterns, or the cost of funding working capital? Would it be prudent to take on fixed-interest long-term debt rather than a floating rate shorter-term facility?

In response to this economic uncertainty, much progress has been made in both macro- and sectorial econometric model-building; leading, *inter alia*, to better inventory control and to a reduction in the cost of corporate capital.

Social Demographic, Attitudinal, and Religious Change

From a corporate perspective, what social changes will affect contemporary strategic positioning and – given robust forecasting –

what competitive advantage could be established? Take, for example, the falling reproduction rates in Western Europe: for every two adults in Italy, 1.3 are reproduced: in Germany and the UK, the figure is approximately 1.6. When combined with an increase in life expectation, who will fund the retirement pension? Can the state fulfil historic provision from the public purse? This social trend has led to the private sector developing new products, particularly private portable pensions, private medical schemes, sheltered housing developments, "third age" holidays, and vocational courses within the university sector.

Consider the rise of pressure groups: the anti-smoking lobby has recorded successes in restaurants, on hotel floors, and on aircraft. The strong positive correlation between smoking and heart disease has been linked to a marked reduction in Western adult male consumption of tobacco products, while – perversely – it has had no impact on female teenagers. Should the tobacco companies re-focus their advertising and promotional activity on a smaller niche and/or diversify more rapidly into related products – see, for example, Philip Morris and Miller?

The third, and increasingly important, category is that of religious fundamentalism, often associated with extreme nationalism. Should Western oil and gas companies invest for the long term in Kakastan? Given the terrorist targeting of tourists in Algeria and Egypt, should holiday companies begin to wind down from hotel contracts in Tunisia? Will the Parsees of India, a minority religion who dominate much of private-sector enterprise, be better long-term joint venture partners than the majority Hindus?

Technological Vulnerability

It is axiomatic that we live in a world of rapid technological change – all the more reason to be proactive in corporate response. Organizations should regularly review the commercial impact of emerging new technologies upon activity costs along the value chain. Take the example of constant-velocity joints: GKN, who claim a 35 per cent world market share, invest heavily in friction research (tribology) in the major technological universities. The reasoning behind this strategy is that, since the 1960s, engine brake horse power, from the same cubic capacity, has quadrupled – and vehicle top speed has doubled. Correspondingy, automobile manufacturers demand component technology of equivalence. Consider advances in data compression and transmission. Will this reduce the need for as many medical general practitioners, or for legal experts? Will neural networks replace branch bank managers? How soon will interactive video disk technology replace ageing professors!

Any company which fails to monitor technological advance within the area of its existing core competencies exacerbates the risk of product/market obsolescence.

Constructing a PEST Framework

PEST analysis is an attempt to reduce strategic risk by SCENARIO PLANNING. It is not intended to be a precise technique in quantification but is specific to individual products and/or markets. It therefore follows that each PEST, although following the same general outline, will specify different item variables, to which different weightings will be allocated. Given the enormous number of potential variables, it is sensible to limit the PEST analysis to no more than five items within each of the main PEST headings in the first instance. The first step is to determine the probability rankings of each item variable; and the second is to evaluate the quantitative and qualitative effect of these occurring upon the achievement of corporate objectives. By multiplying probability by effect, a crude ranking index of corporate vulnerability – or opportunity – is established. This index is next refined by eliminating those items with insufficient impact, so that more detailed analysis can be conducted of the significant variables.

Bibliography

Fahey, L. & King, W. (1977). Environmental scanning for corporate planning. *Business Horizons*, **20** 4.

Hofer, C. W. & Schendel, D. (1978). *Strategy formulation: analytical concepts*. St Paul, MN: West.

Rowe, A. J., Mason, R. O., Dickel, K. E., Mann, R. B. & Mockler, R. J. (1994). *Strategic management*, 4th edn. Reading, MA: Addison-Wesley.

Utterback, J. (1979). Environmental analysis and forecasting in strategic management. In C. Hofer, D. Schendel (eds), *A new view of business policy and planning*. Boston, MA: Little, Brown.

William, R. E. (1976). *Putting it all together, a guide to strategic thinking*. New York: Amacom.

DAVID NORBURN

PIMS structural determinants of performance Profit performance varies enormously from business to business and within a business over time. In developing strategy, both corporate and business unit management need to be able to realistically appraise the level of performance that should be expected for a given business, and to be clear as to what factors explain variations in performance between businesses, and within a business over time. Important guidelines which help address these questions have been developed from the Profit Impact of Market Strategy (PIMS) program. For a fuller description of the background of the PIMS program, see Schoeffler et al. (1974).

Background to the PIMS Methodology

At the heart of the PIMS program is a business unit research database that captures the real-life experiences of over 3,000 businesses. Each business is a division, product line, or profit center within its parent company, selling a distinct set of products and/or services to an identifiable group of customers, in competition with a well defined set of competitors, for which meaningful separation can be made of revenue, operating costs, investment, and strategic plans. The business's SERVED MARKET is defined as the segment of the total potential market which it is seriously targeting by offering suitable products and/or services and toward which it is making specific marketing efforts. On this basis each business reports, in standardized format, over 300 items of data, much of it for at least four years of operations.

The information collected covers, *inter alia*, the market environment, competitive situation, internal cost and asset structure, and profit performance of the business. A full listing of the information captured by the PIMS database is given by The Strategic Planning Institute's *PIMS data manual*. A useful summary of the manual is given in Buzzell & Gale (1987).

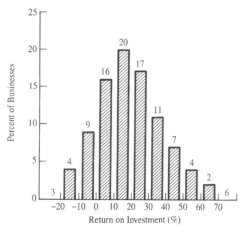

Figure 1   The distribution of return on investment in the PIMS database. ROI is defined as follows: pre-tax after deduction of corporate expenses but prior to interest charges divided by average investment where this is equivalent to the historic net book value of plant and equipment plus working capital (i.e., total assets less current liabilities). Note that four year averages are used for all figures.
Source: PIMS Associates

Table 1   Key determinants of R.O.I. in the PIMS data base

Category of factor	Impact on ROI as factor increases
Marketplace standing	
Market share	+
Relative market share	+
Served market concentration	+
Market environment	
Real market growth	+
Selling price inflation	+
Market differentiation	+
Purchase amount immediate customers	–
Importance of purchase to end user	–
Differentiation from competitors	
Relative product quality	+
Relative price	+
Relative direct cost	–
% Sales new products	–
Marketing/sales revenue	–
R&D/sales revenue	–
Capital and production structure	–
Investment/sales revenue	–
Investment/value added	–
Receivables/investment	+
Fixed capital/investment	–
Capacity utilization	+
Unionization	–
Labor effectiveness*	+

* Based on a productivity submodel.

The businesses in the database have been drawn from some 500 corporations, spanning a wide variety of industry settings. These corporations are based for the most part in North America and Europe.

The distribution of return on investment in the database is shown in figure 1. As can be seen, profit varies widely among the businesses, with 16 per cent of the sample showing negative returns and 12 per cent consistently achieving in excess of 50 per cent ROI. An understanding of why one business should be loss-making while another achieves premium returns lies at the heart of strategy formulation. To explain this variance, cross-sectional analysis is carried out on the database to uncover the general patterns or relationships that account for these profit differentials. The fundamental proposition that underpins this approach is that the name of a business has no bearing on its level of performance. What matters are the structural characteristics that describe the business, factors such as market share, growth rate, customer concentration, product quality, and investment intensity.

Research on the database has identified some 30 factors that are statistically significant at the 95 per cent probability level or better in explaining the variance in profitability across businesses. These factors, which operate in a highly interactive way, collectively explain nearly 80 per cent of the variance in ROI across the database. The more powerful factors are listed in table 1 under four categories: marketplace standing, market environment, differentiation from competitors, and capital and production structure.

It should be noted at the outset that part of the explanation of variance is definitional. This

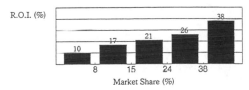

Figure 2   Marketplace standing and profitability are closely related.
Source: PIMS Associates

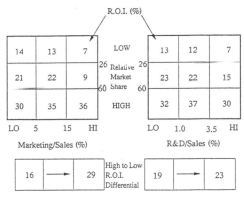

Figure 3   Share tends to have more leverage in marketing and R&D intensive settings.
Source: PIMS Associates

comes about because some of the profit-explaining variables, such as investment/sales revenue, contain elements which are also present in the construction of the dependent variable, ROI. However, the emphasis is on behavioral relationships. Definitional elements are included in the independent variables only when it is impossible to separate out the behavioral and definitional effects of a particular factor.

Key Research Findings from the PIMS Database

The more powerful relationships listed in table 1 are now considered one and two variables at a time in relation to the dependent variable ROI. While this approach sacrifices the insights contained in multifactor interactions, it has the benefit of reducing complexity and helps to develop an understanding of the basic building blocks. To this extent it provides insight and guidelines to aid business judgement rather than hard dogma.

Marketplace Standing

There are several measures of a business's marketplace standing: market share (the business's sales expressed as a percentage of total sales made within the served market), market share rank, and relative market share (the business's market share divided by the sum of the shares of its three leading competitors). Whichever measure is adopted, a strong positive correlation between marketplace strength and profitability is observed. Figure 2 shows the relationship between market share and profit-ability. Businesses with strong market share (above 38 per cent in the upper quintile of the distribution) achieve on average a 38 per cent ROI, compared to only 10 per cent for their low-share counterparts (below 8 per cent in the lower quintile of the distribution).

While the data in figure 2 show that strength of marketplace standing and profitability are strongly related, the question remains as to why we observe the effect. The numbers are a fact, but hypothesis and further examination are required to explain the relationships. It should be remembered that market share in and of itself is not important: it is an output measure which reflects a business's historic and potential ability to gain substantive competitive advantages within its activities and in the marketplace. Factors which explain the underlying reasons why share may help profitability are shown in table 2. For a fuller discussion of the benefits of market share, see Buzzell et al. (1975).

Powerful as these factors are, the fact remains there is nothing inevitable about the relationship between share and profitability. Over 30 per cent of the businesses in the database with market shares above 40 per cent have ROI's below the average of 22 per cent. These businesses have often become victims of their own success, wedded to historic investment decisions and burdened with complexity costs. For a fuller discussion of below average performance for high-share businesses, see Woo (1984).

The benefits of market share are particularly marked in marketing- and R&D-intensive environments, as can be seen in figure 3. The two variable cross-tables divide the database into equal thirds on the basis of relative market share and then into low and high marketing and R&D environments. Each cell contains approximately 300 businesses, and the numbers in the cells

Table 2   Potential benefits of strong market standing.

---

* *"Experience curve" and "learning curve" benefits*
Widely publicized by the Boston Consulting Group, the experience curve effect sees cost per unit come down in a fairly predictable manner as cumulative volume doubles.

* *Economics of scale and scope*
Can drive down cost per unit throughout the cost structure of a business as well as benefitting balance sheet productivity. Key areas for potential benefit are seen to be:

  – purchases: stronger negotiating stance with suppliers leads to preferential terms
  – manufacturing: plant scale and run length
  – distribution: drop size and drop density
  – marketing/R&D: spreading fixed cost component over a larger number of units
  – investment productivity
    • improved asset utilization
    • improved ability to control all current asset components and extend current liabilities

* *Relative perceived quality*
Higher market visibility offering the "low-risk" option for buyers in many instances. Scale benefits should give ability to establish stronger brand and better control distribution.

* *Competitive ability*
  – potential to act as "industry statesman"
  – opportunities to set and administer prices
  – size may deter competitive attack
  – size will heighten ability to control the chain from supplier to customers
  – better ability to spread risk and explore more competitive avenues

---

refer to the average ROI achieved by the businesses that fall into that cell over a four year time period.

When marketing expenditure is below 5 per cent of sales revenue, the ROI's achieved by low-share businesses are 14 per cent, as compared to 30 per cent for their high-share counterparts – a differential of 16 points. On the other hand, in marketing-intensive environments the importance of market share on profit is much more pronounced, with ROI going from 7 per cent to 36 per cent, a 29 point differential. A similar relationship manifests itself in the case of market share and R&D expenditure.

What the PIMS data highlight is the danger of low market share in an environment which is either marketing- or R&D-intensive. This is because both marketing and R&D have many of the characteristics of a fixed cost. Businesses with small market shares often find that they have to spend as much as their larger competitors on these activities, but do not have the same volume over which to spread the costs. The result is that they are trapped in the low-profit cells. When faced with such a trap, the strategic alternatives appear to be to reduce the role of marketing and R&D, to strengthen share either organically or by merger/alliance, or to re-segment to dominate a niche within the market. If none of these possibilities appears to be feasible, the small-share competitor will be faced with the large-share competitor's "virtuous circle," shown in figure 4.

Differentiation from Competitors

A business's value-for-money position versus competitors is a critical determinant of competitive advantage. PIMS assesses this position by judging a business's relative competitive standing in terms of quality and price. It then examines how that offer is supported by new

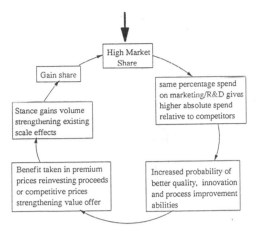

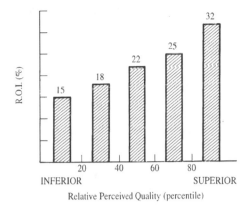

Figure 5   Relative perceived quality is closely related to profitability.
Source: PIMS Associates

Figure 4   High share competitors vicious circle
Source: PIMS Associates

product activity, marketing, and R&D expenditure and the extent to which price is underpinned by the relative direct cost position of the business. "Relative perceived quality" is seen as the key driver of business performance under this category of factor.

Quality in the PIMS database is defined from the perspective of the external marketplace. Customers evaluate the total benefit bundle of products and services offered by the business and rank it relative to leading competitors as being superior, equivalent, or inferior. The "relative perceived quality" measure used by PIMS is then computed by subtracting the percentage of product and service attributes that are judged as being superior to competitors from the percentage which is judged as inferior.

Relative perceived quality has a major positive impact on profitability, as can be seen in figure 5. Businesses whose offer is judged as clearly superior to that of competitors on average achieve more than twice the ROI of businesses whose offer is judged as inferior.

Not only is the relationship between quality and return one of the key determinants of performance in the database, but it is extremely robust in all types of business and marketplace situations. Businesses that achieve a significant quality advantage relative to their competitors can choose to benefit in one of two ways: either they can charge premium prices or grow market share at competitive pricing levels, or some combination of both.

The relationship between market share, quality, and profitability is shown in figure 6. The combination of share and quality is extremely powerful, with ROI in the high-quality/high-share cell averaging 39 per cent.

Figure 6 also shows that quality and share are correlated. Thus, although the database was split into equal thirds on both quality and share, 45 per cent of businesses lie on the top left to bottom right diagonal. The implications appear to be that high-share businesses that offer poor quality weaken in position, while weak-share businesses that offer high quality strengthen in position – both extremes may be transitory in

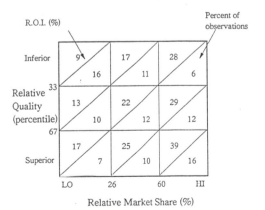

Figure 6   Market position and quality are partial substitutes for each other
Source: PIMS Associates.

nature and represent only 13 per cent of the sample.

Capital and Production Structure

Within this category of factor, the most powerful of the PIMS findings relates to investment intensity. The definition of investment in this context is fixed capital, measured on an historic basis as the net book value of plant and equipment, plus working capital, defined as current assets less current liabilities. Investment intensity itself is measured in two ways: first, investment is ratioed to sales revenue in the conventional manner; and, second, investment is ratioed to the value added actually generated by the business (where value added is defined as net sales revenue less all outside suppliers' inputs).

Both measures are simultaneously employed to assess investment intensity, as many businesses have low levels of investment to sales (turn their asset base frequently) but because of a high bought-in component have high levels of investment to value added. Having cautioned that a balanced view on the overall investment intensity of a business is only achieved by using both measures in combination, on an individual basis each measure is similarly related to profit performance in the PIMS data base, and here the more familiar investment/sales revenue ratio is employed to illustrate the investment intensity effect.

As the investment intensity in a business rises, so the ROI that it achieves falls dramatically. This finding is the most powerful negative relationship in the database, with ROI's averaging only 8 per cent for investment intensive businesses, compared to 38 per cent for low investment intensity businesses. The finding is consistent with the experiences of many businesses in sectors such as airlines, shipbuilding, base chemicals, low alloy steel, refining, smelting, and commodity pulp and paper, which in large degree achieve at best modest rates of return.

Part of the reason for the relationship is definitional. As the investment level in a business increases, it simultaneously increases the denominator of the ROI ratio, hence dragging down the value of the ratio. That there is a behavioral element to the investment intensity effect is vividly illustrated if the return

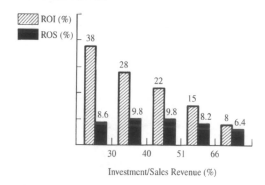

Figure 7   Investment intensity is a major drag on profitability
Source: PIMS Associates

on sales (ROS) achieved at different levels of investment is considered. If a business is to hold ROI as investment intensity increases, ROS should increase smoothly. In practice, ROS is at best flat, and in fact starts to tail off at higher levels of investment intensity. Moreover, it should be remembered that return has been taken pre-tax and pre-interest, with no financial charge made on the amount of investment used in the business. If even a modest capital charge rate is applied to a business's returns to reflect its investment, the relationship would start to turn sharply down. If businesses with high levels of investment are not able to achieve profit margins sufficient to offset the level of investment that they need to sustain their sales, there is indeed a powerful behavioral element to the ROI/investment intensity finding.

What explains this behavioral element? Part of the reason may lie in the fact that management often focus their attention on profit margin on sales, rather than on the more important criterion of return on investment. The more substantive explanation, however, relates to the destructive nature of competition that typically accompanies high levels of investment intensity.

When a business is capital intensive, management not unnaturally becomes concerned about capacity utilization. When this drops, either because of a weakening in demand or because of new capacity addition by competitors, the knee-jerk reaction is to cut price. When one competitor cuts price, the rest of the industry typically follows, and the result is a price war.

The tendency to cut price is particularly marked in fixed capital intensive businesses, because the value of the marginal sale always appears to be so attractive.

The problem is compounded because fixed capital intensity frequently represents a major barrier to exit. When a company has sunk a lot of money into a business, it is often reluctant to exit: it becomes desperate to make the investment come good. It convinces itself that the problems of the business are transitory and that all it needs to do is "hang in" and better times will follow. This is a comforting illusion that does little for a business.

Overview

At the start, it was observed that profit performance varies enormously from business to business and within a business over time. Several of the key research findings arising from the PIMS database that help to explain this variance in performance have been discussed.

Given the richness and diversity of the PIMS database, the findings – when taken individually – direct attention to important areas of strategic strength and flag classic strategic traps faced by businesses. However, care must be cautioned in interpretation. Comprehensive insight is not obtained by examining one or two factors at a time: it requires a multifactor approach in order to start to capture the complexities and tradeoffs in business. To this end, PIMS researchers have developed several models that help assess the level of ROI, cashflow, productivity, and so forth that should be expected for a business, given its structural make-up. Once these benchmarks have been established, attention can be focused on the next stage of strategy formulation; that of managing change. It can be extremely misleading to use the *general* findings presented for this purpose. That market share is generally closely related to profitability is observable; but that is not to argue, of course, that a business should try to grow share in all instances – the feasibility and cost–benefit tradeoff of such a move needs close examination. To this end, other modeling techniques and the database itself, via matched sample analysis, provide important empirical vehicles for the identification and evaluation of particular strategy moves by researchers and practitioners alike.

The authors would like to acknowledge the assistance of John Hillier of the Strategic Planning Institute in researching the PIMS database.

Bibliography

Buzzell, R. D. & Gale, B. T. (1987). *The PIMS principles.* New York: The Free Press. See Appendix A.

Buzzell, R. D., Gale, B. T. & Sultan, R. G. M. (1975). Market share – a key to profitability. *Harvard Business Review*, **53** (1), 97–106.

Schoeffler, S., Buzzell, R. D. & Heany, D. F. (1974). Impact of strategic planning on profit performance. *Harvard Business Review*, **52 (2)**, 137–45.

Strategic Planning Institute (n.d.). *PIMS data manual.* Cambridge, MA: Strategic Planning Institute.

Woo, C. (1984). Market share leadership – not always so good. *Harvard Business Review*, **62** (1), 50–6.

KEVIN JAGIELLO and GORDON MANDRY

poka-yoke Not so long ago, a small English dictionary was published for Japanese schoolchildren to use in studying for their exams. To encourage their efforts, it came with a little printed bookmark that read "A person is an animal that forgets. Learn more than you forget!" The fact is that human beings *are* very forgetful and tend to make mistakes. All too often, we blame other people for making mistakes. Especially in the workplace, this attitude not only discourages workers and lowers morale, but it does not solve the problem. The term "poka-yoke" encompasses a range of techniques for avoiding simple human error at work.

Although the concept of poka-yoke has existed for a long time in various forms, it was the Japanese manufacturing engineer Shigeo Shingo who developed the idea into a formidable tool for achieving zero defects and eventually *eliminating* quality control inspections. The methods that he advocates were formerly called "foolproofing": recognizing that this term might cause offence, Shingo coined the expression "poka-yoke", from the Japanese *yokeru* (to avoid) *poke* (inadvertent errors) – it is generally translated as "mistake proofing" or "failsafing." The idea behind poka-yoke is to respect the intelligence of workers. By taking over repetitive tasks or actions that depend on vigilance or memory, poka-yoke can free a worker's time and mind to pursue more creative and value-adding activities.

Many things can go wrong in the complex environment of the workplace; every day there are opportunities to make mistakes that will result in defective products. Defects are wasteful, and if they are not discovered, they disappoint the customer's expectations of quality. Behind poka-yoke is the conviction that it is unacceptable to produce even a small number of defective goods. To become a world-class competitor, a company must adopt not only a philosophy but also a *practice* of producing zero defects. Poka-yoke methods are simple concepts for achieving this goal.

Types of Poka-yoke Devices

The term poka-yoke is used in a broad sense to describe worker-originated improvements that incorporate one or more of the main components of Shingo's Zero Quality Control system:

1. Source inspection to detect errors at their source – before they cause defects. An example is an additional locator pin to prevent misalignment of the workpiece.
2. One hundred per cent inspection for defects, using an inexpensive sensing device such as a limit switch.
3. Immediate action to stop operations when an error is detected, such as an interlocked circuit that automatically shuts down the machine.

Of course, preventing the defect in the first place is the most effective technique, but devices for catching defects and immediately stopping the action are also valuable parts of the defect reduction process. The "devices" include improvements that should really be regarded as design modifications – alterations that go beyond machine and process improvements to affect the shape of the product itself. Many of these are extremely simple, such as eliminating unused holes in a circuit board to avoid errors when inserting a plug. In many companies, the design function has traditionally been carried out almost exclusively by engineering or design. Although these departments generally take manufacturing factors into consideration, products today often go through several stages of refinement and redesign. Therefore, in keeping with the spirit of poka-yoke, the design refinement process should incorporate the experiences of the production workers, since they are in the best position to discover design elements that cause difficulty and serve no value-adding function.

It is quite possible to take advantage of these ideas without a highly automated factory. These devices – such as an interference pin for a jig or a limit switch to signal correct placement of a workpiece – can be simple and inexpensive. Nor do the devices make an employee's skill unnecessary. Some, such as a color-coded wiring template, simply assist the worker in performing a task correctly. Others, such as a counter, or an alarm to signal a defect, require a worker to take some responsive action. Strictly speaking, these latter innovations are not entirely mistake-proof, since to be effective they depend on the worker to voluntarily respond appropriately. Nevertheless, when employees are motivated and interested in improving the product or process, such helpful devices can significantly reduce the number of mistakes.

The responsibility for a successful "zero defects" campaign ultimately rests with management. The leaders of the company themselves must have a vision of the quality that the company can produce, and must create a company culture and environment that motivates all employees to make that vision their own. This may mean providing time and support resources for work teams to analyze problems. It may mean instituting an incentive-based suggestion system to encourage workers to solve problems that cause defects. At the most basic level, it means recognizing the inherent expertise of the people who are doing the actual work, and creating channels through which they can express this knowledge. Above all, it means maintaining an atmosphere in which they will *want* to express their knowledge for the benefit of the company.

Bibliography

Anonymous (1988). *The idea book: improvement through TEI*. Cambridge, MA: Productivity Press. This is the only English-language handbook on the "continuous improvement" suggestion system (*teian*), which is widely used in Japanese companies not only to improve competitive position by generating and implementing a large number of ideas, but to build a strong, participative environment in which the intelligence and creativity of workers are respected.

Shingo, S. (1986). *Zero quality control: source inspection and the poka-yoke system*. Cambridge, MA: Productivity Press.

PETER DEMPSEY

pricing strategy Historically the main determinant of buyer choice, pricing strategy produces revenue in corporate strategy. The choice of pricing strategy is therefore a key determinant in achieving corporate success. There are many options open to the firm in assessing pricing strategy, which are significantly influenced by a number of key factors. Buyers are less price sensitive under the following conditions:

- unique value effect – when products are unique

- substitute awareness effect – when they are unaware of realistic alternatives

- difficult comparison effect – when they are unable to differentiate between product offerings

- total expenditure effect – when the purchase use is a low part of discretionary expenditure

- end-benefit effect – when the cost is a small proportion of the total cost

- shared cost effect – when costs are shared with another party

- sunk investment effect – when costs are related to a cost which has already been incurred

- price quality effect – when the product is seen by consumers as having higher quality, prestige, and the like

- inventory effect – when they cannot store the product

Given the customers' demand schedule, the cost function of the business, and the pricing strategy of competitors, a number of pricing strategy options are available, including the following:

- *Mark-up pricing.* The most common strategy used in the West involves adding a mark-up to the cost of a product. Many companies compute the cost of producing a product and add a specific margin. This strategy, while widely used, has the serious disadvantage that competitors may reconfigure the value chain (*see* VALUE CHAIN ANALYSIS) and attack cost-plus suppliers.

- *Perceived value pricing.* Many companies presently base their pricing on perceived value as identified by the buyer. The price is set to maximize perceived buyer value by using both price and nonprofit features. Companies such as Dupont and Caterpillar have made heavy use of this method.

- *Target pricing.* The price is based on a target position within the market. This method is widely used by Japanese companies and in industries such as automobiles. From the target price, given a desired rate of return, the required production cost can be calculated and steps taken to remove cost at all stages in order to achieve the target.

- *Value pricing.* A number of companies have charged a low price for high-value products, representing a particular bargain for consumers. In automobiles in recent times, the Lexus was specifically priced lower than comparable Mercedes Benz models, despite its high value. Other examples might include Virgin Airways, Wal-Mart, and Direct Line Insurance.

- *Going rate pricing.* In this form of pricing, prices are decided in relationship to those of the competitors. Such a method may well apply to medium-share companies competing against high-share competitors. Typical examples also apply in relatively undifferentiated products such as gasoline.

- *Sealed bid pricing.* This is widely used in industries such as construction, and increasingly in industries in which OUTSOURCING is becoming important.

- *Penetration pricing.* This is often used to maximize rapid market entry by discounting and special deals. It has been used by recent entrants in automobiles from new countries such as Malaysia and Korea.

- *Skimming pricing.* This is used by some competitors to maximize profit returns by maintaining the highest possible price for as long as possible. Examples might include compact disks.

- *Experience curve pricing.* Some companies have made extensive use of experience effects (*see* EXPERIENCE AND LEARNING EFFECTS) to set future pricing tactics. Texas Instruments has been a major exponent of this technique, and the effect is important in industries such as electronics in which substantial experience effects operate.

Factors Impacting External Price Strategies

The choice of pricing strategy adopted by the firm will also depend on a number of criteria. It should:

- be consistent with overall corporate strategy

- be consistent with buyer expectations and behavior

- be consistent with competitor strategies

- be monitored and modified to reflect industry changes

- be monitored for changes in industry boundaries

There are also constraints on the range of pricing options that are available. These include the following:

- *Corporate image.* The external image of the corporation affects its ability to adopt a specific pricing strategy. For example, a producer of low-cost automobiles would find it extremely difficult to successfully be perceived to be a producer of luxury cars: a downmarket low-priced supermarket chain would find it difficult to move up market in price. The corporation also needs to consider the impact of its pricing strategies on others, such as shareholders, consumer pressure groups, regulatory authorities, and government agencies.

- *Geography.* Many companies charge different prices for goods and services in different parts of the world, depending upon local market conditions and regulations.

- *Discounts.* Many corporations offer discounts based on demand for both volume and value. Large users can usually command significant discounts. Discounts may also be offered for early payments and penalties imposed for late payments.

- *Price discrimination.* Many companies differentiate between customers, product or service form, place and time.

Bibliography

Channon, D. F. (1986). *Bank strategic management and marketing.* Chichester: John Wiley.

Forbis, J. L. & Mehta, N. T. (1981). Value based strategies for industrial products. *Business Horizons* (May–June), 32–42.

Kotler, P. (1994). *Marketing management*, 8th edn. Englewood Cliffs, NJ: Prentice-Hall.

Kotler, P. & Armstrong, G. (1989). *Principles of marketing.* Englewood Cliffs, NJ: Prentice-Hall.

Nagle, T. T. (1987). *The strategy and tactics of pricing.* Englewood Cliffs, NJ: Prentice-Hall.

DEREK F. CHANNON

privatization   Privatization is the transfer of a controlling interest in a state-owned organization to private ownership.

A wider definition also embraces any substantial transfer of state asset ownership or control to the private sector, including any government activity intended to reduce the role of the state, or of central or local government, in any particular industry or organization. This can include the issue of new equity in the capital market, the setting up of independent holding companies to distance government from the management of state enterprises, competitive purchasing practices, or even noninterference pledges made in relation to state holdings. As most privatized organizations used to provide goods or services on behalf of the state while they were part of its administrative structure, it is important to make the distinction between the state's obligation to make available and its obligation to be involved with all aspects of such provision. The logistics of postal services may be delegated, for example, while the financing (subsidy) of uniform national tariffs can remain the responsibility of the government, if this is considered to be desirable.

In summary, although privatization is a concept that, strictly, only has to do with ownership of assets, it is very difficult to understand and explain it without consideration to the related organizational matters of control and the setting of organizational goals, priorities and constraints, and the type and methods of management.

Rationale

There exist a number of different reasons to privatize, and these can typically be understood in ideological, financial, or political terms. Although not necessarily mutually exclusive, tradeoffs are often involved; and the ranking of reasons depends, among other aspects, on the country and industry involved, and the place of any particular privatization in the privatizing country's program.

The ideological rationale is based on the neoliberal view that the market is superior to government planning as a means of allocating resources. Therefore, exposure to the market for corporate capital and control in substitution to the allocation mechanisms employed by most governments encourages the development of a closer link between consumer and producer, and enhances the flow of information as well as accountability, leading to higher allocative EFFICIENCY. In addition, such exposure can enlarge a small national capital market both in terms of size and the number of participants and, in the extreme, be used to convert a planned economy into a market-based economy. Also, privatization can offer the opportunity to introduce or enhance competition in the product market (as the existence of a privileged state-owned competitor may mean that competitive production is unfeasible), with all the beneficial implications which this can have according to the same ideology. Finally, privatization segregates many activities from the all-encompassing state, and this permits more precise measurement of the rationality and cost of government involvement.

The financial rationale for privatization, increasingly implemented by administrations holding a wide range of political beliefs, is based on short-term monetary considerations and justifies the exchange of state assets for liquid funds by the need to raise revenue for the vendor government, often to finance current expenditure and reduce the public-sector borrowing requirement (PSBR). In financial terms, privatization can be seen as the exchange of a perpetual series of cashflows for an up front payment. A short-termist government would always be willing to sell below value, while the private sector would only pay more if it believed that it could undertake the management better. Another, associated, reason to privatize is to allow financial decision making in the organization to be carried out without regard to public spending, thereby often allowing the undertaking of investments which, although sound in their own right, may be deferred in view of more urgent government priorities.

The final privatization rationale involves political and electoral considerations. The ability of the government to reallocate wealth and resources, and through pricing and method of sale to strongly influence the composition of many organizations' ownership, enables it to attack opposition strongholds and form interest groups who benefit from the process (or would be expected to suffer as a result of its discontinuation or reversal), thereby creating a captive electorate.

Related Actions

A number of government actions are often associated with privatization. Although they can often take place without privatization, and privatization can conceivably be implemented without them, these actions are frequently interlinked with privatization in critical ways, particularly as they take an active role in dissipating its effects.

The first such action is liberalization (DEREGULATION). This is discussed in some detail in the appropriate section. In a deregulated market, state-owned firms have no justification for receiving subsidies or any other preferential treatment, so they can only survive if they are as efficient as any other competitor. Public ownership in a deregulated market, therefore, becomes irrelevant. Therefore privatization, although not strictly necessary, may well follow. Similarly, a privatized company cannot be allowed to maintain strong monopoly powers, so it must be controlled by means of competition and/or regulation. As a result, privatization is likely to lead to a combination of REGULATION and deregulation.

A second action is the decoupling of the organization's finances from those of the state, enabling the organization to raise funds directly from the markets. A state-owned organization may be able to raise some project funding directly from the market to circumvent some of the problems of combined funding which have already been discussed but, ultimately, this is likely to lead to loss of state control and, if carried out to any great extent, loss of ownership and privatization. Similarly, and almost by definition, a privatized enterprise ought to have its finances separated from those of the state.

The third action is a change in the employment status of the organization's personnel, who cease to be part of the traditionally strongly protected civil servant family and become private employees. This typically implies reduced job security. Civil servant status for employees of public-sector organizations is often a matter of legal necessity, although it may be possible to alter the employment status of the employees concerned by moving them to private companies which are contracted to perform the same tasks. In essence, however, this is tantamount to partial privatization. Privatization, in turn, is associated with the drawing up of new employment contacts on a private basis.

Economic Theories

A number of economic theories are useful in the analysis of the merits of a particular privatization, and contribute to the understanding of the changes taking place. Three are of particular relevance, and they deal with the relationship between ownership and control.

The public choice theory stipulates that the public sector is unable to efficiently run an enterprise because politicians and state bureaucrats pursue their own objectives rather than the public interest. Government departments, the theory says, tend to implement policies designed to maximize votes and reduce risk, and pursue such goals as budget maximization, higher salaries, over-manning, protective public regulation, power, patronage, and the like, such conduct being facilitated by the fact that bureaucrats tend to have better information about the consequences of budgetary changes than taxpayers do. Opponents of the theory believe that disinterested state officials do

indeed pursue the public interest because, like their private-sector counterparts, they find satisfaction in a job well done and, moreover, they have both developed in the same social and cultural backgrounds.

Such inappropriately self-serving behavior may be the result of a poor link between the interests of those who have the right to control and those who are entrusted to exercise it. This link is the field of interest of AGENCY THEORY. The relevance of agency theory for privatization lies in the fact that a change in ownership implies a change in the requirements placed upon management and, similarly, a change in ownership concentration implies a change in the ability of owners to control management; so that, consequently, the incentive mechanisms that should be employed must also change. Incentives such as performance-related pay, for example, share options, and the like, and disincentives such as the threat of bankruptcy, may become possible and necessary to use for the first time.

The final theory to be discussed is property rights. This essentially views ownership as the right to exercise control over assets in any way other than as specifically provided for by contracts or legislation. Two elements of the theory are of particular relevance.

First, the transferability of the organization's stock implied by privatization enables the market for corporate control to constrain management activity that significantly deviates from profit maximization, thereby aiding the agency mechanisms by establishing the threat of takeover as another disincentive for inadequate performance. Nevertheless, the applicability of the mechanism is limited for practical purposes by transaction costs, free-rider problems, and information imperfections; and, moreover, it is difficult to imagine the takeover of a utility which may be the largest capitalized group in the market.

Second, property rights coupled with private ownership can be useful in helping the government abide by its own or its predecessor's agreements, allowing organizations to receive the *ex post* return required to compensate for their *ex ante* investment. Because government holds legislative power and may possibly influence the judicial sphere too, it may find it difficult to commit itself to a particular policy, particularly so across parliamentary terms, and this can result in the inability of the organization to plan for the long term. This problem is less acute in private organizations, in which the holder of property rights (which are frequently guaranteed by constitutional laws that are more powerful than common legislation) is more clearly identified.

Implications

The planning and implementation of a privatization are affected by the country, industry, and company involved, and the rationale for the particular privatization. The ordering of privatizations within any single country also bears some significance. As a result, different privatizations can have different results. Nevertheless, some key effects are frequently encountered.

Ownership. First of all, widespread trading of the organization's stock allows, in principle, its ownership to be optimized with regard to constitution and concentration. In practice, many privatizations disperse stock to a considerable extent, for reasons that are related to political and privatization success factors rather than to any considerations of economic optimization.

Strategy making and government interference. Another factor has to do with management. When a concern is state owned, particularly as governments and government officials tend to become involved in the operational matters of the industries for which they are responsible – frequently for reasons beyond the benefit of the particular organization – it is often the case that organizations are unable to set clear, long-term strategic goals and to prepare plans to achieve them. This should no longer be the case after privatization, when direct government involvement is restricted to the most important matters and is only justified to take place for the most important reasons. Moreover, as a result of the barriers between government and organization which are erected with privatization, such intervention becomes more explicit, opening the rationale for the intervention for debate.

Strategic choice. One of the most significant influences that privatization can have is on the strategy of the organizations concerned. Assuming that the new owners are more profit oriented, the organization itself will have to adjust and comply with their requirements. As a result, it will begin to look for ways in which to reduce its costs, raise its efficiency and increase its profits and turnover.

The first two of these aspects are reasonably straightforward and, once the appropriate motives are set in place by privatization, efforts to achieve them should be no different than they would be in any other enterprise, using methods such as reduction in the number of unnecessary employees, use of the most appropriate technology, use of best practice methods, and others. The third aspect, however, brings into the discussion the possibility of DIVERSIFICATION. Public-sector organizations in many countries have historically been denied the ability to venture into markets other than those which they were set up to serve. There are many reasons for this. For example, if they were allowed to diversify, they would get into each other's way, or they would start to face competition from private companies. Under their new ownership and profitability culture, however, diversification seems an option that they are eager to explore, even though this may lead them to national and international markets of which they initially have little knowledge. Similarly, privatized businesses are likely to be keen to prune any activities that they find unprofitable.

Having said that, it should be made clear that diversification need not strictly follow privatization, as public-sector organizations can, in theory, be allowed to grow in unrelated ways. Historically, however, very few governments have ever decided that it would be worthwhile to give them this kind of strategic decision making freedom; so diversification does, in practice, often follow privatization. Similarly, there are very few cases in which, given the opportunity to diversify, privatized companies do not take it up, so the association between privatization and diversification seems to be very strong. Where it may appear that is not, this is because the association is moderated by the retention of monopoly powers. Privatized companies which are not immediately threatened by competitors tend to take diversification less seriously, until competitive forces are strengthened.

Structure, systems, and skills. In order to be able to service the new strategies, and to reflect the newly adopted profit orientation, structure and management methods must also change. The kinds of changes involved include the establishment of market facing divisions (*see* DIVISIONAL STRUCTURE) – as opposed to the use of functional integrated structures (*see* FUNCTIONAL STRUCTURE) – the proliferation of profit centers, and the like.

These changes also bring about a requirement for different skills, so privatization is often accompanied by major internal reorganization and the installation of new management teams. The latter, however, is often delayed in order to insure the incumbent management's cooperation in the process of privatization.

The need for regulation. A problem which emerges in the privatization of an organization possessing monopoly power (such as many of the traditionally state-owned utilities) is that the profit orientation of the private sector may lead to socially sub-optimal pricing and output levels. In such cases, and until effective competition can be achieved, if ever, it is necessary for the government to establish an authority to oversee the organization concerned and to ensure that this refrains from using its power in undesirable ways. The management of the relationship between such a regulator and the regulated company requires considerable skill, as the regulator is able to influence and perhaps determine the overall profitability and other key variables of the organization, yet the latter may wish to circumvent any restrictions placed upon it. This, in turn, means that regulation can have its own implications quite apart from those of privatization leading, for example, the regulated organization to adopt strategies that reduce the impact of the regulatory authority on itself.

Finally, regulatory authorities often possess considerable legal powers over the organizations that they oversee and have the right, and indeed the obligation, to request sensitive information to enable them to perform their duties effectively. As a result, regulation is a very potent mechanism for intervention in the organization's affairs, in substitution of direct government involvement, and regulatory regimes may easily become the new instruments of political intervention, this time with the private sector bearing the costs.

Implications for performance. Perhaps the most actively sought outcome of privatization is an improvement in organizational performance, and evidence generally suggests that such improvement is indeed compatible with privatization. This, however, is not sufficient to justify privatization. Financial performance has, with some exceptions, typically and historically been only one of the lower ranking goals of state enterprises, and there is evidence to suggest that state-owned enterprises can perform equally well under certain circumstances.

One of the most important factors influencing the ability and intent of an organization to stretch itself in order to perform well is product market competition, and this often explains much of post-privatization performance variation. This means that liberalization (stronger competition in the product market) becomes at least as plausible an option as privatization (stronger competition in the capital market) if it is just a performance improvement that is required, although privatization usually leads to it anyway. In any case, it should be kept in mind that this is quite distinct from the ability of firms to profit from exploiting their markets, which leads to socially undesirable allocative inefficiency and also promotes productive inefficiency.

This, however, is not sufficient to explain all performance variations associated with privatization. Another factor at work is that the desire to privatize itself acts as a spur to improve the performance of state-owned enterprises in preparation for flotation, in order to maximize revenue for the government, and so performance improvements can also be observed during the period leading up to privatization. These improvements can be achieved not only by better productivity and efficiency, but also by means of simple price increases, particularly in monopolistic markets.

The above discussion is only intended to be a brief introduction to some of the mechanisms which link privatization to performance improvements, and it does not determine whether privatization is the only way to achieve such improvements, nor whether it can be relied upon to deliver them. What can be said, however, is that although it is possible for a determined government to provide strong efficiency and profitability incentives for public enterprises, this outcome remains a matter of discretionary choice. Privatization and deregulation turn this into a matter of necessity. Put another way, it can be argued that privatization, while not strictly necessary for the introduction of enhanced performance incentives, is an effective way of insuring that these incentives are put in place and remain there.

Conclusion

In summary, privatization is a strategy which may be adopted by government in order to reallocate a considerable portion of a country's wealth, with the added bonus of raising revenue by means of the process. It can be used to accomplish a large variety of governmental and political goals, and enables the confrontation of lazy enterprises with competitive pressures in their capital and, indirectly, their product market.

Bibliography

Dunsire, A., Hartley, D. & Dimitriou, B. (1988). Organisational status and performance: a conceptual framework for testing public choice theories. *Public Administration Review*, 66 (4), 363–88.
Goodman, J. B. & Loveman, G. W. (1991). Does privatization serve the public interest? *Harvard Business Review*, 69, 26–38.
Jensen, M. C. (1989). Eclipse of the public corporation. *Harvard Business Review*, 67, 61–74.
Kay, J. A. (1988). The state and the market: the UK experience. Occasional paper no. 23, Group of Thirty, London.
Kay, J. A. & Thompson, D. (1986). Privatisation: a policy in search of a rationale. *Economic Journal*, 96, 18–32.
Vickers, J. & Yarrow, G. K. (1988). *Privatization: an economic analysis*. Cambridge, MA: MIT Press.

STEPHANOS AVGEROPOULOS

process mapping   For many years, theories on business management have been functionally based, but now organizations are viewing themselves as a collection of interrelated and interdependent processes. A process is a coordi-

nated set of activities which meets a customer requirement – it represents the customer's view of the organization rather than the internal view displayed by the organigram. Many organizations are now undergoing Business Process Reengineering (BPR) to change from a FUNCTIONAL STRUCTURE to an HORIZONTAL STRUCTURE.

To achieve this change, time, commitment, and control are required, particularly from the CEO/chairman. Employees need regular communication to convince them of the necessity for change, to gain their commitment and confidence, and to maintain their enthusiasm during difficult stages of projects. Communication is essential not only between team members undertaking the study but also between the team and the business. Effective communication helps staff members understand the purpose of a process, where they fit into it, and how the process contributes to company goals. Successful projects require the participation of cross-functional, trained teams, often supported by an external consultant to act as a facilitator to draw out key goals and objectives.

Most organizations have an "organigram" but very few have analysed the flow of work across the functions or even within them. This kind of analysis is increasing within companies, and is a powerful way of spotting how the organization could work more effectively and either save time/costs or increase quality, or both. However, if improvements are to be made to processes, a clear understanding of them is required before any can be implemented.

One of the most effective ways to gain an understanding of existing processes is to draw them on a "map". Such maps enable them to be easily read and understood and are key in the description, analysis, and communication processes. Typically, between five and 20 major processes are used to encompass the key activities of the organization. These should support the key objectives and goals of the organization.

Use of Process Maps

Within BPR, there are various phases in which process maps may act as a focus.

Process capture and business modelling.   This phase is where the "as is" processes of the

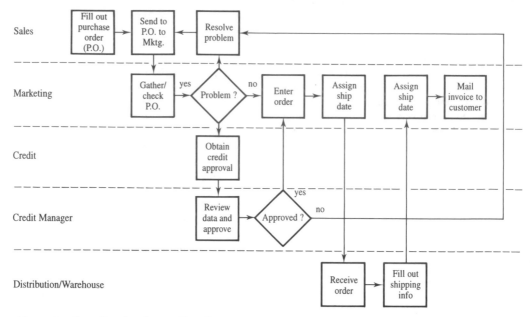

Figure 1   Cross functional map: flow diagram

organization are mapped. This is important for process redesign, as time spent in this phase provides a number of benefits. Specifically, it:

● identifies "quick win" solutions
● provides a common understanding for the team involved
● identifies other potential areas for improvement
● highlights particular failures affecting areas of the organization; for example, customers

Process maps can highlight duplicated activities and interactions in the organization and those which do not add value.

Process redesign.   Following the initial process analysis, the processes are analyzed and redesign opportunities are discussed by the team. Ideas are discussed within the team and simulations may be carried out to investigate the various "what if" possibilities and assess the impact of potential changes.

Process support.   Teams that have been involved in the initial stages of process mapping will be involved in support as changes/new processes are implemented.

Process analysis flows are very effective when overlapped onto organizational structures. Companies are typically organized into functional, vertical hierarchies such as Marketing, Operations, Distribution, Finance, and Human Resources. Organizational charts typically reflect this functionality, with a high degree of hierarchy. Often, status, power, control, ambition, and rank are more important to people than efficiency, lateral cooperation, and customer service. However, organizations delivering to customers depend on key processes that often cut across functional vertical hierarchies. Many companies are thus moving to a CROSS-FUNCTIONAL MANAGEMENT STRUCTURE, to manage and deliver superior CORE PROCESS performance. Process maps help the understanding of the interaction between departments and identify "hand offs" that can then be addressed (see figure 1).

Process Mapping Procedure

Several factors must be taken into account when undertaking a process mapping task.

Differing views within a team.
As teams often contain cross-functional members, tasks being mapped may be viewed

differently. This may be the result of differing ways of working or a resistance to sharing information.

There may also be gaps between what people say they do and what actually happens. The process map can act as a focal point for discussions about the way people work, helping to create a common understanding.

The key is to focus on the inputs and outputs of each step and the "best" ways of working.

Consultants and academics can act as independent facilitators for the BPR programs, but implementation should be undertaken by the organization's own employees, who must own the changes, either in partnership with, or supported by, external people.

Standards.   Before undertaking a process mapping task, it is advisable to set standards for the team, which must be adhered to.

Standards decided at the start of a project help to provide a consistent framework to allow different teams to be able to quickly read and understand each other's maps. Following standards will also allow maps to be easily brought together at a later stage.

It is advisable to start mapping from the top level and work down.

In this way, different groups can work on sections of the process and then bring the findings together. Different levels of processes are essential. This level differentiation enables the complete process cycle to be shown in a manageable way, with each process step being broken down into more detail on separate charts, as shown in figure 2:

- Level 1 map: top-level map – each process symbol identifies a major process chain.

- Level 2 map: process chain map – this map represents a decomposition of one of the process chains; each box represents a process in that chain.

- Level 3 map: process map – this map represents a decomposition of one of the level 2 processes; each box represents a task in that process.

- Level 4 map: task map – each process symbol represents a step taken to complete the specific task.

- Level 5 map: step map – each box represents a specific action to be taken to complete the step.

The topics that generally, should be standardized are as follows.

Symbols.   These must be uniform. The most commonly used are based on the ANSI (American National Standards Institute) type. Rectangles usually indicate activities while diamonds indicate decision points or check points, providing a simple understanding of the process, as shown in figure 3.

- process – group of linked activities

- activity – action taking place in the process

- arrow – direction and order of activities; label output

- boundary – no parent process or immediate scope

- linkage circle – used for linkage within a process

- delay – process waits with no action taking place

- decision – process branching due to results of a decision

Color rules.   These can be used to indicate different departments, sites, or types of process within the organization, and therefore need to be defined at the beginning.

Numbering.   All process symbols must be numbered for easy reference. As process maps are drawn top down, the numbering system should be hierarchical down from the level 0 map. For example, base numbers can be 1.0, 2.0, 3.0 and so on, while for each level down, the next level of numbering can be added:

- subprocess from level 1 – 1.1, 1.2, 1.3 and so on

- subprocess from level 2 – 1.1.1, 1.1.2, 1.2.1, 1.2.2, ..., 1.3.1, 1.3.2, and so on.

Text and lines.   These are important for visual consistency, and particularly important for process mapping tools.

Notes.   Notes referring to the map should be held in the interview notes or an accompanying

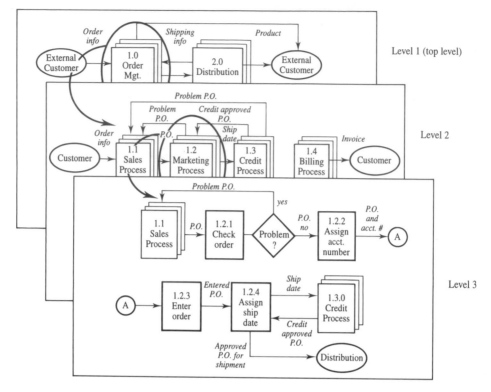

Level 1 (top level)

Level 2

Level 3

Figure 2   Hierarchies displayed within a process map and relationship between them.

document, which should be kept available with the map.

Information. This may be captured at each step of the process:

- *Elapsed and Active Time.* How long the overall process is, and how long it takes to complete each step and inbetween each step. The difference between the active and elapsed time is also a key factor for determining where improvements to processes can be made. *Elapsed time:* the point at which input is received until the point at which output is received by the next customer in the process. *Active time:* the actual time spend performing a task.
- *Dependencies.* Where a task depends on the output of another. These should be clear.
- *Who.* Who is performing each task.
- *Problem areas.* Difficult tasks, time delays, and activities in which problems are frequently experienced.

- *Value added.* Whether a step "adds value" or merely adds cost.
- *Costs.* An element of activity-based costing may be collected.
- *Quality issues.*
- *Cross reference.* To the organization map.

There are a number of methods for collecting data for process maps. These include individual interviews, questionnaires, and discussion groups/workshops. All of these methods provide qualitative data. However, methods such as flow tagging can provide quantitative results. In the example given in figure 4 an order is monitored through the process and times between processes captured. Organizations themselves may also have data on processes that can be used.

During the mapping process, frequent review meetings must occur. These not only solve the purpose of confirming the accuracy of the data that has been collected but also any difficulties/ issues may be discussed and standards re-emphasized. Groups working on different

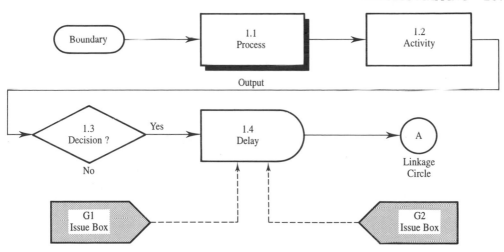

Figure 3

Figure 4

parts of the same map *must* meet regularly to reconfirm the boundaries (see figure 5).

Following the completion and agreement of this "As is" stage, the process redesign stage can then commence. Opportunities are discussed in work groups and various "what if" possibilities assessed. The ideas can then be prioritized based on potential improvement.

Types of Process Maps

Flow diagrams. Flow mapping is the primary mechanism for understanding the order of activities within a process. Process maps are then often developed further by having other information attached to them; for example, roles, departments, value added activities, times, and costs. Flow diagrams permit focus on the inputs and outputs of an activity.

IDEF0. This mapping standard was developed by the U.S. Department of Defense during the 1970s, and stands for International DEFinition. It started life as a software development tool, but is now often used as a general process mapping tool. It can be used to derive a relationship diagram (see figure 6). The boxes represent the activities of the process/system, while the arrows represent the information or products necessary to carry out the activities. Mechanisms are the things used to perform the activity (machine, human) and controls represent the information that influences the way in which the activity is performed.

Role Activity Diagrams. Role Activity Diagrams (RADs) are a relatively new concept in business process modelling. They were first used in 1983. RADs concentrate on the roles and interactions between roles. They are

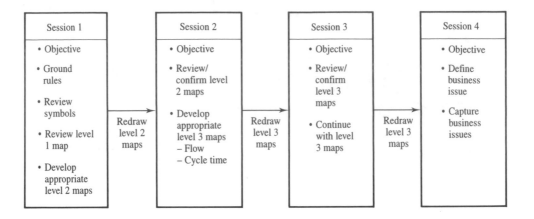

Figure 5

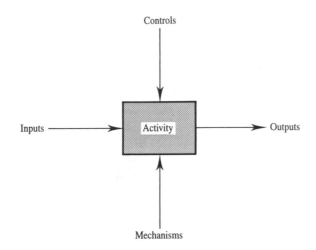

Figure 6

flowcharts that have been ordered so that the responsibility for activities is contained within the diagram. They concentrate on what people actually do within a process (see figure 7).

Action workflow diagrams. This diagramming method represents the person-to-person trans-actions. Each transaction or "workflow loop" is represented by a closed elliptical loop consisting of four phases: preparation, negotiation, perfor-mance, and acceptance (see figure 8). The customer is represented on the left and the performer on the right.

Dependent on the purpose of process map-ping, the different methodologies may be used.

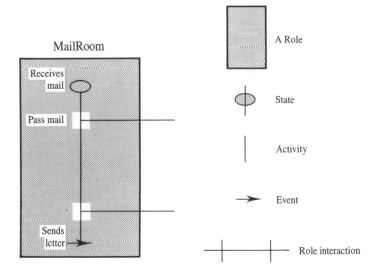

Figure 7   Role interaction

For basic process mappings the simple use of flow diagrams is recommended.

Methods for Developing Maps

Brown paper/Post It™ notes.   One of the most common methods for drawing maps is the use of Post-It™ notes. These have the advantage that the maps can be created in the interviews. The process mapping is therefore quicker; more accurate, as the interviewee can immediately tell if a box is put in the wrong place; better "buy-in", as the interviewee feels that they are part of the process and have more control; and shorter validation workshops are required with less potential for friction, as people will have seen the maps develop.

Post-It™ notes are available in many colors, so that color rules can very easily be introduced to illustrate different departments, manual processes versus technological process, and the like. The data can be captured on a computer *after* the validation workshops.

For visual ease, Post-It™ notes may be stuck on to brown paper put up round a room, or on white boards that may easily be removed and taken into rooms for workshops. This method is ideal for a workshop environment, as it acts as a central focus and facilitates the communication.

When using Post-It™ notes, similar standards to those discussed earlier need to be defined, but some elements may require some modifications.

Software tools.   There are a number of software products available to produce flowcharts and process maps. These range from simple drawing tools, which map to a certain standard, to more elaborate systems.

Various product summary reports can be purchased which analyze all the tools that are available on the market. It is up to the team as to which software is chosen – depending on what information and level is required from the mapping process.

Summary

As more companies move from a functional to a process driven organization, the use of process mapping is important to facilitate this change. Maps often give a clearer explanation of a process than words. Changing the process is a long-term initiative. It needs to be communicated to every level of the business. Staff must understand the purpose of a process, where they fit into it, and how the process contributes to the company's goals. The mapping process is

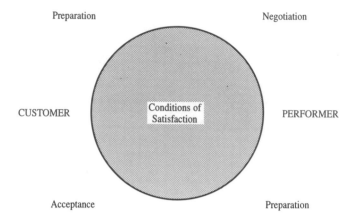

Preparation   Negotiation

CUSTOMER   Conditions of   PERFORMER
                            Satisfaction

Acceptance   Preparation

Figure 8

also often as useful as the maps themselves. When individuals work together to produce an end-to-end map of the processes in which they work, they gain an understanding of other's tasks and problems, and how they contribute to these. This often encourages teams and individuals to improve, as wasteful activities become visible. However, maps do take time to produce accurately. Many companies have invested in producing maps, but do not make use of them fully and are unaware of their true value.

JULIA CHANNON

product market diversification matrix
Originally developed by Ansoff, the product market diversification matrix, shown in figure 1, originally divided a company's product market activities into four key areas, each of which suggested a particular strategy.

Current products produced for current markets suggest strategies of attempting to maintain or increase existing levels of market penetration.

The introduction of current products into new markets suggests strategies aimed at extending product reach. Many new products when first introduced have actually ended up being most successful in markets for which they were not originally conceived. One particular strategy which has proved effective in opening new markets has been the exploitation of new or unused distribution channels.

New products for existing markets suggest a strategy of new product development. These should be introduced taking full cognizance of actual market needs, rather than attempting to force products developed internally, without paying due attention to customer needs.

The diversification cell, that of new products for new markets, is the most dangerous, as the company knows little about either the products or the markets. As discussed elsewhere, many DIVERSIFICATION moves have therefore resulted in strategic failure, and thus great care needs to be taken when embarking on such a strategy. While a RELATED DIVERSIFIED STRATEGY might gain greater stock market acceptance, the concept of relatedness needs careful attention, as experience indicates that what is initially thought of as a related activity may indeed turn out differently. For example, until recently banking and insurance were seen as separate industries, but by redefining industry boundaries both can be categorized as "financial services" and hence related. The ability of each specialist function to absorb the culture and methods of the other is often difficult and fraught with danger.

Ansoff subsequently refined his original concept to include the added complexity of geography (see figure 2). In this three-dimensional format, the matrix can be used to define the strategic thrust and the ultimate scope of the business. As shown, the firm can opt for one of a number of variations of market need, product/

	Current Products	New Products
Current Markets	Market Penetration Strategy	Product Development Strategy
New Markets	Market Development Strategy	Diversification Strategy

Figure 1 The product market diversification matrix.
Source: Ansoff (1987, p. 109).

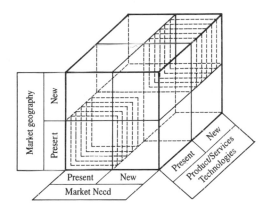

Figure 2   Dimensions of the geographic growth vector

service technologies, and geographic scope to define a SERVED MARKET. The second component of portfolio strategy, as defined by Ansoff, is the competitive advantage that the firm seeks to achieve in each served market. The third component consists of the synergies that might be achieved between businesses (*see* SYNERGY), while the last is the degree of strategic flexibility that can be achieved.

Strategic flexiblity can be achieved in two ways. The first method is external to the firm, through diversifying the firm's geographic scope, needs served, and technologies, so that any sudden change in any of the strategic businesses areas does not produce serious repercussions.

Second, strategic flexibility can be achieved by making resources and capabilities easily transferable among the businesses. Ironically, optimizing one of the four components of the portfolio strategy growth vector is likely to depress the firm's performance with regard to the other components. In particular, maximizing synergy is very likely to reduce strategic flexibility.

Bibliography

Ansoff, I. (1987). *Corporate strategy*. Harmondsworth, UK: Penguin. See pp. 108–11.

DEREK F. CHANNON

Q

question mark businesses In the Boston Consulting Group's GROWTH SHARE MATRIX model, such businesses are seen to indicate opportunity. They are businesses that need to gain share by generating additional market share and hence lower cost via experience gains, while the growth rate in the industry is high. As a result, the primary objective of such businesses should be to gain share rather than maximize short-term profitability. Indeed, starving such businesses of their capital needs is a major reason for failure in companies operating such a strategy. For success, it is imperative that capacity additions and expansions should be added at a rate faster than growth in the market, to allow for share gain. This may mean poor financial performance – or even losses – and cashflow will be considerable and negative. Many companies are very reluctant to tolerate such poor performance and, as a consequence, fail to achieve the cost gains required to convert question mark businesses to STAR BUSINESSES. Due to overall group cashflow capacity, few corporations can support more than a small number of question mark businesses. It is therefore important to carefully select from the range of new business opportunities that are available and to support those selected few to the full.

See also **Growth share matrix**

DEREK F. CHANNON

radar mapping   The radar chart permits management to see at a glance the financial status of the firm. On the chart, an example of which is shown in figure 1, the financial factors influencing strategy are broken down under five key headings of profitability, growth, financial stability, capital activity, and productivity. Many of these measurements are similar to those identified as critically important in the PIMS program.

Within each of these five key headings are a number of lesser measures. Overall, the position of the firm is plotted as a "snowflake" diagram. Circles for "normal," "bad," and "very bad" are shaded to emphasize the critical values and to identify areas for urgent management actions for improvement. The area outside the critical lines can be marked in green to indicate corporate strengths that might form the basis for strategic focus. Comparison of radar charts over time is also useful, to indicate trends which may be focused on or may call for corrective action.

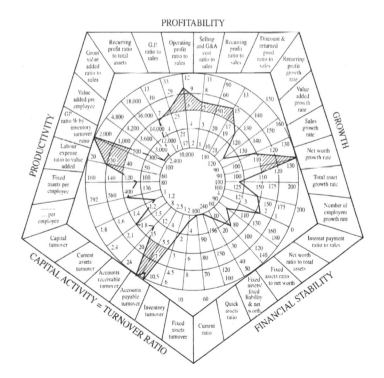

Figure 1 Management analysis radar chart (January 1, 1993 – December 31, 1993).
Source: Nagashima (1992).

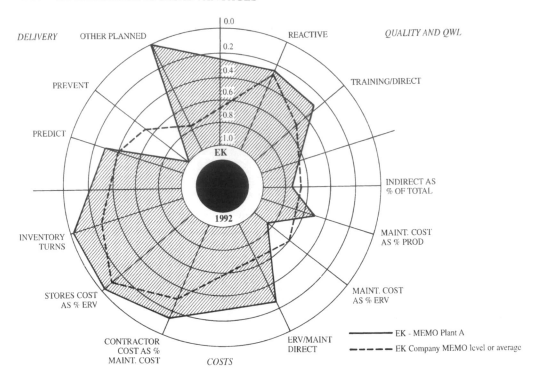

Figure 2   Kodak class MEMO benchmarking M² chart.
Source: Bogan & English (1994).

Some companies have developed charts which illustrate different critical variables. Kodak, for example, has developed its measures matrix, or M-squared chart, illustrated in figure 2, as part of its BENCHMARKING process. In this system:

- Each radial line or spoke represents a measure.

- Concentric circles range from 1.0 at the center to 0.0 at the outermost circle.

- Data are normalized.

- Benchmarks for each measure are set in the center of the chart on its respective line. Consequently, the better an operation's performance, the nearer it is to the center and the further away the greatest opportunity for improvement.

As they allow opportunities to observe performance for an operation from a single graphic, radar charts:

- highlight performance gaps between the company's measures and best practice

- provide a tool to check performance over time

- make management focus on best practice, comparison allowing a series of strategic measures rather than just one

Bibliography

Bogan, C. & English, M. (1994). *Benchmarking for best practice.* New York: McGraw-Hill. See pp. 58–61.
Nagashima, S. (1992). *100 management charts.* Tokyo: Asian Productivity Organisation. See pp. 44–5.

DEREK F. CHANNON

re-engineering disadvantages   Re-engineering is defined by Hammer (1990) as "the fundamental analysis and radical redesign of business processes, to achieve dramatic improvements in critical contemporary measures of performance such as cost, quality service and speed." Research suggests that while re-engineering has had great success, it has also seen great failures (Hall et al., 1993). The benefits of re-engineering are often emphasized, but little is said about its disadvantages, some of which are outlined below.

While the purpose of re-engineering, at a meta-level, is to improve overall performance, in some cases after months, even years, of careful redesign, companies find that they achieve dramatic improvements in *individual* processes, only to watch *overall* results decline. Research shows that re-engineering projects often fail to achieve real business impact, that the resulting improvements in performance are often disappointingly low (Hall et al., 1993).

If a firm is to function effectively, radical changes in business processes require correspondingly radical changes in a whole range of other organizational design variables. These changes cost money and are difficult to implement, while the length of time they take to achieve is uncertain. Companies that rely simply on "re-engineering" as a universal panacea to achieve dramatic improvements in performance are deluding themselves. The dramatic improvements promised are often offset by huge costs, in terms of disruption, retraining, and reworking of systems.

The implementation of re-engineering is easier said than done and a successful outcome is not guaranteed. Indeed, the ingredients needed to insure success still remain unclear (redesign requires careful experimentation). There are no rules and we are told no certain formulas (Ostroff & Smith, 1992).

While companies know that they have to change, in order to adapt to changing market conditions, they are often unsure how they should change, what their new organizational structure should look like, and how it should work in detail. They know they want to become more market-oriented and customer-focused, but do not know how to bring about the desired new behavior (Ostroff & Smith, 1992). They are equally unsure about how the new structure will actually fit together. While the board may have a vision of how this is to be accomplished, it is often not clearly understood at lower levels of the organization. Diagrams may look good on

paper and impress the chief executive, but no-one really knows what their impact will be.

Where initiatives are ill-thought through, at best they only achieve modest levels of success, if any at all. At worst, they lead to failure, disruption, expense, and erosion of employee faith in management (Hall et al., 1993). Where initiatives continually fall by the wayside, they are seen merely as the management's "flavor of the month" and no one takes them seriously.

Many of the changes that are implemented are counter-cultural. They represent a threat to people's working environment and are often met with strong resistance. Many people are reluctant to give up their heritage and that which has always been held sacred to them in the past. Others may appear willing to change, but persuading them to pay more than just lip service is often a major problem.

Re-engineering involves challenging the way in which things have always been done in the past and looking for new, more efficient, ways of doing them. However, long-instilled behavior patterns are difficult to alter. A huge amount of management time has to be spent trying to convince people of the virtue of change. This requires a great deal of communication and reinforcement, a massive amount of effort and commitment of resources. Time has to be spent re-interviewing people for their jobs, re-skilling them, and retraining them, often with uncertain results.

The fact that re-engineering is being undertaken at all is a latent signal to everyone that cutbacks are to be made and almost certainly jobs will be lost. Critically, the way in which re-engineering is carried out and seen to work will both affect and be affected by the culture and climate of trust within the organization.

Re-engineering threatens current jobs, status, and future job opportunities, especially those of long-serving, middle-aged managers, in middle management positions. Indeed, the middle management layers are removed from the organization, as they are no longer perceived to be adding value to the business. However, where re-engineering has not been carried out properly and there are simply fewer people in the company, together with a flatter structure, people can find themselves with a broader job role and an expanded workload. Some may end up with more interesting and varied work, with more responsibility; while others, who are unable or unwilling to cope, may leave the organization.

People become cynical about re-engineering and see it simply as an exercise to reduce the head count and take costs out of the business. They fear they will be re-engineered out of a job. They feel insecure and resentful, as hard work and loyalty no longer appear to be regarded as important. Indeed, people who have been rewarded for good work in the past can find themselves out of work. In a new, "slimline" re-engineered company, there are no longer the same number of jobs to go round. Fewer people are needed. Redundancies are on a scale that would not have occurred in the past, without the company having received bad press. It is a situation in which companies find themselves ill-equipped and lacking in experience.

At IBM in 1993, each wave of redundancies was followed by a fall in morale. At an economic level, it led to a sharp decline in productivity. It was difficult to maintain the commitment and motivation of the remaining staff, and slowed down the cultural change process. Re-engineering was a traumatic experience for the whole company. The situation was compared by the executives to a wake after a funeral. There was massive upheaval and those who survived needed their confidence rebuilding.

Where there are fewer middle management positions, the value system and compensation structure has to be changed. Whereas managers would once have come directly from school or university and been expected to stay with a company for a long time, this is no longer the case. Companies can no longer offer lifetime employment. People's careers are uncertain and their jobs insecure. The view of a career in the future has to change. In the past, it meant going up through the levels of the management hierarchy, whereas in a flat organizational structure these levels no longer exist.

Often, re-engineering is not a once-and-for-all effort, but a series of waves washing over the organization for a period of years (Hall et al., 1993). It takes time and a huge amount of resources to effect fundamental change.

While companies scramble to take costs out of the business – much like throwing sandbags out of a hot air balloon, to see who can be the lightest and fly the highest – they are unsure about how far they should go. How many managers are really needed to manage effectively? And what is the optimum size of their workload? Those companies that shed too many people may save on the payroll, but find themselves unable to cope if they secure a large contract.

A flat organizational structure often depends upon the implementation of new technology. While IT is an enabler for successful re-engineering, it can also be a major constraint. The sheer variety of available IT solutions adds to the complexity of a re-engineering project. The initial capital investment is often high, adding to the net risk of a project. Those who choose to go down the route of re-engineering may find themselves committed to long-term investment in new technology.

A key to successful re-engineering must surely be an appreciation of its disadvantages and weaknesses. In fact, some managers privately conclude that the best way to build a new organization is to start from scratch, and that the best way in which to change all the people – is to change all the people. Companies' visions of the future can be held back by their memories of the past. It is important to remember that these visions are determined by the realities of today.

Bibliography

Hall, G., Rosenthal, J. & Wade, J. (1993). How to make reengineering really work. *Harvard Business Review*, **71**, 119–31. Reprint 93604.

Hammer, M. (1990). Reengineering work: don't automate, obliterate. *Harvard Business Review*, **68**, 104–12.

Ostroff, F. & Smith, D. (1992). The horizontal organisation. *The McKinsey Quarterly*, Number 1, 148–68.

KAYE LOVERIDGE

regulation Regulation is the institution of a set of administrative and legal processes which are designed to ensure that the purposes of particular groups are served and that such groups are protected from forces which tend to threaten them (*see also* DEREGULATION). There are essentially two types of regulation, economic and social. Regulation is typically set up by the government, which appoints a regulatory agency to set the terms for and to implement regulation, although self-regulation – whereby the members of the regulated industry form some sort of organization to regulate themselves – is also common, predominantly in the financial services industry.

Economic regulation, which includes public utility and antitrust regulation, can be further subdivided according to whether it serves to insulate producers from the vigor of market forces (in which case the regulator is said to act as an "environmental buffer"), or to protect consumers from the power of producers (in which case the regulator acts as a "change agent"). Sometimes, however, regulation which has initially been instituted to protect consumers is redirected to the benefit of producers as a result of the latter's actions, in which case the regulator is said to have been "captured by the industry" (Bernstein, 1955). More commonly, economic regulation is instituted to limit excessive competition, to insure that a critical industry is maintained in a healthy condition, or to deal with market imperfections such as asymmetric information, market failures, missing markets, predation, CROSS-SUBSIDIZATION and other monopolistic practices.

Turning to social regulation, this is an increasingly popular activity that often has a scope which goes beyond individual industries and aims for greater social justice overall, addressing matters such as EXTERNALITIES (e.g., pollution) and social change.

The Political Process of Regulation

The distinction between regulation in favor of an industry and regulation constraining an industry was explored in Stigler's (1971) seminal paper, in which a political theory of regulation was advanced which suggested that regulation may not necessarily be the result of forces originating from government to protect groups under threat, but could instead be the outcome of a political process of bargaining whereby pressure groups demand regulation, and government dispenses it to the benefit of those groups for a price, which could be in the form of help with re-election. The pressure groups which are powerful enough to obtain government action to their benefit prefer to receive their benefits in the form of regulation

(e.g., by setting up barriers to entry (*see* BARRIERS TO ENTRY AND EXIT), import tariffs, or other mechanisms to retard the growth of new entrants), and not in more direct ways such as subsidies, as the latter can attract new companies into their market.

The Role and Methods of the Regulator

Because of the difficult nature of their task, regulators are often empowered to interfere at many levels of the regulated firms' decision making, including decisions regarding major investments, the determination of market strategy, and the like. For much of the time, however, the purposes of regulation can be adequately served by controling a few key variables such as prices and the quality of output. This is likely to be preferable because it allows the regulated firm to complete its own decisions, albeit within the framework that the regulator sets, minimizing unwanted side-effects.

As far as price controls are concerned, there are two main methods through which these can be imposed; namely, rate of return pricing and price limit control. Rate of return regulation involves the determination of a reasonable cost base, and the firm is then obliged to price no higher than to meet these costs, plus a fair rate of return which is set by the regulator. This type of regulation allows shareholders to expect a predictable, yet constrained, return and shifts uncertainty from the producer to the consumer. A resultant problem, however, is that management has no incentive to cut costs and, indeed, it may tend to extend the firm's capital base and distort its choice of inputs, particularly if the entire company's activities are grouped together for the purposes of cost determination. Also, rate of return regulation tends to push prices toward being based on average (rather than marginal) costs, and this can prevent the firm from price discriminating and using multipart tariffs.

Price limit regulation, on the other hand, involves the determination of a range of allowable real prices (an upper bound is typically established), leaving the benefit of cost reductions over a set amount with the organization. This system minimizes the incentive to inflate costs and the asset base, but it creates an incentive to reduce the quality of service. This is because a price-capped monopolist may reasonably expect that it can get away with a reduction in the quality of service without significant concurring loss of revenue. To combat this, a combination of price and quality targets may have to be set. In general, because the price limit regime requires the regulator to monitor its industry more closely than under a cost plus regime, in order to obtain the additional information necessary to set maximum prices, it is more appropriate when technology is changing slowly. Another characteristic of the regime is that the shorter the interval is between the rate reviews, the more the regime resembles rate of return and cost plus systems, as the firm does not have enough time to enjoy cost reductions before these lead to price cuts.

In general, the timing and scope of regime reviews, in which rates of return and price limits are regularly re-evaluated, are very important because of their effect on EFFICIENCY and innovation. As far as efficiency is concerned, determination of the review frequency involves a tradeoff between productive and allocative efficiency, as the longer the regulator allows prices to diverge from marginal cost, the more the regulated firm will have an incentive to reduce its costs and improve productive efficiency. Similarly, if the benefits of innovation are taken away from the firm too quickly, then the incentive to develop new products and processes will be reduced. In the longer term, the credibility of the regulator becomes as important as his current conduct. High sunk cost projects, in particular, involve the threat that the regulator will modify his policies as soon as much of a company's (irreversible) investment has been completed and, if the regulator cannot be relied upon to maintain reasonable policies in the future, then the investment may not be undertaken at all.

The Costs and Impact of Regulation

Regulation cannot be implemented without costs. The administration of regulation itself is expensive, and each regulated firm must also incur the costs of negotiating and complying with the regulator. Its impact can be felt at both the industry level and the company level and, indirectly, it can also affect an entire economy.

Impact on market structure. At the industry level, regulation can have a considerable impact on market structure and the level of competition, as it may exclude certain competitors from a particular sector, it may segment a market, place specific limits on geographic expansion, or impede innovation. In addition, it can stifle competitiveness by reducing the surprise element of competition due to disclosure requirements, and it enables firms to contest the actions of their competitors in regulatory hearings.

Impact on the strategy development process. As far as individual organizations are concerned, the effects come through many directions. For a regulated firm, many environmental conditions are articulated through the regulatory agency which, therefore, becomes the focus of organizational attention, to the exclusion of the customer. Similarly, the number of relevant stakeholders is reduced (*see* STAKEHOLDER ANALYSIS), as is the ability of the firm to develop its strategy simply by balancing them off. Instead, the firm must become adept in political analysis and negotiating skills and, in time, traditional planning capabilities are weakened. Characteristics such as centralization, bureaucratic delays (e.g., the need to produce proposals for approval), and the need for procedural uniformity also appear.

Impact on optimal ownership. Another implication of regulation is related to optimization of ownership. As far as control of management is concerned, regulation provides some subsidized monitoring and disciplining as the regulatory agency also keeps an eye on management. This implies that regulation should reduce the need for ownership concentration. Nevertheless, this effect may be counterbalanced by the fact that limited competition reduces the incentive to hold down costs and, with cost plus pricing in particular, as has already been discussed, management may resort to substantial amenity consumption. This danger is all the more realistic as shareholders know that, if alerted, the regulator may squeeze the firm's margins, so they have little to gain by discussing such practices in public. In turn, senior management may tolerate excessive wages, over-manning, and the like as a means of taking out in cost what cannot be expropriated as profit, given the regulatory environment, so the implications of regulation for ownership do vary in practice.

Impact on strategic outcome. One of the most significant ways in which regulation can affect an organization is through its influence on strategic outcome, and DIVERSIFICATION in particular. As long as the interests of the regulated firm and the regulator remain convergent, the firm is likely to remain close to its main line of regulated businesses and may even integrate vertically. When their interests diverge, however, for example due to high contract monitoring costs (*see* TRANSACTION COSTS), the firm may diversify into unregulated businesses, to the extent which is permissible.

Impact on structure. Organization may also be affected, although this is not necessarily the case. Where the regulated enterprise is also active in nonregulated markets, however, practices such as cross-subsidization become possible, so the regulator may require that any nonregulated business is undertaken through separate subsidiaries, to insure that any transactions between the two companies become more visible.

Performance. It is generally acceptable that regulation, by virtue of reducing competition, allows firms to charge higher prices and, consequently, enjoy artificially high levels of profit, although this may be diminished in situations in which manager control is more relaxed, as has already been discussed. Nevertheless, the regulatory process has also been observed to retard price adjustments during inflationary periods, and this can result in diminished performance and increased risk. Overall, however, the risk of a regulated firm is generally lower than for an unregulated one.

Other implications. Finally, certain social priorities (such as cross-subsidization of high-cost areas or low-income groups, or the provision of a universal service) imposed by means of regulation are likely to introduce a number distortions (even though they may be correcting others), as can other constraints imposed on regulated firms, such as the requirement for uninterruptible service (guarantees of constant adequate electricity supply regardless of demand, for example, require companies to prepare for levels of output that may never be required). Technological innovation can also be discouraged with the burden of environmental impact statements and the like, and the regulator's ability to categorize costs in a price ceiling regime can also influence the choice of technology.

Successful Regulatory Regimes

In order to judge the success of a regulatory setup, the criteria set out by Braeutingham & Panzar (1989) can be used: one can consider, for example, incentives for cost misreporting, choice of technology and levels of cost-reducing innovation, choice of price and output levels, and diversification into competitive markets.

Regulation may be unsuccessful: (i) if the regulator possesses imperfect information, knowledge, or foresight; (ii) because of rigidities (regulatory rules are hard to change, yet technology and economic circumstances change constantly); (iii) because of insufficient means (government may fail to choose the least costly means of solving a problem); (iv) because of myopic regulation (if regulators are forced to specialize, regulation may become too forced or rigid); (v) because of political constraints (political realities may prevent the "right" policy from being adopted); or (vi) due to inappropriately set objectives.

Finally, it is worth mentioning that where regulation is instituted in association with PRIVATIZATION, so that direct government involvement is minimized in the relevant industries, the regulatory framework may easily be converted to become the government's instrument for *ad hoc* political intervention in the industries involved.

Bibliography

Bernstein, M. H. (1955). *Regulating business by independent commission.* Princeton, NJ: Princeton University Press.

Braeutingham, R. R. & Panzar, J. C. (1989). Diversification incentives under price-based and cost-based regulation. *RAND Journal of Economics,* **20** (3), 373–91.

Littlechild, S. C. (1983). *Regulating British Telecommunication's profitability.* London: Department of Industry.

Stigler, G. J. (1971). The theory of economic regulation. *Bell Journal of Economics and Management Science*, **2** (1), 3–21.

STEPHANOS AVGEROPOULOS

related diversified strategy   Businesses adopting this strategy are defined as corporations which had diversified into activities with some apparent similarities to their original activities. Such diversification centered on a "core skill" such as a technology. Technologies of this kind included chemical, electrical, and mechanical engineering, and firms in these industries were natural and early diversifiers. They were also early adopters of the multidivisional structure form of organization in response to the growing complexity of the business as product market diversity increased. In the Harvard studies of the early 1970s, such businesses were defined as those in which less than 70 per cent of sales were generated from any one concern.

Firms in technology- or skill-based industries, where the skill or technology led naturally to the production of a wide range of end products meeting the needs of a variety of markets, were amongst the earliest diversifiers. While acquisition was an important element in their diversification strategies, significant growth also occurred as a result of internal development. In chemicals and electrical engineering the level of research expenditure was relatively high, although it was low in mechanical engineering. Nevertheless, the skills of metal manipulation proved to be readily transferable to a wide variety of different end uses.

While overall concentration and capital intensity was high in specific segments, the wide market scope of these industries had not precluded new competitive entries. Furthermore, the constant rapid change of technology frequently transformed the pattern of strategic advantage. In general, despite technical SYNERGY or STRATEGIC FIT, the degree of integration between the different corporate activities was low. There were cases in which one unit supplied raw materials or components to another, but usually all activities had a direct interface with outside markets. Therefore, while some central coordination of interdependent activities might be desirable, this was usually low, relative to the product flow of the corporation as a whole. As a result, while these concerns were early adopters of a multidivisional form of structure and were latterly converted to an SBU STRUCTURE, the large central office predicted for such businesses was sharply reduced during the 1980s and 1990s.

In industries which were historically relatively specialized, such as food, textiles, paper and packaging, and printing and publishing, and without a readily transferable technology, diversification occurred largely by acquisition. While a number diversified to conglomerate strategies, most firms in these sectors of industry endeavored to achieve a strategic fit in which relatedness occurred more through efforts to service common customers, use of common distribution channels, and the like. In addition, as in the textile and paper industries, a number of firms adopted vertical integration strategies by entering additional stages in the processing of materials.

Growth rates and profitability within the nontechnological diversifiers tended to be low. In specific segments, however, there were high-growth segments, such as convenience foods, plastic packaging, and synthetic fibers. Furthermore, competition tended to increase in these sectors as a result of new market entrants, many of which were international operators.

In the 1970s and 1980s, diversification occurred within both the manufacturing industry and service sectors. Moreover, there was a significant volume of activity between these sectors, such that by the mid-1990s it tended to be increasingly misleading to classify businesses as either manufacturing- or service-dominated.

By the mid-1990s, related diversification has become the most important single diversification strategy amongst large corporations throughout the developed world. This applied to both manufacturing-based and service-based businesses, and hybrid strategies are also becoming common. Concurrently with product market diversification, many of these concerns have also adopted international – and an increasing number, global – strategies, dependent upon the industries in which they are engaged. The management of such businesses now almost invariably corresponds to some form of DIVI-SIONAL STRUCTURE, SBU STRUCTURE, or MATRIX STRUCTURE amongst Western concerns while, in the East, Japanese concerns are usually participants in vertical and/or horizontal keiretsu – or chaebol in Korea (see CHAEBOL STRUCTURE; KEIRETSU STRUCTURE).

As identified by Chandler (1966), it was believed that such businesses needed a large central office to coordinate interrelationships between the related divisions, and this was indeed normal until the late 1970s. The impact of improved information technology and the use of the SBU STRUCTURE led to DELAYERING and reduction in the size of such central offices. By the late 1980s, pressures on cost had therefore led to sharp reductions in the central overheads of related diversified corporations, with a strong focus on strategic control and finance. Such thin head office structures should not, however, be confused with the traditional HOLDING COMPANY STRUCTURE, in which no central strategic control was exercised.

Bibliography

Chandler, A. D. (1966). *Strategy and structure.* New York: Anchor Books.
Channon, D. F. (1973). *Strategy and structure of British enterprise.* Cambridge, MA: Harvard Division of Research.
Channon, D. F. (1976). *The service industries: strategy, structure and financial performance.* London: Macmillan.
Wrigley, L. (1970). Divisional autonomy and diversification. Unpublished doctoral dissertation, Harvard Business School.

DEREK F. CHANNON

replacement demand   In the early stages of the product life cycle, most demand is primary or first purchase. However, as markets move toward maturity, to maintain demand it becomes likely that a growing proportion of sales will result from replacement, as initial purchases wear out or new purchases are stimulated by the introduction of product variants, improvements, and the like. The classic strategic example of this was the early development of the US automobile industry. Henry Ford created a mass market for automobiles by cutting cost through mass producing only one model. Unable to compete with the production cost of Ford because of the latter's volume, Alfred Sloan – in rescuing General Motors – decided that each of the different automobile marques that made up the company should be price- and feature-positioned in overlapping ranges which would encourage consumers to trade up when replacing their automobiles. In addition, regular model changes would be made, to stimulate consumers to change their cars more frequently. Therefore, unable to compete head to head, Sloan positioned Chevrolet at a price somewhat above Ford, but offered the consumer the opportunity to have variations which could be personally selected rather than being strictly standard. This strategy stimulated replacement demand, which Sloan further encouraged by helping to create the secondhand car market and introducing credit finance.

The philosophy remains current today, especially in the USA, where the concept of the model year continues to lead to the introduction of new product variants. Manufacturers of many other product categories, including consumer electronics, electrical appliances, and computers and computer software, endeavor to make use of the principle. In a number of these examples, the development of follower strategies is an interesting variant. For example, Amstrad built its consumer electronics and computer business by offering well tried and tested but semi-obsolescent hardware and software to the mass market at markdowns in price, thus opening new and unsuspected market segments via alternate distribution channels. Japanese producers have also stimulated the process of miniaturization, which has encouraged mass market penetration by cost reduction and product portability.

Bibliography

Chandler, A. D. (1962). *Strategy and structure.* Cambridge, MA: The MIT Press.
Channon, D. F. (1987). Amstrad "A" case. Imperial College, University of London
Sloan, A. P. (1963). *My years at General Motors.* New York: Anchor Books.

DEREK F. CHANNON

rule of three and four   An empirical rule observed by the Boston Consulting Group suggests that, at maturity, a stable market never usually has more than three significant competitors, the largest of which has a market share not more than four times that of the smallest.

Originally conceived by observation of the US automobile industry, the rule was based upon the concept that a 2 : 1 ratio between two competitors was an equilibrium point at which neither competitor would benefit from changes in relative share. In addition, it was hypothesized that a ratio of 4 : 1 was about the greatest that the smallest competitor could tolerate and still survive. Beneath this size, the smallest competitor would only be marginal. The rule was based essentially on expected cost structure variations due to relative experience effect positions (*see* EXPERIENCE AND LEARNING EFFECTS), assuming therefore that competitors operated in direct competition in an identical market. Close similarities exist with the premium and oligopoly points identified using the LANCHESTER STRATEGY. It does not, however, allow for the KEIRETSU STRUCTURE of Japanese markets in which, generally speaking, each horizontal industrial group tends to wish to maintain a market entry in each major product market. However, the recommended focus on three major players in each market in the Korean CHAEBOL STRUCTURE is more supportive.

The strategic implications of the rule of three and four are as follows:

- A shakeout is more likely in mature markets in which there are more than three competitors.

- Be number one or number two in a market, or sell it, close it, or fix it (Dr Jack Welch's philosophy at US General Electric).

- Rapid relative share growth is essential during the growth phase of the life cycle to establish a number one or number two position.

- If the two market leaders are not in a 2 : 1 equilibrium share position, the overall market will be less profitable for all competitors, and maturity cashflows will be diminished as the leaders battle for supremacy.

- Under conditions such as deregulation, in which new market entrants are likely, the rule may be an indicator of probable competitive dynamics and a predictor of ultimate market structure. The telecommunications industry currently shows evidence of such a fierce battle for the establishment of global leadership prior to maturity.

Bibliography

Henderson, B. D. (1979). *Henderson on corporate strategy*. Cambridge, MA: Abt Books. See pp. 90–4.

DEREK F. CHANNON

S

5S strategy Companies pursuing quality improvement strategies need to begin with the basics. Many Japanese companies therefore use the 5S's – a strategy dedicated to organizing the workplace, keeping it neat and clean, and maintaining the standardized conditions and discipline needed to insure high quality standards. The name "5S" is derived from the first letters of the Japanese terms for organization (*seiri*), neatness (*seiton*), cleaning (*seiso*), standardization (*seiketu*), and discipline (*shitsuke*). The adoption of these simple principles can yield dramatic improvements in quality and productivity – preventing accidents, reducing downtime, increasing operational control of processes, and creating an improved workplace environment. Japanese observers of Western plants are often amazed at their inefficient layout, untidiness, and lack of workplace discipline. The 5S system is explained in further detail below.

Seiri = Organization

Organization of the workplace is the first discipline to be introduced. It promotes continuous efforts to implement systems which help to eliminate the unnecessary. The concept makes great use of the Pareto diagram (*see* PARETO ANALYSIS) and a Japanese variant, the KJ method (named after Jiro Kawakita), both well established quality control tools used in problem solving, and in prioritizing and organizing information.

Seiton = Neatness

In the 5S model this means having all things in the right place at the right time, thus eliminating the time losses involved in searching. Frequently, the decision is made to start with how often things are used:

- things not used are discarded
- things not used but required as a contingency are kept in use
- things used infrequently are moved far away
- things used sometimes are moved to a specific place in the workplace
- things used frequently are stored at the workplace or on the person

To keep the workplace looking orderly, it is often necessary to draw passage lines and dividing lines on the floor. Time studies are usually continuously undertaken to improve space utilization, on the basis of the "5W's and 1H" (what, when, where, why, who, and how), questions that are posed with regard to every item.

Seiso = Cleaning

In 5S implementation, this term means getting rid of any mark or dirt, and keeping things clean. The emphasis is on keeping things clean, rather than inspection, and on keeping the workplace spotless. While this may seem obvious, it is by no means always practised, and substantial gains in quality are usually obtained by introducing cleanliness as a discipline. For the Japanese this is an historic and traditional concept, in the spirit of "To clean is to inspect." As the factory gate is the interface with the outside world, it applies to the smallest detail, with simple questions to be asked, such as: Is the grass infested with weeds? Is there litter on the premises? and Does the factory look attractive? 5S thus seeks to achieve zero dirt and grime, and to eliminate minor defects and faults at key inspection points.

Seiketu = Standardization

In 5S terms, standardization means continuous and repeated maintenance of organization, neatness, and cleanliness. The emphasis is on visual management and 5S standardization, which is now being used for production, quality, safety, and the like. Ironically, this visual inspection method is both simple and cheap by comparison with more sophisticated computer-based systems often attempted by Western corporations. Thus, for example, management of color coding has become increasingly important, both to improve management systems and to enhance the workplace environment.

Shitsuke = Discipline

In 5S terms, this means instilling (or having) the ability to do the things that were supposed to be done. The intent is to create a workplace and a workforce that conforms to the laid-down mode of operation. Everyone is taught how things should be done, thus eliminating bad habits and reinforcing those deemed to be good.

When explained, the 5S system seems simple. Regrettably, few Western firms tend to practise these principles, partially perhaps because many managers do not have hands-on experience of how to operate at the workplace in the modern production facility.

Bibliography

Channon, D. F. (1993). Canon "C" case. Imperial College, University of London.
Takashi, O. (1991). *The 5Ss*. Tokyo: Asian Productivity Organisation.

DEREK F. CHANNON

SBU structure   In the 1970s, faced with high levels of complexity, the US General Electric Company, in conjunction with McKinsey and Company, developed the organizational concept of the Strategic Business Unit (SBU). The company's departments, which formed the previous operating structure of GE, were subdivided into 43 SBUs.

These units varied considerably in size. Some SBUs were grouped together to form "divisions," while others were large enough to stand alone. However, each unit was essentially a complete business, and contained all the necessary functions to operate independently. To be classified as an SBU, a business had to be able to clearly identify its actual and potential customers and competitors, and to be able to

design comprehensive strategies to reach them, with clearly defined resources, an appropriate management structure and the ability to achieve objectives profitably and at an acceptable measure of risk.

With the introduction of the SBU structure, the then GE President, Reg Jones, was able to personally evaluate the strategic plans of all the units and, at the corporate center, to allocate resources to them on the basis of their position on the COMPETITIVE POSITION – MARKET ATTRACTIVENESS MATRIX. Each SBU was assigned a specific set of strategic objectives and investment policy. A high-growth SBU would therefore perhaps be expected to increase market share when competitively weak, with cashflow profits being deferred. By contrast a strong, low-growth business might be expected to keep investment to the minimum and to operate to maximize cashflow, which could be deployed elsewhere. While maintaining a multi-SBU set of divisions, GE was able to operate a variety of investment strategies within a division. In this case the division had its own small corporate staff which monitored and potentially adjusted the SBU's performance measures and rewards.

The SBU structure was introduced widely throughout the world in the 1980s. With a change in leadership at GE, the incoming regime under Dr. Jack Welch maintained the structure and extended it further. In the late 1980s, DELAYERING was introduced within GE to eliminate corporate staff at every level, leaving business unit/corporate center strategy negotiations essentially between Dr. Welch and a very thin general management team, including himself and the SBU management.

The SBU concept allowed highly diversified corporations to integrate their organizations so as to optimize the STRATEGIC FIT between related businesses and to reduce the complexity of the strategic planning process. The structure also helped to integrate the process of strategy formulation, at both the corporate and business levels, in a form of cascade. It also permitted a hands-on approach by the CEO, which had proven increasingly impossible when the corporation was managed with a departmental structure, as the span of control increased with growing diversity. The SBU form of organization is illustrated in figure 1.

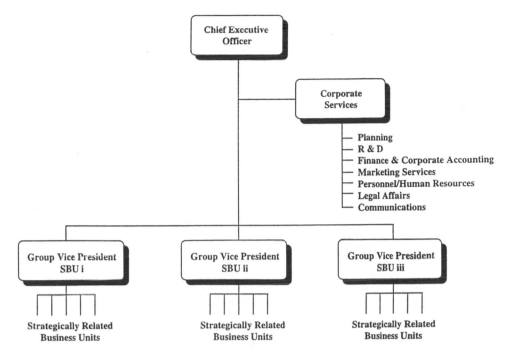

Figure 1 The SBU form of organizational structure.
Source: Hale (1978)

Strategic advantages: provides a strategically relevant way to organize the business-unit portfolio of a broadly diversified company; facilitates the coordination of related activities within an SBU, helping capture the benefits of strategic fits in the SBU; promotes cohesiveness among the new initiatives of separate but related businesses; allows strategic planning to be done at the most relevant level in the enterprise; makes the task of strategic review by top executives more objective and effective; helps allocate corporate resources to areas with greatest growth opportunites.

Strategic disadvantages: it is easy for the definition and grouping of businesses into SBUs to be so arbitrary that the SBU serves no other purpose than administrative convenience. If the criteria for defining SBUs are rationalizations and have little to do with the nitty-gritty of strategy coordination, then the groupings lose real strategic significance; the SBUs can still be myopic in charting their future direction; adds another layer to top management; the roles and authority of the CEO, the group vice president, and the business-unit manager have to be carefully worked out or the group vice president gets trapped in the middle with ill-defined authority; unless the SBU head is strong willed, very little strategy coordination is likely to occur across business units in the SBU; performance recognition gets blurred; credit for successful business units tends to go to corporate CEO, then to business-unit head, last to group vice president.

Unfortunately, many companies introducing an SBU structure have failed to achieve the "hands-on" approach found at GE and, as a consequence, few have actually achieved the relative success found there. The cause of this failure has often been the inability to recognize that each SBU should have an appropriate set of objectives and action plans that are consistent with the strategic position of the business.

Bibliography

Anonymous (1978). SBUs: hot new topic in the management of diversification. *Business Horizons*, **21** (1), 19.

Bettis, R. A. & Hall, W. K. (1983). The business portfolio approach – where it falls down in practice. *Long Range Planning*, **16** (2), 95–104.

Hale, W. K. (1978). General Electric. Reprinted in Thompson, A. A. & Strickland, A. J. (1993). *Strategic management*. Homewood, IL: Irwin. See pp. 228–31.

DEREK F. CHANNON

scenario planning   This technique has become relatively widespread as a way of visualizing alternative futures, and thus of designing flexible strategies that can be developed to cope with these visions of the future.

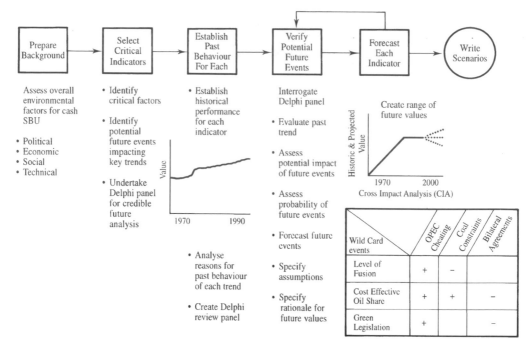

Figure 1 The process of scenario creation.

The success of the method owes much to Royal Dutch Shell's use of scenarios, one of which successfully predicted the first oil-price shock in 1973. Other organizations which make use of future scenarios include the White House, the Pentagon, the Economic Planning Agency, Volvo, and Inland Steel. One definition of a scenario is "a tool for ordering one's perceptions about alternative future environments in which one's decisions might be played out."

Key characteristics of scenarios are that they implicitly incorporate the subjective assessments of individuals or groups, and that they recognize that decision makers have some influence on future development. Scenarios tend to be constructed upon facts and proven assumptions that have been accurate in the past. These positions are then extrapolated to create a series of alternate futures which, in themselves, are mutually consistent.

Within Royal Dutch Shell, every two to three years a series of usually three scenarios about the future are prepared, against which line managers are required to test their own business unit strategic plans. Historically, these scenarios

have tended to predict optimistic, most likely, and pessimistic futures. Most recently, the most optimistic scenario has tended to be dropped, as this has never actually come to pass. Indeed, even the most pessimistic scenario has usually tended to be more optimistic than actual reality.

Most scenarios begin in the present and make assumptions about the future. The process of scenario development is illustrated in figure 1. It commences with a PEST ANALYSIS, which identifies the critical Political, Economic, Social and Technical factors which influence both the present and the future.

From this analysis, the critical indicators of the future environment are selected and any potential future events are impacted against these key trends. The use of a Delphi analysis, and consultations with relative experts, may well be a useful process through which to gain enlightened opinion on likely futures.

For each historical performance indicator, past trends are examined and analyzed to identify the reasons for the past behavior. The future is then assessed and tested against the opinions of the Delphi review panel. As a result, future events may be forecast subject to clearly defined assumptions and an established rationale for the prediction of forward values.

A series of usually no more than three scenarios can then be developed on the basis of alternate predictions. Cross-impact analysis should also be undertaken to examine the effect of contrary variables on alternate futures. At the end of this process, a series of scenarios can be established for issue to line business units, as a background against which they can develop alternate strategic plans for their operations.

To ensure that these scenarios will be useful in strategy formulation, it is important that the following criteria are applied:

• The scenarios must be internally consistent. Any internal contradiction may negate any SWOT ANALYSIS undertaken.

• The scenario must be possible. Any scenario which is seen as highly implausible will tend to be ignored by line business units.

Bibliography

Anonymous (1980). Shell's multiple scenario planning: a realistic alternative to the crystal ball. *World Business Weekly*, April 7.
Schwartz, P. (1991). *The art of the long view*. New York: Doubleday.
Wack, P. (1985). Scenarios: uncharted waters ahead. *Harvard Business Review*, 63, 72–89.

DEREK F. CHANNON

S.C.R.A.P. industries This mnemonic was developed by the Japanese Ministry for International Trade and Industry (MITI) to identify industries which, as a nation, Japan considered should be exited. Each letter of the mnemonic identifies one or more industries as follows:

> S industries are shipbuilding and non-specialist steel
> C industry stands for commodity chemicals
> R for refining
> A for aluminum
> P for pulp and paper

These industries all exhibit a number of similar characteristics. First, they are all high in INVESTMENT INTENSITY; second, they are low

in product differentiation; third, they tend to be high in energy consumption; fourth, they are all relatively heavy polluters; and last, their output tends to be priced in dollars rather than yen. Because of these characteristics and the relatively low value added offered by these industries, MITI recommends that such industries should be based in those countries which enjoy raw material competitive advantage, with Japan purchasing semi-finished products as distinct from raw material itself. For the raw material producers, upgrading their basic commodities allows them to add value: thus, for example, significant elements of the refining and commodity chemical industry have moved to Gulf state producers, with the consequence that heavy rationalization has been taking place in both the refining and chemical industries in developed economies such as Western Europe.

DEREK F. CHANNON

segmentation The choice of which markets to address is a critical strategic decision for the firm. Therefore, the SERVED MARKET is some combination of customers, products, and geography. This choice is based on the segmentation of markets into smaller groupings. Moreover, the development of relational databases and data mining allows firms to define their markets even more tightly. Successful segmentation of markets has proven to be a key source of strategic advantage, especially where this might involve reconfiguration of the value chain (*see* VALUE CHAIN ANALYSIS).

Bases for Market Segmentation

A range of variables can be used for segmenting both consumer and business markets. Typically these involve geographic, demographic, and psychographic factors. Normally more than one variable is used to try to identify a served market segment. Some researchers use consumer response variables such as quality, usage patterns, usage time, and branding. A typical segmentation breakdown is shown in table 1. The main variables are described briefly below.

Geographic segmentation. In geographic segmentation, the market is broken down into differing geographic units, such as nations, regions, countries, cities, and neighborhoods. The company may decide to operate in many or

Table 1 Major segmentation variables for consumer markets.

Variable	Typical breakdowns
Geographic	
Region	Pacific, Mountain, West North Central, West South Central, East North Central, East South Central, South Atlantic, Middle Atlantic, New England
County size	A, B, C, D
City or MSA size	Under 5,000, 5,000–20,000, 20,000–50,000, 50,000–100,000, 100,000–250,000, 250,000–500,000, 500,000–1,000,000, 1,000,000–4,000,000, 4,000,000 or over
Density	Urban, suburban, rural
Climate	Northern, southern
Demographic	
Age	Under 6, 6–11, 12–19, 20–34, 35–49, 50–64, 65+
Sex	Male, female
Family size	1–2, 3–4, 5+
Family life cycle	Young, single; young, married, no children; young, married, youngest child under six; young, married, youngest child six or over; older, married, with children; older, married, no children under 18; older, single; other
Income	Under $10,000, $10,000–$15,000, $15,000–$20,000, $20,000–$30,000, $30,000–$50,000, $50,000 and over
Occupation	Professional and technical, managers, officials and proprietors; clerical, sales; craftsmen, foremen; operatives; farmers; retired; students; homemakers; unemployed
Education	Grade school or less; some high school; high school graduate; some college; college graduate
Religion	Catholic, Protestant, Jewish, other
Race	White, black, Asian, Hispanic
Nationality	American, British, French, German, Scandinavian, Italian, Latin American, Middle Eastern, Japanese
Psychographic	
Social class	Lower lowers, upper lowers, lower middles, upper middles, lower uppers, upper uppers
Life style	Belongers, achievers, integrateds
Personality	Compulsive, gregarious, authoritarian, ambitious
Behavioristic	
Purchase occasion	Regular occasion, special occasion
Benefits sought	Quality, service, economy
User status	Nonuser, ex user, potential user, first time user, regular user
Usage rate	Light user, medium user, heavy user
Loyalty status	None, medium, strong, absolute
Readiness stage	Unaware, aware, informed, interested, desirous, intending to buy
Attitude toward product	Enthusiastic, positive, indifferent, negative, hostile

Source: Kotler, P. & Armstrong, G. (1989).

few areas, or to differentiate between regions or districts. For example, the insurance industry may operate differential pricing policies based on the demographics of different neighborhoods, crime rates, property values, and the like. Some food retailers may divide cities into different areas on the basis of age and/or ethnic mix.

Demographic segmentation. In demographic segmentation, markets are subdivided into groups on the basis of demographic variables such as age, sex, life cycle, education, income, ethnic background, and the like. Historically, demographic variables have been most widely used in consumer marketing segmentation. They are also used in business market segmentation to determine, for example, the size of company that should be attacked, the industry mix to be achieved, and the location areas to be selected. Demographic variables are also amongst the easiest the measure.

• *Age and life cycle stage.* Consumer needs and wealth change with age and position in the life cycle. Historically, this was relatively predictable, but is becoming more difficult to use as a variable. For example, historically, family life cycle could be assessed using the following sequence: single; married with no children; married with young children; married with children up to 18; married, children departed; retired married; retired single. Presently, marriage is a poor predictor due to the high rate of divorce, the growing preponderance of single-person households, and the growing number of working professional women.

Nevertheless, age and life cycle still are important variables for segmentation and the mix of individuals is shifting, particularly toward ageing populations in the developed economies.

• *Gender.* Segmentation by gender has long been an important variable in areas such as cosmetics, magazines, and clothing. It has also been applied in areas not normally associated with gender, such as cigarettes, do-it-yourself materials, automobiles, and liquor.

• *Income.* Income segmentation has always been an important variable for many industries, such as automobiles, clothing, cosmetics, travel, and banking. It is not, however, necessarily a good predictor of profitability or of volume markets. For example, compact disks were originally sold to the market of audio *aficionados* or status seekers, but the market turned out to be driven by young people interested in listening to pop music.

• *Multiple attribute segmentation.* For most companies, markets are segmented by combinations of more than one demographic variable, such as age, income, and education. Thus in banking the young professional has a high income but also a high borrowing requirement in order to establish a professional practice, a mortgage, and the like. Such grouping can be further subdivided by ethnic, locational, and other variables. It is therefore important to attempt to combine variables in a way that clearly identifies an attractive target group profitable for the corporation to service.

Psychographic segmentation. In this form of segmentation, which has become increasingly widely used in recent times, buyers are divided upon the basis of social class, lifestyle, and personality. This form of segmentation has to a degree been used to replace demographic segmentation, as market researchers have discovered wide variations in behavior between subgroups within demographic profiling.

Behavioral segmentation. In this form of segmentation, which is widely used, purchasing behavior may vary significantly according to knowledge, attitude, usage rate, time of use, and attitude to the product.

Requirements for Effective Segmentation

To be useful, market segments should:
• be measurable
• be sufficiently large to provide products or services profitably
• be accessible – distribution/delivery system channels should be open
• be differentiable – segments must be distinguishable from other elements of the market
• be actionable – it must be possible to design strategic marketing programs that permit the segmentation strategy to be implemented

Bibliography

Kotler, P. & Armstrong, G. (1989). *Principles of Marketing* (4th edn). New Jersey: Prentice-Hall.
Kotler, P. (1994). *Marketing management*, (8th edn), Englewood Cliffs, NJ: Prentice-Hall.

Kotler, P. (1994). *Marketing management*, (8th edn), Englewood Cliffs, NJ: Prentice-Hall.

Roberts, A. A. (1961). Applying the strategy of market segmentation. *Business Horizons*, (May), 65–72.

Robertson, T. S. & Barish, H. (1992). A successful approach to segmenting industrial markets. *Planning Forum*, 5–11.

DEREK F. CHANNON

served market   The served market is that segment of the total market that the firm actively attempts to serve. It is difficult to define, but the concept is essential to the measurement of variables such as relative and absolute market share, growth rate, and the like. It is therefore imperative that this task is undertaken creatively before embarking on precise strategy formulation.

Many observers cite market share and relative market share as key determinants of business and profitability, but fail to define the market.

As illustrated in figure 1, the served market is defined as the intersection between a class of customers and the firm's product or service offering, and the desired geographic coverage.

For each market in which the firm is engaged, it should be sufficiently defined such that the following questions can be answered:

• Who precisely are the customers?

• What are their needs?

• What products or services does the firm offer to meet these needs?

• Can these be provided efficiently, profitably, and at an acceptable level of risk?

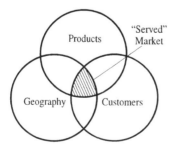

Figure 1 The "served" market concept.
Source: Channon (1986)

• What resources does the firm need to deliver these products or services?

• How will these resources be managed?

In order to evaluate the potential of a served market, it is desirable to complete a customer/product needs grid, on which segments are subdivided and the needs established for each key customer class. An adequate description of a market segment should constitute a set of boundaries on which strategies can be specifically targeted and where a defendable position can be sustained. Geographic boundaries for served markets may also differ sharply. For example, private banking tends to be a regional or global business, while retail banking is mainly a local or national activity.

Bibliography

Buzzell, R. D. & Gale, B. T. (1987). *The PIMS principles.* New York: The Free Press.

Channon, D. F. (1986). *Bank strategic management and marketing.* Chichester: John Wiley.

DEREK F. CHANNON

signaling   The purpose of signaling is to transfer information from one party to another in a credible way. Early work on signals included Schelling's essay on bargaining, which discussed the matter of promise, observed that "bargaining may have to concern itself with an 'incentive' system as well as the division of gains" (Schelling, 1956, p. 300), and also dealt with bargaining tactics such as "tying one's hands" and offering and accepting hostages.

Signaling finds two main applications. The first is in competitive situations, such as where one firm wishes to notify others that it does not welcome them in its market. The second has to do with the provision of information as to the nature and characteristics of a product, service, or even a company for sale, so that the party receiving the information will be convinced to buy or, if such a decision has already been reached, so that a higher price can be extracted from the buyer.

Signaling to Existing or Potential Competitors

In its entry deterrent capacity, therefore, signaling can act as a barrier to entry (*see*

BARRIERS TO ENTRY AND EXIT) (the reverse is also true, and raising other barriers to entry may act as a very effective signal). In order to indicate that entry is unwelcome and that the entrant will be attacked, the incumbent can commit himself to such an attack (by building up EXCESS CAPACITY to credibly indicate readiness to lower prices upon entry, by guaranteeing to match any competitor innovations, or otherwise); it can indicate a low cost function to scare off higher-cost producers (by permanently pricing low); and it can accumulate resources to prepare for retaliation, making such accumulation visible.

In the shorter term, the incumbent may just wish to provide a signal to some particular company which it knows is planning to enter its market. This can be done by means of an announcement of an impending product launch, or a new process or investment, and such actions may well be sufficient to delay entry until the incumbent has had more time to prepare, using methods including those just discussed.

Turning to signals toward existing rather than potential competitors, a firm may wish to indicate its willingness to collude (see CARTEL). Such activity may be illegal, particularly as far as stronger forms of collusion are concerned, but certain modes of independently devised behavior such as promises to match prices, or advance price change notifications, are often observed (it should be noted that practices such as promises to match prices can act both as a signal to indicate willingness to collude and as a signal of willingness to protect one's share of the market).

Signaling to Buyers

Having examined signaling to competitors, the discussion now turns to signaling to buyers. Nevertheless, some of the theoretical arguments presented here can also be used in the context of signaling to competitors.

In asymmetric information situations, parties will be induced to generate information as long as the marginal cost of such generation does not exceed the marginal expected payoff. A consequence of this is that when information is relatively expensive, buyers will refrain from information generation. As a result, the seller of a product the characteristics of which (such as quality) cannot be observed at the time of the sale (even though these may eventually become apparent) may be unable to receive the full value of his product, potential buyers only being willing to accept a price which reflects their beliefs about expected, or average characteristics.

One result of this is that sellers in such a situation are unable to sell high-quality products at prices higher than they can sell low-quality ones, so they have an incentive to reduce their costs and sell low-quality products.

To circumvent this problem and allow sellers of high-quality products to inform buyers of the characteristics of their products, signaling can be used to transmit the information required, so that the buyer is no longer required to generate it. Among the methods which are available for use are: the development of a brand image which conveys the desired characteristics; advertising; the use of sales force and product demonstrations to educate buyers; giving products away to opinion leaders for use and evaluation; or even relying on methods not under the seller's control, such as word of mouth. In principle, the more information there is about a product, and the more its producer/ seller spends on signaling, the more its perceived value will tend to coincide with its real value.

A more generalized view of signaling has been provided by Spence (1973). He observed that if the seller of a high-quality product could find some activity the marginal cost of which was lower for him than for a seller of a lower-quality product, it might pay him to undertake this activity to signal high quality. Offering warranties could act as a such a signal, for example, as this would be cheap for the sellers of reliable products, but more expensive for the sellers of lower-quality products. Similarly, assuming that education is cheaper for productive employees to acquire than for less productive ones, getting an education may act as a signal of higher productivity to employers, and may thus be worthwhile even if it leads to no productivity improvement at all. The exact nature of the signal used is, therefore, not so important in itself, but its most common consequence – giving away money – most certainly is. In the context of stock pricing, for example (particularly when a company is sold in tranches), underpricing, high dividend payments (high tax contributions), the use of expensive bankers, auditors and solicitors, and high advertising expenditure all help to differentiate a high-quality firm from a lower-quality one.

While the above discussion is valid in principle, the conditions under which signaling equilibria are, in practice, free of potential dynamic instability are rather more restrictive than Spence supposed. It has been observed, for example, that Spence's assumption that the potential signaling activity should have a lower marginal cost for high-quality workers is a necessary rather than a sufficient condition. Instead, it appears sufficient for the proportional rate of decline in the marginal cost of signaling with respect to product quality to be sufficiently large.

Moreover, the success of any signaling strategy is affected by several other factors, including the length of time for which agents are committed to announced strategies. Signaling can, for example, be used to deceive the recipient of the information in the short run, where the long-run implications are of no concern. If a seller possesses information that is unfavorable to himself, he may still wish to provide the same signals that he would provide if he had favorable information, albeit at a higher cost. A government, for instance, may underprice bad as well as good companies in a privatization, for fear that investors will infer its private information if it does otherwise. By the time information emerges to prove these signals misleading, the privatization program may already be complete, so it may suffer little harm when its credibility in signaling the quality of stock is dented.

Bibliography

Hart, O. & Holmström, B. (1987). The theory of contracts. In T. Bewley (ed.), *Advances in economic theory*. Cambridge: Cambridge University Press.

Porter, M. E. (1980). *Competitive strategy: techniques for analyzing industries and competitors*. New York: The Free Press.

Porter, M. E. (1985). *Competitive advantage: creating and sustaining superior performance*. New York: The Free Press.

Schelling, T. C. (1956). An essay on bargaining. *American Economic Review*, **46**, 281–306.

Spence, A. M. (1973). *Market signalling: information transfer in hiring and related processes*. Cambridge, MA: Harvard University Press.

STEPHANOS AVGEROPOULOS

single business strategy   Such businesses have been defined as those in which 95 per cent or more of sales came from one business. During the period from 1950 onward, in the manufacturing sector, such businesses have declined dramatically in most developed economies, and in the USA and UK they have been virtually eliminated. Such firms have either diversified or been acquired by more diversified firms. Single business firms are, however, still found in the service industry sector. These service industry firms tend to be of two types. First, there are those for which the strategic potential of the industry makes it unnecessary to diversify by product line. For example, food retailers tend to expand by increasing geographic coverage rather than by entering new product market segments. Second, there are companies that are protected from stock market pressures by factors such as mutual ownership. Such companies include many smaller building societies and mutual life assurance concerns.

Concentration on a single business focuses the attention of management; top management must give its undivided attention to the business. Furthermore, all of the key managers can be given the opportunity to have hands-on experience in all the key functions of the business; most have normally spent time actively involved in field operations. The key danger for the single business firm occurs when the original strategy reaches maturity and, in particular, when opportunities for geographic expansion dry up. At this stage, single business firms usually attempt to diversify or are themselves acquired by diversified firms. This outcome can be especially difficult for the single business firm as the incoming new management may lack experience in purchasing or operating other businesses, which may be quite different from the one that they know. Equally, in the process of acquisition, the single business firm usually has no experience with regard to being purchased or being subjected to subsequent integration.

Single business firms are usually managed according to a FUNCTIONAL STRUCTURE, in which each of the core activities of the firm is the responsibility of a specialized manager.

Interestingly, in recent years the process of PRIVATIZATION has (perhaps temporarily) added to the number of single business concerns. Artificially constrained from diversification, privatized firms have strategically sought to rapidly diversify, tending to face the market rather than integrating backward to restore their single or dominant business origins.

Diversification away from their core business has been both by geography and product market and the early results are still to be counted. Moreover, because of their stable cashflows, in an open market economy many of these concerns have found themselves open to hostile attack by predators interested in gaining access to their attractive cashflow profiles.

Bibliography

Channon, D. F. (1973). *The strategy and structure of British enterprise.* Cambridge, MA: Harvard Division of Research.

Rumelt, R. P. (1974). *Strategy, stucture and economic performance.* Cambridge, MA: Harvard Division of Research.

Wrigley, L. (1970). Divisional autonomy and diversification. Unpublished doctoral dissertation, Harvard Business School.

DEREK F. CHANNON

soga shosha The origins of the soga shosha, Japan's massive international trading companies, date back in large part to the Meiji Restoration of 1868, when the government resumed international trade after over 200 years of self-imposed isolation under the Tokugawa Shogunate. The incoming government encouraged the development of Japanese trading companies to reduce the role of foreign traders; to develop secure supplies of raw materials for the newly industrializing economy, and to help to provide technology, machinery, and other equipment needed to produce manufactured products; and to separate production from supply and marketing, leaving these activities to the trading companies, with their knowledge of overseas markets.

With the exception of the Sumitomo Corporation, the other leading soga shosha were created before World War II. Two of these, Mitsubishi Corporation and Mitsui and Company, were associated with the Mitsubishi and Mitsui zaibatsu, respectively, and were already diversified concerns by the outbreak of war. Both were broken up after World War II by the occupying authorities, but rapidly reformed when this was legally permitted. The other leading groups continued to specialize in particular product markets until the postwar period, but rapidly diversified into general trading companies and associated themselves

Table 1 Sales of Japan's nine soga shosha 1993 (¥ bn).

	Total	In Japan	Exports from Japan	Inputs into Japan	Offshore Trade
Itochu	16,135	8,605	1,768	1,495	4,265
Mitsui	15,862	7,885	1,999	2,119	3,860
Mayuberi	15,156	7,769	2,205	1,736	3,446
Sumitomo	15,032	7,738	2,285	2,158	2,851
Mitsubishi	14,123	6,921	2,268	2,372	2,662
Nisho Iwai	9,588	4,375	1,109	1,756	2,348
Tomen	6,522	3,098	675	769	1,979
Nichimen	5,488	2,583	477	391	2,038
Kanematsu	5,269	1,414	982	2,130	742
Total	103,177	50,388	13,768	14,926	24,191
Share %	100	48.4	13.3	14.5	23.4

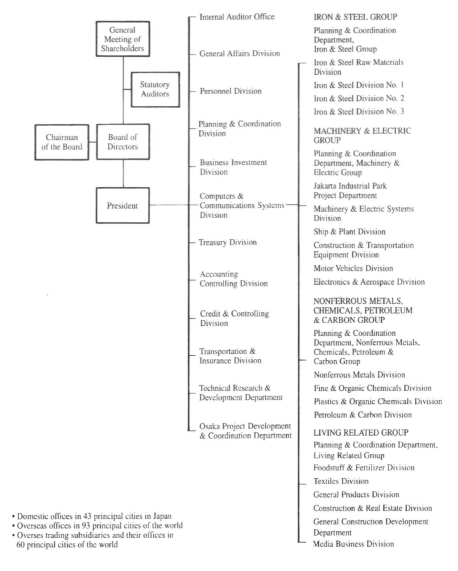

Figure 1 The soga shosha organizational structure.
Source: Annual Reports.

with the emerging bank-related keiretsu (*see* KEIRETSU STRUCTURE). The Sumitomo Corporation was only formed in 1945, as trading was not previously considered to be an ethical activity within the Sumitomo zaibatsu. By the 1950s, therefore, much of Japan's internal and external trade was handled by the top ten soga shosha (subsequently reduced to nine by mergers).

These major trading companies formed key components within the major Japanese keiretsu groups. The leading nine concerns also maintained a major role within the Japanese domestic economy, and in 1993 were responsible for 52 per cent of all imports and 34 per cent of all exports, as illustrated in table 1. While primarily concerned with trade in commodity products, some – depending upon their backgrounds –

20,000–30,000); the degree of product market diversity is illustrated in figure 1, which shows the organizational structure of a typical soga shosha. In recent years they have also been increasing their interests in operating in higher value added products, and in increasing their share in trade between third countries. Overall, in 1993 the leading concerns had a share of world trade greater than most developed economies.

The soga shosha operate in a number of distinct ways. First, they operate as pure traders, buying and selling commodities and other merchandise. While they provide trade finance, they can also act as guarantors for banks and other financial institutions. To stimulate activity they might also pre-pay suppliers. In addition, the soga shosha are skilled at barter trading, which can involve several counter-parties.

Second, the soga shosha can act as project organizers and managers for complex projects. In this scheme, the soga shosha might help to develop an iron deposit by helping provide the necessary finance for infrastructure development, providing project management, arranging construction, providing mining machinery, guaranteeing exports, arranging shipping, insurance and freight, taking the output back to Japan to be sold to steel producers who might be members of the same industrial group, acting as a steel stockholder for the distribution of the product within Japan, and acting as export agent for the manufacturers of finished equipment from the steel.

Third, the soga shosha operate as a market intelligence agent for both itself and members of its industrial group. Each operates extensive global communications networks which, each day, pass millions of words through dedicated lines between all of the world's leading trading centers and Japan, on all the product lines covered. Being trading companies (unlike banks), the soga shosha normally do not require a licence to open in any particular country. Hence they normally operate in all of the major world trading, agricultural, and commercial centers.

Fourth, the soga shosha provide an access route for Japanese companies to overseas markets. Subsequently, such concerns might develop their own overseas distribution systems, but initially the soga shosha make it possible for smaller firms to gain access without the necessity to build expensive infrastructures. More recently, under pressure from Western governments to open domestic markets, the soga shosha have provided a route for Western companies to enter the Japanese market. Such moves have usually been organized as joint ventures between individual Western concerns and specific Japanese companies.

Fifth, the soga shosha have been instrumental in helping to achieve Japanese government policies of obtaining supplies of strategic raw materials. At the time of the first oil-price shock, for example, around 80 per cent of the oil being supplied to Japan was imported via the leading Western oil companies. Keen to reduce this apparent dependency, the government encouraged the soga shosha to help establish energy subsidiaries responsible for achieving secure supplies. By 1993, the share of the Japanese market supplied by Western oil companies had fallen to around 25 per cent, with the leading soga shosha playing a major role in this transformation.

Sixth, the soga shosha are a source of trade finance or can act as a guarantor on the part of suppliers and customers. They are also skilled at barter trade in the case of situations, in which financial credits are unavailable.

In terms of size and scale, this structural form is virtually unknown in the West. It has played – and continues to play – a significant role in Japanese economic and industrial success.

Bibliography

Yoshihara, K. (1982). *Soga shosha*. Oxford: Oxford University Press.

Young, A. K. (1979). *The soga shosha*. Tokyo: Charles E. Tuttle.

DEREK F. CHANNON

specialized businesses In specialized businesses, clear market segments can be defined which are distinct from one another and where overlap is limited. Within each segment, experience effects (*see* EXPERIENCE AND LEARNING EFFECTS) are important determinants of cost structure, but the segments themselves are discrete.

EFFECTS) are important determinants of cost structure, but the segments themselves are discrete.

Industries in which this phenomenon occurs include pharmaceuticals, cosmetics, luxury automobiles, and designer clothing. Competitors may succeed by concentrating on a specific SERVED MARKET segment, in which dominance can lead to extraordinary profits. Within the industry there are typically a number of such successful competitors, each dominating a specific segment. Firms that are not market leaders tend to be less profitable.

While it is unusual, it is possible for competitors to serve more than one market segment and gain SYNERGY for a lower-volume market position. For example, Toyota has successfully penetrated the luxury automobile market with its Lexus brand, using its volume car division position to successfully lower costs relative to specialist producers of luxury segment vehicles, such as Mercedes Benz or BMW.

See also **Advantage matrix**

DEREK F. CHANNON

stakeholder analysis   Stakeholders are all the people (and organizations) that have an interest in a company, and that may influence the company or be influenced by its activities.

Stakeholders may be internal (such as employees) or external (such as suppliers or pressure groups). Most can be identified within the ranks of owners and stockholders, bankers and other creditors, suppliers, buyers and customers, advertisers, management, employees, their unions, competitors, local and state government, regulators, the media, public interest groups, the arts, political and religious groups, and the military. Others may also be identifiable, and their numbers and complexity of interdependence are likely to increase over the life span of the organization.

However, these groups are rarely sufficient to categorize stakeholders themselves, and stakeholders typically form groupings which are subsets of the above (such as secretarial personnel), or even cut across them (such as the group against the introduction of new factory automation technology, which may include some suppliers, some management,

and many employees). In general, the population of stakeholder groups is unstable, with new groups tending to emerge and influence strategy as a result of specific current or expected events, while redundant groups disappear or, in some cases, the members of certain stakeholder groups diverge to such an extent in their views and opinions that the corresponding groups divide and split. It is important to recognize here that while some of the groups are explicitly formed, and may even have their own administrative organization, others may have no such organization, and their members may not even consciously view themselves as part of such a group. Most individuals are likely to belong to more than one stakeholder group.

The Role of Stakeholders

Stakeholders are important to the organization by virtue of their ability to influence it. As a result, their views must be a component of decision making. It is rare, however, that all stakeholders agree on all issues, and some are more powerful than others, so the task of management is also a balancing act.

Given that management hold much of the decision making power, that they need some approval from some stakeholders to retain their power, but also that it is impossible for them to please all, management have a variety of balancing methods from which to choose. In principle, they can attempt to balance all interests equally; or according to their weight and importance; or they can focus on just one group of interests, satisfying all others only to the extent that they permit them to continue in office. This leading stakeholder group could be the organization's owners and shareholders, or it could well be the managers themselves, as they also are a major stakeholder.

In addition to strategy formulation, an analysis of an organization's stakeholders is also a powerful tool for evaluating strategies, by ascertaining the existence of objecting stakeholders and the extent of their power on any issue in question. In addition, a stakeholder analysis can form the basis, if it is so desired, for greater participation in decision making and better communication with stakeholders.

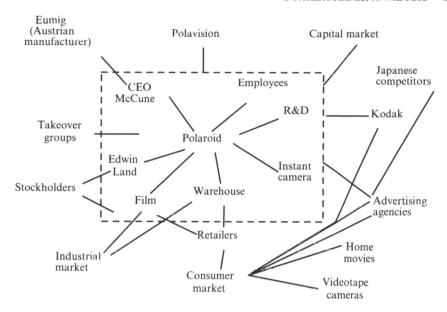

Figure 1   A map of the Polaroid Corporation's stakeholders in 1980.
Source: Rowe et al. (1994).

Stakeholder Mapping

Having established the importance of stake-holders, it is now necessary to find methods of obtaining an accurate picture of what the stakeholder groups are, which interests they represent in relation to the adoption of new strategies, whether they are likely to facilitate or inhibit change, how powerful these groups are, and how they should be dealt with (e.g., by means of side payments, the provision of information, and the like, to insure that they are sufficiently content so as not to take any action that could compromise the established strategies).

Predictability

	Low	High
Low	**A** Fewer problems	**B** Unpredictable but manageable
High	**C** Powerful but predictable	**D** Greatest danger or opportunities

Power

Figure 2   Stakeholder mapping: the power/dynamism matrix.
Source: Gardner et al. (1986)

Level of interest

	Low	High
Low	**A** Minimal effort	**B** Keep informed
High	**C** Keep satisfied	**D** Key players

Power

Figure 3   Stakeholder mapping: the power/interest matrix.
Source: Gardner et al. (1986)

threats, and the identification of the likely impact on the map of any proposed or likely change, so that the ground for this can be prepared. Figure 1 represents a typical stakeholder map.

Having identified who the most significant stakeholders are, a number of methods exist to decide how these should be dealt with. For example, the power/dynamism matrix, shown in figure 2, can be used to ascertain where political efforts should be channelled during the development of new strategies.

In this map, the most difficult group to deal with are those in segment D, since they are in a powerful position, and their stance is difficult to predict. In some cases, they can be dealt with by testing out new strategies with them before an irrevocable decision is made. Stakeholders in segment C are also important, although their stance is predictable and so their expectations can often be met. Groups A and B are reasonably easy to deal with, although their power may increase if it is aggregated on any particular issue.

Similarly, the power/interest matrix, shown in figure 3, classifies stakeholders in relation to the power that they hold and the extent to which they are likely to show interest in the organization's strategies, indicating the type of relationship that the organization will have to establish with each of them.

The acceptability of strategies to the key players D should be an important consideration in the evaluation of new strategies. Stakeholders in segment C are also very important as, although they are relatively passive in general, they may well emerge suddenly as a result of any specific event and become a very interested and significant party, moving to segment D on that particular issue. Similarly, the needs of stakeholders in segment B need to be addressed, largely through the provision of information, as these can influence the more powerful stakeholders.

The author would like to acknowledge the assistance of Diana Winstanley, The Manaagement School, Imperial College for helpful comments on an earlier draft.

Bibliography

Donaldson, T. & Preston, L. G. (1995). The stakeholder theory of the corporation: concepts, evidence and implications. *Academy of Management Review*, **20** (2), 65–91.

Freeman, R. E. (1984). *Strategic management: a stakeholder approach*. London: Pitman.

Gardner, J. R., Rachlin, R. & Sweeny, H. W. A. (ed), (1986). *Handbook of strategic planning*. New York: John Wiley. See pp. 171–8.

Mendelow, A. L. (1991). Environmental Scanning, *Proceedings of the 2nd International Conference on Information Systems*, Cambridge, MA.

Roberts, N. C. & King, P. J. (1989). The stakeholder audit goes public. *Organisational Dynamics*, (Winter), 63–79.

Rowe, A. J., Mason, R. O., Dickel, K. E., Mann, R. B. & Mockler, R. J. (1994). *Strategic management: a methodological approach*, (4th edn), Reading, MA: Addison-Wesley. See pp. 134–44.

STEPHANOS AVGEROPOULOS

stalemate businesses   In these businesses, economies of scale do not produce significant cost advantages, because a variety of factors – such as technology, raw material advantage, and the like – negate the value of high market share. Such industries tend to be low in differentiation and high in capital intensity, with heavy fixed capital – often in specialized plants. This makes exit from such businesses difficult, as the nature of the assets makes them difficult to resell. A further problem today is the impact of environmental legislation, which also makes it difficult to close down such plants, as the cost of clean-up after closure may make it more economic to continue production despite ongoing losses. Examples are Petroleum refining, Gas, Aluminum, Pulp and Paper, Shipbuilding, and Commodity chemicals. Ironically, as part of a national portfolio strategy, the Japanese identify these businesses as SCRAP industries. Many of these businesses have been moved to emerging economies, such as India, South Korea, Indonesia, and Brazil. Japan tends to encourage overcapacity in these industries in order to lower prices. Stalemate occurs as strong competitors erode away any cost advantage in order to maintain capacity utilization, while weaker competitors may well be subsidized or protected by their governments and other parties not subjected to market forces.

See also **Advantage matrix**

DEREK F. CHANNON

See also **Advantage matrix**

DEREK F. CHANNON

star businesses Such businesses are seen as having high market share in a high-growth environment. Because of their high share, they are expected to enjoy a lower cost structure than their lower-share competitors because of the experience effect (*see* EXPERIENCE AND LEARNING EFFECTS). However, cashflow is expected to be either marginally positive or negative, with any surplus being reinvested in the business to continue to add capacity, and thus to maintain or gain market share while industry growth remains high. Research evidence from the PIMS program supports this cashflow expectation but high capital intensity businesses with high growth may be cash negative, and may need to be supported by the funds generated by CASH COW businesses.

See also **Growth share matrix**

DEREK F. CHANNON

strategic alliances These take the form of coalitions and cooperation agreements, formed between a corporation and others in order to achieve certain strategic goals. Joint ventures (*see* JOINT VENTURE STRATEGY) may be seen as a specific form of alliance, but in recent times the term has become more widely adopted to describe a variety of forms of cooperative agreement which may or may not involve shareholdings. In particular they have been formed in some industries in which the cost of new model development, technology investment, and the like has emerged as being beyond the resources of the individual corporation. Japanese corporations have been particular users of alliance cooperative agreements with European and North American firms, partially as a way to enter these markets. Such alliances have been identified as important mechanisms for developing a global perspective in the so-called Triad markets.

With an alliance strategy it has been possible for corporations to swiftly gain access to markets, exchange technologies, form defensive shareholding blocs, enter third markets in combination with other partners, and engage in otherwise prohibitively expensive technologies, production facilities, and the like. They have the advantage of being relatively easily formed and disbanded – more so than joint ventures – and by joining in multiple alliances firms may contain risk and hold down costs.

Despite these apparent advantages, however, their value has been seriously questioned by many corporations; and especially by those with proprietary technology, strategic cost advantage, and high market share. For such concerns it has been argued that the potential loss of technical skills, the provision of competitor access to markets, and organizational and cultural clashes may well outweigh any advantage. As a result, perhaps 50 per cent of such alliances are therefore regarded as failures.

The selection of the right partner is critical to the success of an alliance. Any analysis of such a selection should be focused on fundamental, strategic, and cultural fits.

To achieve a fundamental fit between alliance partners, the activities and expertise of each should complement the other in order to add value overall. Questions which need to be considered therefore include the following:

- What are the risks associated with realizing potential of the alliance within a reasonable period of time?

- Is the partner really interested in eventually mounting a bid?

- How stable is the business environment?

- Is the partner really interested in gaining access to our market, technology, and distribution system prior to entering as a competitor?

Strategic alliances should also always form an integral part of the strategy of the partners. It is therefore important to check the harmony and complementarity of partners' business plans, including strategic goals, product market strategies, technological strategy, the common time frame for achieving goals, and an adequate and clearly defined resource commitment.

Many alliances have failed as a result of differences between the cultures of the partner corporations. This has been especially true

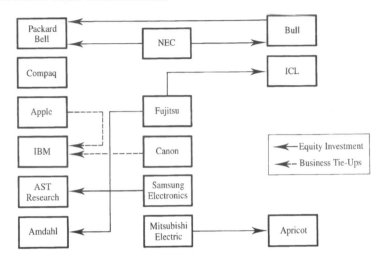

Figure 1 Global networking: international alliances in the PC industry.
Source: companies and Nihon Shimbun.

when they come from countries or regions with significantly different cultures, such as Japan and Western Europe. Regrettably, Western corporations in particular pay too little attention to understanding the underlying cultural and managerial styles of partners from different cultures, despite the fact that this is a major reason for the breakdown of alliances. Analysis of partner cultures is therefore recommended to insure that an acceptable fit is possible before irreversible moves are made.

Bibliography

Bleeke, J. & Ernst, D. (1991). The way to win in cross border alliances. *Harvard Business Review*, **69**, 113–33.
Bronder, C. & Pritzl, R. (1992). Developing strategic alliances. *European Management Journal*, **10** (4), 412–20.
Lorange, P. & Roos, J. (1991). Why some strategic alliances succeed and others fail. *Journal of Business Strategy*.
Ohmae, K. (1985). *Triad power: the coming shape of global competition.* New York: The Free Press.
Ohmae, K. (1989). The global logic of strategic alliances. *Harvard Business Review*, **67**, 143–54.
Sherman, S. (1992). Are strategic alliances working? *Fortune*, 77–8.

DEREK F. CHANNON

strategic core competences "Core speak" has arrived. Hardly a business publication can be read today without finding references to companies focusing on, or retreating to, their core businesses, core activities, core processes – or core competences.

Why should this be so? Is it just a catch phrase? Is it a symptom of the recession? What exactly is meant by "core competences"? What are the ramifications for financial results? Is it easy or difficult? Here, an attempt is made to answer some of these questions.

Over recent years, the pressures of recession have been felt, to varying degrees, by all markets and industries; some companies have triumphed, while others have failed. A large number of those who have succeeded to the greatest extent have done so not by finding market niches but by understanding the roots of their competitive position and exploiting them. Imaginative companies are also seeking ways in which to grow and diversify successfully as they move out of recession without making the mistakes that they, or others, made so spectacularly in the last boom.

It is not an essentially difficult task for senior executives to shrink an organization in response to recessionary pressures, although clearly it can be painful – especially so if the same executives were responsible for the original expansion. What is fundamentally much more difficult is to

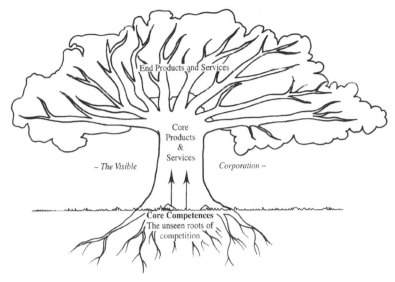

Figure 1 Competences are the roots that support and strengthen business.

develop and implement a successful growth strategy; one that will shape the future competitiveness and form of an organization while fighting off the near-term pressures of shrinking markets. It is the understanding of a companies' competitive roots and how these must be strengthened or replaced in the future – the notion of strategic core competences – that will be explored in what follows.

Background

The term "core competences" first became prevalent following award-winning articles published in the *Harvard Business Review* in 1989 and 1990 by C. K. Prahalad (University of Michigan) and Gary Hamel (London Business School) (Hamel et al., 1989; Prahalad & Hamel, 1990). They have since spoken on and published further developments of the concept, as

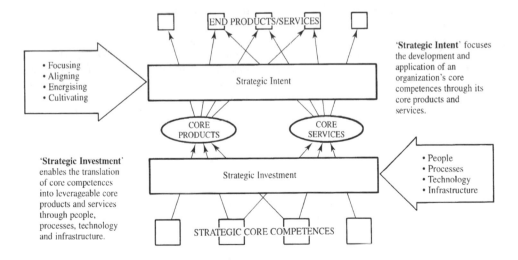

Figure 2 Competence-based strategies are catalysed by strategic investment and strategic intent.

CONVENTIONAL MIND-SET	———————→	CORE COMPETENCE MIND-SET
• Strategic Business Units Framework • Narrow definition of market sectors • Serve specific end-use markets • Compete through head on rivalry	MARKETS	• Strategic Core Competences Framework • Broad understanding of industry factors • Explore new competitive space • Pursue different rules of engagement
• Discrete end product/service portfolios • Aim to dominate brand market share only • Innovation constrained by product applications • Offset development costs through JVs	PRODUCTS	• Flexible core product/service portfolios • Aim to dominate component market share first • Innovation liberated by competence applications • Leverage learning through strategic alliances
• 'Rightsize' by market conditions • Make v Buy decisions on costs • SBU confined resource allocation • Permanent functional organisation structures	RESOURCES	• 'Rightsize' by strategic direction • Make v Buy decisions on competences • Skill-set combination resource allocation • Temporary cross-functional team structures
• Succession of fashionable initiatives • 'Big Bang' change programmes • Take few high risks/executive decisions • Financial target performance measures	CULTURES	• Persistent strategic intent challenges • Build layers of empiric advantage • Take many low risks/encourage experimentation • Strategic intent progress measures

Figure 3 A wholly different strategic mind-set.

well as producing a video, which has brought the subject to a wider audience.

Our definition of core competence is a distinctive combination of applied technologies, skill-sets, and/or business processes, which have evolved and been learned over a period of time in response to satisfying customer needs. We have also coined the term "strategic core competences" to describe the combination of competences required by an organization in the future to dominate its existing markets or create new ones – this may require some existing core competences to be abandoned, others strengthened, and some created. It is the interaction of these strategic core competences and their interrelation with an organization's STRATEGIC INTENT to deliver a competitive but affordable strategy that differentiates this approach from previous strategy models not based on the competence perspective.

This approach, when exploited to its full potential, enables a company to compete in a highly differentiated way that may then allow it to dominate a wide variety of markets through its competence-based strategy.

As Prahalad and Hamel point out, however, "There are major companies which have had the potential to build core competences but have failed to do so because their top management was unable to conceive of the company as anything other than a collection of discrete businesses."

Applying Competence-based Strategies

It is very unlikely that an organization will possess more than a handful of core competences, although it may well own a considerable list of component capabilities. Competences are the roots which give an organization its competitive strengths and which provide the nutrients for future business development through intermediate core products and/or services (see figure 1).

Unfortunately, organizations often think of competences only as technologies or skills that a firm has developed over time; this misses processes or business practices and totally avoids the link with market wants, and whether these will be needed in future end products or services. These issues and emotional ties to the past mean core competences are buried deep within the organization and may be deceptively difficult to identify (and, therefore, to cultivate and exploit) without a strong methodological approach. Once recognized, however, it is the cultivation and exploitation processes that are critical to the organization's success.

Once the strategic core competences have been found, they must be nurtured at board level by strategic investments in people, technology, processes, and infrastructure (such as alliances and facilities). These investments are needed in order to leverage the long-term benefits of a competence-based strategy through its "strategic intent," a congruent concept also developed by Prahalad and Hamel (see figure 2).

"Strategic intent" focuses and stretches the organization toward mobilizing the core competences that it owns, or needs to own, to achieve its strategic objectives, and to liberate it into "new competitive spaces." This means adopting a wholly different strategic mind-set (see figure 3).

Practical Experience

To substantiate and illustrate their thesis, Prahalad and Hamel draw on examples of a number of successful companies that have adopted a core competence approach to competitive strategy, such as Honda, Canon, Motorola, and 3M. They also cite Eastman Kodak as a successful practitioner. However, the Chief Executive of Eastman Kodak – who is featured in their videotapes – has subsequently been replaced because shareholders were unimpressed by the results of the strategy that he pursued. Why was this?

While we remain convinced that Prahalad and Hamel's work is of immense importance and practical relevance to executives worldwide, we have – through practical application of the principles – recognized some shortcomings in the approach they have so far adopted to developing a strategy based on core competences.

We see four principal areas of difficulty – some of which have already been alluded to:

- *The concept gap.* Some executives still think of core competences as a process of rejigging a portfolio of end products. Others think of their competences only in the narrowest terms of the most obvious technological competences that they possess. These misconceptions must be exposed and dispersed for the concept to take root.

- *The change gap.* Even more organizations fail to recognize or anticipate the impact that significant changes in the market have on the competences that they must develop or acquire in order to remain competitive in the future (the original reason for us devel-

oping a strategic core competence methodology). Our simple way of modeling these impacts greatly facilitates the importance of core competences to strategy development.

- *The opportunity gap.* By far the most powerful aspect of the strategic core competences concept is the potential to leverage the technologies and skill-sets that an organization possesses into new markets – to release the constraints of "served market" and "strategic business unit" thinking. Although Prahalad and Hamel make much of the opportunities in this area, we found that they offered little practical guidance on how to identify and realize them until we applied our future mapping and vision design techniques (not covered here).

- *The methodology gap.* In our opinion, the published work does not yet prescribe a reliable method to effectively identify core competences, or to overcome the deficiencies described above. *If competences cannot be correctly and readily identified at the outset, the whole philosophy collapses and falls into disrepute.* A way of bridging this gap is most important of all in finding solutions to the shortcomings that we have described.

In short, the need is for a practical, structured method to identify core competences, model the effect of changing market conditions, and leverage competences into new competitive spaces.

Our Approach: QFD

The basis of the methodology that we have developed provides an effective solution to the needs. Simply, it adapts the framework of the Quality Function Deployment (QFD) "house of quality" matrix – a technique most commonly used for improved product development (principally in the automotive and other engineering industries) – and applies it for the purposes of strategic planning (see figure 4).

This came about through our becoming increasingly aware that strategic core competences needed to be developed from core competences which had evolved from solutions that companies had built up over time to satisfy or create customer wants in their markets. We also saw that QFD, an emerging technique that

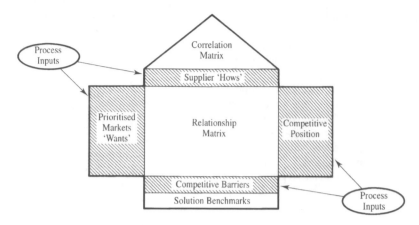

Figure 4 An adaptation of the Quality Function Deployment (QFD) matrix provides an effective tool – and database – to define competences and challenge assumptions. This technique provides quantitative evidence of the importance of competence elements in providing competitive solutions to the market's present and future demands.

we had applied in other project work, was also about interrelationships (sympathies and anti-pathies) between customer "wants" and supplier "hows" which led to engineering solutions.

We found that if the QFD tool is used appropriately, it does bring a highly structured approach to the process of defining both present and future core competences. Its great advan-tage is that it provides a database against which the dynamic effects on optional solutions of different, changing, or new customer "wants" within markets can be easily modeled.

3-E categorization. We also developed a method for categorizing the principal solutions that the company had devised to satisfy market needs. These were the empiric technologies and skill-sets learned; the enabling competences such as business processes and capabilities; and those that could be emulated – that could be most easily copied or bought by competitors. This categorization, along with understanding the layering of competitive advantage, helped to define the combinations of competences most clearly differentiated from those of competitors and which, therefore, could be defined as *core* competences.

Benchmarking. A further advantage of apply-ing the QFD technique is that it also provides a structured framework for BENCHMARKING. Not only are the relative successes of the company's solutions in satisfying the market's perceived needs measured, but also the relative strength of its technologies and business processes.

Cross-functional workshops. By using a series of cross-functional workshops for gathering the key inputs to the matrix, we also found that as these progressed a much greater consensus was achieved between the functional managers within the organization (e.g., between engineer-ing and commercial viewpoints) than in the early stages of the project work (as shown from the results of our initial internal questionnaire). We believe that this is as a direct result of applying a rigorous structural framework to the definition of core competences.

Future mapping and vision design. Lastly, by applying this methodology, we observed a much greater willingness to explore the poten-tial for diversification into new markets, as well as how to focus the technical and marketing research roles.

There is insufficient space here to describe in detail how to apply the QFD technique to the definition of strategic core competence. Suffice it to say that we were able to prove conclusively that it is a powerful tool, the potential of which has not yet been adequately recognized in this type of application.

Conclusion

This method builds upon the concept of core competences, introduced by Prahalad and Hamel, by providing a structured approach to formulating a competence-based strategy. It also facilitates an ability to model the outcomes of strategic decisions and test alternative solutions through comparative benchmarking.

What is unique about our contribution is the marriage of the core competence concept to a practical technique that allows the entrepreneurial and innovative skills of a company to be focused on a truly competitive strategy.

Bibliography

Hamel, G. & Prahalad, C. K. (1994). *Competing for the future.* Cambridge, MA: Harvard Business School Press.
Hamel, G., Doz, Y. & Prahalad, C. K. (1989). Collaborate with your competitors – and win. *Harvard Business Review*, 67, 133–9.
Prahalad, C. K. & Hamel, G. (1990). The core competence of the corporation. *Harvard Business Review*, 68, 79–81.

CHRIS ADAMS and DAVID JOHNSTON

strategic fit Strategic fit occurs usually in related diversified concerns (*see* RELATED DIVERSIFIED STRATEGY) as a result of superior competitive position arising from overall lower cost and the successful transfer of core skills, technology, and managerial know-how between businesses. The earlier concepts of SYNERGY and shared experience have similar meanings.

Strategic fit, however, may apply in apparently unrelated businesses where financial synergy may be found. For example, a high cashflow business may financially complement a business that is a high capital user. Examples of this phenomenon include Reo Stakis – a combination of casinos and hotels – the Ladbroke Group, and Donald Trump's empire, all of which are engaged in similar sets of activities.

Diversification into businesses in which shared technology, marketing, and production skills are required can lead to ECONOMIES OF SCOPE when the costs of operating two or more businesses are less than operating each individually. The key to such cost reductions is therefore diversification into businesses with strategic fit.

Market-related fit occurs when the activity cost chains of different businesses overlap such that they attempt to reach the same consumers via similar distribution channels, or are marketed and promoted in similar ways. In addition to such economies of scope, it may also be possible to transfer selling skills, promotion and advertising skills, and product positioning/differentiation skills across businesses. Care must, however, be taken to insure that market-related fit is possible. Successful examples include Canon's strategic position in cameras and photographic equipment being logically extended into copying and imaging equipment, and Honda's position in motorcycles being extended into other activities using engines, including automobiles and lawnmowers. However, not all such moves are successful. Thus BAT found that selling branded cosmetics was different than selling branded tobacco items.

Operating fit is achieved where the potential for cost sharing or skills transfer can occur in procurement, R&D, production, assembly, and/or administration. Cost sharing amongst these activities can lead to ECONOMIES OF SCALE. Again, successes such as the sale of life insurance policies by retail banking branches can be identified. Similarly, failures are frequently due to inabilities to insure integration between activities from different businesses brought together by acquisition.

Management fit occurs when different business units enjoy comparable types of entrepreneurial administrative or operating problems. This type of gain is very difficult to achieve due to differences in corporate culture. Classic failures in achieving such fit gains occurred in the attempted diversification moves by the oil industry majors after the first oil-price shock in 1973. Redefinitions of their businesses into "energy" and "raw materials" encouraged moves into minerals, coal, and gas. Most of these moves were serious failures, or the expected strategic fit did not materialize.

Ironically, the only strategic fit which is almost certain to be achieved is the financial one. The operational strategic fits have lower probabilities of success, that for marketing being higher than that for production which, in turn, is higher than that for R&D.

The strategic fit concept has also been criticized as being too static and limiting, focusing as it does on existing resources and the existing environment rather than seeking out the future opportunities and threats which are the focus of firms with STRATEGIC INTENT.

Bibliography

Ansoff, H. I. (1965). *Corporate strategy*. New York: McGraw-Hill. See chapter 7.

Kitching, J. (1967). Why do mergers miscarry? *Harvard Business Review*, November–December, 84–101.

Ohmae, K. (1983). *The mind of the strategist*. New York: Penguin. See pp. 121–4.

Porter, M.E. (1985). *Competitive advantage: creating and sustaining superior performance*. New York: The Free Press. See pp. 318–19 and 337–53.

DEREK F. CHANNON

strategic groups   A strategic group consists of those rival firms with similar competitive approaches and positions in the market. The identification of strategic groups within an industry enables the competitive structure of the industry to be redefined to compare strategies of various competitors for similarities and differences. Thus some firms may have comparable product lines, be similarly vertically integrated, focus on similar customer segments, use the same distribution channels, sell with the same product positioning, and the like. If all competitors within an industry have similar strategic characteristics, then there will be only one strategic group. However, in most industries with a significant number of competitors it is common for more than one cluster of competitors to emerge. This is illustrated in the strategic group map of the US brewing industry, shown in figure 1, which positions the major competitors along the two dimensions of price/perceived quality and image and geographic coverage.

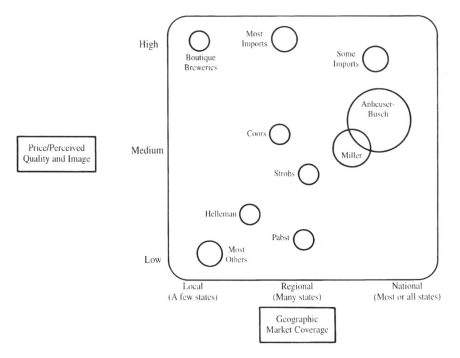

Figure 1 A strategic group map of the US brewing industry.
Source: Thompson & Strickland (1993), p. 77.

To construct such a strategic group map it is necessary to follow the procedure set out below:

1. Identify the key strategic characteristics which differentiate competitors, such as SERVED MARKET, product range, distribution channels used, price, and quality.
2. Plot firms on a two-dimensional map, using selected pairs of differentiating variables.
3. Cluster firms that fall in a similar strategic space into strategic groups.
4. Map the groups in terms of importance, by indicating the level of group total sales by the area of the circle surrounding clustered competitors.
5. If more than two significant strategic variables can be used for axes, draw a number of maps to identify alternate positions of competitive relationships.

This form of analysis helps to improve understanding of the degree and nature of competitive rivalry. As a generalization, the closer that strategic groups are to one another, the greater is the likelihood of competitive rivalry between the firms within the group. Firms that are strategically distant from the main groups may be subject to much less competitive pressure. As a result, the profit potentials of different competitors may be radically different and not necessarily correlated with size. Thus, a large competitor, despite enjoying the advantage of a high market share, may operate within a group in which competitive rivalry is intense, thus leading to profit erosion. By contrast, a number of competitors operating in a smaller market of strategic space may enjoy superior margins due to the lack of other competitors. Thus competitive pressures will tend to significantly favor some groups over others.

Bibliography

McGee, J. & Thomas, H. (1986). Strategic groups: theory, research and taxonomy. *Strategic Management Journal*, 7 (2), 141–60.
Porter, M. J. (1980). *Competitive strategy*. New York: The Free Press. See chapter 7.
Thompson, A. & Strickland A. J. (1993). *Strategic management*, 7th edn, New York: Irwin.

DEREK F. CHANNON

strategic impact of information technology see INFORMATION TECHNOLOGY, STRATEGIC IMPACT OF

strategic intent It has been argued that US firms seeking STRATEGIC FIT have often found themselves overtaken by firms, especially the Asian conglomerates, driven by long-term visions of the future, which are then relentlessly and ruthlessly pursued with *strategic intent*. The strategic objectives of such firms are to achieve a specific business position at some time in the future. This may be to exercise long-term industrial leadership on a national or global scale. For example, in the 1960s Komatsu, the largest Japanese producer of earth-moving equipment, but then less than a third of the size of the US industry leader, Caterpillar, adopted a strategy of "Maru-C," or "Surround Caterpillar." At the time the US company probably hardly recognized the existence of the Japanese firm. By the late 1980s, however, Komatsu had developed as the second largest global competitor after Caterpillar, and had also produced a diversified range of products, including specialist plastics, and industrial robots and electronics. The company had extended its product range further by the mid-1990s, and expected earth-moving equipment to account for no more than 50 per cent of sales by the millenium. By then, the company's vision had evolved to actually exclude its ancestral earth-moving equipment market, and Komatsu was marshalling its energies to become a "total technology" enterprise. This involves:

- an enterprise that operates globally
- an enterprise that supplies leading edge technologies to diverse industries
- an enterprise that supplies systematized products integrating hardware and software
- an enterprise with creative and vigorous employees that makes broad contributions to society

Within Japanese companies, a long-term perspective is commonplace. Protected from short-term stock market pressures partly because of their membership of keiretsu groups (*see* KEIRETSU STRUCTURE), Japanese companies can focus on their long-term positions. Strategic plans, which usually run for three years, each have an inspirational name, such as "first global company by 2000": there may even be a series of three-year plans. The basic elements of such plans are universally known and understood by all employees and each therefore shares the common strategic goal. Such strategic intent targets are much less common in Western concerns.

Strategic intent can thus be used as a psychological target which provides a focus that all members of the organization to adopt. Becoming the industry leader or dominating a specific segment are frequent missionary goals. The prophecies can therefore become self-fulfilling provided that employees have faith in their leadership and that, in many cases, the existing industry leaders fail to recognize that the challenge is on.

Bibliography

Hamel, G. & Prahalad, C. K. (1989). Strategic intent. *Harvard Business Review*, **89** May–June, 63–76.

DEREK F. CHANNON

strategic management   This concept consists of that set of decisions and actions which result in formulating a strategy, and its implementation to achieve the objectives of the corporation. The process of strategic decision making is illustrated in figure 1. The process consists of a number of specific steps:

1. Determination of the MISSION of the corporation, including statements about purpose, philosophy, and objectives.
2. An assessment of the internal environment of the corporation, including an assessment of its culture, history, and informal as well as formal organization.
3. An assessment of its external environment by PEST ANALYSIS.
4. The matching of external opportunities and threats with internal strengths and weaknesses via SWOT ANALYSIS.
5. The identification of desired options from this analysis in the light of the corporate mission.

6. Strategic choice of a relevant set of long-term strategies and policies required to successfully achieve the chosen options.
7. The development of short- and medium-term strategies and action programs that are consistent with the long-term strategies and policies.
8. Implementation programs based on budgets, and action plans based on budgeted resource allocations and monitored via appropriate management information, planning and control systems, and reward and sanction systems.
9. Review and evaluation systems to monitor the strategy process and to provide an input for future decision making.

The process may or may not be articulated formally via a STRATEGIC PLANNING system. In addition, strategic management occurs at a number of hierarchical levels within the firm, dependent upon the complexity of the corporations – this usually involves three levels. At the top is the corporate level, at which decisions are taken by the senior executive officers and, in particular, the CEO in conjunction with the board of directors. This group is responsible for providing the vision of deciding where the company wants to and does go. They are also responsible for financial performance, legal structure, and for establishing overall corporate image and social responsibility, which reflect the views of the various stakeholders of the firm, including employees, shareholders, and society as a whole.

The corporate level also establishes an overall strategic perspective across the business activities of the firm. For multibusiness firms – which includes most large corporations – the corporate level determines: the portfolio balance and the position of each business within it; sets performance objectives; allocates resources; makes key appointments and sets human resources policies; creates the formal organizational structure (and influences the informal structure); sets the management information, planning, and control systems; and creates the reward and sanction systems. The corporate level is also usually responsible for the identification and implementation of any major acquisitions, although some companies delegate "fill in" acquisition strategy to the business unit

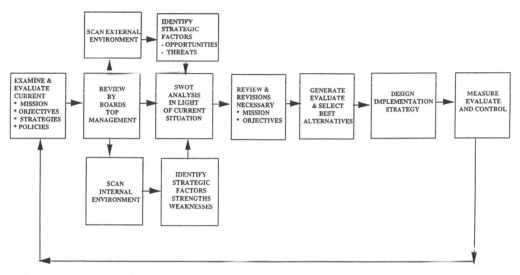

Figure 1   The strategic decision making process.

level. Any new fields of activity, however, are normally determined at the corporate level.

The second main tier of strategic management occurs at the level of the business unit, although an intermediate division level may exist in some organizations, comprising a cluster of business units. At this level managers translate the general direction and thrust of the corporation into specific strategies relevant to their businesses and consistent with the overall portfolio investment strategy determined for them. At this level multifunctional strategies are formulated and implemented for the specific product market area in which the business operates. Such strategies might vary greatly in terms of commitment to growth. While some businesses may be expected to strive for growth, others may be expected to release resources by adopting harvesting or divestment strategies. A number of portfolio models to position businesses, including the ADVANTAGE MATRIX, COMPETITIVE POSITION – MARKET ATTRACTIVENESS MATRIX, DIRECTIONAL POLICY MATRIX, GROWTH SHARE MATRIX, LIFE CYCLE STRATEGY, and VALUE-BASED PLANNING, are discussed elsewhere. All these models have been designed to aid the corporate center in identifying the appropriate position of each business within the corporate portfolio, and the development of appropriate strategies is dis-

cussed throughout many of the other entries in this volume.

The third tier of strategic management applies at the functional level of each business, at which managers from the principal functions of the business, such as marketing, production, operations, R&D, information technology, accounting, and human relations, develop operational strategies and tactics to implement the selected business level strategy. The overall process thus represents a cascade approach.

The characteristics of strategic management decisions vary with the hierarchical level of activity. Corporate level decisions tend to be value oriented, conceptual, and less precise than those at lower level. In particular, the CEO's vision about how the corporation should develop is exceptionally important. This is especially true in large corporations which attempt to change direction, and in which overcoming the effect of historically established corporate inertia is perhaps the most challenging managerial task – unless the corporation is in crisis and a TURNAROUND STRATEGY is called for. Corporate level decisions are also characterized by greater risk and determine future profitability and the ability of the corporation to survive and prevail. Such decisions also cover all aspects of financial strategy, including capital structure, dividend

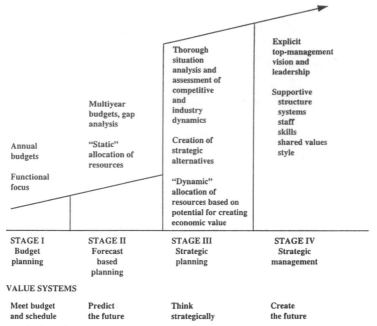

Figure 2   The evolution of strategic management.
Source: Gluck, F. W., Kauffman, S. P. & Wallek, A. S. (1980, p. 4).

policy, growth priorities, and selection of the business portfolio.

By contrast, functional decisions are effectively made up of action programs which, hopefully, support the overall corporate position. However, this is not always so, and in conditions of corporate level led radical change, serious dysfunctional behavior may be experienced, especially when shifts in the existing power structure may be experienced during programs such as re-engineering (*see* RE-ENGINEERING DISADVANTAGES; VALUE-DRIVEN RE-ENGINEERING). Functional level decisions are, however, normally concerned with relatively short-term, lower-risk, moderate-cost activities. They do not usually cut across businesses within the corporation unless interdependencies exist, and therefore tend to be confined to the individual business.

Decisions at the business level bridge those at corporate and functional levels. They are more risky and costly than those at the functional level and may involve significant changes in existing behavior, including factors such as plant location, segmentation strategy, geo-

graphic coverage, and the choice of distribution channel.

Evolution Toward Strategic Management

Relatively few companies can be said to have developed a full strategic management perspective, in which the whole corporation thinks strategically and has a clear vision of where it wants to go – and knows how to get there. Rather, companies evolve toward this position, as shown in figure 2.

McKinsey and Company believe that companies proceed through four stages of development. They start with simple financial planning (stage I); move through forecast-based planning (stage II); then externally oriented or strategic planning (stage III); and finally arrive at stage IV, strategic management.

In stage I, budgets and financial objectives dominate the planning process, and managers and planners are preoccupied with setting an accurate budget and achieving it. In such companies, senior management assumes that the status quo will continue, that industry change will not affect the way things are done, and that industry boundaries are clear and will not be breached by new competitors or technologies. The question of change of corporate direction is seldom raised and the firm's approach is inward-looking and execution-oriented. The process of planning is dominated by financial numbers rather than strategic variables and the development of budgets is usually undertaken by the finance and accounting function.

Movement of the company from stage I to stage II is an indication that management recognizes the need to extend the time horizon of the corporation beyond the single financial year and to think about the future. Usually, future forecasts extend for three years. In the 1970s and early 1980s such forward extrapolations often extended for longer periods, but the rapid growth of environmental turbulence, coupled with a recognition that future financial forecasts were relatively meaningless projections of the present position, has caused most managements to cut back to three-year projections. Even so, most such plans remain dominated by financial projections rather than strategic considerations. In many companies some managers also believe that senior management is mainly concerned with the first year of such a projection, and therefore tend to consider that extrapolations beyond this point are relatively meaningless. Again, the exercise tends to be dominated by the finance and accounting staff, with line management rarely participating in strategic decisions regarding operations, focusing instead on how to avoid or fill any profit gap.

A quantum leap in the effectiveness of strategic planning and decision making usually occurs with the transition of the corporation from stage II to stage III. At this point the corporation becomes more focused on the external environment in which it operates, and the focus switches from the forecasting of volume and revenues toward obtaining a better understanding of customer needs, competitive position, technological developments, and market characteristics. At this stage, line management become significantly involved in the development of strategy, professional corporate planning staff are introduced, and the system of developing strategy tends to become formalized with the introduction of detailed procedures and timetables.

The stage III company thus adds conceptual and analytic skills which theoretically enable it to develop strategies for sustainable competitive advantage. Many new variables are considered other than financial. Plans are sophisticated and resource allocations may be determined on the rational basis of the strategic positions of individual businesses. Despite these efforts, however, many such strategies fail to achieve necessary strategic changes in the corporation. This is due, in large part, to the fact that many line managers do not regard themselves as the owners of the plans and, as a result, fail to implement them. Moreover, many do not wish to change their perspective and in particular accept the organizational, cultural, and power relationship changes which may be necessary to transform the corporation when faced with major shifts in the external environment.

In examining the reasons why companies in leadership positions went into decline, McKinsey and Company concluded that such firms fell into one or more of three major traps. First, they used unrealistic or obsolete criteria to assess company strengths and/or weaknesses. Second, they became complacent about their leadership position – and as such became inflexible and assumed that the status quo would go on indefinitely. Third, they failed to recognize industry change and take action to respond to it.

Companies making the transition from stage III to stage IV did recognize these traps. They understood that change was continuous and permanent, and that unwillingness to meet the challenge would ultimately result in failure. Moreover, change within the corporation might be radical. Within corporations such as IBM, Citicorp, and GE, this acceptance has been clearly led from the office of the CEO.

In stage IV companies therefore, strategic management is inculcated throughout the corporation. The corporation is continually adjusting its competitive strategy in response to the market and competition. Such firms are also constantly changing the rules in the markets in which they compete, in order to win. They are also low on bureaucracy, with strategic responsibility passing throughout the corporation. Planning becomes a line rather than staff function and line managers own the plans.

uncompromising in their commitment to com- petitive success and develop a management style and system to support this commitment. They are also able to both institute continuous incremental change and make that quantum leap when considered necessary. As such, their leaders are prepared to make big and bold decisions, while planners are expected to provide insights for adapting the vision rather than mere descriptions.

Bibliography

Gluck, F. W. (1986). Strategic management: an overview. In J. R. Gardner, R. Rachlin, & H. W. A. Sweeny (eds), *Handbook of strategic planning.* New York: John Wiley.

Gluck, F. W., Kaufman, S. P. & Wallek, A. S. (1980). Strategic management for competitive advantage. *The McKinsey Quarterly,* Autumn, 2–16.

Hofer, C. W. & Schendel, D. (1978). *Strategy formulation: analytical concepts.* St. Paul, MN: West.

Hunsicker, J. Q. (1980). Can top managers be strategists? *Strategic Management Journal,* 1, 77–83.

DEREK F. CHANNON

strategic planning   Most corporations today have some form of corporate plan. However, very few are successfully implemented. In theory, strategic planning is the mechanism whereby the corporation organizes its resources and actions to achieve its objectives. It is a formal rather than an informal process, the usual contents of which are illustrated in table 1, while the process of strategic planning is illustrated in figure 1.

Planning will be conducted at hierarchical levels within the corporation, dependent upon its complexity. For the multibusiness firm, plans will be established at the corporate, business unit, and departmental or market segment levels.

At the corporate level, for example, the overall MISSION is established consistent with internal resources and external opportunities and threats. The direction in which the corporation will go is determined in large part by a corporate vision of where it would like to be. The CEO plays a disproportionate role in the establishment of such a vision.

At the business unit level the concept of mission translates into the markets and activities that the business unit would like to address, subject to corporate level constraints such as resource allocation. At the market segment level, mission is less ambitious and more constrained, being based on the scope of activities assigned to that segment. Similar cascades apply to the other elements of a plan, as shown in table 2. The system is an iterative process, involving a repetitious sequence of strategic developments, strategic planning, plan implementation, and strategic performance measurement. The cycle is normally repeated on an annual basis, with plan horizons presently tending to be around three years in Western companies. Normally, the procedures are standardized with schedules also phased throughout the planning cycle. A typical cycle is illustrated in figure 2.

The main steps often consist of the following elements, although the precise timing and content vary from company to company:

Executive briefing. The starting point of the plan commences with a senior management review which includes:

- assumptions about the external environment
- changes from previous assumptions
- alternate futures/scenarios – (*see* SCENARIO PLANNING)
- a review of progress against the existing plan and an update of performance against goals
- a possible theme for the forthcoming plan cycle

General management meeting. This establishes the mission, goals, and objectives of the corporation, and decisions reached are then broadly communicated to operating managers at business unit level and to other operating managers.

Strategy assessment meeting. Follow-up meetings are held between corporate and SBU executives to discuss issues and options, and policies and guidelines.

Plan overview. Plan submissions from SBUs are consolidated and reviewed with corporate management.

Strategy review meetings. The corporate center and SBU management negotiate to

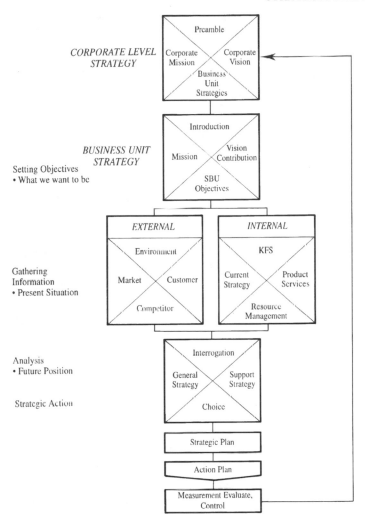

Figure 1 A Strategic plan flowchart.
Source: Channon (1994).

at business unit level and to other operating managers.

Strategy assessment meeting. Follow-up meetings are held between corporate and SBU executives to discuss issues and options, and policies and guidelines.

Plan overview. Plan submissions from SBUs are consolidated and reviewed with corporate management.

Strategy review meetings. The corporate center and SBU management negotiate to develop shared views on SBU plans by selecting strategic options, plan modifica

tions, resource allocations, and performance targets.

Plan resubmission. Resubmitted plans by SBUs are then consolidated with any corporate level adjustments and given a final review by corporate incentive management.

Board presentation. The final plan is then summarized in strategic terms, formally submitted to the board of directors for discussion, and usually approved.

The plan and planning cycle are never fully finalized in the sense that both internal and external events may cause them to change.

Table 1   Strategic plan components.

Mission	Defines the present and desired position of the corporation. Similarly, a mission will apply at the business unit level.
Objectives	Qualitative and quantitative statements of what the corporation wishes to achieve over a measurable future. These should be internally consistent and fit the mission.
Goals	Specific short- and long-term quantitative results which directly support the objectives measured as key performance indicators. They should also reflect the critical successful factors for each business within the corporation.
Strategies	These will apply at both the corporate and business unit levels.

Strategic planning

- Corporate level – establishes strategy for the total corporation

- Business unit – applies in three phases, as follows:

  1. Formulating strategy

  What are the critical factors for success?
  What are the external opportunities and threats?
  What are the relative strengths and weaknesses?
  What strategic alternatives are available?
  What assumptions have been made?
  What sensitivities need to be tested?

  2. Detailed strategic programs

  What specific programs achieve objectives?
  What resources will these require?
  What are the risks/rewards of each program?
  How will these programs be managed?

  3. Strategy implementation

  What organization/human resources will be adopted?
  What milestones will be used to monitor progress?
  Is the MIS system appropriate?
  Is the reward and sanction system appropriate?

some cynicism about the plan unless it is clearly taken seriously by top management.

Interestingly, perhaps, the literature on strategic management in the 1990s pays little attention to the practicalities of the mechanics of strategic planning; unlike in the 1970s, when formal systems were emphasized. Moreover,

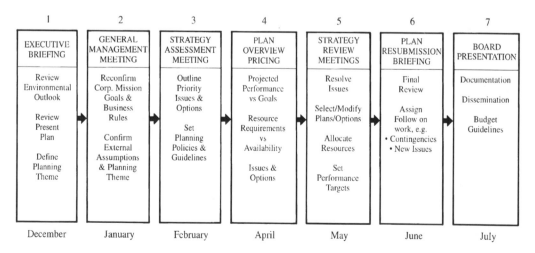

Figure 2 An annual planning cycle.
Source: King (1986).

attention more on the budget than the longer-term plan, and as a consequence there is often some cynicism about the plan unless it is clearly taken seriously by top management.

Interestingly, perhaps, the literature on strategic management in the 1990s pays little attention to the practicalities of the mechanics of strategic planning; unlike in the 1970s, when formal systems were emphasized. Moreover, while during the 1980s many corporations built up substantial central planning units, these have lost considerable credibility, since line management believes that they are the operational component of the corporation needed to imple-ment plans. In addition, many line managers believe that top management in the West has become relatively obsessed with short-term rather than long-term performance.

Interestingly, Japanese corporations have built significant planning departments. Employees in these departments, however, have rarely been trained as specialist planners; rather, they are assigned to planning departments as a regular element in their development, based on job rotation, and many come to such departments from anywhere in the company. While plans themselves tend to have a three-year time horizon, they are not seriously

Table 2 Hierarchical plan requirements.

	Corporate level	*Business unit*	*Market segment level*
Mission	Corporate mission	Markets, activities assigned to divisional constraints	Scope of activities assigned to develop market segment
Objectives	Corporate objectives	SBU objectives supporting corporate objective	Segment objective
Assumptions	Specific to corporation capabilities, opportunities, threats	Specific to scope of divisional activities	Specific to market: demand, competition, service
Competitive strength	Corporate strength, weakness	SBU strength, weakness	Specific share, strength, weakness
Assessment of market opportunity		As evaluated and reviewed at all levels	
Market portfolio strategy	Overall corporate mix and priority, including new areas of interest	Mix for markets assigned to SBU	Specific investment priority for this segment
Changes desired in controllable variables	Attack plans for change in corporate capabilities	Attack plan for change in SBU capabilities	Attack plans to change factors
Programs to implement change, specific to corporation	Specific to corporation	Specific to SBU capabilities	Specific to segment
Expected financial results	Corporate financial measures	SBU financial measures	Segment financial measures

changed each year. Furthermore, such plans, all of which have a formal name, usually form elements in much longer-term "visions" established by the president of the corporation. These visions may have time horizons spanning 20 years or more, and rather than being driven by financial objectives, have broader technical and social goals.

Bibliography

Channon, D. F. (1986). *Bank strategic planning and marketing*. Chichester: John Wiley.

Channon, D. F. (1994). Strategic management workbook. Working paper, Imperial College.

Chinn, W. D., Yoshihisa, M. & Vanderbrink, J. D. (1986). Strategic planning: a view from Japan. In J. R. Gardner, R. Rachlin & H. W. A. Sweeny (eds), *Handbook of strategic planning*. New York: John Wiley.

King, W. C. (1986). Formulating strategies and contingency plans. In J. R. Gardner, R. Rachlin & H. W. A. Sweeny (eds), *Handbook of strategic planning*. New York: John Wiley.

Toyohiro, K. (1992). *Long range planning in Japanese corporations*. Berlin: De Gruyter.

DEREK F. CHANNON

strategic square   This technique invokes concepts of military strategy in a competitive environment. There are some similarities with LANCHESTER STRATEGY. Four key strategies are identified in the strategic square illustrated in figure 1.

Defensive Strategy

This strategy is only normally available to an industry leader. It is important, therefore, that any company wishing to adopt such a strategy should be sure that it enjoys a clear leadership position. This will involve careful market analysis to define its precise boundary. In particular, care should be taken when geographic coverage or channel shifts are possible. It is also important to remember that defense is a negative strategy unless it restricts the future intentions of a competitor. Examples from military history include the Battle of the Somme, which developed as a stalemate, and Waterloo, where reinforcement of the defense ultimately gained a British/Prussian win. Superior force can, however, overrun a defense provided that firepower is sufficiently superior (*see* LANCHESTER STRATEGY).

Offence

In an offensive strategy, head-on attack should

DEFENCE	OFFENCE
1. ONLY MARKET LEADERS SHOULD PLAY 2. THE BEST DEFENCE IS A GOOD OFFENCE 3. STRONG COMPETITIVE MOVES SHOULD ALWAYS BE BLOCKED	1. THE MAIN CONSIDERATION IS THE STRENGTH OF THE LEADER'S POSITION 2. THE ATTACK SHOULD BE LAUNCHED ON AS NARROW A FRONT AS POSSIBLE 3. THE ATTACK SHOULD BE LAUNCHED AT THE LEADERS WEAKEST POSITION
1. SUCCESSFUL FLANKING MOVES MUST BE MADE INTO UNCONTESTED AREAS 2. TACTICAL SURPRISE OUGHT TO BE AN IMPORTANT ELEMENT 3. THE PURSUIT IS AS CRITICAL AS THE ATTACK ITSELF	1. FIND MARKET SEGMENT SMALL ENOUGH TO DEFINE 2. NEVER ACT LIKE THE LEADER NO MATTER HOW SUCCESSFUL 3. BE PREPARED TO MOVE OUT AT SHORT NOTICE
FLANKING	GUERRILLA

Figure 1 The strategic square.

be avoided unless clear supremacy of force is achievable. Rather, the "indirect" approach should be adopted by focusing the attack on an area of competitive weakness. Successful armies operate on the principle of the line of least resistance/expectation.

Flanking Strategy

Flanking strategies also require innovation via the development of new products of markets. Moves to re-segment markets often therefore form the basis for successful flanking attacks.

Guerrilla Strategy

This is the strategy for most competitors in a market, as they are too small to tackle market leaders head on. Guerrilla attackers should identify and seek to dominate small segments which are not seen as especially important to the industry leader. If the guerrilla competitor is attacked by a market leader, a rapid retreat may be called for and a willingness to exit from a chosen market is therefore important. Flexibility in such positions is therefore desirable. Unfortunately, all too often, niche domination leads many such companies to adopt the mistaken belief that they can take on an industry leader. It is better to adopt the philosophy of Mao Tse-Tung:

> The enemy advances, we retreat
> The enemy camps, we harass
> The enemy tires, we attack
> The enemy retreats, we pursue

Bibliography

Davidson, H. (1987). *Offensive marketing*. Harmondsworth, UK: Penguin. See pp. 161–70.
Liddell Hart, B. H. (1968). *Strategy*. New York: Praeger.
Ries, A. & Trout, J. (1986). *Marketing warfare*. New York: McGraw-Hill.

DEREK F. CHANNON

strategic use of information systems   *see* INFORMATION SYSTEMS, STRATEGIC USE OF

structuring organizations   Mintzberg has suggested that an organization consists of five basic components that differ in size and importance. These components are illustrated in figure 1.

The first component, the *operating core*, consists of those personnel who undertake the basic work of the organization which is related directly to operations or the production of products/services. This component conducts four key functions:

● securing inputs

● transforming inputs into outputs

● distributing outputs

● providing direct support to the production process

The second main component is the *strategic apex*. This consists of managers responsible for the overall direction of the corporation. They manage the organization to achieve the objectives of those who own or control it. Their primary functions are as follows:

● direct supervision, resource allocation, structure planning and control system design, conflict resolution, and strategic decision making

● managing and monitoring relations with the external environment

● formulating organizational strategy

The third component is the *middle line*. This comprises the chain of managers with formal authority and connects the apex with the operating core. Historically it was seen as essential, because the apex could not directly supervise all the line operators. In addition, the middle line:

● provides feedback to the hierarchy about performance in the operating core

● makes some, basically operational, decisions and allocates some resources

● manages the relations of business units or functions with the external environment

As a result of re-engineering (*see* RE-ENGINEERING DISADVANTAGES; VALUE-DRIVEN RE-ENGINEERING) and the adoption of the HORIZONTAL STRUCTURE, the role of the middle line

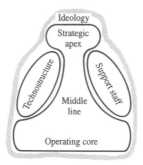

Figure 1   Six basic parts of the organization
Source: Mintzberg (1989)

has come under serious threat, as the span of control of the apex has been considerably enlarged as a result of improved IT systems. Moreover, there is some feeling amongst senior management in firms with operating horizontal structures that middle line managers act as an often undesirable block on the information flow between the apex and operations.

The fourth organizational component, *support staff*, provide support for line operations and include functions such as property, social affairs, legal industrial relations, payroll management, accounting, and the like. Historically, support staff were added to enable the firm to gain greater control over boundary activities in order to reduce perceived risk and uncertainty. These activities were usually loosely coupled to core processes and could be located at various levels in the hierarchy.

In recent years the size and scope of support staff numbers and duties have come under serious scrutiny in many corporations as part of re-engineering projects and cost reduction drives. As a result many concerns are turning to OUTSOURCING as an alternative to operating their own support functions. While this poses no serious threat in nontechnical areas, a number of strategic and/or specialized functions have been outsourced, including computer systems.

The final component is the *technostructure*. This consists of analysts who evaluate and influence the work of others. Many technostructure personnel are control specialists who attempt to increase the level of operational standardization, so reducing the level of skill required in the operating core. Three types of analysts are identified:

- work study analysts, whose task is to standardize work processes
- planning and control analysts, who attempt to standardize outputs such as planning, budgeting, quality systems, and the like
- personnel analysts, who seek to standardize organizational skills via training and recruitment

In order to accomplish the total task of the organization, it is also necessary to integrate the activities of the key components. Mintzberg identifies five specific coordinating mechanisms which help to achieve this:

- mutual adjustment – whereby work is coordinated through direct informal communication between related personnel

- direct supervision – a formal mechanism whereby an individual or manager is given authority over and takes responsibility for the work of others and for monitoring their activities

- standardization of work processes – whereby the content of work is specified or programmed

- standardization of outputs – which insures that the results of work conforms to predetermined standards and specifications

- standardization of skills – which is accomplished via appropriate training and recruitment

Bibliography

Galbraith, J. K. & Nathanson, D. A. (1980). *Strategy implementation*. St Paul, MN: West.
Mintzberg, H. (1979). *The structuring of organisations*, Englewood Cliffs, NJ: Prentice-Hall.
Mintzberg, H. (1989). *Mintzberg on management*. New York: The Free Press.

DEREK F. CHANNON

substitute products   Substitutes are goods or services which are consumed instead of one another. They can be identified by their positive cross-price ELASTICITY of demand (i.e., the quantity demanded for one product increases as the price of the other increases). Two products can be strong or weak substitutes, according to how easy it is to switch between the two, although substitutability is a continuous measure, and the distinction between the two is quite arbitrary. COMPLEMENTARY PRODUCTS are consumed together, and have a negative cross-price elasticity of demand.

Products offered by the same company can be substitutes, as can products offered by different companies in the same industry, or even those offered by different companies in different industries. There is no requirement that substitutes are in any way similar as far as their producers are concerned, except that they must broadly fulfil the same purpose as far as their

buyer is concerned. Not only is the Channel Tunnel a substitute for ferry boats, therefore, and fizzy water for still water, but also restaurants for cinema, as they both often compete for the same entertainment budget.

Perhaps the most important function of substitutes is that they enhance the competitive forces in the industries concerned. By allowing the buyer to compare the attributes of the products involved, and switch between the two, the manufacturers or service providers involved are kept in check in terms of the prices they can charge, and the quality, performance, and other attributes of the products.

Although good for competition, this may act to the detriment of the firms involved. Indeed, the threat from substitute goods is one of the forces in Porter's FIVE FORCES MODEL.

Another importance of substitutes lies in the fact that a measure of the degree of substitutability can be helpful in determining the likely impact on pricing and demand of a change in prices of a substitute product, whether under the control of the same firm or not.

Measuring the Threat from Substitutes

The strength of this danger for any given product is related to the cost, price, quality, and performance of the substitute, the buyer's propensity to switch, and his SWITCHING COSTS. These must be evaluated over the entire lives of the products concerned, as the running and maintenance costs of certain products are much higher than their initial purchase costs.

Even where switching costs for any individual buyer are prohibitive, the threat from substitutes remains. The costs of changing between electricity and gas for industrial and domestic heating, for example, are such as to lock in many consumers once they have made their initial investment in equipment. Over the long term, however, the two energy sources are substitutes for each other and as purchasing decisions are repeated (perhaps by other buyers), switching costs become less relevant and it is the attributes of the substitutes themselves that maintain the two industries in balance, and deserve the most attention.

When evaluating the threat of substitution, the entire value chain of the buyer must be looked at. In addition, covert threat from substitution can also be the result of substitution further downstream, a good secondary market for recycled or reconditioned goods or, at the extreme, from the buyer no longer requiring the product at all, or manufacturing it himself or performing its function internally. The threat of substitution varies by geographic area, product varieties, buyer segment, and channel.

In general, the number of substitutes in an industry increases over time, with young industries often tending to have fewer substitutes. As far as the proactive development of substitutes is concerned, it is often observed that substitutes are attracted by industries earning high profits. Substitute-producing industries are likely to enter into another market and become a threat if they become more competitive in their own right, or if they are still financially healthy although they have been forced out of their industry, and the target industry appears more accommodating. Early indication of substitute products which are about to become significant may be provided by growing sales and profits, and (planned) capacity growth.

Implications for Strategy

Substitute analysis can be used proactively in three main ways: to defend an industry's position if it is threatened by them; to increase its sales if it is producing them; or to determine their pricing if it is involved in the marketing of a range of products acting as substitutes for one another.

Where substitutes limit a company's flexibility, an attempt to develop strategies to minimize their influence will have to be made. This can be done by: (i) modifying the product's image, e.g., by means of differentiation in product design, innovation, quality enhancement, careful marketing, and the like; (ii) redefining competition away from the strengths of the substitute (e.g., by focusing on service rather than price); (iii) finding new, unaffected uses for the original product; (iv) raising buyer switching costs; or (v) in the short term, acting opportunistically to counter any attempts by competitors to enter the market. Retaining customers while a more fundamental improvement is being searched for along the lines of the above methods is more important where switching back costs are high. In addition, (vi) other firms adversely affected by the substitute, such as competitors, suppliers, and other stakeholders, can be encouraged to organize themselves and help with the defense by such means as industry-wide advertising or R&D, the enforcement of standards, getting regulatory or legislative approval or protection, and the like. Otherwise, the company may decide to enter the substitute industry itself, putting the company's future ahead of the business unit's, or to exit from that area entirely if it has become too unattractive.

In order to promote substitution, on the other hand, a firm may help its product by: (i) aggressively targeting the likely early switchers on the basis that it is they who will influence the subsequent take-up of the product, SIGNALING to them necessary information about the new product, and trying to lower their switching costs, and perhaps even subsidising them; (ii) by integrating forward in a limited way to create demand from the end users (especially where these face lower switching costs than any intermediate buyers), informing them, or helping them to lower their switching costs, or inducing limited backward integration to bypass intermediate parties unwilling to take on the new substitute; (iii) by insuring adequate capacity, perhaps in combination with other companies, to assure prospective buyers that this is a strong industry on which they can rely for a long time after switching; (iv) by promoting investment in complementary goods; or (v) by otherwise acting to enlarge the substitute's market. The speed of entry is a function of barriers to entry. Where there are first-mover advantages, early entry on a large scale and the setting up of protective barriers is warranted, while if the firm faces high barriers, then it may be best to attack the high-value segments first.

As far as the management of product line substitutes is concerned (i.e., where a firm chooses to produce a number of products which may act as substitutes for one another), then the optimal rates of output for each good will be less than the rates that would maximize profits if there was no demand interdependence, as sales of one good preclude sales of the other.

Bibliography

Porter, M. E. (1979). How competitive forces shape strategy. *Harvard Business Review*, **57** (2) (March–April), 137-45), Reprinted with deletions in H. Mintzberg & J. B. Quinn (1991). *The strategy process: concepts, contexts, cases*, 2nd edn Englewood Cliffs, NJ: Prentice-Hall. See pp. 61–70.

Porter, M. E. (1980). *Competitive strategy: techniques for analyzing industries and competitors*. New York: The Free Press.

Porter, M. E. (1985). *Competitive advantage: creating and sustaining superior performance*. New York: The Free Press.

STEPHANOS AVGEROPOULOS

sustainable growth rate A company's sustainable rate of growth depends in part on, and is limited by, the rate at which it can generate funds that can be invested to achieve growth targets while at the same time paying interest and dividends, accounting for depreciated assets and inflation. The sources of these funds are generally retained earnings, debt, and new equity capital. Improved efficiency, which reduces capital intensity by superior asset turnover and greater productivity, can also be an important source of new funds for growth.

Debt, risk, dividend, and return policies and intentions should therefore be determined before overall corporate goals are established. These factors will essentially determine the limits to growth. The sustainable growth rate of the firm can then be calculated as follows.

The rate of growth is equal to the firm's return on equity if no dividends are paid. This is the rate of return (profit) less interest on debt, as follows:

$$\text{profit} = r(TA) - iD$$

where r is the rate of return, TA is the total assets, i is the interest rate, and D is debt. Since total assets are equal to the sum of debt and equity (E), their expression may be rewritten as:

$$\text{profit} = r(D + E) - iD$$

or

$$\text{profit} = rD + rE - iD$$

Dividing through by E, this becomes:

$$\text{profit/equity} = (\tfrac{D}{E})(r - i) + r$$

or

growth rate $(g) = (\tfrac{D}{E})(r - i) + r$.

However, the payment of dividends reduces this rate of growth due to the disbursement of funds. The effect of dividend payout can be accounted for by multiplying the expression by the percentage of earnings retained by p, the dividend payout ratio. The growth formula thus becomes:

$$g = (\tfrac{D}{E})(r - i)p + rp.$$

Each of the financial variables in the growth formula can be used strategically to influence the growth rate of the firm. The sensitivity of the growth rate to the key variables of rate of return, interest rate paid, the debt : equity ratio, and the dividend payout ratio is demonstrated in table 1. In the table each of these variables has been changed in turn by 10 per cent with other variables remaining constant.

Table 1 Sensitivity analysis of four variables influencing corporate growth rate.

Variable	Growth rate	Growth rate in response to 10% change in variable
Earning power		
6.3%	4.8%	
7.0%	*5.5%*	*12.7%*
7.7%	6.2%	
Interest rate		
3.3%	5.35%	
3.0%	*5.50%*	*2.7%*
2.7%	5.65%	
Debt : Equity		
ratio	5.30%	
0.9 : 1		
1.0 : 1	*5.50%*	*3.6%*
1.1 : 1	5.70%	
Dividend payout		
45%	4.95%	
50%	*5.50%*	*10.0%*
55%	6.05%	

Source: Boston Consulting Group (1971)

As expected, the most sensitive variable is return on assets. Most surprising for most observers is that the dividend payout ratio is the second most powerful variable, and not the debt : equity ratio. Interest rates tend to be relatively inconsequential. As a result, a significant increase in the debt : equity ratio may be a viable strategic alternative, even if higher interest rates are incurred as lenders perceive the firm as becoming more risky. Interestingly, perhaps, high leverage has been a significant reason behind the success of Japanese corporations, where the strength of the yen has also provided low rates of interest. Similarly, reduced dividend payment ratios help to accelerate corporate growth – again a characteristic of Japanese concerns. Indeed, by operating with a high debt : equity, a low dividend payout ratio, and constant attention to improved asset turnover – the inverse of lower capital intensity – Japanese companies have been able to achieve superior investment performance compared to their nearest US counterparts during the past two decades.

The relationship between financial strategy and market share growth suggests several important conclusions: high margins do not necessarily indicate an attractive business while reported earnings are not always meaningful. However, since most managers perceive margins as an indication of market attractiveness, the aggressive growth firm might seek to keep margins down in order to discourage. competitive market entry.

Firms using debt aggressively and reducing dividend payouts can both cut price relative to competitors and finance an increase in market share. Provided that such growth achieves a satisfactory return, greater than the cost of equity, such a policy also builds shareholder value.

Bibliography

Boston Consulting Group (1971). *Growth and financial strategies*. Boston, MA: Boston Consulting Group.
Rowe, A. J., Mason, R. O., Dickel, K. E., Mann, R. B. & Mockler, R. J. (1994). *Strategic management*, 4th edn. Reading, MA: Addison-Wesley. See pp. 375–6.

DEREK F. CHANNON

switching costs   Switching costs are the fixed costs that buyers face in order to change between SUBSTITUTE PRODUCTS (the costs of changing suppliers are typically excluded from the definition).

Switching costs arise from all impacts that a substitute can have on the buyer's value chain, including any linkages with the supplier's value chain. They can be the result of investment by the buyer in high-cost specialized equipment, investment in learning how to operate such equipment, or even the result of product specifications which tie the buyer to particular inputs.

Typical switching costs include the costs of identifying, evaluating, and testing the substitute, the costs of product or process redesign, the costs of purchasing additional equipment, employee retraining costs, and the costs of the technical help needed to effect the changeover. Other, indirect, costs may arise from the changing role of the user: these include resistance to the substitute, and the cost of failure, which includes any costs incurred in switching back.

Switching costs typically change and fall over time. Early adopters of a new substitute have to develop their own technologies, procedures, and standards, and so – in effect – they subsidize subsequent adopters, who may find it easy to copy the early work. Similarly, products and processes using substitutes can be redesigned to reduce the costs, and thus increase the demand for and acceptability of the substitute, and reduce its costs. The propensity to switch can also change over time, as success with a substitute will induce other companies to try it.

As switching costs can lock in buyers, they constitute effective barriers to entry (*see* BARRIERS TO ENTRY AND EXIT), so they are pursued by the company which already has the business, and reduced by the company which aspires to win the business. Establishing high switching costs, however, may foster inflexibility. IBM, for example, has long strived to make its systems incompatible with those of any other supplier. This strategy has meant that repeat business was almost guaranteed, but as open systems became more commonplace, buyers were reluctant to purchase IBM products for fear that they would be unduly restrained by the company. To overcome switching costs, suppliers of substitute goods may initially have to offer buyers considerable price concessions or extra quality of service, which can mean lower profit margins.

Bibliography

Porter, M. E. (1979). How competitive forces shape strategy. *Harvard Business Review*, **57** (2) (March–April), 137–45, Reprinted with deletions in H. Mintzberg & J. B. Quinn (1991, *The strategy process: concepts, contexts, cases*, 2nd edn, Englewood Cliffs, NJ: Prentice-Hall. See pp. 61–70.

Porter, M. E. (1980). *Competitive strategy: techniques for analyzing industries and competitors*. New York: The Free Press.

Porter, M. E. (1985). *Competitive advantage: creating and sustaining superior performance*. New York: The Free Press.

STEPHANOS AVGEROPOULOS

SWOT analysis An acronym of Strengths, Weaknesses, Opportunities, and Threats, SWOT analysis provides a simple but powerful tool for evaluating the strategic position of the firm. It is especially useful for senior executives undertaking a fundamental reappraisal of a business, in that it permits a free-thinking environment, unencumbered by the constraints often imposed by a finance-driven budgetary planning system. It also allows a test of perceived common purpose within an organization when carried out at various levels within the firm. The requirements for undertaking such an analysis are relatively simple and, at the end of the exercise, key information needs can usually be identified which might prove to be the subject of further research.

A list of common strengths, weaknesses, opportunities, and threats is shown in table 1. This list is not comprehensive and other critical factors may be identified. In terms of usage, executives may be divided into groups to initially identify – first as individuals and second as groups – their views as to the firm's SWOT. It may well be useful to focus on only a prioritized list of these and also to assess the cross-impacts of strengths and weaknesses on threats and opportunities, utilizing a form such as that shown in figure 1.

For strategy formulation, the firm attempts to build upon its strengths and eliminate its weaknesses. When the firm does not possess the skills required to take advantage of opportunities or avoid threats, the necessary resources needed may be identified from the SWOT analysis and steps taken to procure the strengths or to reduce any weaknesses.

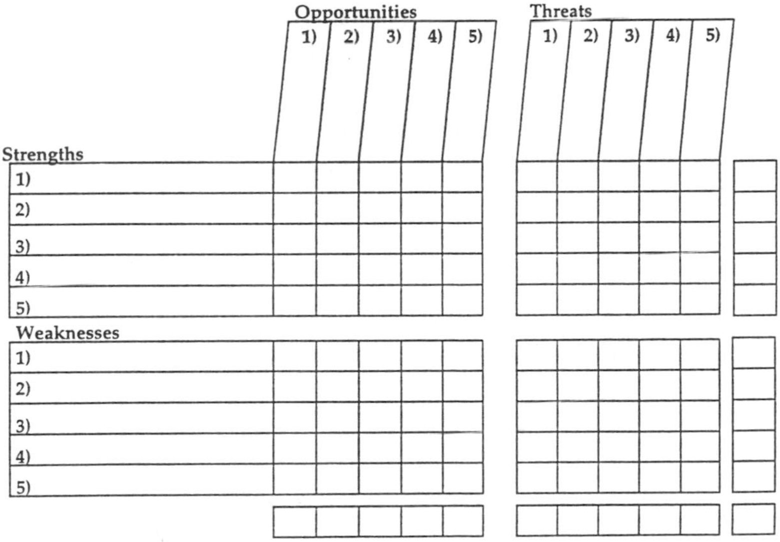

Figure 1 SWOT analysis.

Table 1   SWOT analysis – potential key factors.

Potential strengths	Potential weaknesses
Core skills	Lack of strategic direction
Adequate finances	Obsolete plant
Good customer perception	Weak IT systems
High market share	Weak control systems
High productivity	Lack of finance
High product/service quality	Lack of management skills
Low production costs	Internal power struggle
Superior R&D	Weak marketing skills
High innovation record	Lack of raw material access
Good top management	Poor access to distribution
Proprietary technology	High cost structure
Access to distribution	Poor product quality
Political protection	Poor record on innovation
Well established strategy	Others?
Others?	
Potential opportunities	Potential threats
Entry to new markets/segments	New low cost competitors
Diversification to related activities	Technological substitutes
Vertical integration (forward or backward)	Slow growth
High growth prospects	New regulatory requirements
Export markets	Foreign exchange rates
Weak competitors	Bargaining power of customers/suppliers
Government contracts	Adverse demographic shift
Deregulation	Vulnerability to recession
Others?	Changing consumer needs
	Others?

Bibliography

Channon, D. F. (1986). *Bank strategic management and marketing*. Chichester: John Wiley.

Channon, D. F. (1994). *Strategic management workbook*. Imperial College, London. See pp. 87–9.

Thompson, A. & Strickland A. J. (1993). *Strategic management*, 7th edn, New York: Irwin.

DEREK F. CHANNON

synergy   As originally conceived by Ansoff, synergy was seen as one of the major components in a firm's product market strategy. It was the extra value added achieved when two businesses were integrated together such that the sum of the whole was greater than that of the constituent parts. It was popularly described as "2 + 2 = 5." The concept lost some credibility when expected synergistic effects were found to be elusive, and it became said that in many situations "2 + 2 = 3." More recently, the term has tended to be less widely used, its nearest modern equivalent being STRATEGIC FIT. Ansoff classified synergy in terms of the components of the formula for return on investment:

- *Sales synergy*. This could occur when products used common distribution channels, sales administration, or warehousing. Similarly, a full line of related products enhanced sales force efficiency, while advertising, promotion, and reputation were also enhanced.

- *Operating synergy*. This occurred as a result of higher facilities and staff utilization rates, spreading of overheads, shared experience effects, and greater purchasing power.

- *Investment synergy*. This could result from joint use of plant, common raw materials stocks, R&D transfers, a common technology base, and common plant and equipment.

- *Management synergy*. Less apparent than the other forms of synergy, management synergy was seen as an important element in the total synergy effect. This could come about when entry into a new industry allowed managers to transfer their skills into industry structures and problems similar to those experienced in the firm's original areas of business expertise.

However, if problems in an acquired business are not familiar, not only can positive synergy be low, but it can actually have a negative effect. Ansoff has recognized, in a more recent version of his original work, that management synergy quickly becomes negative when a firm diversifies into a product market area in which environmental turbulence is significantly different from that to which it has historically been accustomed.

Ansoff originally did not discuss financial synergy, which has been reported elsewhere as the most easy form to release. For example, blending two balance sheets together is easily achievable and quick. Other functional synergies are much more difficult to release and, due to internal organizational conflicts and incompatible cultures, may never be attained.

Ansoff also differentiates between *start-up synergy* and *operating synergy*. In the start-up phase, apart from identifiable physical costs, such as facilities and working capital, there are one-off costs associated with setting up a new business, such as the creation of a new organization, new hirings, errors made due to lack of familiarity with the new business, and costs of establishing awareness in the market. Most of these costs are not capitalized but rather are charged as operating costs incurred during the start-up phase.

The degree to which new activities are similar to the firm's existing operations, and for which there are transferable skills, in part determines the scale of these start-up costs. When the new situation is very different from existing operations, the costs of start-up are likely to be significantly higher. This is especially true when management believes that new activities are similar to existing ones and then belatedly

discovers that this is not so, after market entry. In these cases, substantial diseconomies may result in many functional areas. Start-up business situations may therefore exhibit negative or positive synergy effects, and firms with a positive effect may gain significant competitive advantage over those that do not.

Apart from set-up costs in start-ups, new market entries often experience a penalty for the delay. Those firms which contain the required skills, such as production facilities, access to distribution channels, and sales force capabilities, are likely to be able to enter related markets much more rapidly than concerns which have to start afresh. Timing advantage synergy can therefore be especially significant in highly dynamic, fast growth markets.

Ansoff also identifies a second category of costs incurred as a result of new market entry. This is concerned with the operating costs and investment required to support the new activity. Two basic effects can produce synergy in this area. First, there may be the advantage of scale, whereby overall costs may be reduced as a result of extra volume (such as volume discounts in purchasing, improved machine capacity utilization, distribution cost savings, and the like).

Second, it may also be possible to spread corporate overhead over a wider range of activities. The use of ACTIVITY-BASED COSTING is important in insuring that overhead is correctly allocated, however; otherwise new activities may be disproportionately burdened with overhead which is not in reality consumed in the new business.

Top management talent, which is usually a scarce resource, may be better employed by adding new businesses, provided that it is not fully utilized. The synergy generated from this resource is, however, difficult to measure. Moreover, in switching top management resources to new business activities, care must be taken to insure that existing operations do not suffer from excess withdrawal of any necessary attention. It is also important to insure that any such talent deployed is actually appropriate to the new activities. For example, the disastrous record of the attempts by oil companies to diversify can, in part, be attributed to the appointment of oil industry managers to new business activities for which they were poorly equipped in terms of their skills and understanding.

As a generalization, synergy effects during start-up tend to complement operating synergy, although the respective effects may differ according to the specific circumstances.

Ansoff suggests that the effect of synergy should be measured and mapped on one of three variables: increased volume of dollar revenue to the firm from sales, decreased operating costs, and decreased investment requirements – with all three being viewed in perspective over time. In practice, such mapping is rarely possible, especially for unrelated diversification moves. Here, although the primary variables affecting synergy can be identified, it is rarely possible to quantify and combine their effects. The same criticism can be leveled at the concept of STRATEGIC FIT. Thus, while the concept of synergy is seductive, making the concept operational has proved to be more problematic.

Bibliography

Ansoff, I. (1987). *Corporate strategy*. Harmondsworth, UK: Penguin. See chapter 5.

Kitching, J. (1967). Why do mergers miscarry? *Harvard Business Review*, **45** (November–December), 84–101.

DEREK F. CHANNON

T

target-based costing Japanese producers have made extensive use of target-based costing. Market research is undertaken to establish what consumers might be prepared to pay for the functions offered by a new product. Once this is established, the retail price minus any discounts is set. After allowing for the required level of profitability, this establishes the cost at which the company must produce in order to achieve a satisfactory level of profit. Sony calls such prices "magic price" points.

Having established the target price and corresponding costs, designers, engineers, and procurement officers set out to achieve the desired cost level using techniques described elsewhere, such as JUST IN TIME, KAIZEN,

TEAR DOWN, TOTAL QUALITY CONTROL, and VALUE ENGINEERING. The process also involves techniques such as ACTIVITY-BASED COSTING and BENCHMARKING and is illustrated in figure 1. The process is conducted in extreme detail, with consideration given to component re-engineering, changes in assembly methods, function elimination, pressure applied to suppliers, and the like; and – quite literally, in some cases – to chip away, yen by yen, at the fundamental cost structure of individual products. If the target cost is not reachable, then the product may need to be aborted. A further practice by Japanese producers, however, is strategic miniaturization. This involves reducing the size of products, such as office

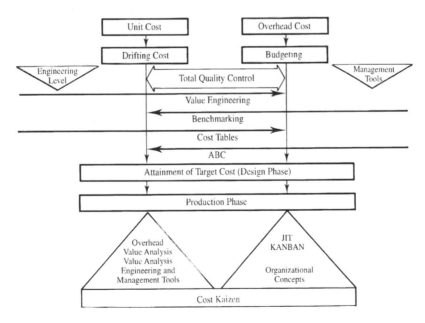

Figure 1 Attainment of target cost (production phase).

machinery and electronic products. A major result of this technique is to both reduce costs and also increase market penetration. For example, the reduction in size of office photocopiers has encouraged distributed photocopying, rather than centralized processing on large machines. The ultimate miniaturization is to make such equipment portable, or purchasable by the individual household. This has already occurred with fax machines, personal computers, personal copiers, and mobile telephones. This results in dramatically increased volumes, new purchasers, new distribution channels, and substantially reduced production costs as a result of shared experience, and deliberate attacks on costs due to target costing procedures.

Bibliography

Channon, D. F. (1993). Canon B case. Imperial College, London.
Kotler, P. (1994). *Marketing management.* Englewood Cliffs, NJ: Prentice-Hall. See pp. 497–8.

DEREK F. CHANNON

tear down   This is a method of comparing products and components with those of competitors. Originating in the US automobile industry, the technique involves the systematic analysis of a competitor's product in terms of materials, parts, function, manufacture, coating, and assembly.

The approach used by the US General Motors Corporation (GM) was modified by Isuzu Motors and became the basis for the Japanese tear down method. The major difference between GM's original method and that of Isuzu is the scope of the Japanese approach.

The Japanese tear down program contains eight different methods. The first three of these were designed to reduce the direct manufacturing cost of a vehicle. The next three seek to reduce capital intensity by increased productivity, while the last two are integrations of tear down and value engineering techniques. These techniques are as follows:

- *Dynamic tear down.* This method seeks to identify ways in which to reduce the number of assembly operations required to produce a vehicle in the time required.

- *Cost tear down.* The objective of this method is to reduce the cost of components used by comparing the components used with those of a competitor. Cost reduction techniques are then used when costs are higher and cannot be compensated for with greater functionality.

- *Material tear down.* This approach compares materials used and surface treatments. Any innovations observed in competing products are adopted.

- *Static tear down.* This basic approach consists of the disassembling of competing products to their components, which are then laid out for observation by design engineers.

- *Process tear down.* This process consists of comparing the manufacturing processes for similar parts and reducing the difference between them, with the long-term objective of producing multiple products or components on the same production line.

- *Matrix tear down.* In this method a matrix is developed of all components used in the company's products. This matrix is prepared on an as-needed basis and identifies the volume of each component used per month by model and the total usage across all models. Low-volume components are identified, designed out of existing products, and banned from future ones.

- *Unit kilogram price method.* In this method parts produced by similar production processes are treated as a product group and analyzed for possible savings. The efficiency of the product or component is expressed in terms of its value per kilogram. Products requiring further analysis are identified by plotting the value per kilo for all the products in the same group against their weight. Outliers are carefully examined with a view to identifying why their costs are higher than the group's average value.

- *Group estimate by tear down method (GET).* This method is a combination of basic value engineering and tear down procedures and a modified version of the unit-kilogram price method. The method consists of treating, as a group, parts that have similar functions and analyzing them for possible cost savings.

Bibliography

Cooper, R. & Yoshikawa, T. (1994). *Isuzu Motors Ltd, Cost Creation Program,* Case no. 9-195-054. Harvard Business School.

DEREK F. CHANNON

technology assessment In many industries, technology drives strategic decision making, with new products, and new production systems, distribution channels, and markets, often stemming from technological advances. Today, increasingly, industries may be transformed by the impact of information technology, provided that it is not merely used to automate the business practices of the past. The monitoring of technological development can therefore be a critical factor, and many companies have woken up too late to recognize that their historic competitive advantage has been rapidly eliminated by a technological bypass. For example, the camcorder eliminated amateur cine film in about three years, xerography eliminated diazo copying in a similar period, and automated teller machines now process over 90 per cent of cash withdrawals and some 65 per cent of deposits in Japan.

There are two basic components to technology. The first of these is tangible in the form of machines, tools, and materials. Second, which is more important, is the intangible component of technological knowledge. This factor drives skills and techniques which need to be learned and adopted by employees; plant layouts; machine operating procedures, computer software; and the like. It also forms the basis for achieving competitive advantage via patents and distribution know-how.

Assessing technological capability involves collecting data on the firm's relative technological position (technology scanning) and analyzing this position (technology evaluation). The outcome of this analysis is shown in figure 1.

To undertake technology scanning:

• Divide the corporation into SBUs

• For each SBU, determine (i) the technology currently in use and (ii) the technology used by key competitors' potential new technologies. A widespread scan is important at this point, and is where many companies succumb to BLIND SPOTS.

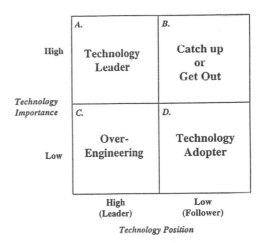

Figure 1 *The technology evaluation matrix.*
Source: Rowe et al. (1994).

• Investigate sources of new technologies and their effects on all stakeholders.

To undertake technology evaluation, check the following:

• Is the technology important to the success of the business unit? Does it add value? Is it changing? Will it open new markets? Does it threaten existing markets? Does it significantly change cost structures?

• How strong is the company presently and in future with respect to the technology? This can be assessed by consideration of R&D expenditure, patents, R&D personnel employed, and adaptability to change. The company's relative position as a technological leader or follower should be evaluated.

From this analysis the SBU's position is mapped on the technology evaluation matrix (see figure 1). Businesses which, in general, are high in both technology importance and technology position represent a strong position, which should be pursued aggressively in order to maintain competitive advantage. Businesses in which technology is important but the firm is in a follower position suggest several strategic alternatives. First, resources can be committed to strengthen the firm's technology position and attempt to gain competitive advantage. Second, the firm can exit and deploy released R&D resources to other businesses. Third, enough resources can be committed to maintain an adequate follower strategy position while monitoring opportunities for potential future technology shifts.

Businesses in quadrant C are probably guilty of over-engineering. The resource commitment is probably too high for the needs of the business, and consideration should be given to redeploying such resources to improve their effectiveness.

Businesses in quadrant D have a weak position in an important technology. Involvement in such an area should be reconsidered, and any technical requirements might be outsourced (see OUTSOURCING).

While technology alone usually does not sustain long-term competitive advantage, it can be a vital ingredient, especially during the early stages of the business life cycle. It may also be important in industries with short product life cycles. The role of technology at maturity might be one of transforming industry cost structure via substitution, rejuvenation by opening new market segments, and by product development to stimulate replacement demand.

Bibliography

Birnbaum, P. H. & Weiss, A. R. (1974). Competitive advantage and the basis for competition. Strategic Management Society Seventh Annual Meeting, Boston, MA.

Gould, J. M. (1983). Technology change and competition. *Journal of Business Strategy*, **4** (2), 62–73.

Rowe, A. J., Mason, R. O., Dickel, K. E., Mann, R. B. & Mockler, R. J. (1994). *Strategic management*, 4th edn, Reading. MA: Addison-Wesley. See pp. 116–21.

DEREK F. CHANNON

technology fusion This involves the combination and transformation of a number of different core technologies in order to create new product markets. The term was popularized by Fumio Kodama of Japan's Science and Technology Agency (STA) in the 1980s: "The fusion of technologies goes beyond mere combination. Fusion is more than complementaries, because it creates a new market and new growth opportunities for each participant in the innovation... it blends incremental improvements from several (often previously separate) fields to create a product."

The key elements of technology fusion are that it is both complementary and cooperative. Typically, it is the result of reciprocal and substantial R&D expenditure by companies from a range of industries and with different technological competences. For example, in the 1970s, the fusion of research by companies from the mechanical and electronic engineering sectors created what the Japanese call "mechatronics." A group of Japanese companies from a wide range of industries combined efforts. Fanuc, a spin-off from the computer company Fujitsu, led the group with the development of an electrohydraulic servomotor and a new controler; Nippon Seiko (NSK), Japan's leading bearing manufacturer, developed a new type of ballscrew; and material suppliers developed a new low-friction coating. This spawned the Japanese robotics and numerically controled machine tool industries, which now dominate world markets.

Technology fusion is of increasing importance in a wide range of industries in which American and European companies are currently strong. In the telecommunications sector the fusion of optics and electronics technologies has been critical. In the automotive industry the integration of electronic and mechanical systems has become a major locus of innovation, particularly in engine, transmission, and braking systems. In aerospace the development of fly-by-wire systems demands the fusion of electronics and hydraulics technologies – and the next generation of fly-by-light systems will also require expertise in optics technologies.

Significantly, Japanese companies have considerable expertise in electronics, opto-electronics, and hydraulics technologies and appear to be able to recognize and exploit the potential of technology fusion. Japanese companies are reflecting the importance of technology fusion in their slogans and company missions. For example, NEC uses "computers & communication," whereas Toshiba uses "energy and electronics." This is more than marketing alliteration, and reflects an explicit strategy of related diversification.

However, there are a number of potential problems with the concept of technology fusion, which must be resolved: the measurement of technology fusion; the level of analysis; and the organizational constraints. The first two issues are closely related. Most of the current analysis of technology fusion has been undertaken at the level of the industry or sector, and has been based on levels of R&D expenditure. In Japan, companies are required to report their R&D expenditure to the government, disaggregated into 31 different product fields. Studies suggest a that growing proportion of R&D expenditure lies outside the traditional core business. Two ratios are of particular significance:

$$\frac{\text{R\&D expenditure by industry A in other industries}}{\text{R\&D expenditure by industry A in itself}}$$

and

$$\frac{\text{R\&D expenditure by other industries in industry A}}{\text{R\&D expenditure by industry A in itself}}$$

The ratio of R&D in outside industries to that in the core business can be used as an indicator of technology fusion. Similarly, the R&D from outside industries into an industry as a ratio of the R&D within that industry can be calculated. However, strictly speaking, these ratios may simply indicate diversification; but, by definition, technology fusion involves reciprocal investment by companies in the respective industries. Combining the two ratios for specific pairs of industries provides a better measure of reciprocal investment. For example, a coefficient of technology fusion (CTF) can be defined as follows:

$$\text{CTF} = \sqrt{R_A R_B},$$

where

$$R_1 = \frac{\text{Total outside R\&D by A}}{\text{R\&D in B by A}}$$

and

$$R_B = \frac{\text{Total outside R\&D by B}}{\text{R\&D in A by B}}$$

Defined in this way, the closer the CTF is to unity (one), the greater the level of mutual R&D investment. Therefore one can construct year-by-year fusion maps based on the level of reciprocal R&D investment. Kodama has done this for several periods, and claims to have identified the emergence of mechatronics and biotechnology in the mid-1970s.

In Japan, the MITI now conducts fusion surveys on a periodic basis. However, there are several problems in applying this analysis. First, the standard industrial classification adopted may obscure occurrences of technology fusion. Second, the reliability of data on R&D is uncertain; for example, numerous studies suggest that the definition of R&D is variable, despite the OECD "Frascati" guidelines. Moreover, the precision of allocation into the different product groups is unknown. Third, only aggregate R&D expenditure by principal industries is published outside of Japan. Any attempt to allocate to different product groups would have to be based on primary data collection from companies, or estimates from annual reports and other sources.

For these reasons, other measures of technological capability and activity may be more appropriate at the level of the firm. Of the techniques available, patent analysis and bibliometric measurements based on publications are the most promising. Patent analysis will typically involve detailed study of between 1,000 and 10,000 patent applications, depending on the company and field of technology. For example, in the US 1,000 new patents are issued every day. A leading high-tech company, such as Hitachi, will be issued almost 2,000 patents each year. Patent data can be used in a number of ways, the most common being to measure changes in the number of patents granted in specific fields. In addition, maps of technology fusion and the associated organizational linkages can be generated by examining the cross-citation of related patents.

Finally, there may be significant organizational barriers to technology fusion at the level of the firm. Past strategic choices clearly shape existing organizational structures and processes, and these structures and processes may constrain future strategic options. For example, most large firms are organized into strategic business units (SBUs), based on past product market linkages, but these linkages may no longer be relevant, and may prevent technological synergies across SBUs. This suggests a potential barrier to the recognition and exploitation of technology fusion. Independent strategies to optimize the performance of each division may not necessarily produce optimum corporate performance.

Bibliography

Kodama, F. (1991). *Analyzing Japanese high technologies*. London: Pinter.

JOE TIDD

time-based competition   The technique of time-based competition addresses the complete order to delivery cycle. It analyzes each element of time used and questions the right to use it. It involves much more than JUST IN TIME, ELECTRONIC DATA INTERCHANGE, or any single technology. It helps to compress time in the whole organization. This means that one has to change processes, information, and decision flows from the customer, to engineering, to procurement, through manufacturing, order processing, and distribution, and back to the customer. In all these stages of the business cycle, actions and the use of time are driven by the voice of the customer.

It is important to establish the relationship between time and money. The fact is that profit is typically reduced by one third for every six months by which a capital goods product is late to market. A computer game has only a six month life anyway, so time is even more vital. The relationship between time and quality is also vital. Doing everything faster means doing this right first time. One cannot afford the time for rework. Quality is inextricably linked to customer satisfaction, which is a number one requirement of time compression management. Achieving the required quality standard first time does not mean rushing the job and cutting time out. Time compression management may mean deliberately taking longer on tricky aspects in order to insure that "right first time" is achieved.

Companies that compress time out of their business cycle or pipeline understand that, throughout it, materials, direct labor, handling and transportation, interest, and overheads contribute to overall costs. The longer the business cycle takes, the greater the costs are and the slower is the response to the customer. The trick is to speed up the flow of all events. The process flow consists of all of the operations of the business, the information flow consists of all of the data in the business, and the decision flow consists of all of the actions taken by people in the business.

Responsiveness refers to the ability to satisfy customer requirements quicker than one's competitors. However, satisfying customer requirements has a variety of interpretations, such as:

- filling an order from shelf stock
- assembling to requirement
- engineering to order
- bringing a new product to market

Other variations also exist, but what they all share is cycle time (elapsed time) as the common measure of performance.

As a result of the emerging competitive importance of responsiveness, cycle times are beginning to have unprecedented significance. As emphasis shifts from product-based competition, a major rethink of the roles of traditional functions is taking place. It is becoming increasingly clear that competitiveness is a "whole enterprise" problem.

In the past, it was relatively easy for nonmanufacturing functions to abdicate responsibility for enterprise competitiveness. After all, their impact on product quality and price was thought to be quite minor. Product quality and price were regarded as "blue collar" variables, whereas they were "white collar" people. However, when various cycle times are seen as determinants of competitiveness, "white collar" staff become extremely important in the enterprise competitiveness scheme (see figure 1). Therefore, let us examine a typical enterprise and identify the three main time cycles to be managed.

Three main activity cycles control the responsiveness of a manufacturing company:

- new product introduction
- value adding pipeline
- customer service

Their interrelationships with key functions of the business are shown in figure 1.

New Product Introduction Cycle

This is the product specification/design/develop/component specification cycle, which is vital to response to customer product needs. It is the subject of all the current work on concurrent or simultaneous engineering, with Quality Function Deployment (QFD) as an

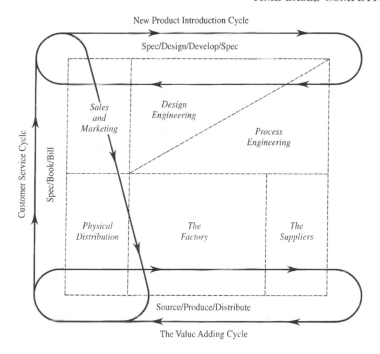

Figure 1 Responsiveness activities and business functions.
Source: Ed Heard & Associates.

important tool in reducing risk through prioritization of effort.

This is a major area of potential competitive advantage. Notice that Japanese competitors are very open about how things must be done, except in this area. Some manufacturing enterprises engineer to order; they have no stock products as such. Still others introduce new products periodically for strategic reasons. The design/develop cycle is a major competitive factor in both cases. In the engineer to order case, the design/develop cycle is a major contributor to the customer service cycle. That fact is widely appreciated.

The potentially negative impact of longer design/develop cycles in new product introduction is not as well understood. When the nature of market demand cannot be predicted very far in advance, the inevitable result of long design/develop cycles clearly takes the form of missed market opportunities. However, when the nature of market demand can be predicted, why not just start earlier?

The specification elements of new product introduction are special, as described below.

Unlike other elements of the three major cycles, *more* time spent on them frequently results in a shorter overall cycle time, because such work that is done subsequent to good speculation is well targeted.

Regardless of the reasons for longer design/develop cycles, larger total expenses are generally the result. What is not so clear is that longer design/develop cycles also require more borrowing or longer periods of negative cash-flow. Therefore, long design/develop cycles pack a triple negative competitive punch: they limit responsiveness, raise expenses, and increase capital requirements.

But what takes so long? The answer just consists of a list of a few incidental processing activities, such as market analysis, marketing production definition, technology analysis, engineering product definition, product design, prototype development, functional verification, model development, performance evaluation, field test, process planning, and process verification.

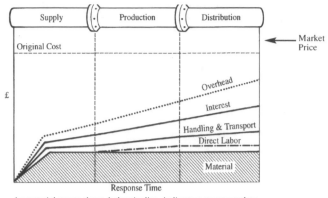

As material moves through the pipeline, indirect costs accumulate

Figure 2 Time and the pipeline – the problem.
Source: Andersen Consulting.

The Value Adding Cycle

This is the source/produce/distribute cycle, often described as a pipeline, as shown in figures 2 and 3. These activities start at the second specification stage of the product introduction cycle. Fit, function, performance, quality, delivery, and price requirements must be established. Make or buy decisions must be made. Potential suppliers of purchased items must be identified and preliminary contacts initiated. Visitations must be arranged and completed. Suppliers must be evaluated and selection decisions made. Specific issues must be negotiated and long-term agreements worked out. Ultimately, actual releases (requests) must

be initiated and transmitted to suppliers. Materials must be shipped from suppliers to the enterprises' facility, unloaded, and received. Packing slips must be verified against releases; orders must be unpacked, and counts and quality checks must be completed before materials are put away or taken directly to the line for use.

If materials are stored, some form of requisition must be prepared to trigger removal. Pick lists may have to be generated and storage locations identified. Materials often have to be picked, counted, and issued, and inventory transactions usually have to be prepared before material leaves the storeroom and is transported

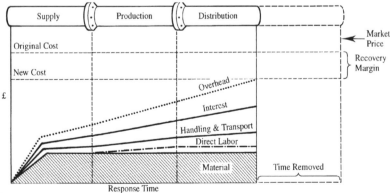

Take out time – manage your pipeline to recover your margin

Figure 3 Time and the pipeline – the opportunity.
Source: Andersen Consulting.

Table 1   Elements of customer value

Product orders	C/E transactions	Design
Promised lead times	* Sales calls	Form, fit, function
* Actual lead times	* Information requests	* Reliability
Promised quantity	* Order initiation	* Maintainability
Actual quantity	* Credit application	* Upgradability,
Promised quality	* Billing and collection	robustness
Actual quality	* Service and support	Selling price

Key: * Time Related

Source: Ed Heard & Associates.

to the places where it is used on the floor. On the floor itself, materials must be processed, inspected, counted, and moved. Machines must be maintained, changed over, and cleaned. Parts must be counted and inventory transactions prepared. Tools, fixtures, and dies have to be located, retrieved, transported, and put away. Orders must be opened and closed. Typically, the finished product must be checked and approved for shipment before it can be picked, packed, and loaded for shipment.

At entry to the distribution system a whole program of activities is set in motion in terms of interface with the customer service cycle for order processing, stock allocation, and billing arrangements. Then follow all of the activities related to the outbound logistics, inventory management, warehousing, transportation, and replenishment.

All of these activities take time and cost money. The opportunity to improve responsiveness and margins is clearly demonstrated in figures 2 and 3.

As material moves through the pipeline, indirect costs accumulate.

The value adding cycle time is critically important to enterprise competitiveness. To be viable in the long term, the gross margin for an enterprise's products must be large enough to provide an adequate return on assets. Inventory is one of those assets. The longer the total cycle time, the greater is the amount of inventory. In turn, the greater the inventory, the larger are the gross margin requirements, and the higher and more uncompetitive the necessary price becomes.

For enterprises that must build in whole or in part to order, the source/produce cycles packs a double punch. Not only do longer manufacturing cycle times – the major portion of the source/product cycle – mean less competitive prices, they also mean less competitive response times. This is the case because any portion of the purchase/product cycle cannot be completed until the customer order is in hand as a part of the customer service cycle, a major competitive factor.

The Customer Service Cycle

Customers demand value:

$$value = \frac{what\ customer\ gets}{what\ customer\ pays}$$

Some of the activities related to customer service are listed in table 1. Those asterisked are time-dependent or rely on responsiveness and directly affect customer value.

The customer service cycle comprises all the activities from the initial and very critical new product requirement specification, which is supplied by the marketing department, to the new production introduction cycle.

In the book/bill part of the customer service cycle, customer requirements must be translated into actual sales orders and delivery promises. In turn, sales orders must be added to the open order field. Customer credit must be checked, and pricing must be verified. Even if the necessary products are available on the shelf, picking, packing, and shipping must be scheduled. Pick lists and shipping documents must be prepared. Ultimately, the order must be picked, packed, and shipped and the customer must be invoiced.

Clearly, most of the activities that comprise the customer service cycle are white collar activities. Just as clearly, those activities take time, even when the necessary products are available on the shelf. But what if they are not? In some cases, preparing an inventory of finished goods may not be economically impractical. In other cases, products may have to be assembled, configured, or fabricated to order. In the extreme case, products may have to be engineered to order.

Regardless of the environmental reason why orders cannot be filled from stock, the net effect is the same. The customer service cycle consists of a larger number of activities and the critical path through them is longer. Whether long or short, the customer service cycle represents a discrepancy between when the customer would really like to have his order (now) and when he can actually get it. Consequently, customer service cycle time is a major competitive factor.

The importance of the customer service cycle extends even further.

Clearly, the historic trends in traditional manufacturing enterprises are inconsistent with marketplace trends. Not only is conflict between the two inevitable; it is already occurring in market after market around the world. High-quality and low-price products are becoming the price of admission and customers are demanding quicker response. But that is not all that is happening.

Industrial customers and the consuming public are becoming more discerning. They are beginning to think in terms of total cost, not just product cost. Low prices accompanied by unwieldy order entry and customer service processes that raise the effective cost of doing business are not very impressive. Incorrect invoices and unreadable owner's manuals become new determinants of quality once product excellence is assured. Even the definition of responsiveness is changing.

Customers are beginning to notice how long it takes to get questions answered, employee attitudes, and how many times the telephone rings before someone answers. In short, the customer is beginning to measure cost, quality, and responsiveness at all of the interfaces between him- or herself and the enterprise.

Clearly, enterprises must adapt to the new reality and begin to think: "Low Cost, High Quality and Short Cycle in Everything We Do!"

Time Management versus Time Cutting

Success in the pursuit of responsiveness can be elusive unless one key principle is understood: *Managing time in the three key cycles sometimes means spending more time on one element in order that the total cycle is shorter.*

In this case – although this is a generalized statement – the fact that significantly more time is spent by the Japanese in the product specification stage results in half the total amount of time being spent in the overall activity. Provided that the total calendar time remains about the same, the benefits are obvious.

A second example concerns inventory levels and the cost of their finance. There are two kinds of inventory. Highly visible inventory consists of raw materials, work-in-progress, and finished goods. Invisible inventories consist of money paid for various processing cycle activities, in advance of the recovery of those expenses through sales. Cycle time reductions can be shown to always lead to inventory reductions under certain conditions, regardless of whether the inventory is visible or invisible. In general:

$$\text{average units in process} = (\text{throughput rate}) \times (\text{cycle time})$$

The first requirement is that the number of units being processed per unit time interval must be the same before and after the hypothetical change. The second requirement is that the processing cost rate per day must not increase such that the total cost of processing a single unit is greater than it was before the hypothetical change. If, in fact, the processing cost rate does not increase that much, or even decreases, reductions in cycle time will also reduce both cost and inventory since, generally:

$$\text{average \$ in process} = (\text{average units in process}) \times (\text{average cost of units in process})$$

Clearly, cycle time reductions increase competitiveness by increasing responsiveness. The previous discussion makes it obvious that not all cycle time reductions are cost-effective. Likewise, some means of reducing cycle time can make quality worse, not better. However, this discussion has also raised the possibility of simultaneous improvements in responsiveness, visible and invisible inventory, capital requirements, and total cost. Suppose that certain principles could be found that not only could be used to do all that for both white collar and blue collar processing activities, but that would also improve quality at the same time. That is exactly the magic of the time management principles referred to earlier.

Close examination of the JIT/TQC/TPM concepts, tools, and techniques incorporated in time management suggests that the primary criterion for their selection was their ability to complement one another. In every case in which one of those concepts, tools, or techniques has a potentially negative outcome, some other one has obviously been developed and incorporated to offset it. Smaller processing batches and changeover reduction provides an obviously instructive example of this approach. There are numerous others, the interactions between which are too subtle to detail here.

Summary and Conclusions

Low-cost, high-quality products are beginning to be simply the price of admission to some markets. Likewise, customers are beginning to think in terms of total enterprise cost, quality, and responsiveness. These changing market needs are on a conflicting course with current and past trends in traditional manufacturing enterprises. Meeting the responsiveness challenge depends on an enterprise's ability to identify and shorten the three primary business cycles – new product introduction, the value adding pipeline, and customer service. Some approaches to shortening cycle times impact cost, quality, and capital requirements negatively. Short cycle management incorporates numerous JIT/TQC/TPM principles selected to complement one another. Those principles can be used to dramatically improve competitiveness by simultaneously improving white collar and blue collar processing cycle times, cost, quality, and capital requirements. In short, if a structured approach is taken to reduce wasted time in designing, developing, producing, and distributing, then: costs will decrease; less capital will be tied up; and customer value

will increase. This is so provided that capital is not substituted for intelligence, people are not thrown in at the deep end, and necessary activities are not eliminated. Time compression is therefore managed, and the vision of the customer as king is maintained.

Bibliography

Stalk, G. Jr. & Hout, T. M. (1990). *Competing against time*. New York: The Free Press.

PETER DEMPSEY and ED HEARD

total quality control   The founder of TQC as it has developed in Japan was the influential US quality expert, W. Edwards Deming. An annual award named after him, for the most significant quality performance in Japan, is still highly prized. Deming's work strongly emphasized statistical techniques of quality control, and although these are widely used and Japanese workers are highly trained in their use, TQC is today much more than this. It has become a fundamental philosophy which guides all aspects of Japanese manufacturing strategy.

TQC may stand alone but, more commonly, it may be used in conjunction with other concepts, such as KAIZEN and JUST IN TIME. To implement TQC, all plant personnel are inculcated into the philosophy, and implementation is achieved by the use of a CROSS-FUNCTIONAL MANAGEMENT STRUCTURE and processes. In particular, under the Japanese system all individuals are responsible for their own actions rather than being overseen by quality inspectors and accountants. The concept has been widely used in Japanese industry since the early 1960s, and has been constantly elaborated on and improved such that many companies are still seeking real gains in productivity of 10 per cent or more per annum.

An attempt is made in table 1 to group a number of TQC factors into specific categories.

Organization

This consists of the key concept of assigning the primary responsibility for quality to production workers rather than a staff quality control department.

After organizing for TQC, the rate of quality improvement can be accelerated by introducing the items in categories 2–5. These include new

Table 1 Total quality control: concepts and categories

TQC category	TQC concept
1 Organisation	Production responsibility
2 Goals	Habit of improvement • Perfection
3 Basic principles	Process control • easy-to-see quality • insistence on compliance • line stop • correcting one's own errors • 100 per cent check • project-by-project improvement
4 Facilitating concepts	• QC as a facilitator • small lot size • housekeeping • less than full capacity scheduling • daily machine checking
5 Techniques and aids	Exposure of problems • foolproof devices • $N = 2$ • analytical tools • QC circles

Source: Schonberger (1982, p.51).

goals, principles, facilitating concepts, and techniques for successful implementation of TQC. Some of these concepts are alien to Western production practice, while others have been copied from the West and adapted to Japanese business culture.

Goals

• *The habit of improvement.* While most Western companies accept one-off improvement programs, Japanese companies have developed the habit of KAIZEN – continuous improvement, day after day, year after year at all levels within the organization. For example, in some Japanese corporations the workforce meets each morning to confirm and consolidate productivity gains made the previous day.

• *Perfection.* The goal of perfection is treated differently between Japanese and Western concerns. There is agreement that quality needs to be regularly monitored to insure adherence to specification. However, while Western concerns accept a given standard of defects, Japanese concerns continue to work toward absolute perfection. Similarly, both Japanese and Western concerns accept that quality depends on the efforts of all functions within the corporation. However, while Western concerns place a limit on the costs to be incurred in the pursuit of quality, Japanese companies believe that ever better quality will continue to improve market share and expand the overall market. It must also be seen that for Japanese concerns the TQC concept may well include continuous cost reduction as well as product perfection.

Basic Principles

A number of basic principles are listed as components of TQC. The first two of these are closely related and equally important.

- *Process control.* The concept of process control is a standard Western quality control technique. However, it is undertaken by the inspection of only a number of processes in the production system, together with final inspection. Moreover, this activity tends to be undertaken by the quality control department. In the Japanese system all processes are continuously checked, but by the workforce, who have been trained to undertake this task themselves, thus allowing every work station to become an inspection department.

- *Easy-to-see quality.* This principle, which is an extension of the Deming and Juran concepts that there should be measurable standards of quality, has been finessed by the Japanese such that display boards are located everywhere in Japanese plants. These convey to workers, management, customers, suppliers, and visitors what quality factors are measured, recent performance and what current quality improvement projects are in progress, which groups have won awards, and the like. Many of the displays are graphic rather than numerical and are completed regularly by the workforce. These have much more impact than pages of computer print-out, which may well be unread by Western management and perhaps not even shown to the workforce.

- *Insistence on compliance.* In many Western concerns, while lip service is paid to achieving consistent quality standards, these may be sacrificed on occasions for short-term expediency. In most Japanese concerns, the pursuit of quality standards is paramount and takes precedence over output standards and pressures.

- *Line stop.* Closely related to the compliance principle, in Japanese production systems every individual worker has the facility to stop the production line if quality standards are compromised. By contrast, in many Western plants the production line is not expected to stop, and any production identi-fied as deficient is despatched to rework areas. While the Japanese system is initially slow when a new production process is started, as quality problems are gradually resolved, the line speeds up, quality improves, and rework costs are eliminated.

- *Correcting one's own errors.* When errors do occur in the Japanese system, unlike in the West, it is the responsibility of the worker or workgroup to correct its own errors by undertaking its own rework. While the output rate is unimportant in the Japanese system with, for example, the line stop system being open to all workers, daily output is important and in the event of line stops and needed reworks, the workforce is expected to work late to make any necessary corrections. In this way, workers assume full responsibility for quality problems. In general, however, these are limited while JIT keeps lot sizes small, so that any defects detected apply to only a small number of units.

- *100 per cent check.* In Japanese systems this requires every item of output to be inspected – not merely a random sample. This principle applies rigidly to all finished goods and, where possible, to components. When it is impossible to inspect all components, the $N=2$ concept is used (see below), with a long-term goal of achieving a 100 per cent check. By contrast, in Western companies statistical sample inspections are the norm. This technique, which was developed by the US military in World War II, was used initially by the Japanese but later rejected because the concept of a lot implied long production and hence the build-up of inventory – the antithesis of JIT. Second, the Japanese adopted much tighter standards of defects and ultimately were aiming for true zero defects, which made sampling tables irrelevant. Third, sampling itself was considered inadequate.

- *Project-by-project improvement.* Schemes for project-by-project improvement are visible throughout Japanese production units. The displays may also show partly completed projects, on a type of "scoreboard." Western visitors find such displays impressive, but are skeptical when they understand the number of such projects being undertaken. While it is true that individual projects make little contribution, the overall number, coupled with the cultural environment induced toward quality, results in a massive continuous level of improvement which most Western firms find impossible to replicate.

Facilitating Concepts

The effect of quality improvement can be enhanced by making use of the facilitating concepts once the organizational and quality principles are in place. These facilitators are as follows:

- *Quality control as facilitator.* In Japan, as responsibility for quality is assigned to the line function, specialist quality control departments are reduced in size and used as facilitators for the total process. As a result, they promote the removal of the causes of defects, keep track of quality achievements, monitor as standard procedures are followed, and observe procurement to insure that supplier factories have similar quality standards and conduct QC training. The inspection of goods inwards parts is also passed back to suppliers and, as such, goods inward are sent straight to the production line. One exception to this practice is that parts received from Western suppliers may be inspected by the quality department.

- *Small lot sizes.* This is a key element in JIT production. It is also important in ensuring that any defects are detected early. As such, it also forms a basic concept in quality control.

- *Housekeeping.* Japanese factories are carefully laid out to insure scrupulous tidiness and cleanliness. While individual workers are expected to keep their workplace tidy, any production workers not required for their line production jobs may be temporarily assigned to cleanliness and hygiene tasks elsewhere in the factory.

- *Less-than-full-capacity scheduling.* Having available spare capacity insures that the daily production schedules will be met. It is also a quality control concept, as it permits the line to be stopped for quality or other reasons. Moreover, capacity slack avoids over-pressuring the workforce, tools, and equipment – so reducing the probability of errors.

- *Daily machine checking.* Unlike in the West, where production machinery is used as hard as possible and maintenance is the responsibility of specialists, in Japan production workers are expected to perform routine maintenance on their machines at the beginning of each day. Each morning, therefore, the Japanese normally go through a checklist, insuring that the machine functions correctly, oiling, adjusting, sharpening, and the like before operations commence.

Techniques and Aids

In Japanese TQC there are fewer techniques and aids than those found in the West, where specialists using various techniques and aids are common. In Japan, the commonly used tools are fewer and different. They include the following:

- *Exposure of problems.* In the TQC system, discovery of a defect triggers a detailed investigation to discover the cause of the defect and correct it. This process is so valued that management may deliberately remove workers or buffer inventories to expose problems affecting quality. Exposure of problems and correction of causes are also sought out before there is actual evidence of problems. This might involve very careful analysis of product designs and checks at the product start-up phase, before volume production commences. Similarly, workers – both individually and in small groups or quality circles – are constantly seeking ways in which to improve quality.

- *Foolproof devices.* The work process can be redesigned to eliminate many mistakes. Many machines are fitted with *bakayoke*, which automatically check for abnormal production. When such defects are found, the machines stop automatically – the process of "autonomation." The monitoring mechanisms may therefore check for malfunction, excess tool wear, and the like, in addition to dimensions and tolerances. Such devices are also sometimes used in final assembly or when manual systems are used via the line stop system or via worker triggered warning lights.

- $N = 2$. While foolproof devices are useful for high-volume operations, for lower volumes manual inspection may be required. High percentages of production are inspected – even as high as 100 per cent, in the case of unstable processes. For more stable processes, sample inspection may be used. Unlike in the West, where random sampling is normal, in Japanese TQC inspection is not random. In practice, the first and last pieces in a production run are inspected – hence the term $N = 2$. The argument is that in a stable process if the first and last units are good, then those produced in between should also all be good.

- *Tools of analysis*. Statistical tools are used in both Western and Japanese quality control systems. In Japan, however, these tend to be used by superiors and workers who have undergone extensive training in their preparation and use. Many Japanese variants of such tools, however, show greater detail. The cause–effect, or Ishikawa, diagram was less known in the West, but is now a normal tool used in quality analysis.

- *QC Circles*. QC circles are used throughout Japanese corporations and almost all employees are members. Such groups meet to develop ideas for quality improvements on a regular basis. Their output is prodigious, with ideas for quality and kaizen improvement often running into millions of suggestions each year per company. Most of these ideas are implemented. While successful ideas are rewarded, the gains in monetary terms are usually small, with prestige awards being more highly thought of.

The TQC concept has been accepted by a number of Western companies, but few have adopted the depth of commitment to the principles and practice found in Japanese concerns. Without such commitment, the constant improvements in quality and costs experienced in Japan are unlikely to materialize in the West, leading to a continuous loss of competitive advantage.

Bibliography

Kusaba, I. (1981). Quality control in Japan. *Reports of QC circle activities*, no. 14, pp. 1–5. Union of Japanese Scientists and Engineers.

Ishikawa, K. (1985). *What is total quality control? The Japanese way*. Englewood Cliffs, NJ: Prentice-Hall.

Juran, J. M. (1978). Japanese and Western quality: a contrast in methods and results. *Management Review*, 26–45.

Monden, Y. (1983). *Toyota production system*. Atlanta, GA: Institute of Industrial Engineers.

Schonberger, R. J. (1982). *Japanese manufacturing techniques*. New York: The Free Press.

DEREK F. CHANNON

transaction costs   These are the costs involved in any transaction between two parties relating to the transfer or exchange of goods or services.

Initially, transaction cost principles were used in a debate regarding the role of government in promoting economic EFFICIENCY with respect to EXTERNALITIES. In 1920, Pigou took the view that common law needs to be applied to force the internalization of social costs in the quest for efficiency (Pigou, 1920). His view was contested by Coase (1937), who claimed that externalities are sometimes self-correcting, and suggested that holding the party which created the externality liable under common law was not necessarily efficient; instead, efficiency would be best achieved by balancing costs and benefits, to which the role of causality was not decisive.

The transaction costs theory was considerably extended and gained its widespread appeal through a series of publications by Oliver Williamson, who applied it to the organization of the firm. Williamson suggested that there are three generic governance structures; namely, the market (in which, for example, a firm subcontracts a certain task to another firm), hierarchy (in which, for example, a firm asks a salaried employee to undertake some task that is required), and a hybrid one which combines elements of both. According to this model, hierarchies (surrendering authority to a single party) are expected to emerge where the costs of drawing up an all contingent contract are high, typically due to an unusually uncertain environment. These structures differ in two principal respects; namely, the form of contract law that they support (an employee, for example, has no access to the courts for most intents and purposes), and the applicable incentive and control mechanisms (from the automatic coordinating role of prices in a market, to the conscious and deliberate considerations in hierarchies).

Nature of the Costs

Transaction costs consist of two main components, namely transaction uncertainty and performance ambiguity. Transaction uncertainty exists to the degree to which transactions are unstandardized and unpredictable, and is influenced by factors such as the frequency of transactions, their duration, and the degree to which parties to the transaction have made transaction-specific investments. Performance ambiguity refers to the ability of the parties involved to monitor and evaluate the performance of the other parties and to determine the value of the objects of exchange, and is influenced by the intangibility content of the objects of exchange, the simultaneity of production and consumption, and the involvement of skilled and specialized personnel.

Transaction costs relate to all aspects of a transaction, including negotiating, monitoring, and enforcing the exchange. Typical costs in a market organization are discovering what the relevant prices are, learning and haggling over the terms of the trade, and negotiating and concluding a separate contract for each exchange transaction; they typically increase with long-term agreements. Similarly, costs in an internalized (hierarchical) organization include increased organizational rigidity and often higher management costs too; these increase with the number of hierarchical levels involved, by virtue of the latter adversely affecting the quality and quantity of the information transmitted.

Implications

Transaction costs can affect a firm in many ways, and can even explain its existence. When the costs of determining market prices are substantial, a firm emerges and workers surrender the right to use their labor by contract (Coase, 1937). Similarly, high transaction costs (such as in the form of difficulty in forecasting input or output prices) may lead the firm to internalize activities further upstream or downstream (i.e., to integrate vertically; *see* VERTICAL INTEGRATION STRATEGY), can explain multinationalization (as a way of producing cost savings by internalizing markets across international boundaries), and can modify organizational structure so that the level of task interdependence is reduced to lower the transaction uncertainty and performance ambiguity and allow prices to emerge as the principal governance system.

In addition, high transaction costs may lead to allocative inefficiency, if they feed through to higher prices. Similarly, they may necessitate the establishment of rules and regulations, and the government may have to intervene to limit the impact of a harmful transaction cost (*see* REGULATION).

Bibliography

Coase, R. H. (1937). The nature of the firm. *Economica*, **4**, 386–405. Reprinted in Stigler, G. J. & Boulding, K. E. (eds) (1952). *Readings in price theory*. Chicago, IL: Irwin.

Pigou, A. C. (1920). *The economics of welfare*. London: Macmillan. 4th edn, 1932, reissued by St. Martin's Press, New York, in 1952.

Williamson, O. E. (1975). *Markets and hierarchies: analysis and anti-trust implications*. Glencoe, IL: The Free Press.

Williamson, O. E. (1979). Transaction cost economics: the governance of contractual relations. *Journal of Law and Economics*, **22** (October), 232–61.

Williamson, O. E. (1981). The economics of organisation: the transaction cost approach. *American Journal of Sociology*, **87**, 548–77.

STEPHANOS AVGEROPOULOS

turnaround strategy Turnaround strategies can be applied when a business is in decline but is worth saving. It is important to recognize the conditions under which an otherwise successful business may go into decline. Such recognition can suggest the appropriate solutions which might aid recovery.

Causative Factors

A number of factors have been identified as leading to decline.

1. Poor management. The personal characteristics of the chief executive and key management play a major role in causing decline. Apart from incompetence, the principal factors identified as poor management reasons for decline include the following:

- *One man rule.* This is acceptable while the company is successful, but rapid decline ensues when the leadership is seen to fail.

- *Combined chairman and chief executive role.* In this case there is no counterbalance over the activities of the CEO.

- *Ineffective boards of directors.* The board constitution is important. All too often, nonexecutive directors do not know enough about a business and/or do not participate. In addition, executive directors may be ineffective or only participate when topics specifically affect their area of interest.

- *Management neglect of core businesses.* This occurs especially when the core business matures and top management time becomes diverted by attempts at diversification.

- *Lack of management depth.* This may well occur in newly diversifying concerns, where traditional skills have tended to be functional and the firm lacks general management or succession skills.

2. Inadequate financial control. Apart from poor management, lack of adequate financial control is the most common characteristic of declining firms. Such a lack of control comes about because the control systems lack one or more of adequate cashflow forecasts, costing systems, and budgetary controls. In smaller firms all three items may be missing and only statutory financial information is prepared. In larger firms the problem is more likely to be due to inadequate systems. Four common problems have been identified:

- *Many management accounting systems have been poorly designed.* Often, control systems are too complex, produce poorly presented information, and may even produce the wrong information. The blame for this lies with top management but, regrettably, many may not understand the information that they really need, nor what can be provided by the information systems in place.

- *Management accounting information is poorly used.* Many senior managers do not understand how to use accounting information, actually running the business on heuristics or "rules of thumb."

- *The organizational structure hinders effective control.* In many corporations, centralization has been identified as a causal factor in decline and, in addition, the hierarchical level at which control is located may well be too high.

- *Methods of overhead allocation distort the costs.* Correct overhead cost allocation is not undertaken by many companies. ACTIVITY-BASED COSTING is a modern tool which tries to improve this problem.

3. Competition. Both price and product competition are seen as common causes of corporate decline: usually they occur together.

- *Product competition.* Firms which fail to revitalize their product offerings in response to changing market needs and competition ultimately end up in decline. Other problems are due to poor product introduction strategies; to mistaken beliefs about the viability of the old product; to a lack of financial and technological resources to pursue the introduction of new products; and to a failure to develop new product ideas.

- *Price competition.* Severe price competition is a common cause of decline in Western corporations, especially in those sectors targeted by Japanese and other Asian competitors. While the problem is especially acute in undifferentiated product markets, it has also occurred in areas in which product differentiation is important, such as automobiles and consumer electronics.

4. High cost structure. Firms with a substantially higher cost structure than major competitors usually experience a seriously competitive disadvantage. Six major sources of cost disadvantage have been identified. These are as follows:

- *Relative cost disadvantages.* There are two such disadvantages. First, there are those associated with experience effects (*see* EXPERIENCE AND LEARNING EFFECTS), while the second is due to ECONOMIES OF SCALE.

- *Absolute cost disadvantages.* These may be due to a number of factors, such as competitive cost disadvantage due to ownership or control of critical raw materials or components by competitors; access to cheaper labor; proprietary production know-how; and favorable site location.

- *Cost disadvantages due to diversification strategy.* Diversified firms may experience a cost disadvantage due to the allocation of corporate overheads. This can occur especially in industries with shared costs, where overheads are allocated in an arbitrary fashion without an activity-based costing system.

- *Cost disadvantage due to management style and organizational structure.* Some organizations deliberately lower costs by improving productivity, reducing labor costs via OUT-SOURCING, reducing central staff overheads, and the like. Those concerns that do not so reduce overheads may suffer serious cost disadvantages.

- *Operating inefficiencies.* Such inefficiencies are usually the result of poor management and can occur in any function of the business.

- *Unfavorable government policies.* Some businesses may be placed at a disadvantage as a result of direct and/or indirect government policies, such as subsidies, tax differentials, exchange rates, preferential procurement, environmental controls, social policies, and the like.

5. Changes in market demand. An important causal factor in decline can be a reduction in demand or a change in the pattern of demand, to which the firm fails to respond or simply cannot respond. A drop in demand can be due to market obsolescence, such as buggy whips and gas lamps; cyclical demand, such as recession, which may cause serious but probably temporary decline; and seasonal decline, such as for ice cream in winter. This is not usually fatal unless the firm is in a weak financial condition. Failures to monitor secular decline trends regrettably often occur because the firm does not really want to see and acknowledge that this is happening, because of the resulting change in strategic behavior and the adjustment it may entail. Cyclical decline failures often result because of price wars in which competitors attempt to grow or maintain market share.

Insurance is a classic example of an industry with such a pattern.

6. Adverse movements in commodity prices. Major changes in commodity prices which can occur suddenly have been responsible for many business failures. Examples include changes in the price of oil, as in the case of the first and second oil-price shocks; rapid changes in the prices of metals such as copper, aluminum, and steel; and significant movements in exchange rates, as with the rapid appreciation of the yen in the late 1980s, and again in the mid-1990s.

7. Lack of marketing effort. While most firms suffering serious decline have managerial problems throughout their organizations, the problem is often especially acute in the sales and marketing functions. Such problems occur as a result of:

- a poorly motivated sales force and weak sales force management

- ineffective and wasted advertising

- efforts not targeted on key customers and products

- poor after-sales service

- poor product quality

- lack of research/knowledge of customer buying habits

- loss of access to distribution channels

- weak or nonexistent new product development

- lack of marketing orientation

8. Large projects. Large projects that go wrong because costs were underestimated and/or revenues overestimated are a common cause of failure. There are a number of ways in which such projects can go wrong:

- *Underestimates of capital requirements.* These may arise because of: poor cost estimates at the project planning stage; poor project control; late design changes; and external factors such as strikes, bad weather, technical delays, and late delivery of equipment. Civil engineering and defense projects, such as the Channel Tunnel and the Eurofighter, regularly seem to be examples of such failures.

However, the real losers may be banks, shareholders, and taxpayers.

- *Start-up difficulties.* Even after completion, projects may experience a variety of start-up problems which increase expense above forecast levels. Technical problems with plant and equipment can lead to high wastage, significant downtime. and losses in customer confidence and volume. For example, introductory problems with Eurostar trains thus compound the problems of the Eurotunnel.

- *Capacity expansion.* This problem occurs especially in process industries such as oil and chemicals, when competitors all add capacity at the same time, resulting in overcapacity, price wars, and losses when each endeavors to maximize capacity utilization.

- *Market entry costs.* Problems may occur with the entry of new products, both to existing markets and, especially, to new markets. Each results in different risks, but DIVERSIFICATION carries particular risk.

- *Major contracts.* Poor cost estimating and pricing on major contracts are also a common cause of failure, especially in the construction and capital goods industries.

9. Acquisitions. Acquisitions play a major role in corporate strategy, especially for firms attempting to diversify. However, most acquisitions are considered to be failures. Three aspects of ACQUISITION STRATEGY have been identified as causes of decline for the acquiring company:

- the acquisition of losers – firms with weak competitive positions in their own markets

- paying an unjustifiably high purchase price for the acquired firm

- poor post-acquisition management and control

10. Financial policy. There are at least three direct causes of failure due to financial policy:

- *High debt : equity ratio.* Financial structures which contain moderate debt are perfectly rational, although the level of debt depends to some extent on the industry structure. In acquisition situations in recent years, high debt levels have often been incurred by the use of junk bonds and mezzanine subordinated debt, which has proved a serious problem for companies using these instruments during recession and periods of rising interest rates.

- *Conservative financial policies.* When a firm is characterized by a lack of reinvestment, a high dividend payout ratio, high liquidity, and low gearing, this conservative financial strategy effectively ends up by liquidating the firm and turning it into an acquisition target.

- *Inappropriate financing sources.* While some borrowing term mismatches are acceptable, this can be taken too far, as with the secondary banking crises of the 1970s and over-investment in commercial property in the late 1980s and early 1990s.

11. Overtrading. Overtrading occurs when a company's sales grow too rapidly, such that cashflow becomes inadequate to finance operations. The phenomenon can occur quickly when financial controls are inadequate to accurately identify the possibility of a decline situation. The problem is an important cause of failure in very high growth firms, in which the increased scale and complexity of such a business can rapidly outstrip its control systems.

Summary

The symptoms of decline are often easier to identify than the causes. The most common symptoms include the following:

- decreasing profitability, as measured by declining profits before tax and interest, and reduced ROI, ROE, and ROS

- declining sales volumes, and in particular sales per employee, sales per square foot, and the like at constant prices

- increased debt

- declining liquidity, measured by falls in current test and acid test ratios, plus rising stocks and debtors as a percentage of sales

- reduced dividends and dividend cover

- accounting practices which delay publishing accounts and auditors' qualification of accounts
- rapid turnover of management
- a decline in market share
- a lack of strategic thinking by top management
- an unsatisfactory Z-SCORE and trend

Successful Recovery Strategies

A number of generic successful turnaround strategies have been identified. It is common that a number of these will be deployed at the same time. They include the following:

- *Change of management.* This usually involves a change of CEO or chairman, or both, to provide a new vision for the corporation and to inspire confidence in shareholders and bankers.
- *Strong financial control.* This is essential for successful turnaround. All cash needs to be centralized initially, and every effort should be made to improve cashflow to reduce debt, including possible asset disposals.
- *Organizational change and decentralization.* This is not a short-term turnaround policy, but might be expected once new top management has been installed and often involves DOWNSIZING. Decentralization should also not occur until adequate financial controls are in place.
- *New product market focus.* This may well include: addition or deletion of product lines; addition or deletion of customers according to profitability potential; changes in the sales mix by focusing on specific products and customers; complete withdrawal from unattractive segments; and entry into new product market segments.
- *Improved marketing.* This is usually essential, as declining businesses tend to be weak in marketing.
- *Growth via acquisition.* This does not necessarily mean diversification, but the purchase of firms in the same industry, or in closely related industries. This alternative may not be open to firms in serious financial crisis.
- *Asset reduction.* This is usually an integral part of any turnaround strategy. In the short term, strict cash control and reduction in working capital assets are priorities, and in the medium term fixed asset disposals and sales of whole businesses may well be necessary.
- *Cost reduction strategies.* These are designed to increase product profitability and cashflow.
- *Investment strategies.* These should involve moves to reduce costs by asset reduction or by promoting growth.
- *Debt restructuring.* Frequently, financial problems may require restructuring any outstanding debt and reaching acceptable revised terms with lenders, or raising additional equity.

The precise management actions required for a successful turnaround will depend on the position of the firm. The combination of the above generic strategies will therefore be a function of the following factors:

- the causes of decline
- the severity of the crisis
- the attitudes of the stakeholders involved in the turnaround process
- the firm's historic strategy
- the characteristics of the industry or industries in which the firm competes
- the firm's cost–price structure

Bibliography

Argenti, J. (1976). *Corporate collapse: the causes and symptoms.* New York: McGraw-Hill.
Grinyer, P. & Spender, J. C. (1979). *Turnaround: managerial recipes for strategic success.* London: Associated Business Publications.
Hofer, C. W. & Schendel, D. (1978). *Strategy formulation: analytical concepts.* St. Paul, MN: West Publishing. See pp. 172–4.
Slatter, S. (1984). *Corporate recovery.* Harmondsworth, UK: Penguin. Very good: this entry was heavily influenced by this work.

DEREK F. CHANNON

V

value-based planning Since the early 1980s, an increasing number of corporations have adopted the concept of value planning. An alternate model to other portfolio systems, value-based planning seeks to maximize the value of the corporation for shareholders. By examining the corporate portfolio with this objective, individual businesses may be seen as creating, sustaining, or destroying shareholder value. Those businesses which create value should be invested in, those sustaining value should be supported, and those destroying value should either be divested or closed.

The Concept of Value Planning

The fundamental economic relationship underlying value-based management is that share-holder value in developed economies with established stock markets is determined by the net present value of the future cashflow streams that can be expected from the corporation. At the same time, the value of the equity of the firm is given by the market value of the common stock. This assumes that the market is efficient, and that the market value represents a consensus of the expected present value of future cashflow streams based on the portfolio of existing assets and the returns that can be expected from future investments. Over the long term, and despite short-term market fluctuations, there is strong evidence to support this view. This market value can be contrasted to the book value of the corporation, which is based on the accountant's view of the value of

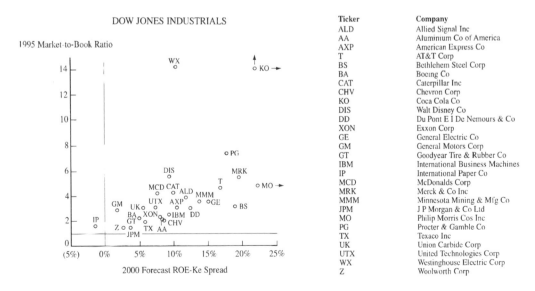

Ticker	Company
ALD	Allied Signal Inc
AA	Aluminium Co of America
AXP	American Express Co
T	AT&T Corp
BS	Bethlehem Steel Corp
BA	Boeing Co
CAT	Caterpillar Inc
CHV	Chevron Corp
KO	Coca Cola Co
DIS	Walt Disney Co
DD	Du Pont E I De Nemours & Co
XON	Exxon Corp
GE	General Electric Co
GM	General Motors Corp
GT	Goodyear Tire & Rubber Co
IBM	International Business Machines
IP	International Paper Co
MCD	McDonalds Corp
MRK	Merck & Co Inc
MMM	Minnesota Mining & Mfg Co
JPM	J P Morgan & Co Ltd
MO	Philip Morris Cos Inc
PG	Procter & Gamble Co
TX	Texaco Inc
UK	Union Carbide Corp
UTX	United Technologies Corp
WX	Westinghouse Electric Corp
Z	Woolworth Corp

Figure 1 Market-to-book versus forecasted spread (note that Ke = Tech Ke).
Source: Value Line Investment Survey, Marakon Associates (1995).

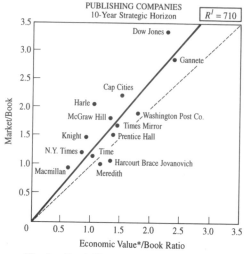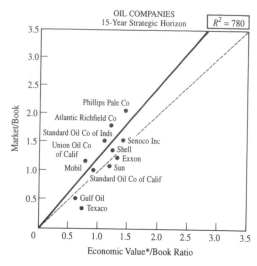

Figure 2 *McKinsey's (M/B) versus (E/B) graph*
Source; Lai (1983)

historic contributions by shareholders. The market to book model has been derived from the comparison between these two values of the firm. The market/book (M/B) ratio is calculated as follows:

$$\frac{\text{market value}}{\text{book value}} = \frac{\text{expected future payments}}{\text{past capital invested}}$$

From the calculation the basic message is as follows:

- If M/B = 1, all future payments are yielding the expected rate of return required by the market, and the firm is neither creating nor losing value.

- If M/B > 1, the rate of return is greater than that expected by the market, and the firm is creating value.

- If M/B < 1, the rate of return is less than that required by the market, and the firm is destroying shareholder value.

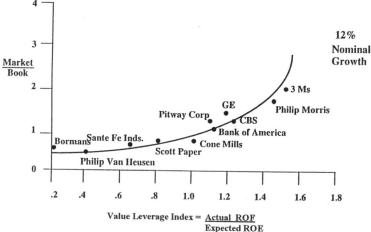

Figure 3 *Across industries the higher the VLI the higher the market/book.*
Source: Mercer Management Consultants.

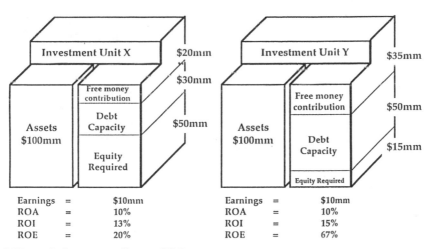

Earnings	=	$10mm
ROA	=	10%
ROI	=	13%
ROE	=	20%

Earnings	=	$10mm
ROA	=	10%
ROI	=	15%
ROE	=	67%

Figure 4 The capital structure effect on ROE.

Utilizing this basic principle, a number of portfolio models have been developed which compare market to book with the rate of return on equity compared with the cost of equity. This latter factor is calculated roughly by the risk-free bond rate of return and adding a premium for equity risk. This in turn is finalized by multiplying by a beta value risk factor, which is based on the industry and the individual company. The precise calculation of the cost of equity varies slightly between consultancy company models. Comparing this calculated cost of equity with the full return on equity provides a term against which to compare M/B. Marakon Associates thus calculate the "spread," which is the actual return on equity minus the calculated return on equity. The combination of M/B versus spread is illustrated in figure 1, which indicates a positive association between the two. This model provides the basis for a useful comparison between competitors.

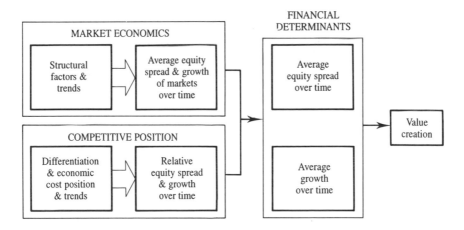

Figure 5   Strategic determinants of value creation
Source: Marakon Associates

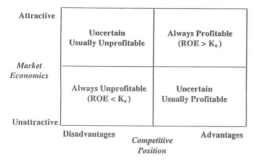

	Disadvantages	Advantages
Attractive	Uncertain Usually Unprofitable	Always Profitable (ROE > K$_e$)
Unattractive	Always Unprofitable (ROE < K$_e$)	Uncertain Usually Profitable

Figure 6 Linking strategic position to value creation.
Source: Marakon Associates.

By contrast, McKinsey and Company use a different way of comparing the economic performance of a group of firms. In this method M/B is plotted against an indicator called the economic-to-book value ratio (see figure 2). This is calculated on the basis of historic performance projected into the future but, again, the measure is based on future cashflow streams discounted plus a residual term.

Strategic Planning Associates, a pioneer of the technique but subsequently acquired and now Mercer Management Consultants, used a term called the Value Leverage Index (VLI) index and by comparing this with the M/B one can construct the value curve illustrated in figure 3. The VLI is estimated by dividing the actual to expected return on equity. The implications of the value curve are similar to those from the Marakon calculations. Only when the actual to expected ratios of return are equal will the market value of the corporation be equivalent to the book value. When the VLI is less than one, the curve flattens out, which is assessed as an underlying value and thus a potential acquisition premium, while a VLI greater than one indicates a growth in shareholder value and the market essentially rewarding the performance with a share premium. As shown, these models are all static.

Using Value Planning at the SBU Value Level

When growth is added it can have a positive, negative, or neutral effect on the market/book ratio. Corporations adding shareholder value enhance M/B, those sustaining it remain on the curve in the case of SPA, while those producing

negative value have a reduced level of M/B. Growth itself, therefore, is not necessarily seen as attractive, except when it leads to increased shareholder value.

When applied within the multibusiness firm, these methodologies attempt to evaluate the contribution of each business unit to the overall value of the firm. When SBUs are free-standing and independent, the value of the firm is equal to the sum of the units.

The evaluation of the contribution of each business unit is critical to assessing the desired strategy at the SBU level. In particular, the impact of growth is critical. SBUs with a positive value contribution are candidates for investment, while those that destroy value should not be invested in, as further growth will accelerate this trend. However, the calculation of positive or negative value is complex, and may be subject to interpretation dependent upon how return on equity at the business unit level is calculated. Thus, if the capital structure of each business unit is seen as proportional to that of the parent, return on equity may be substantially affected by the allocation of debt, equity, and risk. However, if each SBU is treated as if it were a microfirm, its capital structure might reflect the nature of the industry in which it operates rather than that of the firm as a whole.

For example, as shown in figure 4, for two businesses with the same asset size and profitability, the return on assets value may be the same, while the return on equity value may be dramatically different, due to different capacities to generate free debt and apply leverage. Moreover, relative risk values may be quite different, and the future prospects of the business units may also vary widely. Similarly, risk, while a function of industry, will also vary according to the competitive position of both the corporation and the business unit itself. For example, selective segmentation in insurance may result in reduced risk, which is unrecognized by industry regulators.

In assessing the portfolio position of each business, Marakon notes that its capability to generate value is determined by a combination of market economics and competitive position (see figure 5). Market economics are determined by competitors, that determine the average equity spread and growth rate over time for all competitors in its product market. Competitive position is based on factor 3, or on forces that jointly determine a specific competitor's equity spread and growth rate over time relative to the average competitor in its product market, where competitive position is defined in terms of a combination of product differentiation and economic cost position.

These two key variables can be used to assess the SBU's current and expected profitability of the business, as shown in figure 6. Business units with sustainable competitive advantages in attractive markets will always be substantially profitable: ROE will always exceed the cost of equity capital and M/B will always be greater than one.

SBUs with weak competitive positions in unattractive markets will always be unprofitable: they will produce economic losses and they will destroy existing shareholder value.

In the remaining two cases the linkage is less clear, although competitive position tends to have a greater influence on profitability than market economics. Marakon notes that when a business enjoys substantial competitive advantage but participates in unattractive markets, it still tends to generate value over time, although long-term profitability tends to be a function of size and the sustainability of its competitive advantage. Those businesses with a competitive disadvantage in attractive markets are usually unprofitable.

From this form of financial and strategic analysis combination, value planning advocates that business units should be assigned one of four strategies – grow, hold, invest, or divest. Ironically, by eliminating portfolio losers, divestiture results in an increase in market capitalization despite a reduction in corporate assets, as future expected cashflows increase long-term shareholder value.

Bibliography

Anonymous (1981). *Strategic and shareholders' value: the value curve.* Washington, DC: Strategic Planning Associates.
Copeland, T., Koller, J. & Murri, J. (1990). *Valuation.* New York: John Wiley.
Day, G. S. & Fahey, L. (1990). Putting strategy into shareholder value analysis. *Harvard Business Review,* 68, 156–62.
Hax, A. C. & Majluf, N. S. (1991). *The strategy concept and process.* Englewood Cliffs, NJ: Prentice-Hall.
McTaggart, J. M., Kontes, P. W. & Mankins, C. M. (1994). *The value imperative.* New York: The Free Press.
Rappaport, A. (1986). *Creating shareholder value.* New York: The Free Press.

DEREK F. CHANNON

value chain analysis The activities that a firm performs become part of the value added produced from a raw material to its ultimate consumption. Individual actors may operate over a greater or lesser extent of the total value generated within an industry. The value chain for the firm is shown in figure 1, in which are also illustrated many of the key issues associated with each of the main functions within the value chain. At the same time, the firm does not exist in isolation but merely forms part of the industry chain. Thus suppliers have value streams, as do customers and the channels that supply them. Moreover, in multibusiness firms there may well be a variety of value chains with different dimensions in which the firm is involved. The value system for single business and multibusiness firms is illustrated in figure 2.

The value chain concept allows the firm to be disaggregated into a variety of strategically relevant activities. In particular, it is important to identify those which have different economic characteristics; those which have a high potential for creating differentiation; and those which are most important in developing cost structure (PARETO ANALYSIS may be a useful tool for this purpose). The value chain concept thus helps to identify cost behavior in detail. As such, a number of the Japanese cost analysis techniques are useful in gaining this information. From this analysis, different strategic courses of action should be identifiable in order to develop differentiation and less price sensitive strategies. Competitive advantage is then achieved by performing strategic activities better or cheaper than competitors.

Value is the amount that buyers are willing to pay for the product or service that a firm provides. Profits alter when the value created by the firm exceeds the cost of providing it. This is the goal of strategy, and therefore value creation

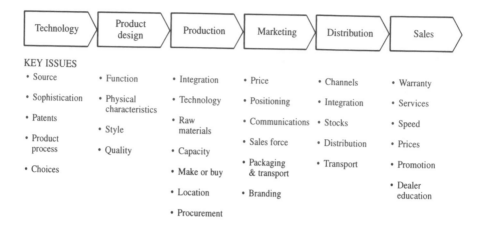

Figure 1   The business value chain

becomes a critical ingredient in competitive analysis. Every value activity employs costs such as raw materials, and other purchased goods and services for "purchased inputs," human resources (direct and indirect labor), and technology to transform raw materials into finished goods. Each value activity also creates information that is needed to establish what is going on in the business. Similarly, value is created by producing stocks, accounts receivable, and the like; while value is lost via raw material purchases and other liabilities. Most organizations thus engage in many activities in

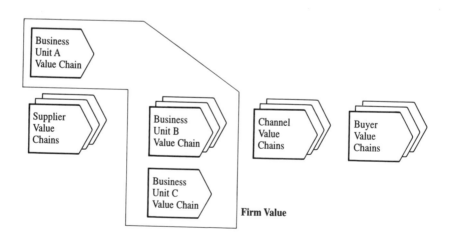

Figure 2   Competitive advantage value system for a diversified firm
Source: Porter (1985)

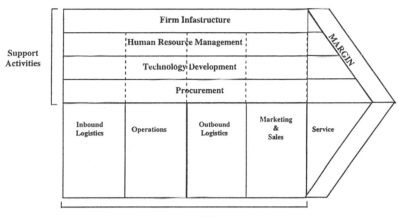

Figure 3 The generic value chain.
Source: Porter (1985).

the process of creating value. These activities can generally be classified into either primary or support activities. These are illustrated in figure 3, which details the view of Michael Porter, who states that there are five generic categories of primary activities involved in competing in any industry. Each of these is divisible into a number of specific activities that vary according to the industry and chosen strategy of the firm. These categories are as follows:

- *Inbound logistics.* Activities associated with receiving, storing, and disseminating rights to the product, such as material handling, warehousing, stock management, and the like.

- *Operations.* All of the activities required to transform inputs into outputs and the critical functions which add value, such as machining, packaging, assembly, service, testing, and the like.

- *Outbound logistics.* All of the activities required to collect, store, and physically distribute the output. This activity can prove to be extremely important both in generating value and in improving differentiation, as in many industries control over distribution strategies is proving to be a major source of competitive advantage – especially as it is realized that up to 50 per cent of the value created in many industry chains occurs close to the ultimate buyer.

- *Marketing and sales.* Activities associated with informing potential buyers about the firm's products and services, and inducing them to do so by personal selling, advertising and promotion, and the like.

- *Service.* The means of enhancing the physical product features through after-sales service, installation, repair, and the like.

While each firm provides these activities to a greater or lesser degree, they do not do so to the same extent; nor is each function as important to all competitors, even within the same industry. This is illustrated in figure 4, in which is shown the value chain positioning of a variety of

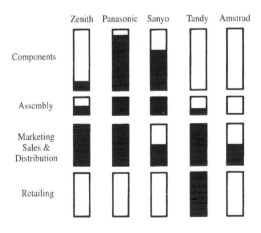

Figure 4 Value added activity structure.

competitors in the consumer electronics industry. The chart is meant to be illustrative rather than definitive.

Porter has also identified four generic support strategies. These are broad concepts which support the primary activities of the firm:

1. *Procurement.* This concerns the acquisition of inputs or resources. Although technically the responsibility of the purchasing department, almost everyone in the firm is responsible for purchasing something. While the cost of procurement itself is relatively low, the impact can be very high.

2. *Human resource management.* This consists of all activities involved in recruiting, hiring, training, developing, rewarding, and sanctioning the people in the organization.

3. *Technology development.* This is concerned with the equipment, hardware, software, technical skills, and the like used by the firm in transforming inputs to outputs. Some such skills can be classified as scientific, while others – such as food preparation in a restaurant – are "artistic." Such skills are not always recognized. They may also support limited activities of the business, such as accounting, order procurement, and the like, and in this sense may be likened to the value added component of the experience effect (*see* EXPERIENCE AND LEARNING EFFECTS).

4. *Firm infrastructure.* This consists of the many activities, including general management, planning, finance, legal, external affairs, and the like, which support the operational aspect of the value chain. This may be self-contained in the case of an undiversified firm or divided between the parent and the firm's constituent business units.

Within each category of primary and support activities, Porter identifies three types of activity which play different roles in achieving competitive advantage:

- *Direct.* These are activities directly involved in creating value for buyers, such as assembly, sales, and advertising.

- *Indirect.* These are activities that facilitate the performance of the direct activities on a continuing basis, such as maintenance, scheduling, and administration.

- *Quality assurance.* These are activities that insure the quality of other activities, such as monitoring, inspecting, testing, and checking.

To diagnose competitive advantage, it is necessary to define the firm's value chain for operating in a particular industry and compare this with those of key competitors. A comparison of the value chains of different competitors often identifies ways of achieving strategic advantage by reconfiguring the value chain of the individual firm. In assigning costs and assets it is important that the analysis be done strategically rather than seeking accounting precision. This should be accomplished using the following principles:

- operating costs should be assigned to activities where incurred

- assets should be assigned to activities where employed, controled, or influencing usage

- accounting systems should be adjusted to fit value analysis

- asset valuation may be difficult, but should recognize industry norms – particular care should be taken in evaluating property assets

The reconfiguration of the value chain has often been used by successful competitors in achieving competitive advantage. When seeking to reconfigure the value chain in an industry, the following questions need to be asked:

- How can an activity be done differently or even eliminated?

- How can linked value activities be reordered or regrouped?

- How could coalitions with other firms reduce or eliminate costs?

Successful reconfiguration strategies usually occur with one or more of the following moves:

- a new production process

- automation differences

- direct versus indirect sales strategy

- the opening of new distribution channels

- new raw materials used

- differences in forward and/or backward integration

- a relative location shift

- new advertising media

Bibliography

Porter, M. E. (1979). How competitive forces shape strategy. *Harvard Business Review*, 57, 137–45.

Porter, M. E. (1985). *Competitive advantage; creating and sustaining superior performance.* New York: The Free Press.

DEREK F. CHANNON

value-driven re-engineering Much has been written and said about Business Process Re-engineering (BPR) since Michael Hammer's paper in the *Harvard Business Review* in 1990. He defined the term as a "fundamental rethink and radical re-design of business processes to achieve dramatic improvements in critical contemporary measures of performance, such as cost, quality, service and speed." He does not claim to have invented the concept, but merely to have discovered it.

Value Driven Re-engineering was pioneered by Andersen Consulting and is by necessity a broad, sweeping approach to strategic change, but it is based on practical, workable principles. It focuses on integrated processes, not piecemeal results. It combines innovation, creativity, and strikingly new perspectives with guiding principles, best practices, and a pragmatic appreciation of how customers, employees, and organizations really behave (see figure 1).

Compared to conventional quality improvement programs, it blends the best of two worlds; comprehensive change throughout the core processes of a business, and a profound respect for the smallest but most important details that make a company successful in the eyes of customers.

When do our customers feel they really get "value" from us? Why? How do we keep making that happen?

By focusing on end-to-end business processes rather than narrowly defined functions, re-engineering concentrates all of a company's resources on insuring that the costs of delivering excellent products and services are in complete harmony with the value that they provide to customers. In the early stages of a re-engineering effort, a company may be surprised to learn, for instance, that the "premium" service that it provides is costing far more than it is actually worth to certain customer segments.

While most businesses can be described in terms of 20–50 separate processes, re-engineering focuses on the five to ten that are critical to the company's ability to balance cost/value trade-offs. Instead of becoming trapped in one or more of the "functional silos" of sales, marketing, manufacturing, and distribution, re-engineering reveals a broad view of how all of these together, as integrated processes, affect a firm's management of those trade-offs.

As a result, Value-Driven Re-engineering becomes a powerful methodology for exploiting change rather than being overwhelmed by it.

Re-engineering considers the entire business enterprise, including the company's suppliers and customers. It is constant and relentless in its focus on integrating four key drivers – people, processes, technology, and infrastructure – to create and sustain value for customers while managing costs.

There are normally three specific steps in a re-engineering program. They all relate to managing change and are targeted to balance the goal of long-term change with the need for practical, quick payback opportunities. These steps start with creating an environment to enable change to occur.

Typically, this involves formulating a shared vision for the enterprise that links the business strategy to operational realities. This vision becomes the foundation for defining and managing cost/value trade-offs. It is necessary to design the new processes and define the people skills, organizations, technology, and infrastructure needed to turn the vision into a reality. The first step concludes with a well-structured plan for implementing these changes.

The second step is to achieve change. The use of innovative change management techniques is important to help a company navigate from today to tomorrow. As appropriate, this

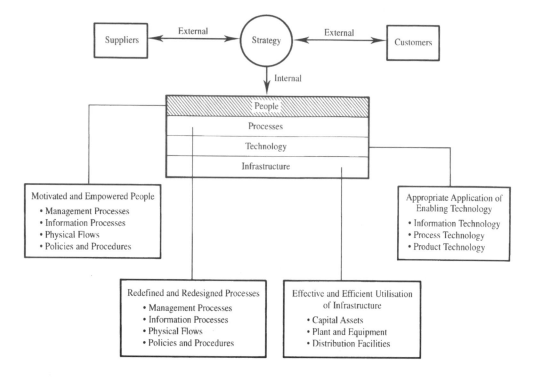

Figure 1 Value-driven re-engineering.
Source: Andersen Consulting.

involves the design and conduct of pilot programs. Most importantly, it involves implementing the comprehensive transformation of the organization and its skills, core processes, mission-critical systems, and infrastructure.

As this 12–36 month transformation is implemented, it is important to integrate the re-engineering effort with the company's culture and competitive strategy. To sustain the change – which is the third step – it is vital to complete the necessary changes in organization, processes, technology, and infrastructure. It is also necessary to establish measures for monitoring performance to insure continuous cost control and consistently high levels of customer satisfaction for many years beyond the re-engineering project itself.

To sustain change it is also necessary continuously to question how further improvement can be achieved. For example, when he successfully re-engineered Woolworths in the UK, Sir Geoffrey Mulcahy, CEO of Kingfisher, said that – even now – if ever a day passed when he did not imagine that company still to be in a turnaround situation, he would be failing his shareholders.

The guiding principles throughout all these steps are clear.

Guiding Principles of Value-Driven Re-engineering

• maintain a customer orientation

• think outside the box

• focus on outcomes and results

• challenge the rules

• empower people

• build in quality at the source

• define end-to-end solutions

• set stretch targets and goals

- eliminate non-value-added activities

- compress time

- communicate, communicate, communicate
Source: Andersen Consulting.

Why do BPR Initiatives Fail?

In reviewing some of the many re-engineering programs that have been undertaken, it is evident that the most common cause of failure or slowdown in the process is through failure properly to manage the "people" aspects, to demonstrate organizational commitment and build shared visions. A company must have a view of its longer-term strategy and its core skills. Without that focus, the substantial effort and resources dedicated to BPR are likely to be wasted on areas of the business which are not critical to success. Another cause of failure is "analysis paralysis" – companies over-analyze situations and attempt to quantify costs and benefits to an unnecessary degree.

Will BPR Fizzle out or Flourish by the Millennium?

BPR will continue to evolve during the 1990s until the majority of companies have incorporated new modes of operation that are consistent with today's environment. Successful BPR is an ongoing rather than one-off project, as well-managed BPR programs encourage organizations to see beyond their current mental models and continually challenge themselves to learn and generate new processes that support continual improvement.

In conclusion, to meet the competitive challenges of the 1990s and beyond, most companies need far more than steady, incremental improvements. They require, in fact, nothing less than strategic change.

Streamlining and automation used to be enough. A company could rely on reorganized operations, new or upgraded information systems, or more efficient production or distribution techniques. Taking comfort in the cliche, "If it ain't broke, don't fix it," many companies thought that they could keep their businesses competitive just by "tweaking things here and there."

Unfortunately, that relatively stable world is no more. Today, unless a firm is a notable exception, success is impossible without an order-of-magnitude improvement in all measures of performance – especially in the way in which the company balances the competing demands for added value to customers on the one hand and cost efficiency on the other.

Achieving such a goal requires a fundamental re-evaluation of the company's basic purpose. The question is not just "How do we cut costs without losing business?" but "Why are we in business? What do our customers really expect from us? How do we meet those expectations at a reasonable cost?"

Over many programs, Andersen Consulting has found that Value-Driven Re-engineering is the best methodology for performing such a sweeping re-evaluation. It has proven itself as the most efficient and reliable means of implementing strategic, sustainable change in today's fast-moving, highly competitive marketplace.

Bibliography

Hammer, M. (1990). Reengineering work: don't automate – obliterate. *Harvard Business Review*, 68, 104–12.

Hammer, M. & Champy, J. (1993). *Reengineering the corporation*. New York: Harper Business.

Johansson, H. J., McHugh, P., Pendebery, A. J. & Wheeler, W. A. III (1993). *Business process reengineering*. Chichester: John Wiley.

PETER DEMPSEY and BILL LATTIMER

value engineering   Japanese companies have made heavy use of value engineering in their pursuit of cost reductions. One such approach, used by Isuzu Motors, has eight aspects to its value engineering program:

- *Value target*. This term is used at Isuzu for its procedures developed to identify target costs of components purchased from suppliers. At the planning stage, the target cost of an entire vehicle at the concept proposal stage is distributed among the company's many thousands of component suppliers. Target costs for major functions and components are determined using monetary values or ratios. Monetary values are determined from customer-based market research, although factors such as technical, safety, and legal considerations are often used to adjust these values. Once target costs are established, outside contractors are invited to bid to supply. Creative suppliers can add value by increasing component functionality.

- *Zeroth look value engineering.* This involves the application of value engineering techniques to the earliest state of product development. By this process the company expects to find revolutionary solutions to improve the functionality of the firm's products.

- *First look value engineering.* Defined as developing new products from concepts, this method is applied during the second half of the concept proposal stage and during the entire planning stage. In the planning stage, the key components or major functions are identified, the commodity value is determined, a design plan submitted, target costs distributed to major functions, and a degree of component commonality set. The objective is to increase a product's value by increasing its functionality without a corresponding increase in cost.

- *Second look value engineering.* This technique is applied during the second half of the planning stage and the first half of the development and product preparation stage. In the development and product preparation stage, the components of the main functions are identified and a first handmade prototype produced. The objective is to improve the value and functionality of existing components rather than to create new ones. Improved components are then incorporated into new products.

- *Manufacturing value engineering.* The objective of this approach is to identify the best method to produce a part, with the critical trade-off being quality versus cost. This approach is applied during the second half of the development and product preparation stage and the first half of the development and production – sales preparation stage.

- *Wate method.* This is a mechanism to systemically incorporate value engineering techniques into small group activities such as quality control and industrial engineering. It

is applied on a continuous basis during the development and product preparation stage, the development and production – sales preparation stage and the production – sales preparation stage. The method utilizes a working group approach, with each analyzing problems encountered with new products.

- *Mini value engineering.* This is a simplified approach to second look value engineering, and applies to specific parts or very small inexpensive parts. The technique is applied during the development and product preparation stage, the development and production – sales preparation stage, and the production – sales preparation stage.

- *Value engineering reliability program.* This is designed to insure that the most appropriate form of value engineering is applied during the development and product preparation stage, the development and production – sales preparation stage, and the production – sales preparation stage.

Bibliography

Cooper, R. & Yoshikawa, T. (1994). *Isuzu Motors Ltd, Cost Creation Program.* Case Study no. 9-195-054. Harvard Business School.

DEREK F. CHANNON

vertical integration strategy   Vertical integration strategies aim to increase the firm's coverage of the value added chain of an industry by extending backward into the production of components or raw materials or forward into wholesaling and distribution toward end users. Such moves can aim at full integration participating in all stages of the value chain (*see* VALUE CHAIN ANALYSIS) to one of partial integration where the firm is engaged in part of the process.

Advantages of Vertical Integration

It has been claimed that the only good reason for investing company resources in vertical integration is to strengthen the firm's competitive position. Thus, unless such a strategy produces competitive advantage or produces cost savings which create shareholder value, it should not be undertaken.

Backward integration is therefore only viable when the volume needed is sufficient to gain the same ECONOMIES OF SCALE as those of suppliers and when it can match supplier efficiency. This may be possible when suppliers achieve high margins, when the item supplied is a high value added component, and when the firm possesses – or can readily gain access to – any necessary technology. The strategy can be valuable when, by producing its own components, the firm can achieve a competitive advantage for its primary product or gain industry dominance for a strategic component. For example, Canon holds some 80 per cent market share in the production of laser beam engines, although the company's share of the market for laser printers is much lower.

Backward integration may also be advantageous when the firm is faced with dependency for critical components or raw materials from a monopoly supplier, or where there are few powerful suppliers bent on maximizing their own profitability.

Forward integration offers similar potential advantages. Poor access to existing distribution channels may lead to an expensive built-up in inventory and poor capacity utilization, so reducing economies of scale. Forward integration offers the firm greater control over the distribution function and may provide an opportunity to gain competitive advantage by opening new channels. When it is realized that some 50 per cent of value added in consumer products can occur at the distribution stage, this option may well be attractive provided that the firm has the requisite skills to manage this function. For example, until the late 1980s personal computers were sold by professional sales persons or from specialized computer stores. By lowering prices and opening a mass volume segment, a firm such as Amstrad transformed the market by supplying its products through consumer electronics stores. In the early 1990s, however, this channel was superseded by manufacturers adopting a strategy of direct selling off the page, so dramatically weakening the position of the mass market retailers.

Integrating forward into production may assist raw materials producers to achieve product differentiation and higher value added while avoiding the price competitive market for undifferentiated, commodity products. In high capital intensity businesses with specialized fixed assets, in the early stages of the value

chain products are sold primarily on specification. As a result, differentiation is often minimal and competitors compete away possible margins in order to maximize capacity utilization. Where excess capacity exists, therefore, margins are often too low to provide an adequate return on equity – as, for example, in oil products and bulk commodity chemicals. Forward vertical integration therefore may improve the possibility of differentiation and so avoid margin pressures. In areas such as refined oil products, backward integration by hypermarket and superstore operators has proven to be especially attractive, as the oil companies themselves have fought to supply the distributors because of their high-volume sites and in order to maintain or strengthen refinery capacity utilization.

Disadvantages of Vertical Integration

There are also a number of actual or potential disadvantages from the pursuit of a vertical integration strategy. First, vertical integration adds to the level of capital investment involved in a business, and unless the additional level of value added covers the extra capital required, overall capital intensity will be increased, with consequent pressure on margins and profitability, and shareholder value will be destroyed.

Second, integration introduces additional risk in that the firm's strategic scope across an industry is increased. Third, vertical integration makes it more difficult for a firm to exit an industry and to resist changing technology and production facilities because of losses likely from investment write downs. Such firms are therefore vulnerable to shifts in technology or methods of production.

Fourth, vertical integration may well require careful coordination of each stage of an integrated activity chain. Efficient economies of scale may also vary significantly for different processes within the chain. One interesting characteristic of integrated strategies occurs when such a chain is broken or where each process is opened to the external market. In the aftermath of the first oil-price shock, for example, BP lost control of 94 per cent of its crude oil supplies. While the company subsequently made important new discoveries on the North Slope in Alaska and in the North Sea, the integrated flow of the company's operations was severely disrupted. As a result, BP's tanker fleet was largely disposed of: it became a net purchaser of crude in some markets, and a crude supplier in other markets in which it lacked refining capacity and retail outlets to engage in downstream value added activities. In other companies such as Booker McConnell, where similar sudden environmental shifts have broken up integrated strategies, companies have moved to create separate businesses from their previously integrated functions, thus essentially becoming conglomerates.

Vertical integration as a strategy therefore has both strengths and weaknesses. The value of such strategy depends on how compatible it is with the long-term interests of the firm; how much it strengthens the firm's strategic position within an industry; and the extent to which it generates competitive advantage. Therefore, unless such a strategy creates shareholder value it is unlikely to be attractive.

Bibliography

Harrigan, K. R. (1984). Formulating vertical integration strategies. *Academy of Management Review*, **9** (4) 638–52. Lexington, MA: Lexington Books.

Harrigan, K. R. (1985). *Strategic flexibility*. Lexington, MA: Lexington Books. See p. 162.

Stuckey, J. & White, D. (1993). When and when not to vertically integrate. *McKinsey Quarterly*, no. 3 3–26.

Thompson, A. & Strickland A. J. (1993). *Strategic management*, 7th edn, New York: Irwin. See pp. 120–2.

DEREK F. CHANNON

volume businesses   Identified as one of the environments in the BCG ADVANTAGE MATRIX, in volume businesses, basic costs make up the key element in overall cost structure and, as a result of low product differentiation, the experience effect is important (*see* EXPERIENCE AND LEARNING EFFECTS). Moreover, margins tend to be reduced in the drive to maximize capacity utilization. Examples of volume businesses include basic consumer electronics products such as television sets, VCRs, and cassette recorders. Others include fast foods, microcomputers, commodity chemicals, and electronic banking.

For success in volume businesses it is imperative to achieve volume leadership,

which is translated into a lower-cost structure. This allows the business to achieve competitive advantage. However, many industry leaders adopt umbrella pricing strategies, negating their potential cost advantage and encouraging low-share competitors, and this often leads to stalemate strategies. To maintain strategic advantage, therefore, it is imperative that leaders in volume businesses maintain share by investing in adequate capacity additions until market maturity occurs, to avoid undue cost increases due to business complexity, and to monitor the environment carefully to avoid any technology bypass or market redefinition, such as that caused by globalization.

See also **Advantage matrix**

DEREK F. CHANNON

vulnerability analysis   An alternate method of evaluating the threat to a company is to conduct vulnerability analysis. When executives undertake a SWOT ANALYSIS there is a tendency to play down the potential impact of threats. Vulnerability analysis assesses the potential damage to the firm of removing its key strategic underpinnings. These have been identified as:

- customer needs and wants served by the firm's products or services

- resources and assets – people, capital, facilities, raw materials, and technology

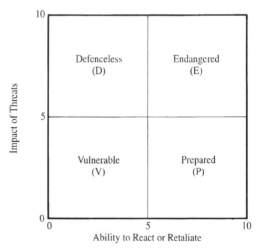

Figure 1 The vulnerability assessment matrix.
Source: Rowe et al. (1994).

- relative cost position compared with those of competitors

- consumer base – size, demographics, and trends

- technologies required

- special skills – systems, procedures, and structures

- corporate identity – image, culture, and products

- institutional barriers to competition – regulations, patents, and licensing

- social values – lifestyles, common norms, and ideals

- sanctions, supports, and incentives to do business

- customer goodwill, product quality, safety, and corporate reputation

- complementary products or services in the stakeholder system

Conducting vulnerability analysis involves the following steps:

1. Identify the key underpinnings.
2. Identify the threat caused by their removal.
3. State the most conservative consequence of each threat.
4. Rank the impacts of the worst consequence of each threat.
5. Estimate the probability of each threat occurring.
6. Rank the firm's capability to deal with each threat.
7. Determine whether the company's vulnerability to each threat is extreme or negligible.

Having conducted this assessment, rank the impact on a scale of 0 to 10, where 0 denotes no impact on the organization and 10 represents catastrophe. Similarly, the firm's ability to respond to each threat should also be ranked from 0 to 10, where zero represents defenselessness and 10 means that the company can easily absorb the threat.

From these assessments, the company's overall vulnerability to each threat can be plotted on a vulnerability assessment matrix, as shown in figure 1.

The firm is virtually defenseless against threats that fall in quadrant D. Any entry falling in this box thus requires immediate management action to reduce the threat. This should be done by abandoning plans or strategies which might result in the threat materializing. In the event that this is not possible, the firm's ability to react must be appraised.

Threats in quadrant E are still dangerous, but the capabilities exist for the firm to react. For such threats, contingency plans should be developed, to be brought into play as and when such a threat materializes.

The firm is well prepared to deal with threats in quadrant P, and little monitoring is therefore required. While threats in quadrant V have limited impact, the company is not well prepared to deal with them. Such threats should therefore be monitored to insure that they do not escalate, although detailed contingency plans are not likely to be necessary.

Bibliography

Hurd, D. A. (1977). *Vulnerability analysis in business planning.* SRI International Research Report no. 593.

Rowe, A. J., Mason, R. O., Dickel, K. E., Mann, R. B. & Mockler, R. J. (1994). *Strategic management*, 4th edn. Reading, MA: Addison-Wesley. See pp. 202–6.

DEREK F. CHANNON

W

waste elimination In many Japanese concerns, waste elimination is a key objective in production management. Within Toyota, great effort is expended on eliminating seven identified areas of waste. In Canon, nine forms of waste were identified and employees at all factories were asked to try to identify waste, quantify it, and suggest ways of removing it. Employees continuously put forward suggestions to achieve this. The nine areas of waste identified at Canon were as follows:

- *Waste caused by work in process.* This occurred between the times at which raw materials were purchased and finished products were despatched. Thus warehousing space, stock control management, tied up working capital, and the like all occurred due to waste in work in process.

- *Waste caused by product defects.* When parts or products were outside specification, waste occurred due to the use of labor which was not productive, waste of raw materials, the cost of correcting deficiencies, disposal, and the indirect costs associated with these activities.

- *Waste in capital equipment usage.* This form of waste occurred when facilities, capital equipment, and operations management were inefficiently used or wrongly selected. All equipment was expected to be operated at optimum efficiency. An operating ratio measured the expected usage of equipment and was compared with the actual working ratio, which measured differences between actual usage and unproductive operations, such as producing defective parts or products, unscheduled stops, and overly lengthy changeovers.

- *Waste in expenses.* This waste included all indirect manufacturing costs, such as personnel, power, heat and light, tooling, and the like, where the cost of providing the product or service exceeded the benefits obtained. Zero-based budgeting was used to help eliminate such waste.

- *Waste in indirect labor.* This form of waste occurred in all indirect operations or employment which did not add value. Such waste was usually a result of inefficient management systems, planning, and control systems. JUST IN TIME cost savings occurred largely as a result of the elimination of indirect labor waste.

- *Waste in planning.* Such waste was looked for in the areas of manufacturing processing and purchasing.

- *Waste in human resources.* This occurred when individual manpower was not fully used or could be replaced efficiently by machines.

- *Waste in operations.* This occurred when standard procedures in production were not followed, or where the incorrect standards had been adopted.

- *Waste in start-up.* With careful planning, start-up times and costs could be sharply reduced.

The improvement resulting from the elimination of waste was calculated as the "waste elimination profit," which was defined as the degree to which expected profits had improved over the previous year. All areas of waste elimination were therefore measured in financial terms, with gains in each area either adding value or cutting historic costs.

The waste elimination program was designed to reduce waste in the short term. Canon believed, however, that it was also important to plan for waste elimination in the future. This involved top factory management being concerned with the careful reinvestment of waste elimination profits, in the Four Investment concept. This involved selecting projects for investment in four key areas, thus:

- new technology
- equipment
- developing human resources
- human welfare

The first of these involved investment in new manufacturing technologies which improved manufacturing flexibility, speed, and efficiency. Investments in human resources included job and other educational training programs designed to provide a superior workforce for the future. Investment in human welfare was designed to produce a people-oriented workplace environment, which was healthy and attractive to those working in it.

In 1988, this very successful system was significantly modified. While maintaining many of the features of the earlier system, Canon revised the Elimination of Waste concept to the more positive concept of "improvements." The new concept was concerned with preventing wastes from occurring. New management policies were adopted showing six improvements and four innovations.

The first "improvement" focused on "quality" characteristics aimed at changing the conditions amongst the 5M's of a business (man, machine, material, method, and measurement) in a way that could be clearly measured against set standards. The second improvement, "work," centered on changing work methods and conditions of work, with the aim of improving efficiency in less time while maintaining quality standards. "Equipment" improvement set out to change processing conditions so as always to maintain operating equipment in the best condition and to operate in less time. "Inventory control" improvement endeavored to change the impact of processing methods to reduce inventory levels to the minimum. "VALUE ENGINEERING" improve-

ment sought to change designs to achieve lower costs for the same function, or higher functions for the same cost. The final improvement looked for was "purchasing," by seeking technical possibilities in reducing manufacturing stock of supplies, which could then be reflected in the reduction of purchase prices.

The four innovations concerned production, technology, production start-up, indirect operation, and worker motivation. The first of these sought to introduce new technology to achieve cost reductions and quality and productivity improvements. Much cost was incurred in production start-ups and hence the second wave of innovation sought to improve the efficiency of start-ups. Innovation in indirect operations sought to achieve maximum efficiency in overhead systems to yield higher value added work. Finally, innovation in worker motivation was designed to establish the working style and behavior of active workshops, in which improvements were constantly being made.

The system put into practice within Canon was by no means unique. Similar systems are also in use at other leading Japanese producers, such as Toyota, Nissan, Sony, and the like.

Bibliography

Channon, D. F. (1993). *Canon C.* Imperial College London, SM, 93 01.
Japanese Management Association *The Canon production system.* Cambridge, MA: Productivity Press.

DEREK F. CHANNON

workout   This was a process designed in GE as a mechanism to radically shift the corporation's corporate culture. Dr. Jack Welch, the CEO, found that despite all his efforts it was proving almost impossible to convey his perceived sense of urgency for corporate change throughout the corporation. In particular, there was an apparent blockage, caused by middle management, in conveying his message to lower level employees. As a result, the process of workout was developed with a view to achieving a major change in attitude and culture. The concept began with four major goals:

- *Building trust*. GE employees at all levels had to find that they could speak candidly without

The sessions included people from multiple levels and functions, and were facilitated by trained internal staff and/or external consultants. To create trust and positive emotional energy, the process initially focused on "bureaucracy busting." One method developed was the CRAP detector (Critical Review APpraisal) of unnecessary work. Individuals were asked to look for CRAP, which could take the form of unnecessary plans, approvals, policies, measurements, meetings, and reports; since, despite delayering and downsizing, GE had attempted to maintain many of its previous bureaucratic systems, hence adding great pressure to the remaining employees. The CRAP detector is illustrated in figure 1.

To make use of the technique, workout participants were asked to complete a four-stage process:

Step 1. Review a typical working week and identify activities that do not add value to the customer.

Step 2. Determine who needs to be involved to change it.

Step 3. Indicate the degree of impact and difficulty of change – place each item on the matrix.

Step 4. Create action plans to attain the "low hanging fruit" items that could be changed quickly and which had impact.

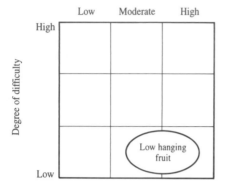

Figure 1   The CRAP detector (Critical Review Apraisal – take work out).
Source: Tichy & Sherman (1993).

jeopardizing their careers. Only in this way was it believed that their ideas would be forthcoming.

● *Empowering employees.* In order to release their intimate knowledge of the job, the CEO wanted to give the employees more power in return for more responsibility.

● *Elimination of unnecessary work.* The quest was for higher productivity, but in addition it was necessary to provide some relief for GE's overstressed workers.

● *A new paradigm for GE.* Ultimately, the CEO wanted workout to define and nurture a new organization that had no internal boundaries.

The workout program began at the end of 1988, with a series of local gatherings patterned on New England town meetings. In groups of 30–100, the hourly and salaried employees spent three to five days off site to discuss their problems. Executives were locked out during these discussions to reduce any worker fears.

On the final day, the executives returned to hear these proposals, and under the workout rules were required to make instant on-the-spot decisions about each proposal in front of the whole group. Some 80 per cent of proposals were given an immediate yes or no decision, with the remainder that needed study being decided upon within a month. At the end of each workout session, individuals and functional teams signed written contracts to implement the new procedure. Hundreds of workouts took place, involving thousands of people throughout GE and leading to a massive demand for change.

In 1990, phase two commenced, involving people who would normally work together, such as cross-functional teams of finance, manufacturing, purchasing, and marketing personnel, collectively responsible for a specific product. These groups were expected to examine and solve a well defined problem. These solutions relied heavily on tools acquired from the BEST PRACTICES initiative. In many businesses the employees would gain control over the CORE PROCESS by process mapping in great detail. Customers and suppliers were also invited to join these sessions.

Phase three of workout began in 1992. Called the Change Acceleration Programme (CAP), this was a systematic attempt to use workout to breed a new type of GE manager. Jack Welch's objective was to make all GE leaders professional change agents rather than mere managers. The idea was to disseminate to top management all GE's accumulated knowledge and wisdom about the change process itself.

The workout process is an interesting example of a massive attempt to involve the great majority of employees in a major corporation in a dramatic shift in its culture.

Bibliography

Tichy, N. M. & Sherman, S. (1993). *Control your own destiny or someone else will*. London: HarperCollins.

DEREK F. CHANNON

Z

Z-score The Z-score was developed in the USA by Altman (1968), as a predictor of corporate failure. The concept has been extended to other countries, and provides a useful tool for predicting bankruptcy or financial difficulties largely in manufacturing businesses (or those with significant working capital intensity). The formula makes use of ratios derived from standard financial statements and can therefore be applied to the analysis of competitors, customers, suppliers, acquisition candidates, and the like. However, care must be taken to insure that financial statements provide a realistic estimate of the financial health of companies investigated. The tool can also be used as a predictor for business units or the corporation in multibusiness concerns.

A company's Z-score is calculated using the formula

$$Z = (1.2)X1 + (1.4)X2 + (3.3)X3 + (0.6)X4 + X5$$

where the individual variables are defined as follows:

$X1$ = working capital/total assets, i.e., net current assets divided by total book value.
$X2$ = retained earnings/total assets. Virtually by definition, retained earnings are less for younger companies, and the lower value of this ratio for such concerns can be seen as a higher risk effect of failure for them.
$X3$ = EBIT/total assets, i.e., earnings before interest and tax divided by all capital employed.
$X4$ = market value of equity/book value of total debt, i.e., market capitalization of all classes of equity divided by total short and long debt. This ratio is not available for companies that are not listed on the stock market.

$X5$ = sales/total assets, a measure of capital term. Note the similarity to the capital intensity term used in PIMS.

Using historic data from 85 failed US companies, Altman calculated that 95 per cent of these had a score of less than 1.81 a year before failure and 72 per cent up to two years before. However, only 4 per cent of firms had such a low score 3 years prior to bankruptcy. By contrast, scores above 3 had a low likelihood of failure.

While Altman's model was essentially a short-term predictor of bankruptcy, many companies have used it as a trend predictor, plotting Z-scores on the vertical axis and time on the horizontal. A significant downward trend in Z-scores may therefore be a predictor of future trouble and potentially highlights the cause of such a problem. For private companies, for which the $X4$ ratio is not relevant, such concerns will, by definition, tend to have a lower Z-score.

Bibliography

Altman, E. (1968). Financial ratios discriminant analysis and the prediction of corporate bankruptcy. *Journal of Finance* (September).

DEREK F. CHANNON

zaibatsu structure These concerns formed the basis for the foundation of Japanese industrialization. They developed from a variety of sources, but emerged as highly diversified, family-dominated concerns from the late nineteenth century. Today they would be defined as conglomerates (*see* CONGLOMERATE STRATEGY), although at the time diversification moves tended to be seen as related, albeit opportunistic in some cases. The businesses within a zaibatsu were not necessarily legally independent concerns, but were sometimes organized as internal divisions (indeed, the Mitsubishi zaibatsu seems to have been the first recorded corporation to adopt a multidivisional structure in 1908, some 15 years before this structure developed in the USA). Nor necessarily, were zaibatsu large, although the largest formed the core of Japanese industry. Moreover, not all Japanese large corporations were zaibatsu, with joint stock companies also being relatively undiversified in industries such as power generation and textiles. All of the large concerns were located in one of the major central cities – Tokyo, Osaka, Kobe, and Yokohama – with location being a subsequent influence on corporate evolution.

After the Meiji Restoration in Japan in 1868 eight major zaibatsu groups – Mitsui, Mitsubishi, Sumitomo, Yasuda, Furakawa, Okura, Asamo, and Fujita – had begun to develop. Two further groups, Kuhara and Suzuki, emerged around 1910. These ten concerns exerted substantial influence over the Japanese economy both qualitatively and quantitatively and in the industries in which they operated (and frequently dominated).

The rise of the zaibatsu was based around the concept of the family firm, despite the fact that the joint stock company concept was introduced early in the Meiji period. The main sources of wealth for the founding families which enabled them to embark on their diversification strategies came from profits generated as a result of government patronage and mining. The families invested their fortunes in new activities because of strong internal pressures, in part from family members, such as in the case of the Iwasaki family in Mitsubishi, but mainly from professional managers employed by the concerns.

By the early 1920s all the major zaibatsu had a multisubsidiary form of organization. In this structure, each of the businesses into which the zaibatsu diversified took the form not of a division but of a subsidiary company and, as in a multidivisional structure, each subsidiary functioned autonomously within the framework of the zaibatsu overall policy. This was established by the central office, which controled the subsidiaries via share ownership. Although historically family businesses, the leading zaibatsu were also progressive in employing more educated managers who guided the affairs of the organization.

The four leading prewar zaibatsu, Mitsubishi, Mitsui, Sumitomo, and Yasuda, accounted for around 24 per cent of all Japanese industry. Created by Iwasaki Yatoro, a low-order samurai, the Mitsubishi zaibatsu was born out of shipping operations and diversified into trading, shipbuilding and heavy engineering, and banking and insurance. By 1945, Mitsubishi was engaged in virtually all sectors of manufacturing industry. The Iwasaki family still owned 55.5 per cent of the Mitsubishi Holding Company, which in turn owned more than 52 per cent of the subsidiary and affiliated companies. The Iwasaki family, however, owned directly only 0.4 per cent of subsidiary and affiliated companies. Under Iwasaki management control was strongly centralized and this tradition continued with his sons. Professional managers were, however, given a great deal of power over operations.

Mitsui was initially concerned with the textile industry and money exchange, and dated back to the late seventeenth century. Following the Meiji Restoration, Mitsui developed with government encouragement as a bank, spinning off its dry goods retail business into a new family branch, Mitsukoshi, which – while outside the Mitsui clan – developed properly as a major retailing organization. Mitsui itself diversified by adding a trading company, which in turn diversified into mining and traded in a wide range of products. By the end of World War II, Mitsui had diversified substantially and consisted of some 22 subsidiary and affiliated companies. The Mitsui family owned some 67 per cent of the group holding company and over 50 per cent of the stocks of all subsidiaries and affiliates. As the group expanded and diversified away from its money exchange activities to become a major zaibatsu, management was passed to professional managers. Indeed, the family imposed a strict rule against the participation of family managers in company management.

The Sumitomo zaibatsu had its roots in copper mining and smelting, but after the Meiji Restoration diversification occurred into metal and commodities trading, shipping, warehousing, and financial services, and other areas of metal processing and timber. By 1946 the Sumitomo family held 29 per cent of the group's holding company and 13 per cent of the subsidiary and affiliated companies. However, the family had gradually dissociated itself from direct management of the businesses, and by the end of World War II Sumitomo was essentially managed by professionals.

The Yasuda zaibatsu, like Mitsui, had its origins as a privileged provider of fiscal services to the government. Founded by a low-rank samurai, Yasuda Zawjuro, at the end of the Tokugawa period, the organization began as a money changing concern before becoming a political merchant. After the Meiji Restoration, Yasuda cooperated with the new government in introducing unconvertible paper money. In 1876, Yasuda created a bank, which became the foundation of the group. Nonfinancial businesses were less significant than in the other three major zaibatsu.

After World War II, the zaibatsu became a target for the occupying powers. Eighty-three zaibatsu holding companies were initially identified for dissolution. This focused on breaking their ownership of banks, subsidiaries, and affiliates, freezing their assets and imposing a capital levy on their wealth. Where family interests remained, these linkages were also broken. The four largest zaibatsu, Mitsubishi, Mitsui, Sumitomo, and Yasuda, voluntarily made dissolution proposals and, to prevent the groups from reforming, US-style anti-monopoly laws were introduced. The deconcentration of 1,200 companies was planned at the end of 1947, but this policy had to be abandoned in the face of Japan's critical economic condition.

In 1957 a final treaty was signed which restored Japan's independence. The post-occupation government, anxious to restore the economy, allowed the former zaibatsu to re-establish links with banks of their former groups; defensive cross-shareholdings began to be established as a protection against acquisition, and soon the former Mitsubishi, Mitsui,

and Sumitomo zaibatsu began to come together in the late 1950s. Unlike the prewar zaibatsu, however, these newly emerging groups had no family ownership and no overall holding companies. These new groups were the first of the postwar horizontal keiretsu groups (see KEIRETSU STRUCTURE).

Not all of the prewar zaibatsu re-established connections with former related companies. Partially in response to the emergence of the three leading former zaibatsu groups, other keiretsu groups formed around the major city banks, who were key providers of funds for redevelopment. The Yasuda zaibatsu thus reformed in part, to become a key element within the Fuyo group, centered on the Fuji Bank. The other leading keiretsu groups developed around the Sanwa and Dai Ichi Kangyo banks. By the mid-1960s the zaibatsu conglomerates had been superseded by keiretsu groups. The historic family structures of these groups, however, can be seen today to some extent in the evolution of chaebol groups in Korea (see CHAEBOL STRUCTURE) and the CHINESE FAMILY BUSINESS elsewhere in Asia. By contrast, the concept of family- or clan-based industrial conglomerates has not developed in the West, and an understanding of these two alternate structural modes helps to explain major differences in strategic evolution.

Bibliography

Bisson, T. A. (1954). *Zaibatsu dissolution in Japan.* Berkeley, CA: University of California Press.

Hattori, T. (1989). Japanese zaibatsu and Korean chaebol. K. H. Chung & H. C. Lee (eds), *Korean managerial dynamics.* New York: Praeger. See pp. 79–88.

Min Chen (1995). *Asian management systems.* London: Routledge.

Morikawa, H. (1992). *Zaibatsu: the rise and fall of family enterprise groups in Japan.* Tokyo: University of Tokyo Press.

DEREK F. CHANNON

—— INDEX ——

Compiled by Meg Davies (Registered Indexer)